SOUTHERN BIOGRAPHY SERIES

# GENERAL EDMUND KIRBY SMITH, C.S.A.

General Edmund Kirby Smith (from a portrait in possession of
Dr. R. M. Kirby-Smith, Sewanee, Tennessee).

# General
# Edmund Kirby Smith,
## C.S.A.

By

JOSEPH HOWARD PARKS

LOUISIANA STATE UNIVERSITY PRESS

BATON ROUGE AND LONDON

Copyright © 1954, 1982 by Joseph H. Parks
All rights reserved
Manufactured in the United States of America

ISBN 0-8071-1800-1

Louisiana Paperback Edition, 1992
01  00  99  98  97  96  95  94  93  92     1  2  3  4  5

The paper in this book meets the guidelines for permanence and durability of the Committee on Production Guidelines for Book Longevity of the Council on Library Resources. ∞

TO

THE MEMORY OF

MOTHER, DAD, AND HORACE

# ACKNOWLEDGMENTS

No adequate study of the life of General Edmund Kirby Smith could be made without unrestricted access to the Kirby-Smith family papers. For the privilege of such access to these papers I am indebted to Dr. R. M. Kirby-Smith of Sewanee and Mrs. Nina Kirby-Smith Buck of St. Augustine, Florida, the only survivors of the General's eleven children, and to Drs. J. G. deRoulhac Hamilton and J. W. Patton of the Southern Collection, University of North Carolina. I wish to thank Dr. Kirby-Smith and Mrs. Buck for their gracious reception and enthusiastic cooperation when I visited them in search of material. Their interest in the publication of an adequate biography of their father was exceeded only by their desire that the writing be free from family influence. Drs. Hamilton and Patton made research in the Southern Collection a pleasure. They also greatly contributed to the ease of research by arranging for the microfilming of the Kirby-Smith papers.

On the "Mountaintop" at Sewanee members of the University staff were eager to contribute what they could. To Mrs. O. N. Torian, Archivist, and Arthur B. Chitty, Director of Public Relations, I owe thanks for their efforts in rounding up scattered items of information.

As will be noted in the Critical Essay, other materials were located in depositories extending from Washington, D.C., to Austin, Texas. For kind reception and patient and efficient assistance I wish to thank the staffs of the Texas State Archives, the University of Texas Library, the

Louisiana State University Archives and Library, the Manuscript Division of the Duke University Library, the Manuscript Division of the Library of Congress, and the Southern Collection of the Birmingham Public Library.

To Dr. Bennett H. Wall of the University of Kentucky and Mr. Thomas R. Hay, Locust Valley, New York, I again say thanks for bits of information furnished. Mr. Hay, Dr. Frank Owsley of the University of Alabama and Dr. T. Harry Williams of the Louisiana State University have read the entire manuscript. Their knowledge of Civil War history made their criticisms invaluable.

Generous grants-in-aid from the Social Science Research Council, Birmingham–Southern College, and the Committee on Carnegie Grants helped to finance the research connected with this study. For this assistance I am grateful.

Joseph H. Parks

# CONTENTS

# ILLUSTRATIONS

# GENERAL EDMUND KIRBY SMITH, C.S.A.

## CHAPTER I

# THE KIRBYS AND THE SMITHS

ECHOES OF THE shots fired at Lexington on April 19, 1775, were soon heard by young Ephraim Kirby in the neighboring colony of Connecticut; he reached the vicinity of Boston in time to aid the colonials in the battle of Bunker Hill. Born in Woodbury, Connecticut, February 23, 1757, the eldest of twelve children of Abraham and Eunice (Starkweather) Kirby and a lineal descendant of Joseph Kirby of early Hartford history, Ephraim Kirby had moved to Litchfield shortly before the outbreak of hostilities, had begun reading law in the office of Judge Reynold Marvin, and had fallen in love with the judge's only daughter, Ruth.

Throughout the Revolution Kirby saw almost continuous service, participating in nineteen engagements, including Brandywine, Germantown, and Monmouth, and receiving thirteen wounds. In the fall of 1782 Lieutenant Kirby's [1] regiment, along with Olney's Rhode Island battalion, was transferred to Saratoga on the northern frontier. Kirby himself was assigned to Lord Sterling's guard at Albany. This was a most pleasant assignment, for he could now drive with "his Lordship" and attend many public entertainments at the Albany playhouse, including

[1] The title of "Colonel" by which he was later addressed was his rank in the postwar Connecticut militia.

the tragedy of the *Mourning Bride,* which inspired him to write more often to his sweetheart, "Ruthy." [2]

When the fighting ended, Kirby returned to Litchfield, resumed his study of law, and married Ruth Marvin on March 17, 1784. Ruth had been born in Litchfield, December 20, 1763, and was a descendant, five generations removed, of Reynold Marvin, who had migrated from England to Connecticut in 1635. The family had moved from Hartford to Farmington and then to Saybrook before coming to Litchfield. [3]

Ephraim Kirby now settled down to a career of legal practice, politics, land speculation, and the rearing of a family which soon included six children. In 1789 he published the *Reports of the Decisions of the Superior Court of Errors of the State of Connecticut.* With the launching of the new United States government under the Constitution, he became an ardent Jeffersonian Republican in a Federalist stronghold. In 1791 he was elected to the Connecticut legislature, where he continued to serve for fourteen semiannual sessions, an accomplishment which drove humiliated Litchfield Federalists to fury. "Kirby is, to the disgrace of this town, again chosen deputy," wrote Uriah Tracy following the election of 1799, "but he has no cause of triumph . . . all the solid, respectable part of the town, without any preconcert or intrigue, voted against him." His victory was by the "aid of every tag-rag who could be mustered, and a whole winter of intrigue." [4] Tracy's statement was correct only if one accepted the Federalist defini-

<hr />

[2] Ephraim Kirby to Ruth Marvin, October 18, 29, November 24, 1782, in Kirby-Smith Papers, Southern Collection, University of North Carolina. (All manuscript letters cited in this study are in the Kirby-Smith Papers unless otherwise noted.) Sketch of Ephraim Kirby, *ibid.;* Melatiah Everett Dwight, *The Kirbys of New England* (New York, 1898), 172; Kirby-Smith Genealogy (manuscript in possession of Dr. R. M. Kirby-Smith, Sewanee, Tennessee).

[3] Dwight, *Kirbys of New England,* 175; Kirby-Smith Genealogy.

[4] Quoted in George Gibbs, *Memoirs of the Administrations of Washington and John Adams* (New York, 1846), II, 232.

tion of respectability. But Kirby's popularity did not extend throughout the state, and he was unsuccessful in his desire to become governor.[5]

An original member of the Society of the Cincinnati in Connecticut, Kirby took seriously the activities of the order, particularly the opportunities for land speculation in the Western Reserve. In 1795 he became a director in the Connecticut Land Company and during the next two years spent considerable time in Philadelphia and Virginia, attending meetings of the Cincinnati and "negotiating with the first characters in the United States." Believing that success depended upon the impression one made, he felt compelled to employ a personal servant. The cost was high, but he hoped to net several thousands of dollars, he assured his wife, for "fortune" had thrown his way "several very fortunate negotiations." In Philadelphia he dined with Aaron Burr, whom he had met at Albany during the Revolution, and along with other Cincinnati, called upon President Washington, who "shook us all cordially by the hand and welcomed us as old brother soldiers." On another occasion he joined a group of prominent men at dinner with the President and enjoyed considerable conversation with the "Old Planter." However, he soon tired of the display of wealth and luxury in Philadelphia and longed for his little domestic circle, although he did not relish thoughts of a future in the town of Litchfield. That town, he exclaimed, was "the hotbed of envy, malice, and every other dissocial feeling of the mind." [6]

Although he had assured his wife of "good prospects of acquiring property . . . as fast as all my boys can spend it," [7] Kirby's bubble of speculation burst in 1802, and

[5] Richard J. Purcell, *Connecticut in Transition* (Washington, 1918), 238, 247.

[6] Ephraim Kirby to Wife, May 1, 7, 1796.

[7] *Id.* to *id.*, February 4, 1796.

only his yeoman service in the Republican cause saved him from financial distress. President Thomas Jefferson came to the rescue with an appointment to the collectorship of revenue in the state of Connecticut. Then in July, 1803, he and Robert C. Nicholas of Kentucky were designated United States commissioners in the Mississippi Territory "for the purpose of ascertaining the rights of persons claiming lands in the said territory East of Pearl River." After four months of travel Kirby arrived at Fort Stoddert in January, 1804. By August the commissioners had completed their work, and Nicholas had returned to Kentucky.

In the meantime, Congress had authorized the appointment of an additional judge for the Territory to reside near the Tombigbee settlements. President Jefferson requested Kirby to accept a temporary appointment to this judgeship, which he did, though there is no evidence that he tried any cases. Kirby desired a judgeship at New Orleans, but Jefferson, fearing his knowledge of French insufficient, suggested the governorship of the Mississippi Territory instead.[8] This offer, dated December 1, 1804, was never received by Kirby; he had died at Fort Stoddert on October 20.[9]

Before leaving Litchfield, Ephraim Kirby had become well acquainted with Joseph Lee Smith, who, fresh out of Yale University, had come to Litchfield to study in the famous law school conducted by Tapping Reeve. Smith, born in New Britain, Connecticut, May 28, 1779, was the son of Elnathan and Chloe (Lee) Smith and a descendant of William Smith of Farmington and John Lee of Shrop-

[8] Thomas Jefferson to Ephraim Kirby, December 1, 1804, in *The Territorial Papers of the United States* (Washington, 1934——), V, 296. For the full correspondence between Jefferson and Kirby see *ibid.*, 222, 223, 296, 297, 303, 316, 317, 329–332.

[9] Joseph Chambers to Mrs. Ephraim Kirby, October 27, 1804.

shire, England, who had come to New England in 1634. Already an aggressive Republican Joseph Lee Smith immediately plunged into the political fight which Ephraim Kirby had been waging for several years.

When Selleck Osborn, editor of the newly established Republican *Witness,* was severely beaten by a prominent Federalist, attorney Joseph Lee Smith took Osborn's case. The court ordered Osborn to post bond as guarantee that he would restrain himself in his newspaper attacks upon Federalists. Osborn refused and was sent to jail. Smith and his associates, declaring the editor a martyr to the Republican cause, began publishing daily accounts of his jail life. Parading friends marched by the jail with their heads uncovered. A mammoth mass meeting of protesting Republicans was planned for the Litchfield meetinghouse. Among the early arrivals were Judah Champion and Dan Huntington, two divines of Federalist leanings who had explained from their pulpits the close connection between Republicans and the Devil. As they were about to enter the meetinghouse, attorney Smith stepped forward and suggested their withdrawal. The reverends later claimed that Smith had subjected them to both physical abuse and humiliation, and their Federalist friends caused him to be arrested for remarks alleged to have been made at the mass meeting. The Federalist-controlled court fined Smith $250 and $123 in costs.[10]

Meanwhile, on August 25, 1804, Joseph Lee Smith had married nineteen-year-old Frances Kirby, the eldest daughter of the late Ephraim Kirby, who, according to her father, was possessed of passions "finely strung, tempered with much warmth, and exquisitely alive to feeling." [11]

[10] Samuel H. Fisher, "Why Two Connecticut Yankees Went South," in *The Florida Historical Quarterly* (Jacksonville, 1908——), XVIII (1939), 32–45.

[11] Joseph Lee Smith to Ephraim Kirby, January 12, 1804; Ephraim Kirby

The next half dozen years brought a meager income from the practice of law and two additions to the Smith family —Ephraim Kirby, born 1806, and Frances Marvin, born 1812.[12]

Then came the War of 1812, and Joseph Lee Smith, good Republican that he was, joined the service. Rising rapidly to the rank of lieutenant colonel, he chose to continue a military career after the war rather than return to legal practice. A similar decision in favor of army life was also made by Smith's brothers-in-law Reynold and Edmund Kirby and Francis S. Belton, who had married Harriet Kirby.

Soon tiring of life at frontier army posts, particularly the long periods of forced absence from his family, Colonel Joseph Lee Smith resigned his commission in 1821 and accepted appointment as Federal judge for the eastern district of the recently acquired Florida Territory. Leaving his family in Litchfield, Judge Smith left for St. Augustine early in 1822. As his boat eased over the bar into the shallow harbor, the soldier within him must have been stirred by the sight of old Fort San Marco, whose battered shell rock walls, now turned dark with age, had absorbed the shock of many bombardments. Behind it stood the open gates of the oldest town in the United States. Its plaza, narrow streets, Spanish houses, and orange groves, so thick as to exclude the sunlight, were at least new to a New Englander.

The new judge found St. Augustine rather dull, but he attributed this more to the absence of his family than to unfriendliness of the people. As he expected, "the good

---

to Joseph Lee Smith, April 10, 1804; *id.* to ?, January 23, 1797. Ephraim Kirby's other children were Reynold Marvin (born 1790), Harriet (1798), Edmund (1794), Helen (1800), and Katherine (1802).

[12] These are the dates given in the Kirby-Smith Genealogy. Dwight, *Kirbys of New England,* gives 1807 and 1809.

and the bad commingled both in its normal & physical texture." Society was "more extensive than in Litchfield," but "heterogeneous transitory & collected from all parts of the World—some with polished intellects & more with neither intellects nor polish." Great love for pageantry was in evidence almost daily. During the first few months of Judge Smith's residence there he witnessed "a succession of masquerading shows of the most grotesque & ludicrous character," with selections of kings and queens for nine consecutive nights. The approach of Lent alone terminated these festivities. "Alas for the finny tribe for 40 days," the judge remarked to his wife.[13]

Judge Smith returned to Connecticut in the summer of 1823 and accompanied his wife and children to St. Augustine in the fall. The Smiths took up residence in the Segui House on Hospital (Aviles) Street, which was rented from the heirs of Bernardo Segui. The family now consisted of Frances, age eleven, and Josephine, age five. Ephraim Kirby, the eldest, had been admitted to West Point in July, 1822.

In St. Augustine Judge Smith became a legal associate of young Benjamin Alexander Putnam. Georgia-born, Harvard-educated Putnam had come to St. Augustine to read and practice law. In 1830 he journeyed to Connecticut to claim as his bride Helen Kirby, a younger sister of Mrs. Smith, whom he probably met while she was visiting in St. Augustine. Putnam later served as speaker of the Florida house of representatives, major in the Florida militia, United States surveyor general for the state, and Confederate judge.[14]

Although he had lost some of the rashness of his earlier

[13] Joseph L. Smith to Wife, February 25, 1823.

[14] Notes recorded by Putnam himself. Copy in the Florida Historical Society Collection; R. M. Burt, "Benjamin Alexander Putnam," (manuscript in possession of Florida Historical Society).

days as a Litchfield lawyer, Judge Smith could never live a quiet life. Scarcely had he become settled in Florida before he became involved in controversies with Marshal Walter Smith and District Attorney Edgar Macon. In 1826 he made a trip to Washington to explain matters to President John Quincy Adams. The President received him with *"marked* civilities," he reported to his wife, and expressed approval of his conduct "in all particulars." Smith did "not feel disposed to bragg," but would certainly be disappointed if the district attorney returned to Florida.[15]

In the midst of these feuds a contemporary judge, who knew Judge Smith well, described him as "a gigantic man, both mentally and physically, who, but for his unbounded prejudices and ungovernable passions, would have been qualified to fill any, even the most exhalted station in the government. He had the advantage of an excellent education, was a sound lawyer, read much, had fine conversational powers, a highly discriminating mind, and could equally adorn the bench or the drawing room." [16]

In the old Segui House, on May 16, 1824, another son was born to Judge and Mrs. Smith. They christened him Edmund Kirby. He immediately became the idol of the family, particularly of the father who affectionately referred to him as "Ted" or "Ned." Writing his wife while on a trip to Washington two months before Edmund's second birthday, he commented: "I hope you are mistaken as to *Ted*—I shall be quite disappointed if he be not competent to strut Pantaloons on my return—if he governs the home, I think his mother must be *impeached* for mal administration." [17]

During his early years Edmund was almost constantly

[15] Joseph L. Smith to Wife, March 25, 1826.

[16] Manuscript Autobiography of Judge Thomas Douglas, quoted in Rowland H. Rerick, *Memoirs of Florida* (Atlanta, 1902), II, 64–65.

[17] Joseph L. Smith to Wife, March 25, 1826.

under the affectionate, if sometimes domineering, care of his sister Frances. Twelve years his senior, she had for him a feeling akin to that of a mother. Mrs. Smith was none too happy in her Florida home and made frequent and extended visits to relatives in Connecticut and New York. Josephine, very delicate of body and tastes, a musician of some promise, often accompanied her mother. At other times she lived with her Aunt Harriet Belton, whose husband, Major Belton, was stationed at Charleston. The eldest of the Smith children, Ephraim Kirby, graduated from West Point at the foot of his class in 1826 and entered upon an army career at a frontier post. He subsequently married Mary Jerome of Syracuse, New York.

Young Edmund Kirby Smith, an aggressive lad, lively and mischievous, kept his sister Frances in a dither. Though he was the first child to be baptized in Trinity (Episcopal) Church, as a boy he was not fond of attending church and Sunday school. "Frances says I must attend Sunday School again and . . . I do not intend to be so irregular as I used to be." He preferred to commune with nature outside; the woods, streams, and flowers fascinated him, and the fruits of the extensive orange groves whetted his appetite. Again and again he promised Frances not to play hooky and to be a better boy in general. Yet how could she expect him to refrain from climbing the big fig tree near Deacon Gould's wall and spattering his chickens, and perhaps the deacon himself, with overripe fruit?

In mental development Edmund was much above his age. Few Florida boys of eleven years could write letters like this to their mothers:

". . . We had a very pleasant but long passage to Indian Key. We saw several villages on the coast before we reached Indian Key, but they were all deserted, the people at Indian Key very much frightened, under arms and expecting an attack daily. There was a

family by the name of Cooley just below the light house at Cape
Florida murdered by the Indians. And it was very singular their
mother was almost an Indian herself and the children were named
after Indians and could speak Indian better than they could speak
English. The father had gone to Indian Key and left his family at
home as they expected no danger from the Indians They heard the
Indians and attempted to fly The boy and girl were shot down as
they made the attempt The mother who had an infant in her arms
received a ball through her and her infants body. The father took
a canoe and returned in a few days and found them all dead as before mentioned.

.     .     .     .     .     .     .     .     .     .     .

We arrived in Tallahassee on the 28 instant 15 days from St.
Augustine. Father has had the Rheumatism for 4 or five days very
bad in his knee, but it is now getting a little better he still walks
very lame and the knee is very much swelled. Father is writing a
letter to Kirby about the Indian war and he says he expects that
Kirby will be ordered on to Florida We have heard the news of
Major Putnams severe fight with Indians—We think his command
fought bravely—What a pity they had not ammunition and force
sufficient to conquer the Indians We, that is father and I are sad
and grieved for poor Edward Gould—he was such a fine young
man, how can his parents bear it.[18]

Edmund was more alive to nature than the average boy.
He strolled the beach, collecting shells of all sizes and
shapes, and watched the fishing boats, accompanied by
hopeful sea gulls, come and go. Now and then a supply
boat docked at old Fort San Marco, now known as Fort
Marion. Though the beauty of it all made its impression,
he developed no great desire to go to sea. In after years
he longed for the hot sands, fresh mullet, and orange groves
of his native Florida but said nothing of a desire to be a
skipper.

It was the countryside that young Edmund loved most.
When the judge bought him a pony, which the lad named
"Rocket," only the fear of Seminole Indians held his coun-

    18 Edmund K. Smith to Mother, January 31, 1836, in possession of Dr. R. M.
Kirby-Smith, Sewanee, Tennessee.

try rambles within bounds. In the boy's estimation, Rocket was the fastest horse on foot, and a very determined and restless animal, too. "Rocket was very restless and as soon as I turned towards home he galloped all the way to the stable without stopping," he excitedly related to his mother.[19]

[19] *Id.* to *id.*, January 25, 1835, in possession of Dr. R. M. Kirby-Smith.

## CHAPTER II

# WEST POINT YEARS

THE CAREFREE AND exciting life in St. Augustine was terminated when Edmund was twelve. The family, apparently without very much assistance from the boy, had decided upon a military career for him; therefore, he must be sent to a school that would prepare him for entrance into West Point. Benjamin Hollowell's school in Alexandria, Virginia, was selected, and the future general was admitted in 1836.

Several long years were to elapse before he saw his childhood home again, and many were the changes among family and friends. The year before he left for school his sister Josephine died of tuberculosis. She and her mother had gone north in June, 1835, to escape the summer in that *"hot sandy unprofitable place"* called Florida. Both longed for an "Eden" such as Uncle Edmund Kirby's country place near Brownsville, New York. Josephine died there in the fall of 1835.[1] Sister Frances married Captain Lucien B. Webster in December, 1837, and accompanied him to Hancock Barracks, Maine.

Edmund did well at Alexandria, although he sometimes expressed disgust and resentment over the actions of the headmaster. "Benjamin has behaved very singular lately

[1] Josephine Smith to Joseph L. Smith, July 21, 1835; Ephraim Kirby Smith to Mother, December 25, 1835.

having expelled two or three of his students and in two cases he acted unjustly," he wrote Frances. He had just passed another strict examination, he explained on another occasion. "Benjamin" was becoming more precise daily. He came out with "flying colors," but had been "obliged to get up about three or four o'clock and study by candle light." [2]

The report cards preserved show excellent grades, "First Rate" deportment, commendable application to study, and attention to orders. He liked mathematics best and Latin least.[3]

No doubt the boy studied too hard. His good scholastic record was attained at a sacrifice of physical activities. There was nothing he liked better than skating, he wrote Frances, but he had not had an opportunity to learn very well. He envied those boys "who seem to glide by as if they went by steam." [4]

Sister Frances, his former tutor, was complimentary of her brother's record and constantly urged him to do still better. His spelling and sentence structure should be improved, she insisted. More pains should be taken in making the corrections indicated by her. His "last *corrections* were incorrect." "We all fear that you do not pay sufficient attention to composition." He must improve his style and learn to express himself "*clearly,* concisely, and elegantly." Nothing was needed but "diligent application," for nature had endowed him bountifully. Money, drawing paper, and other supplies were being sent. Would he not save his drawings for her? She was glad to learn that he was developing an interest in botany and mineralogy.[5]

[2] January 2 (?), 1837, November 26, 1839.
[3] See Kirby-Smith Papers under date of October 25, 1839; Edmund K. Smith to Frances Webster, February ?, ?.
[4] *Id.* to *id.*, ?, 1837.
[5] Frances Webster to Edmund K. Smith, September 18, October 15, 1837; April 8, July 26, 1838.

While in St. Augustine, Frances kept her brother posted on the happenings there. His pony had run away and probably been picked up by the Indians. The Seminole war was under way, and she had visited the fort to view the sad and forlorn savages who had been captured. They had many brave and noble qualities, she thought, and "if they were any other than poor unprotected Indians they would be considered martyrs in the cause of patriotism and justice of their cause would every where find champions." [6]

Edmund irritated the whole family by his negligence. Months passed without his writing a letter, and when Frances visited Washington he failed to go to see her even though he had been notified of her coming. She was offended. Nothing but "your own inclinations prevented your coming," she charged.[7] He should consider it a pleasure, his mother admonished, to write home frequently, "at least every other week." Brother Kirby also complained, and Mrs. Smith urged Edmund to write him a long careful letter, not forgetting to mention his little nephew, Joseph Lee Smith. She then offered her young son some motherly advice. He must be *"perfectly sincere"* in all his actions and careful to "preserve an undeviating regard for truth in all things. Never *shuffle* or do a mean thing to save your life." She wished him to write in detail of his friends and of himself—studies, pleasures, dislikes, books, and so forth. He must be nice to Edward Dummett (a schoolmate from St. Augustine) but take care not to imitate him, for he had "too many Augustine ways & habits." Edmund must ever be aware of too intimate companionship with "any noisy fighting or swearing boys." [8]

Judge Smith, ill and discouraged since being forced to resign his judgeship under political pressure in 1832, con-

[6] *Id.* to *id.*, September 18, 1837.        [7] *Id.* to *id.*, ?, 1837.
[8] Mrs. Joseph L. Smith to *id.*, July ?, 1838.

tinued his intense interest in "Ned." He, too, felt neglected but was willing to settle for a letter "every fourth Sunday" in order to "lessen the immense burden of the task" of writing. If one hoped for respectability and competency in afterlife, he advised his son, then in youth he must "be regular methodical studious and punctual." [9]

By 1841 Edmund's instructors considered him prepared to take the West Point examinations. Captain Webster examined his record, especially in mathematics, and pronounced it good; and sister Frances began to dream. How wonderful it would be if her baby brother could graduate from the Military Academy with a rank high enough to get into the artillery. With Captain Webster's influence, he could no doubt be attached to the First Artillery and assigned to his brother-in-law's company. He could then come to live with her. But before he entered the Academy, she urged Edmund, he must try to improve his style of writing. His orthography also required attention. [10]

The appointment to West Point was secured without serious difficulty. The "power of becoming respectable, of continuing to be so, and of causing affectionate parents to rejoice and exalt in your good fortune and prosperity now rests with you," Judge Smith reminded his son. However, the immediate objective was to pass the entrance examinations. Edmund must learn not to "spell operation with two p's"; neither should he spell warrant "with an e in the last syllable." "Do not by any *inattention, self indulgence* or *lack of exertion* and *industry mar your own fortune.*" Furthermore, Judge Smith explained, Edmund, in receiving an appointment, had been favored over many Floridians, particularly his classmate Edward Dummett. He should prove himself worthy of that honor by exhibiting candor,

[9] Joseph L. Smith to *id.*, October 27, 1839.
[10] Frances Webster to *id.*, February 12, 1841.

uprightness, and gentlemanly conduct. These character-istics plus neatness in person would give him high rank with West Point authorities. Then he must also learn econ-omy. His ill and aging father would be unable to furnish unlimited funds, but he would see to it that his son was properly attired when he appeared at the Academy—noth-ing showy, however, for he considered plainness and neat-ness always most becoming and proper.[11] The dutiful son took this advice in the manner in which it was intended, for Edmund greatly admired his father.

Frances arranged for Captain Webster and herself to accompany Edmund to West Point. She trusted that her little brother would be *"man enough"* to get from Alex-andria to New York without losing his baggage. She and her husband cut short their vacation in St. Augustine and rushed to New York, sending advance instructions for Edmund to meet them at the American Hotel near the Astor House. All would then journey to West Point together. Edmund must write in care of Aunt Kate's husband, Dr. Joseph P. Russell,[12] of Governor's Island, when they should expect him.

Judge Smith promised to forward necessary funds to Dr. Russell but was soon forced to notify Edmund of his ina-bility to raise the required $50 or $100 at once. Uncle Ira Smith, Judge Smith's brother, who divided his time be-tween New Britain, Connecticut, and New York, came to the rescue with the needed funds, for which the judge ex-pressed deepest appreciation. Edmund was "an honest and big hearted affectionate boy," he assured his brother.[13]

At West Point arrangements were made with a Mr.

[11] Joseph L. Smith to *id.*, March 1, 1841.

[12] Dr. Russell had married Katherine Kirby, Mrs. Joseph L. Smith's young-est sister.

[13] Frances Webster to Edmund K. Smith, April 20, June 15, 1841; Joseph L. Smith to *id.*, April 2, 1841; *id.* to Mary Smith, June 15, 1841.

Kinsly to tutor Edmund for his examinations, and the Websters then left for Houlton, Maine. Reports from Kinsly were encouraging, even complimentary, both as to Edmund's scholarship and conduct. As for Edmund himself, he studied but did little writing. Frances grew anxious and showered him with questions. How did he like West Point? What about his examinations? Who examined him? What were some of the questions asked? Would he not write her all of the particulars? He must not hesitate to tell her all of his troubles, for she would give him sympathy and understanding. While passing through Boston en route to Maine, she had seen Cousin Winfield Belton, Aunt Harriet's son. "Winfield is a fine looking young man," she observed, "but I fear is pursuing a downward, disgraceful career owing to a want of truth & strict integrity of principle & character."

Young Belton had once been a cadet at West Point and had apparently been dismissed because of improper conduct. Frances knew the details, and so did Edmund; she did not discuss them in her letters. Frances had also heard from her husband, a graduate in the class of 1823, many stories about cadet life. She was horrified that young men would have so little respect for themselves and their families. He must shun every deviation from the path of honor and integrity, she urged Edmund. "The impositions which the cadets are frequently in the habit of practicing upon their professors & the means which they take to evade their duties & violate regulations even though connived and laughed at by each other are anything but honorable creditable or justifiable. I hope my dear Edmund you will never be induced to make use of any subterfuge however witty & cunning they may seem at the time." [14]

Judge Smith also sent suggestions. Edmund must write

[14] Frances Webster to Edmund K. Smith, June 15, 1841.

his Uncle Ira, taking pains with his spelling and composition, for his uncle's quick eye would immediately detect errors. During vacation time he might visit his uncle in New Britain, but he must never remain longer than two or three days. "Do not make those you visit twice glad"— once at arrival and again at departure. He might also pay short visits to other relatives in New York and Connecticut. "I mean by *a short time a few hours.*" [15]

Cadet Edmund K. Smith got off to a good start at West Point. Owing to the publicity given the Seminole war in Florida, his associates nicknamed him "Seminole." Flattering reports both as to work and conduct soon reached the family. Indeed it appeared that he would be among the leaders of his class. Frances, bubbling over with "pride & pleasure," urged him on to higher things and again insisted that he submit all of his problems to her. She would refer them to her husband, for "Capt. Webster's long residence at West Point has given him such knowledge & experience in all the *ways* of the institution that he is competent to give you advice in any emergency." However, if he would but let honor, integrity, and truth be his guide there would be few serious difficulties. She was delighted with the manner in which he spoke of his roommates, Davidson and Russell. They were sons of fathers who had been martyrs to the hardships of frontier Florida. Like her late sister Josephine, Frances had no compliments for Florida. "Poor St. Augustine seems to be doomed [as a result of fever]," she commented, "and all that are bound to it seem driven to some wretched fate, rejoiced am I that *your* destiny leads you from it; and would that all our friends could *shake its dust* from their feet & bid farewell to it forever—there is no longer anything desirable or profitable in it." [16]

---

[15] Joseph L. Smith to *id.,* quoted in a letter to Mary Smith, June 15, 1841.
[16] Frances Webster to *id.,* December 21, 1841, and March 20, 1842.

At the Academy Edmund again neglected to keep the members of his family informed to the extent they desired. "Why don't you write me," inquired Frances again and again. "I have written several letters to him—he treats them with silent contempt," complained Kirby. Cadet Smith, on the other hand, must have enjoyed receiving mail, even the numerous letters from Frances. Born with a collector's instinct, he carefully preserved most of those received.

Judge Smith was one of the fortunate few to receive a letter from Edmund during the winter of 1841–42. He replied with family news and some more sound advice. Frances, he had learned, had another baby girl, and the plan was to name her Frances Catherine. Josephine, Frances' other daughter, was said to be an *"intellectual* prodigy." Kirby also had a new baby at his home. It might be a promising lad, but could hardly be expected to equal the older one—Joseph Lee Smith. But Uncle Reynold Kirby had beat them all; his new baby weighed thirteen and a half pounds at birth! This husky fellow was to be named Joseph Lee Smith Kirby.

In his recent letter Edmund had indicated considerable discontent with life at the Academy and expressed a youthful doubt as to the value of it all. "Say not again that you have *no ambition,"* his father urged. "Strive *honorably virtuously* and *ardently* to be distinguished—and God will give you *distinction."* Although, when viewed superficially, it seemed neither "remarkably sensible nor philosophical" to censure or charge a cadet with demerits "for a button off his coat, or for one unbuttoned or because his clothes, bed, windows, room, mantle, shelves, books, face, hair, hands, or nails were out of order," he knew the "importance of these things *in the aggregate."* "They go far to *make the man;* much farther to make the officer and gentleman." Many years of army life had clearly demonstrated to him that strict attention to these seemingly small matters improved the health, efficiency, courage, and morality of both officers and soldiers. If such rules were not enforced at the Academy, "the filth, the irregularity, *the vermin even,* would become intolerable."

Then My Dear Son, as it will benefit you so much; as it will save you from the discounts for demerits; as it will ensure for you a higher standing in your class; as it will advance you in the Army and in reputation,—do I pray you, be scrupulously attentive to each and *all of these small things; small indeed individually* but *in the aggregate* I repeat of vast importance. . . . Let no temporary discontent indifference, ennui, or despondence check your forward course for a single day; never again say or think *that you feel indifference as to your success.*

In closing his long letter of advice, the anxious father stressed that Edmund was no longer a boy and must now make decisions for himself, determining his own moral principles. He wished to relieve his son from a previous promise not to play cards. Although he most earnestly desired that Edmund not play, even for amusement, he preferred to "confide in your upright principles, rather than on a verbal promise." [17]

This fatherly advice was not accepted in its entirety, and in the fall of 1842 the family learned indirectly that Edmund and his roommates were running high in demerits. Only nine other cadets had received more during the year. "Now as this is the case it would appear as if you aided each other in obtaining these demerits," observed Frances. Therefore the solution to the problem would be for each to locate himself with "some steady, studious pains-taking young man," who would furnish better example and influence. Although he had "reposed no confidence" in her and perhaps would not appreciate her advice,

[17] Joseph L. Smith to *id.,* February 25, 1842.

she hoped he would not be offended. If he wished, Captain Webster would use his influence at the Academy in effecting the change in roommates. "All now depends upon yourself. . . . You surely will not for the sake of a little *personal* enjoyment refuse to exert yourself to afford . . . consolation to the last days of a father who has always been kind and affectionate to you." [18]

Edmund wanted neither Frances' advice nor the use of Webster's influence at West Point. He did not reply. But Frances did not quit. Her brother must be aroused and the good name of the family saved. For the sixth time without an answer, she began on December 12, 1842, she was appealing to him not to disgrace his old father. "Your success will soothe his troubled spirit, and confer a balm upon his declining years." Furthermore, a scrupulous course on Edmund's part would "wipe out all remembrance of the stain . . . cast upon the family" by Winfield Belton's "disgraceful career at the Point." But she would offer no more advice, "for I almost begin to think that you do not reply to my letters because their contents are not agreeable to you." [19]

On the same date Captain Webster wrote a friend at the Academy: "If you can either by advice or admonition or in any other way, contribute to Edmund Smith's well doing at the Academy you will confer a lasting obligation on us; and I shall esteem it an act of friendship if you inform me, should you observe any thing amiss, either in his conduct or studies." [20]

Before Frances' and Captain Webster's letters reached West Point, brother Kirby had also written "dear Ted." "I am not willing to believe," he began, "that you have no affection for any of us or that you can entirely forget your

[18] Frances Webster to *id.*, September 6, 1842.
[19] *Id.* to *id.*, December 12, 1842.
[20] L. B. Webster to A. E. Church, December 12, 1842.

Mother and only brother who both so dearly love you. Yet you take no pains to evince your regard for us. Indeed you entirely neglect us, and if by this you do not deliberately insult us, you show an utter disregard of our feelings and a great indifference to our esteem." He was pleased with Edmund's class standing, but regretted the accumulation of demerits. He trusted they were for petty neglect rather than serious offenses. "My own *sad experience* [21] in the institution enables me to make all allowances for any boy there, as well as to increase my anxiety for you, who are passing through that severe ordeal." If his number of demerits did not prevent a leave next summer, why not come to Dearborn for his vacation? Kirby would furnish necessary funds. Their mother was now visiting at Dearborn and was eager to see her baby boy.[22]

In far away St. Augustine, Judge Smith, lonely and discouraged, had heard nothing from his "Ted" for months. Age and illness had softened, if not improved, the old judge's manner. He was now alone, except for a few trusted servants, in the Segui House, which he had purchased in 1838. All of his children were at distant points, and his wife had gone north several months earlier and had shown no inclination to return. Her leaving St. Augustine was prompted by more than just a desire to visit Northern relatives.

Early in May, 1843, the judge finally received a letter from West Point. Edmund wished permission to visit Kirby during the coming summer. Judge Smith suggested a visit to his uncle Ira's instead. It would be less expensive, and he had no funds to send his son. He was willing, however, to leave the decision to Edmund's judgment.[23]

Edmund made the trip to Detroit, after first visiting his

---

[21] Kirby had graduated at the foot of a class of forty-one.
[22] Ephraim K. Smith to Edmund K. Smith, December 16, 1842.
[23] Joseph L. Smith to *id.*, May 12, 1843.

uncle Ira. He found his mother still with Kirby, and after ten days together she accompanied him back to his uncle Edmund's home at Brownsville. Kirby was much impressed with his younger brother, whom he had not seen since a small boy. "He is about my height, will be a little larger man," he wrote their father. "He is a noble young gentleman, amiable well mannered and intellectual." [24]

While visiting with Kirby, Edmund probably heard his mother's version of the difficulty between herself and his father. Possibly at her request, he wrote his father a long touching letter after returning to West Point. The letter has been lost but its contents are revealed in the judge's reply: "Your letter my dear Son, makes me love you, if possible, more than ever; at least, it adds to my respect, and also evinces a very respectable intellect." He had already written Edmund's mother "in a kind and uncomplaining manner," requesting that she come home without delay. All he knew of a "separation" was from reports. "Your mother never told me." "*Cause of complaint* certainly existed; but at my advanced stage of life, I never thought of making it *cause* for *separation*." He hoped his wife would return by autumn. As for his part, he would do nothing "to mar a quiet, peaceable, and even an affectionate old age—such as we ought to pass together."

In the same letter to which the above was a reply, Edmund had also referred to the subject of cards and drinking, a topic of previous discussion between them. If his father requested, he would promise never to drink spiritous liquors or play cards. This worried the old judge. Had Edmund been drinking and playing cards? Could his demerits have resulted from such conduct? "Dear Edmund," he replied, "I think you, now in your nineteenth year, too much of a gentleman, and far too intelligent, to be *re-*

[24] Ephraim K. Smith to Joseph L. Smith, n.d.

*quested, I mean requested* in the nature of a command. I
do most earnestly *entreat* that your duty and good sense
may check you both as to *drink* and as to *cards*. . . . I
thought dear Edmund, that both were prohibited at the
Academy." Surely his son "would not be guilty of violat-
ing such important *rightful* injunctions." He had no idea,
he continued, that his son touched liquor. Edmund had so
stated to him shortly before entering the Academy. "I am
surprised that you have *there* commenced and yielded to
this *bad habit*." Cards too, he thought, were "very dangerous and discreditable." Since Edmund had brought up
the subject, his father now requested a monthly statement
as to his son's success "in conquering and *treading under
your feet,* these bad practices." [25]

Judge Smith immediately wrote again to his wife, who
was now in Brownsville, New York, enclosing Edmund's
letter to him, both of which were sent to Edmund for examination prior to being forwarded to Brownsville. "I en-
close you Edmund's eloquent letter," he wrote. "It makes
my heart bleed with love and grief for him—Read it, and
listen to the warm outpouring of his loving heart. Come
home without delay—and unite in the exertion to live
quietly and decently with your husband till death which at
my age from me cannot be far distant. Let our latest impress on the memories of our children at least not be painful to them." He was sending funds to cover her transportation to St. Augustine. [26]

In an appended note to Edmund he added: "If any
added reason for kindness to your mother could influence
—it would be your request, and my love for you and pride
in you." And now since he had complied with his son's request he urged him to comply with that of his father—

[25] Joseph L. Smith to Edmund K. Smith, September 2, 1843.
[26] *Id.* to Wife, September 8, 1843.

would he "strive in every particular to comply with all orders—neglect no duty—" and use his faculties in rising from twelfth in class to among the highest five? "If you do your duty & try, though you fail, it will not lessen your father's love—it will touch his pride only." [27]

Weeks passed and Judge Smith heard nothing from his wife. The Kirbys on the one side and the Smiths on the other had now entered the controversy, and Edmund was caught in the cross fire. In September there came a long letter from Aunt Kate Russell, of Governor's Island. She began by mildly reprimanding him for his loss of standing in his class. "Your dear Mother will be most sadly disappointed & grieved when she finds that you have fallen off for dear Edmund her whole heart & soul are wrapped up in you that you are to be her all in all—she is almost heart broken at the treatment she has received from her children & husband's relatives . . . it is wrong very wrong in you to neglect so kind & devoted a mother. Your letters are a great comfort to her—if your silence has been occasioned by the influence of your fathers connexions I can soon prove that the[y] should not have that influence—I have felt too *indignant* at the steps taken to annoy & distress your Mother to make her wretched and unhappy—Ed he is your father still I cannot but speak plainly it is due to your Mother that you should know, how he is endeavoring to injure her now she is away from him—his conduct is shameful beyond anything the steps he has taken to turn her friends from her are the very ones to bind them more closely to her. She is worthy of being loved & cherished— While he by the life he leads & his *outrageous ungovernable temper* has lost the respect of every one—You have yourself young as you are witnessed his outbreaks of temper . . . [Your Mother's] friends will not allow her to be sub-

[27] *Id.* to Edmund K. Smith, September 10, 1843.

jected to it any longer & her home must for the future be
with them, or her children." [28]

Next came a letter from Uncle Ira Smith of New Britain. "You are the son of our beloved brother," he began,
"and by his long sickness you are in some measure deprived of those affectionate attentions which his ardent love
for you would gladly bestow, and which we therefore
would the more joyfully afford, and which, having become
more particularly acquainted with you, we rejoice to find
are justly your due for your kind disposition and goodness
of heart. . . . You cannot conceive, much less can I express the warmth of the love he feels for you . . . & his
ceaseless anxiety concerning you." On his last visit to relatives his father was "greatly enervated in body, and his
vigorous intellect was in some measure unstrung, and he
was almost hopelessly desponding, still his affectionate
heart clung to you and Kirby and Frances with a tenacity
that death only can relax. Of such a father dear Edmund
you cannot be too fond, and your whole life of kindness
can hardly repay his affection. Oh how I wish he would
leave that hateful Florida where he never found health,
friendship or kindness, and that he would return to the
home of his youth, and those friends which his affectionate
heart has ensured to him." [29]

Winter came and passed, and Mrs. Smith remained
with her brother Edmund at Brownsville. Frances was still
isolated at Fort Kent, Fish River, Maine. Her letters to
Edmund made no mention of the rift between their parents.

[28] Mrs. Katherine Russell to *id.*, September ?, 1843.
[29] Ira Smith to *id.*, October 27, 1843. The ties between Judge Smith and his
brother Ira were very close. In view of the judge's declining health, Ira's wife
Mary urged him to become a more religious man. The Judge promised that
he would "read the Bible attentively & without delay make peace with God."
Should he die, he urged his brother Ira to bestow upon Edmund the kindliness
of a father. Joseph L. Smith to Ira Smith, June 30, 1841; *id.* to Mary Smith,
June 15, 1841.

She seldom mentioned her mother at all but was constantly reminding Edmund of his duty to his aged father.

Edmund corresponded with his mother at fairly frequent intervals. He was delighted that the New York winter was passing so pleasantly for her. As for himself, since he had become an anchorite, he had "bid adieu to pleasure and amusements." His "only gratification is in hearing of the enjoyment of others, and the happiness of those I love." But he warned his mother not to rank him among "the philanthropists," "for as you know I much prefer being a prime mover in all pleasures and amusements and it was really quite a stoical effort that induced me to think with indifference of my present privations but as one of my next door neighbors says, *nil desperandum.*" Others at West Point were enjoying sleighing, at least Dr. Hitchcock who dashed by with "bells jingling and his good natured face glowing with delight. I passed him . . . the other day, made him a most polite bow a la Paris but bad manners to him—the Heathen! the Turk!! he didn't ask me in.!!"

Edmund described at length his meeting with Miss Margaret Robinson, the first mention he had made of interest in the ladies. While returning with a group of boys from a chestnut hunt and pleasant stroll in the woods, they passed a number of ladies. "I heard someone exclaim— why really there's Edmund Smith— In consternation at being caught in such a plight for I was rather deshabile & with a mouth full of chestnuts I shook her warmly by the hand, but in my first attempt to express my pleasure at the meeting out flew the chestnuts bountifully distributed on *all* sides; had it not been for her open countenance beaming with delight I should have felt rather awkward—as it was I had a hearty laugh over it on my return to quarters." But it was now time for drumbeat and attendance at drawing class. His mother should have his best pieces in her portfolio, for she would value them more than he.[30]

A few weeks later Cadet Smith was less cheerful. Continued bad weather and bad news from Washington, where in the House of Representatives a vicious attack was being made upon the Academy, made him "feel more like writing a satire and venting my spleen on some poor wight, than taking pen in hand to write you even the state of the weather." He could scarcely believe that Congress would blast the hopes of the Academy's graduating class, yet Captain J. A. Thomas, the commandant, who had just returned from headquarters, saw slight hope for commissions and advised against the purchase of uniforms. "O tempora! O Mores!" Now the cadets, huddled about their fires and enveloped in the smoke from their own pipes, must decide "whether to seek a home on the wild prairies of the far west in the unrestricted freedom of the Pioneer life or with the recklessness of the Buccaneer on the boundless expanse of water in the depths of the gulf of Mexico as of old to rob the Spaniards of their treasure."[31]

His mother replied with sympathy and advice. Since no one could foretell what that "vile Jacobin portion of our body politic may do," Edmund should occupy himself with the acquisition of general knowledge. "This is a 'working day world,' " she explained, "and you will have to carve your own future." Did he have an ear for music? If so, she begged him to cultivate it. The labor would not be lost, for "the cultivation of music is one of the refinements of life—and is always a passport to society." A singing school was then in session at Brownsville, and Uncle Edmund was "a regular attendant with book in hand." His daughter Frances was also doing well on the

---

[30] Edmund K. Smith to Mother, February ?, 1844.
[31] *Id.* to *id.*, March 16, 1844.

piano. His son Jake was expected home from West Point for a visit, she slyly added. He stood first in his class and his father was justly proud of him.

Now that the fierceness of winter had passed, Mrs. Smith concluded, and the season for making maple syrup had come, young and old were having fun at "Sugar Bush." Soon she would be able to take walks along the river and "throw off care and depression of spirits in the excitement I always feel in these romantic rambles." [32]

Down in Florida the old judge, after two months in Tallahassee, returned to St. Augustine early in February, 1844, and found neither wife nor letters from his children. He complained to Edmund that he had not received a line in six months. But his son's monthly report cards for October and November were before him. In all subjects except natural philosophy, he noted, Edmund had dropped from two to seven places in class rank. Furthermore, he had received thirteen demerits in November as compared to nine and a third for the academic year through October. Would his son not strive to regain his loss of standing and avoid "these *black demerit scores?*" the father asked.[33]

At the close of his third year Cadet Edmund K. Smith ranked twenty-fifth in his class. His family was worried, and he was sick and disgusted even to the point of wishing to resign. That he had lost respect for the authorities and the rules was clearly indicated in his letters. Demerits were accumulating at a rapid rate. He apparently was not permitted a leave during the summer of 1844, for in September he wrote his mother at Brownsville expressing great disappointment over not being able to see her. The "fates were adverse." For months, he explained, his own illness and disgust had rendered him incapable of either study or

[32] Mrs. Frances K. Smith to Edmund K. Smith, April 2, 1844.
[33] Joseph L. Smith to *id.*, February 4, 1844.

pleasure. On two or three occasions he had seriously contemplated applying for resignation. His only restraint had been the lingering hope that he might still gratify his parents by securing a diploma. However, he was still not convinced that resignation would have been unwise. The Academy doctor had recommended him for sick leave, but "cogent reasons prevented notwithstanding my desires to the contrary." He now felt much improved, and was anxiously waiting for the few months of his imprisonment "to glide by in their certain and eventful course."

He had received a letter from his cousin Frances Kirby urging him to visit Brownsville and enjoy the winter sports. "I believe its all fudge! give me the sunny clime of the South; though her presence would lend enchantment to any scene." He dreaded the dreary winter now approaching.

The Point had taken on a bit of social color as a result of the visit of Mrs. Winfield Scott and her daughters, Edmund reported. "Camille Cornelia & Ella cary [sic] the day here at present—If I was the Old General I should be dreadfully jealous—Mrs. Scott holds her levee to forty or fifty cadets at Koscuisko's. Gives them parties sends them daily fruit, cakes &—and never seems at ease till she gets a crowd of cadets (her heart's corps as she calls them) around her. She is very much liked and would make quite a popular Superintendent— From the length of time she has been here, and her apparent aversion to leaving, I expect she is fully inclined to supercede Major Delafield in the regal chair of tyranny." [34]

Edmund also wrote his father of his disgust and threatened resignation. In the same mail went the official report of his conduct and standing at the Academy. The judge hastily tore a blank page from the report and dashed off

[34] Edmund K. Smith to Mother, September 24, 1844.

a reply. There must be no thought of resignation before graduation, he urged. After receiving a commission resignation could be accomplished "more advantageously & reputably." The report on his son's conduct greatly alarmed the old man. Forty-five demerits for the month of August! "9 times 45 for your *nine* remaining months at the academy," the judge figured, "will be 405 which added to the 60 already charged against you will constitute a Total of *465*!! And *200* I thought, was the *ne plus ultra*. Be careful my dear Son, and rein in your prancing steed, or you will be thrown headlong from the Academy."

Edmund had asked for $300 or $400 by the following June to pay up his little debts and buy uniforms. There must be some mistake about the need for so much money, the judge replied. Cash was very scarce. He had provided Kirby with about $250 to cover his mother's expenses and had also sent some money to her. Further, he had made "liberal presents" to Captain Webster who had suffered an accident and had been rather harshly treated "as to his quarter master's amts." But if Edmund would put forth his best efforts, his doting father promised all of the financial aid possible.[35]

Frances had also heard a portion of the news in faraway Hancock Barracks, Maine. A friend returning from West Point and a letter from Edmund both arrived on September 29. Frances put a letter in the next mail. She had set her heart on having her brother with her after graduation, she explained. But only the highest five could get into the artillery. Edmund's fall to twenty-fifth position almost blighted her hope, even though "it seems as if it *ought* to be *impossible* that such bright dreams should be disappointed." She now realized that her "ambition and anxiety" for him had exceeded his own. Yet the artillery was

[35] Joseph L. Smith to Edmund K. Smith, October 9, 1844.

so worth striving for. It had so many advantages over the infantry in "point of station, society, manners and morals." She had wanted so much to welcome him as part of the Webster household and show him "as much domestic happiness as is commonly allotted to mortals." And with Captain Webster's standing and influence, he could be of great assistance to a young officer. Edmund must guard his health, Frances insisted, yet she urged him neither to resign nor take a sick leave unless absolutely necessary. Why not go to Dr. Russell for examination and prescription? In whatever action he took he should ever remember his old father, troubled in mind, sick in body, and with his "future completely shattered."

Edmund had complained of Captain Thomas' attitude toward him. This should not worry or disgust him, Frances insisted, for Captain Webster thought Thomas "weak & deficient in judgment & apt to carry any thing too far." Webster would write Thomas a friendly letter and probably turn the scales in Cadet Smith's favor. "Of course you will *not mention* this." [36] Frances had not yet learned about the forty-five demerits in August.

After talking more at length with the friend lately returned from West Point and learning of Edmund's demerits, Frances was at him again. Twenty additional demerits, she cautioned, would result in his dismissal, and there were still four months remaining. "Think of the *nominal* if not real disgrace, which will cling to you through life for this failure." Few persons would understand and be willing to "attribute it to the folly and heedlessness of youth." Many would exaggerate and attribute it to "vice and incapability." Surely he would not let early indiscretion dim his resources and close to him the avenues of preferment. A little discretion now could avert this

[36] Frances Webster to *id.*, September 29, 1844.

catastrophe. Since he was now officer of the guard, maybe there would be less chance of being caught "visiting after taps."

All along, Frances had urged him to graduate at the top of his class, but she had recently decided that graduation even "at the very foot" would be better than not graduating at all. What would he do if dismissed? she inquired. The family had no money. And even relatives who might be inclined to help him would consider dismissal from West Point a poor recommendation. "I cannot sleep at night so filled am I with anxiety for you. . . . I am almost sick now with very dread of the future, and I shall not rest until I hear from you." [37]

As winter came, Cadet Smith was no more contented at the Academy, but he had become more careful. Probably he had taken his Uncle Edmund Kirby's advice not to be "found out." However, he was still rebellious under the restraint. "If I obeyed the regulations to the letter," he wrote his mother, "I should make a perfect anchorite of myself. The Professors—Superintendent, etc.—twist-turn & change them to suit their fancies & should not we poor devils evade them to meet our necessities." Only recently an order had forbidden the use of dressing gowns in quarters. "Would you have me throw out that beautiful gown *you* took so much trouble to make for me— Would you [have] me keep my coat buttoned to the detriment [of my] health." They "would indeed be a stiff-n race" should the collar regulations be followed.

Edmund had no great expectations for Christmas, but he wished his mother a merry one. Until she mentioned it, he remarked, he had just about forgotten the old gentleman who goes about visiting folk at Christmas time. The "Old Chap" had become "entirely obsolete in these regions, for he would indeed fare but badly, with his goods & chattels amongst a band of hungry and rapacious Cadets." There was some hope for an interesting Christmas party, however. He recalled that last Christmas Eve "the Major indulged us with one, but taking advantage of his permission we obtained such a supply of Brandy peaches, that many were taken off to bed—thusly proving they preferred brandy to peaches any day."

Examinations were approaching. This hurdle once passed, the three roommates in No. 6 North Barracks would add astronomy to their course and begin the last grind. Edmund wished his mother could know his roommates—William Farrar Smith, better known as "Baldy," and Richard Howard. The former he described as "a Yanky by birth but as fine a fellow as ever graced a short tail." Howard was "a Mississippian full of pistols & bowie knives but now tempered down by the cooling effects of a northern clime to quite a gentle & rational being with black hair & eyes that look through & through a person & in the tout ensemble quite a handsome young man." [38] The Smiths undoubtedly settled down to serious work. What happened to Howard is not known; he was not later listed among the graduates.

Edmund's last year was most satisfactory, Judge Smith wrote him on February 1, 1845. He must keep up all of his improvements and "*Strive without fainting* till you actually graduate." Would he not prefer the infantry after graduation? Chances for rapid promotion were much better in that branch of the service. However, if he preferred the artillery he must strive toward that end with a determination to attain it. Whichever should be his choice, would Edmund let him know in his next letter. A close friendship between himself and Adjutant General Roger

[38] Edmund K. Smith to Mother, December 19, 1844.

Jones would assure the desired placement, if Edmund's class rank was satisfactory. The Negro boy Alex, the father added, was developing rapidly and should make a useful servant. Edmund might have him immediately after graduation.[39]

When Edmund's February report reached his father the old gentleman was beside himself with joy. "But 3 marks for *demerit* in the month God be praised!" he wrote Edmund. Continuing at that rate, his son would have only 180 at graduation. "God be thanked a second time; now you will surely escape the rocks and whirlpools of both Scylla and Charybdis." And Edmund's letters had also improved, the father commented, although he was still using "laying" instead of "lying." His son would do well to study Shakespeare and Ben Jonson as authorities.[40]

Edmund's preference as to the branch of the army or regiment is not expressed in his extant letters, but on April 6, 1845, Judge Smith wrote Adjutant General Jones, requesting that his son be attached to the Eighth Regiment then stationed at St. Augustine. Since Cadet Smith had been away from his aged father for nine years, the judge hoped General Jones would appreciate the special request.[41] The judge then notified his son of the request and suggested that after graduation he and his mother might journey to St. Augustine together. A draft on either New York relatives or Uncle Ira would be sent to cover the expense of a new uniform and pay his son's little debts. Free board awaited Edmund in St. Augustine.[42]

Captain Webster urged Judge Smith to meet him at West Point for Edmund's graduation, but the judge was not able to make the trip. Webster left Hancock Barracks on

[39] Joseph L. Smith to Edmund K. Smith, February 1, 1845.
[40] *Id.* to *id.*, April 2, 1845.
[41] *Id.* to General Roger Jones, April 6, 1845.
[42] *Id.* to Edmund K. Smith, April 7, 8, 1845.

May 25, Frances informed Edmund, and would be present for his examinations. She was still hoping against hope that Edmund might get into the artillery. At any rate, Captain Webster could be of assistance in purchasing his new equipment. There would be no need to buy a large number of shirts, for she was making a dozen for him. He must accompany Webster to her home immediately after graduation before he reported to any regiment. His little niece Josephine was eagerly awaiting his arrival and wanted him to bring her an atlas.[43]

Cadet Edmund K. Smith graduated twenty-fifth in his class. As the family awaited the good news another message was received instead. The Board of Examiners had found him too near-sighted for active duty as an officer.[44] Kirby and Frances sent letters of condolence. Kirby refused to believe that such an unjust decision would be sanctioned by the Secretary of War. However, in any case, Edmund should not become disheartened, for

the army in our country is certainly not a desirable profession for any young man who has ability and perseverance to succeed in any other. With your talents and education, a few years of industry will most certainly place you in a position far in advance of your classmates, who will lead the enervating and indolent lives of subalterns, and I by no means desire that *my* sons should ever wear a sword. I would certainly prefer that they become honest, industrious mechanics. So, my dear brother, be not cast down. You can get a better profession than the one I fear you have lost.

Kirby himself was expecting to be transferred from Detroit to an even more isolated post on Lake Superior. Nothing but war with Mexico, he reasoned, could prevent this unpleasant banishment from his family.[45]

Frances was even more severe in denouncing the type

[43] Frances Webster to *id.*, May 24, 1845.
[44] See report in Kirby-Smith Papers under date of June 20, 1845.
[45] Ephraim K. Smith to Edmund K. Smith, July ?, 1845.

of life that Edmund had apparently escaped. She had lived many years at army posts in isolated areas and had observed much. "The Army opens no career which a man of talent can desire—It to be sure (and I am sorry to say it) offers a safe harbour for indolence and imbecility." Since he had escaped this type of life, he had only to choose a profession, apply himself, and become distinguished. She suggested the medical profession as more desirable and certain than law. It would also be more ennobling. Edmund might make his home with her and study under doctors there before going to New York for advanced study. All their friends at Hancock Barracks sent sympathy for the injustice suffered.[46]

When Edmund's letter telling of the "injustice" reached his father, the old judge was furious. Such an action was retroactive, he declared, and "forbidden by all law public and private—human and divine." He hastily wrote the Board of Examiners a stinging censure and unwisely incorporated quotations from Edmund's letter in his own. An anonymous member of the Board replied: "I can make any allowance for a father's feelings and solicitude for the welfare of a son—but the style of your letter is such that it would not deserve a reply, but to correct an error that brings down upon the guiltless, the burden of your wrath." The Board was not just a group of medical men, as had been charged, but included a number of Academy officials headed by the Superintendent. Edmund had appeared before that group and was thoroughly examined and found to be perfect except for his vision. He himself admitted that his sight was bad and growing worse. Even his mother, on a recent visit to the Academy, had expressed great concern over her son's defective vision. For the father's information, the Board would like to say that

[46] Frances Webster to *id.*, July 5, 1845.

Edmund was "a general favorite with all who knew him."[47]

Before Judge Smith received this letter Edmund had already received his commission in spite of defective vision. Several persons at the Academy came to his assistance, at least two of them being members of the Board. The surgeon stated that Edmund had never complained of defective vision or asked to be excused from his duties. From the commandant of cadets came a statement that no defect of vision had prevented his performance of duty and he had frequently commanded a company. The instructor of sword exercises had observed no interference with his horsemanship.[48] These testimonies were apparently sufficient.

The judge was now suffering from both remorse and fear. Suppose the War Department should hold his letter, particularly the excerpts from Edmund's letter, against his son. He decided upon a letter of explanation and apology. "If there be severity in your letter without date or signature," he began, "I deserve that severity." For nine long years he had seen his son only once and that for only a few hours. But in all of his son's correspondence, save his most recent letter, there had been nothing critical of the authorities at the Academy. "My letter, for these reasons, I admit, was the less excusable." The news that an alleged weakness, of which he himself had "never heard even a lisp," had wrecked the youthful aspirations of his son had astounded the father. It seemed unjust that the boy should have been allowed to continue so long in ignorance of his fate. The "*fiat* of the Board" seemed "unsound in its very origin"; therefore, he hastily wrote his "silly and pragmatic letter." Now he wished to tender to

---

[47] "One of the Board" to Joseph L. Smith, n.d.
[48] See Kirby-Smith Papers for these testimonies.

all who might have been offended "the *amende honorable*."
"If more need to be said, recollect that I am an old man,
near to 70—and that my son, most *assuredly* should not
be held responsible for what naturally belongs to the
senility of his father." If his other letter, as had been indicated, had been sent to the War Department, then would
the receiver please give this one a place beside it.[49]

A copy of this letter accompanied by a note of apology
was forwarded to Edmund. That portion of his son's letter
which was included, the judge explained, was not correctly
transcribed; therefore, it was not actually Edmund's.
Should anything come of this affair, "no principle of
*morality* or *honour*" could compel him to acknowledge the
authorship of something that was not fairly his.

Edmund was commissioned brevet second lieutenant
and assigned to the Fifth Regiment of Infantry which was
already making preparation to move with General Zachary
Taylor into the disputed zone on the Texan border. Judging from the tone of a letter from his sister Frances, he
had been given his choice and had chosen the infantry.
She rejoiced at his having received a commission, but was
"pained and chagrined" by his choice. He had certainly
proved himself "verdant & inexperienced." His decision
placed between them forever "an insurmountable barrier
of forest and lake." She suspected that want of affection
for her had assisted him in choosing the infantry. "And
with this I resign the most cherished dream of my later
years, the hope of having my much loved brother *with* us,
and *one* of us." He had voluntarily chosen life on the
frontier where soldiers gradually became a part of the
"demi civilized" people about them and married ignorant
and illiterate girls. However, since he had chosen the in-

---

[49] Joseph L. Smith to "The Unknown Member of the Medical Board at
West Point," September 29, 1845.

fantry, she was pleased that he would be with Kirby.[50]
There was no evidence of a want of affection on Edmund's
part; however, he quite likely did not wish to pass under
the domination of Frances and Captain Webster.

[50] Frances Webster to Edmund K. Smith, July 26, 1845.

# CHAPTER III

# TO MEXICO WITH TAYLOR

EDMUND K. SMITH received his commission at a critical time. On March 1 Congress had adopted a resolution admitting the Republic of Texas into the Union as a state. Since Mexico had never recognized the independence of Texas and had warned the United States that annexation would mean war, the Mexican minister immediately left for home. As a part of the annexation agreement the United States promised to protect Texas against Mexico. Rumors of a concentration of Mexican troops along the Rio Grande made the Texans uneasy. In order to quiet these fears and to be ready for action if necessary, President James K. Polk ordered General Zachary Taylor to move his troops from Fort Jessup to the mouth of the Sabine River or some other point on the Gulf of Mexico which would be convenient for a possible movement to the Texas frontier.

Taylor received these instructions of June 29. Troops began immediately to move toward the Sabine. But when Taylor received assurance that Mexico undoubtedly planned an attack upon Texas, he decided to establish camp at Corpus Christi on the Nueces River.[1] This river, Mexico insisted, was as far as Texas had ever extended,

[1] Brainerd Dyer, *Zachary Taylor* (Baton Rouge, 1946), 153; Holman Hamilton, *Zachary Taylor, Soldier of the Republic* (Indianapolis, 1941), 159–63.

but Texas claimed the territory to the Rio Grande. The United States was now obligated to protect Texan boundaries.

Following a visit with his mother at the home of Aunt Kate Russell, on Governor's Island, Second Lieutenant Edmund K. Smith and his newly acquired dog "Ponto" set out through New York to join his regiment. He had pleasant visits with friends and relatives along the way in spite of a brief illness which resulted from having two teeth filled with an amalgam and which almost cost him both of the teeth and one eye. His face became so badly swollen that his eye was closed. One tooth was then extracted and the abscess on the other lanced. Ponto behaved well through it all and soon became closely attached to the young lieutenant. From Fort Ontario Edmund sent both his and Ponto's greetings to his mother.[2]

Back at Governor's Island his mother was deeply grieved. "I almost feel as if the last tie that binds me to life was broken," she wrote, "and as if I had nothing more to do in this world." She was alarmed at the great confusion and the movement of men and materials at Governor's Island. Horses were being crowded into transports, and many men were soon to take passage on the sloop of war *Lexington*. Most of them, she observed, appeared "down in the mouth."[3]

Lieutenant Smith was too late to join his regiment before it left Detroit. On August 28, four days after he wrote his mother from Ontario, the Fifth was moving toward Cincinnati by way of the Ohio Canal. Uncle Edmund Kirby had urged his nephew to hurry to Jefferson Barracks, Missouri, before the Fifth left that place, but it does not appear that a stop was made at the Barracks.

[2] Edmund K. Smith to Mother, August 24, 1845.
[3] Mrs. Frances K. Smith to Edmund K. Smith, August 27, 1845.

In the published correspondence of Captain Ephraim Kirby Smith there is no mention of the time of Edmund's arrival. It is quite likely, however, that he caught up with the regiment before it reached New Orleans. When the Fifth reached Cincinnati it found orders to proceed immediately to Corpus Christi. Embarking on August 29, it was at Cairo by September 1, and at New Orleans about a week later. The post temporarily occupied at New Orleans was described by Captain Ephraim Kirby Smith as "by far the most beautiful I have ever seen. The quarters are fine and airy, completely protected from the sun by beautiful tropical shade trees, with extensive yards and gardens about them, and a large shaded parade ground clothed with a rich greensward." [4] He made no mention, however, of Edmund being present to enjoy this ideal camp site.

There was only a short delay at New Orleans. The men of the Fifth, hearing that Corpus Christi was "the most delightful spot on the globe, cool, healthy, no insects, not a mosquito, an abundance of oysters, fish and venison," were eager to get moving.[5] They took passage on the steamship *Alabama,* and were off the bay by September 13. The *Alabama* drew too much water to enter the bay; so small steamers were used in disembarking. On the night of September 14, during a storm, the Fifth Infantry dropped anchor opposite the Corpus Christi camp. For a mile or more along the south side of the Nueces River could be seen the camp fires blinking in the rain.[6]

Taylor's army remained at Corpus Christi for several months.[7] During the midwinter young Lieutenant Edmund

[4] Ephraim K. Smith to Wife, September 9, 1845, in Emma Jerome Blackwood (ed.), *To Mexico With Scott: Letters of Captain E. Kirby Smith to His Wife* (Cambridge, 1917), 14–16.
[5] *Ibid.*     [6] Ephraim K. Smith to Wife, September 18, 1845, *ibid.,* 17–19.
[7] *Ibid.*

K. Smith went on a hunting trip that took him thirty miles up the Nueces. He probably accompanied his brother, Captain Smith, who wrote about a similar trip.[8] Shortly after their return Lieutenant Smith began a series of interesting reports to his mother. He had just received word of his mother's intention to return to St. Augustine. "O my dear Mother," he exclaimed, "you do not know how anxiously I have wished, how fervently prayed that those I love best on this earth—My Own Dear Parents—might once again in all honor and amity, be united under the same roof." Oh how he longed for a reunion with them in the home of his childhood. But the war clouds were growing darker, and every day widened the gap between him and those he loved. Army life thus far, however, had not been too bad, although he had suffered from two attacks of bilious fever and one of jaundice. He had recently returned from a hunting trip up the Nueces, where the country was alive with myriads of game. The climate at Corpus Christi was delightful and the town itself, though a bit isolated, had a daily newspaper, two theaters, and a boat line to New Orleans. He would regret exchanging these comforts and pleasures "even for the Fandangos and black-eyed senoritas of Matamoras." There were no regrets over the decision to enter the infantry instead of the artillery.

The army was about ready to move to the Mexican border, Lieutenant Smith assured his mother. A few weeks hence would find their tents on the Rio Grande or else their "bones whitening on the plains" between. There was much excitement and eagerness for action. "Such sharpening of swords, repairing of firearms, such a demand for revolvers and bowie knives, Corpus Christi never saw." Many were the rumors of the size and positions

[8] *Id.* to *id.*, November 2, 1845, *ibid.*, 20–21.

of Mexican forces; all were considered unreliable. On the other hand, the American camp was filled with spies who no doubt relayed to Mexican commanders not only the strength and position of troops but even the names of officers and "the very gossip of the camp." [9]

General Taylor, although originally opposed to the annexation of Texas, had now become eager for action, and notified Washington authorities of his desire to occupy Point Isabel and Laredo on the Rio Grande River.[10] He willingly held his army at Corpus Christi, however, until the John Slidell peace mission to Mexico proved a failure.

On January 13, 1846, President Polk ordered Taylor to begin movement toward the Rio Grande and instructed Commodore David Connor to stand by, ready to seize Tampico and Vera Cruz in case war should be declared. Taylor's advance column under Major Samuel Ringgold moved out of Corpus Christi on March 8. The Fifth Infantry, which was attached to the Second Brigade, began the march on March 10. This was four days after Lieutenant Smith had written his mother. Twelve miles were covered the first day, much of the distance in sight of the Nueces, "winding through the prairie like a blue ribbon carelessly thrown on a green robe." [11] The prairie was covered with wild flowers—"spiderwort, phlox, lupin, fireplant, lobelia inflata, primrose, etc." The second day's march was in the rain and mud, but the soldiers were much impressed with the abundance of game—"deer innumerable, geese, ducks, curlew, cranes, wild turkeys, etc." In camp that night Captain Smith observed "a rabbit, a rat,

[9] Edmund K. Smith to Mother, March 6, 1846.

[10] Excellent accounts of Taylor's activities are found in Dyer, *Zachary Taylor;* Hamilton, *Zachary Taylor;* Justin H. Smith, *The War With Mexico* (New York, 1919); Robert S. Henry, *The Story of the Mexican War* (Indianapolis, 1950).

[11] Ephraim K. Smith to Wife, March 17, 1846, in Blackwood (ed.), *To Mexico With Scott,* 22 ff.

a rattle snake and a tarantula" living together in the same den. He killed a six-foot rattler in his tent.[12]

Then came several days of marching over parched plains. Captain Smith broke out in an irritating rash. On March 19 General Taylor sent back an announcement: "The enemy is on our front, threatening to attack us if we advance." Fatigue and suffering were immediately forgotten as guns were made ready for action. But the enemy, wishing to do no more than threaten, rode away. The dusty march was resumed. The heat and barrenness were made more oppressive by the enemy fires which destroyed even the scanty grass. All day the troops were engulfed "in clouds of black sooty dust and ashes" which clung stubbornly to beards and perspiring bodies, and the sun burned down upon man and beast "like living fire." Late in the afternoon a pool of brackish water was sighted and the troops plunged in like so many hogs. As they dragged themselves out not even their closest relatives could have recognized them.[13] The Rio Grande was reached on March 28.

How young Lieutenant Smith fared on this march is not recorded. His next letter to his mother was written after the battles of Palo Alto and Resaca de la Palma. Too much real excitement had now been experienced for him to dwell upon either hardships or pleasures of the march.

After pitching camp along the Rio Grande opposite Matamoras the troops settled down to light drill and watching the Mexicans across the river. Captain Smith was shocked at the boldness of Mexican girls swimming in the nude opposite his camp.[14] What the much younger Lieutenant Smith thought of it is not a matter of record. On the night of April 8 a tropical storm struck the camp. The Smith brothers and friends were at mess. Kirby ran

[12] *Ibid.*    [13] *Ibid.*    [14] *Id.* to *id.*, March 29, 1846, *ibid.*, 33–35.

from the tent as the storm approached. The others cheered him for his speed. A moment later the tent came down upon them, and men, food, dishes, and sundries became "one amorphous mass under a perfect deluge of rain." Edmund came crawling from under it all. He had stayed with the food. The two brothers held Kirby's tent, preventing its blowing out of the muddy cornfield in which camp had been pitched.[15]

The Mexicans across the Rio Grande gave evidence of warlike activities, and General Taylor prepared for defense. Leaving Major Jacob Brown and the Seventh Infantry to construct fortifications opposite Matamoras, he took the remaining troops, including the Fifth, and hurried down the river toward his base of supplies at Point Isabel, which was being threatened by General Mariano Arista. Advance scouts brought back reports that a Mexican force of "near ten thousand" blocked the way. A forced march of two days brought Taylor's troops to the vicinity of Point Isabel, but nothing had been seen of the enemy. Lieutenant Smith thought they "passed the enemy's encampment in the night." There was considerable grumbling because of such unnecessary exertion, but young Smith voiced no criticism.

After four days spent loading supplies at Point Isabel, the return march was begun on May 7. Taylor, hearing that he was now cut off, declared: "If the enemy oppose my march, in whatever force, I shall fight him." His men applauded, and with the passage of each hour they became more determined to cut their way through. On the following day Taylor's advance came face to face with the enemy in a well-selected defensive position, "having their rear and flanks strongly protected by dense chaparral, and an open prairie, covered with tall thick grass on their front."

[15] *Id.* to *id.*, April 9, 1846, *ibid.*, 35–37.

The advancing column halted, parked its wagon train, went into battle formation, and began moving cautiously across the prairie. The enemy opened with a cannonade from eleven pieces. Duncan's and Ringgold's batteries unlimbered and returned the fire. A half hour later the Fifth Infantry received orders to move forward from the extreme right. Simultaneously, a body of Mexican cavalry with two pieces of artillery rushed forward from the enemy's left. The Fifth halted, stood its ground, received the enemy's fire "at thirty paces," and returned devastating volleys which emptied "upward of forty saddles." Two pieces of Ringgold's battery had now come up and begun "sweeping down" the Mexican cavalry as it fled. Darkness ended the battle of Palo Alto, and the Fifth Infantry lay down for a night's sleep on the field it had taken.

By dawn of the following day Taylor's troops were again on the march, stepping over numerous enemy dead and new-made graves. By midafternoon, after marching nine miles under a burning sun, they were again upon the enemy. Re-enforcements arriving during the night had increased the fighting strength to an estimated eight thousand. "Here they had long contemplated fighting us," Lieutenant Smith later related. "A deep ravine, rendered difficult of passage by a marshy slough extended along it, formed their front, while all approaches through the open chaparral were raked by their batteries established at different points." Embankments had been thrown up further to strengthen this natural position.

The Fifth Infantry was again thrown forward, moving to the left of the road; the Fourth came up on the right. The order was to rush the enemy's batteries. Charging, falling back, and charging again, the troops became scratched, torn, and confused, but refused to stop. Regiments became mixed and men separated from their officers, but they fell in behind the leadership of others and continued the charge. On they went "yelling, shouting, killing and carrying everything before them." "I never saw such perfect demons in all my life . . ."; Lieutenant Smith exclaimed, "they rushed through the showers of grape, round and canister, to the very mouths of the enemy's pieces, bayoneted their artillerists, completely routed the infantry drawn up for the support of the batteries; capturing every piece, some fifteen hundred stands of arms, 240,000 rounds of musket cartridges, all their camp equipage and five or six hundred pack mules."

Lieutenant Smith had nothing but praise for those Mexicans who "fought bravely, fell at their posts, were bayoneted at their pieces and formed piles of dead within their entrenchments before they gave way." "Thus ended the battle of Resaca de la Palma," reported the excited Lieutenant, "a victory without its equal in our history, and fought without the aid of militia."[16]

Captain Smith also made a lengthy report of the two battles and added: "Edmund and myself, though in the thickest of the fight—men falling around us on all sides—were unhurt." "Edmund behaved with great gallantry taking a piece and bringing it from the midst of the enemy." Kirby, like his brother, reflected the regular's distrust of volunteers: "It is a glorious fact for the army that there were no volunteers with us," he explained to his wife.[17]

Great confusion followed the battle of Resaca de la Palma. The Mexicans, Lieutenant Smith believed, not calculating on defeat, had made no preparation for retreat. When they realized their danger of being completely de-

16 Edmund K. Smith to Mother, May 13, 1846.
17 Ephraim K. Smith to Wife, May 10, 13, 1846, in Blackwood (ed.), *To Mexico With Scott*, 45–53.

stroyed, they threw away their arms and fled in wild disorder. Taylor, too, was unprepared for such an overwhelming victory and had made no plans to intercept the retreating enemy at the Rio Grande ferry. Much to young Smith's disgust, Taylor did not follow up his victory but set out again for Point Isabel, leaving Colonel David E. Twiggs in command with instructions to remain on the defensive. A period of inaction followed even though Twiggs was informed by scouts that two hundred men could take the Mexican town on the other side.[18] It is generally agreed that Taylor might have made a successful crossing at this time had he been interested in hastening an entrance into enemy country.[19]

After another week of camp talk and reflection upon the recent battles, Lieutenant Smith thought the victories even more glorious and was confident of complete destruction of Mexican opposition. "You may banish all concern for our safety," he assured his mother. "The war is pretty much over. Two thousand men, were it our policy, could with ease march to the City of Mexico." Almost overcome by the excitement and glamour of it all, young Smith could not refrain from telling his mother more of the highlights of the struggles. The Mexicans had "staked their all upon the turn of a die, and at one fell swoop," had been rendered helpless. The American artillery had plowed through their lines, and the infantry, expecting no quarters, "fought with perfect desperation." "It was a hand-to-hand conflict— a trial of personal strength in many instances. Where the bayonet failed, even the fists were used (Kirby, in the thickest of the fight, got tired of using the sword and knocked a man down with his fist)." Courage, moral and

[18] Edmund K. Smith to Mother, May 13, 1846.
[19] Hamilton, *Zachary Taylor*, 191; Dyer, *Zachary Taylor*, 178.

physical, had proved its superiority and taught "a lesson which ages cannot obliterate." [20]

In neither of his interesting accounts did the modest Lieutenant refer to his own heroism. During the second day of fighting he and his immediate command captured a Mexican cannon and dragged it off into the chaparral near a pond. Immediately they observed a formidable enemy force bearing down upon them. Smith ordered the cannon spiked. A ramrod was broken off in the vent but the cannon was still serviceable. He then ordered it thrown into the pond, but Sergeant Abraham Vanderhoff of New Jersey observed that it would be a pity to destroy a beautiful cannon when it could be protected by bayonets. Lieutenant Smith accepted the suggestion and ordered his men to stand their ground. The piece was saved.[21]

Congress officially declared war on Mexico on May 12, 1846. But General Taylor had not waited for a declaration. Returning from Point Isabel, where he had gone to confer with Commodore Connor, he began preparation for crossing the river. On May 18 a portion of his force, including the Fifth Infantry, ferried the river unopposed. So swift was the current, Lieutenant Smith related, ten hours were required to get eighteen hundred men across. The Mexican army had destroyed most of the public property and retreated toward Monterey "in a dreadful state of mutiny and disorganization." And Smith heard it rumored that General Arista had been arrested and "charged with having delivered up the army to General Taylor." [22]

The Stars and Stripes were soon floating over Mata-

[20] Edmund K. Smith to Mother, May 20, 1846.
[21] Statement of Sergeant Charles Becker, August 12, 1846, in Baltimore *Sun*, September 5, 1846.
[22] Edmund K. Smith to Mother, May 20, 1846.

moras and soldiers were busily engaged searching out hidden materials of war, including artillery pieces believed to have been thrown into the river. Captain Kirby Smith strolled into town for some bread and coffee. He thought the city resembled St. Augustine, "only with larger, wider streets and finer public buildings." [23] Lieutenant Smith gave a more detailed description. Matamoras was a large city and contained enough able-bodied men to whip all the Americans present, if they but possessed the courage. Narrow streets were lined with Moorish style houses "with flat roofs, terraced floors and thick walls." The inhabitants—a mixture of Spanish, Indian, and Negro bloods—were "apparently a great deal below and more ignorant than either race." [24]

It was now rumored that the Rio Grande was to be used as a base for pushing the war into the interior. Orders to advance were expected daily. Volunteer and regular reenforcements were arriving. Captain Webster and his artillery company were at Barita, eighteen miles down the river. [25]

On June 2 Captain Smith reported the expected arrival of Major Belton with other companies of artillery. But he was not so hopeful of the outcome as his younger brother. The Mexican government would not make peace, he thought, until the Valley of Mexico was invaded. "What long marches, bloody sieges, and dreadful battles are to be encountered before then cannot be foretold but all will have to be met is most certain." [26]

Shortly after the news of Taylor's victories reached Washington he was promoted to major general and offi-

[23] Ephraim K. Smith to Wife, May 19, 1846, in Blackwood (ed.), *To Mexico With Scott*, 53–55.

[24] Edmund K. Smith to Mother, May 20, 1846.   [25] *Ibid.*

[26] Ephraim K. Smith to Wife, June 2, 1846, in Blackwood (ed.), *To Mexico With Scott*, 57.

cially placed in charge of the armies of Mexico. He was left much upon his own as to plans for action, Secretary of War William L. Marcy merely suggesting that Monterey be taken and that both sides of the Rio Grande be held as far up as Laredo.[27] The Eighth Artillery and the Fifth and Seventh infantry, under the command of General William Worth, made ready to move toward Monterey, 250 miles to the southwest. "We are all busily engaged in making our preparations for crossing the mountains," reported Lieutenant Smith. "We are in fine health and excellent spirits. The camp resounds with the heavy hum of our voices; jokes and hilarity circle round; while with that carelessness—that recklessness of the future which seems characteristic of the soldier's life—all seem busily engaged with their mules, mustangs, and Mexican *amigos*, in preparing for some pleasure excursion." These men would not likely be disappointed in their desire for action, "for the General sits cross-legged in his tent, as glum as an old bear—sure indication of the coming storm." The camp site along the San Juan was beautiful, but the soldiers longed for the "mountain winds—the bracing breezes of the Sierra." [28]

On September 19 General Taylor halted his army three miles from Monterey. Retaining two divisions for a frontal attack, he then sent General Worth, with the Fifth and Seventh infantry and the Eighth Artillery, to storm the heights to the rear. Five days later the fighting was all over and Lieutenant Smith was in "Don Garcia's house, where our brave fellows picked their way yesterday morning." Again he wrote assuredly to his mother that the war was practically over. Taylor's frontal attack was repulsed with heavy losses, the First and Third infantry and the Balti-

[27] Hamilton, *Zachary Taylor*, 195; Dyer, *Zachary Taylor*, 183, 187.
[28] Edmund K. Smith to Mother, August 18, 1846.

more Battalion being "literally cut to pieces." Worth was more successful. Approaching the rear of the city "with consummate skill," he "carried each height with its battery, stormed the Bishop's Palace . . . , successfully advanced to the town, driving the Mexicans before him into the plaza, [and] cut them off from their communications." Within the town the going became harder. "Our men were shot at from the tops of houses, each of which is a fort in itself," Lieutenant Smith related. "Their artillery swept the streets with a destructive fire. A great mistake was made somewhere. Two divisions were marched into town, against stone walls, with nothing in the whole command for breaking into a house. Even Yankees can't butt down stone walls, and every Spanish house is build like a fort. Our officers fell and died like heroes. . . ." [29]

The victory was costly but complete. As Lieutenant Smith stood on the edge of the plaza and saw thousands of defeated enemy troops walk out, he was amazed that such fine physical specimens could ever be persuaded to surrender as long as guns and ammunition were plentiful. And as he viewed the ruins of fine buildings and what should have been impregnable fortifications, he was more convinced than ever of the superiority of American courage and skill. Nature had done its part for the defense of this beautiful city. The Mexicans alone had failed. "Commanded in rear by almost inaccessible heights, surmounted by batteries and a large bastion fort in front and a superior garrison of regulars in the town, we have much reason to congratulate ourselves, that without a siege train, with inferior force and separated from our supplies, we have successfully obtained possession of this point." [30]

Captain Ephraim Kirby Smith was not in the battle of Monterey. Early in June he and Edmund had learned of

---

[29] *Id.* to *id.*, September 24, 1846.  [30] *Ibid.*

the death of their father. Kirby secured a sixty days leave and went to visit the family. Numerous misfortunes in travel and a serious illness at New Orleans delayed his return. It was October 23 before he arrived in Monterey. "I shall be much mortified and distressed should there be an engagement before I join [my regiment] and after the expiration of my leave," he wrote his wife from near St. Louis on his return trip. He was off Brazos when he learned of the terrible fighting at Monterey. "I could lie down and cry of vexation and grief at not being there," he exclaimed. Then, thinking of his numerous comrades who had fallen, he added: "Though it is perhaps all for the best and we shall have more fighting." [31]

Major Edmund Kirby (uncle of the Smith brothers), a member of General Taylor's staff was in the midst of the heavy slaughter, remaining under fire for eight hours. Taylor had called to him early that morning: "Get up, Kirby, and come with me and I will give you a chance to be shot." [32]

Edmund Kirby Smith, lively, intelligent, and amiable, made friends everywhere he went, even within those larger groups which were classed as his enemies. During his few weeks stay in Monterey, he lived in the home of a prominent Mexican, a lawyer of talent and education and a man of science, who was well known for his benevolence. Through the family of this friendly gentleman, he became acquainted with the *buenos y decentes* of the city. "Never in my life had I met so much real kindness, warmth of feeling and interest in my welfare," he confided to his mother. "They were constantly giving me proofs of their regard, sending me sweetmeats and other nice things, and during my sickness, an old lady, who always called me her

---

[31] Ephraim K. Smith to Wife, September 5, 30, 1846, in Blackwood (ed.), *To Mexico With Scott,* 58–60, 62–63.

[32] *Id.* to *id.,* November 2, 1846, *ibid.,* 68–72.

son, visited me and attended my bedside with all the interest and anxiety that a mother could manifest. I found a great deal of refinement, some talent and education, with a kindness of heart and warmth of feeling quite universal among the higher classes." But the great masses he found steeped in ignorance and superstition and "much darker in morals than they are in complexion." [33]

Captain Smith also reported on Edmund from Monterey. Arriving on October 23, he had gone straight to headquarters of the Fifth Regiment. There he met Edmund and received an account of his activities. "Ted is quite ruddy from the mountain air," he wrote his wife. "He has become quite a Spaniard and is decidedly the most popular officer of the army with the natives. He is a guest, and through his influence, I am, also, of one of the most distinguished men of the place, a member of Congress and once Governor of the Province." [34]

The terms granted by General Taylor to General Pedro de Ampudia were extremely liberal. Not only was the Mexican army allowed to march out with arms, but an eight weeks armistice was agreed upon. Clearly Taylor was more interested in preventing further bloodshed than he was in the effect his magnanimity might have upon the continuation of the conflict. At Washington his action was disapproved by the administration, and although Congress gave him a vote of thanks, much opposition was manifested. President Polk, with the unanimous approval of his Cabinet, notified Taylor to terminate the armistice at once.[35] He wished additional victories before the next session of the Mexican congress.

The administration finally decided that Taylor should

---

[33] Edmund K. Smith to Mother, January 5, 1847.

[34] Ephraim K. Smith to Wife, October 26, 1846, in Blackwood (ed.), *To Mexico With Scott*, 65–68.

[35] Milo M. Quaife (ed.), *The Diary of James K. Polk During His Presidency, 1845–1849*, 4 vols. (Chicago, 1910), II, 181–86.

not advance beyond Monterey, but should hold that point and make secure a line southeastward to Tampico. The heart of Mexico would then be invaded from Vera Cruz.[36] By the time these instructions reached General Taylor he had already made preparations to move on Saltillo a few miles to the southwest. General Worth was sent to carry out this plan. Lieutenant Smith did not make the trip, however, for he had been promoted to second lieutenant in the Seventh Infantry on August 22, 1846. The Seventh remained with General Twiggs. In mid-December this regiment, plus a number of volunteer regiments under General John A. Quitman, took up march toward Victoria. Rumor circulated among the officers that General Taylor intended moving on Santa Barbara and then along the road to Tula and San Luis where a strong Mexican force was said to be concentrating.

While en route to Victoria, Taylor received word from General Winfield Scott that he was on his way to Mexico to direct an attack upon Vera Cruz. A number of Taylor's veterans would be needed. This notice of Scott's intention and the recently acquired knowledge that there was "no practicable route across the Sierra from Tampico to San Luis" changed the plans. General Taylor, Lieutenant Smith reported, had decided to make no move beyond Victoria until further orders from Scott.

Lieutenant Smith enjoyed the thirteen days march from Monterey to Victoria, a distance of about eighty leagues. Natural beauty always delighted him. "We passed through three large towns averaging five thousand inhabitants (Cadereita, Morelos, and Linares), besides villages and haciendas," he wrote his mother.

The road skirts along, at ten or fifteen miles from the base of the Sierra, and excepting in the neighborhood of the towns and haci-

[36] *Ibid.*, 198–99.

endas, which lie along water courses, through a dry, parched and unproductive country is entirely destitute of trees, but abounding in rocks and the thorny chaparral bush.

At the towns and haciendas, where the country admits of irrigation, the orange, lime, lemon, and various other trees and fruits, flourish in all the exuberance of a tropical clime. Fields of cotton, coffee and sugar-cane, the broad leafed banana, with the dark, rich foliage of orange and aguacate, there greet our arrival after a long and toilsome day's march over a dusty waste.

Along the march he delighted his comrades by speaking to the natives in the Spanish he had learned at Monterey.

He found little that was attractive in the town of Victoria, the capital of Tamaulipas, situated at the base of the Sierre Madre.

Its population is about 4,000, and like all Mexican towns, speaks of times gone by. Old and ruined houses, dilapidated walls, crumbling churches, or the unfinished foundations of some magnificent cathedral, meet the view on every side. A miserable, ignorant and beggarly people, half naked, lounging around or squatting like Indians, at the street corners and on the main plaza, form two-thirds of the population of the towns east of the Sierra, and of the ranchos —the peons of the haciendas of the rich. The whole country from Monterey to Matamoras and Tampico exhibits a people lapsing deeper and deeper into ignorance and superstition. Ruined houses, deserted fields and ranchos, crumbling cathedrals and the dilapidated condition of the towns, all mark how great has been the decrease in population, how rapid the decline since the rule of the Spanish. Indeed the inhabitants all refer to the times of the Spanish Governor as those of peace and plenty. Then, at least they were secure from the depredation of the *Indio*.[37]

Scott's order soon came. All of Taylor's troops at Victoria, except a small escort for his return to Monterey, were to proceed to either the mouth of the Rio Grande or Tampico. The regulars at Saltillo, which included the Fifth, were to proceed down the Rio Grande. The Seventh marched from Victoria to Tampico and embarked for Vera

[37] Edmund K. Smith to Mother, January 5, 1847.

Cruz. The boats carrying the Fifth and Seventh became mingled, and Captain Smith began a search for his brother Edmund. He found the young lieutenant on board a brig with Colonel F. Plympton. The two then spent a pleasant evening together on the *Huron*. Edmund was in fine health and spirits.[38]

Early in March the transports anchored at Anton Lizardo, a dozen miles from Vera Cruz. On March 9 a landing was effected three miles from the castle San Juan de Ulua. "The surf boats of the first line struck the beach in beautiful order," Lieutenant Smith reported, and General Worth led his three thousand men to position "amid deafening cheers from the fleet and transports, and the soul-inspiring strains of our Navy band." General Twiggs' command, including the Seventh Infantry, followed immediately, moving to the left wing, and forcing its way seven miles "through thickets and marshes and over sand hills." Enemy skirmishers offered feeble resistance, and heavy shells occasionally sailed overhead. A captain immediately in front of Lieutenant Smith was decapitated by an eighteen-pounder. To one side a surgeon was busy amputating a leg of another unfortunate victim. "We moved on rapidly," the lieutenant later recalled, "leaving a few men to bury the brave man where he fell, and with a silent prayer for his soul, all was soon forgotten—even that such might soon be the fate of any of us."

The Seventh debouched on the Jalapa road and began seizing provisions destined for the besieged city. Frightened natives ran for their lives as half-starved men "dashed into the deserted ranchos." One of Lieutenant Smith's men emerged with a bag of Mexican sugar. The Lieutenant raised his sword and assumed a "ferocious look," but his

[38] Diary of Captain Ephraim K. Smith, in Blackwood (ed.), *To Mexico With Scott*, 84 ff.

indignation was "completely subdued" by an offer to divide the sugar with him.

A week of bombardment by American artillery convinced the defenders of Vera Cruz of the advisability of surrender. A major portion of the city was heavily damaged, a part in complete ruins. An estimated four hundred Mexicans, including many women and children, lay dead or wounded. Such was the destruction wrought by bombardment.

Young Lieutenant Smith was much impressed and recorded the results with considerable pride: "We have just achieved a result stupendous in itself and grand through the influence it must have on our future operations; and most joyfully do we hail it as the harbinger of a change in the system hitherto pursued in our campaign. Rashness, unflinching determination and bull-dog courage, have achieved results glorious for our arms, honorable for the Nation, and I may almost say, unparalleled in the history of the world." But with all the greatness of the victory, he was conscious that it would have been far more glorious had it been accomplished with less bloodshed and destruction. "Science, with the long and sad experience of the other continent," he reasoned, "teaches what is truly the military maxim, that the greatness of the victory is measured, not by the immensity of the loss on either side, but by the accomplishment of the result with the smallest possible loss." However, he added, had the old method of storming fortifications been used the cost in lives would have been much greater.[39]

All of the military men of the Kirby-Smith relations were at Vera Cruz except Captain Webster, who had remained with General Taylor and recently seen action at

[39] Edmund K. Smith to Mother, April 3, 1847; F. S. Belton to Wife, March 22, 1847.

Buena Vista. Major Edmund Kirby had a brief visit with his nephews shortly before landing. Later he spoke of seeing Kirby often but Edmund very seldom, since they were in different divisions. He was less enthusiastic about the bombardment than his young nephews. "This is war in its most dread form . . . ," he wrote his sister. "I pray God I may never have occasion to witness another bombardment."[40] Captain Kirby Smith also reported the battle in detail. He had not seen Edmund since the engagement but had heard much of him indirectly. "Ted is a gallant glorious fellow & a universal favorite."[41]

By April 3 General Twiggs had received orders to move on La Puente Nacional some thirty miles to the northwest along the road to Mexico City. A few days later he stormed the fortification at Cerro Gordo. Both Edmund and his Uncle Edmund were active. When the firing began Lieutenant Smith was confined to his cot by illness. The thought of missing the excitement immediately became more oppressive than his ailment; he rushed from his tent and reported to his company. When the Seventh Infantry broke into the enemy's works, he was among the first. ("I verily believe the first," he later stated) to enter. Racing ahead, he was the first to reach the entrance to the Stone Tower, the heart of the fortification, where he saved three defending Mexicans from being bayoneted by those immediately behind him. Yet when Colonel Plympton made his official report he failed to list Lieutenant Edmund K. Smith among those specifically cited for bravery.

Young Smith was astonished. His professional reputation was involved, he complained to General Scott's headquarters, and he owed it to himself to bring the facts to the attention of higher authorities.[42] After reading this

---

[40] Edmund Kirby to Mrs. Frances K. Smith, April 7, 1847.
[41] Ephraim K. Smith to Mother, March 24, 1847.
[42] Edmund K. Smith to Franklin Gardner, July 23, 1847.

vigorous protest and examining the accompanying evidence, Colonel Plympton amended his official report. Recent and unquestionable information, he explained, had established the fact that "2nd Lt. E. K. Smith, of the Infy, was, if not the first, one among the first officers of the 7th Regt in the enemy's works on Telegraph height on the morning of the 18th of April; in whose case I am doubly gratified, 1st having in my power to assure him that no individual neglect was intended and 2nd in having an opportunity of conveying his name, with the facts connected, to the Genl. in chief . . . as an officer of much merit and promise." [43] A brevet first lieutenant's commission "for gallant and meritorious conduct" was soon on its way from Washington.

This made Lieutenant Smith and his relatives very happy. "My glorious brother, I learn," wrote Captain Smith to his wife, "has a paragraph especially dedicated to his praise in Plympton's report. He fully deserves anything complimentary which can be said of him." [44]

The army moved on. On June 22 the Seventh Infantry took position near Lieutenant Colonel Charles Ferguson Smith's Light Battalion to which Captain Smith was now attached. The brothers could again see each other often. Both were active in the battle at Contreras. After the fighting Edmund sat down with his company to rest, and Kirby, after aiding the wounded, "supped with Uncle Edmund and slept in a monks cell in an old convent." [45] But the rest period was short; Mexico City must be reached. "Tomorrow will be a day of slaughter," wrote Captain Smith to his wife late at night on the eve of the battle of Molino Del Rey. "I firmly trust and pray that victory may crown

---

[43] F. Plympton to H. L. Scott, July 27, 1847.
[44] August 22, 1847, in Blackwood (ed.), *To Mexico With Scott*, 197 ff.
[45] *Ibid.*

our efforts though the odds are immense. I am thankful that you do not know the peril we are in. Good night." [46] This was his last letter.

Lieutenant Colonel Charles Ferguson Smith was ill and unable to command his battalion. Captain Smith, as second in command, took over. At dawn, September 8, he led the Light Battalion to the foot of Chapultepec, and there he fell "in the moment of victory." A ball entered the left eye and emerged at the ear and he toppled forward on a pile of stones, severely injuring the right side of his face. He was taken to Major Kirby's quarters in Tacubaya and given the best care available. At times he showed signs of being rational. On the eleventh he was moved to marine corps headquarters at Miscoique, but on the previous day he had sunk into a coma from which he never recovered.

Edmund had advanced as far as Piedad, a post near Mexico City, when he learned of his brother's wound. He made frequent visits to his Uncle Edmund's quarters but did not arrive at Miscoique until shortly after Kirby's death. "Edmund, noble, generous fellow is most deeply distressed," wrote Major Kirby to Mrs. Smith. "He has borne himself with the most distinguished gallantry in all the battles, and is loved and admired by all; but his rank is too low for him to be benefitted by his gallantry as he ought." [47]

Captain Ephraim Kirby Smith was buried near the place of his death. Later the citizens of Syracuse, New York, sent for the body and moved it to that place. [48] The news of Kirby's death cast a great shadow over family circles. In Syracuse he left a wife and three children—Joseph Lee, Emma Jerome, and George Geddes. His aging mother in

[46] *Id.* to *id.*, September 7, 1847, *ibid.*, 215–17.
[47] Edmund Kirby to Mrs. Frances K. Smith, September 12, 1847.
[48] L. B. Webster to Mrs. Frances K. Smith, March 11, 1848.

St. Augustine and childless Aunt Mary and Uncle Ira Smith in New Britain now became increasingly apprehensive lest Edmund also should fall in battle. In view of the great uncertainties of life, wrote Aunt Mary, he should strive to be a better Christian. She had understood that in his father's last illness he had calmly committed himself "to the care of his God & Savior." [49]

Lieutenant Edmund Kirby Smith moved with his regiment into Mexico City. He wrote no account of his part in breaking through the defenses; there was little chance of getting his letters out even if he had. "Edmund is well. I see him every day," reported Major Kirby from the Halls of the Montezumas. "He will not write now for want of opportunity. Our only chance for sending letters is by smuggling them into the valise of the courier of the British Legation." [50]

The Mexican War came to an end with the signing of the Treaty of Guadalupe Hidalgo on February 2, 1848. By April 21, Major Edmund Kirby was in Washington lobbying in the interest of pensions for widows and orphans of soldiers who lost their lives in the recent war. When he arrived, there was already before the Senate a list of officers recommended for special recognition. Among them were Belton for brevet colonel, Webster for brevet lieutenant colonel, Edmund Kirby Smith, for first lieutenant, and Edmund Kirby for brevet lieutenant colonel. General Twiggs had also arrived, Major Kirby reported to his sister, and the two of them would attempt to get Edmund the brevet of captain. Had her son Kirby survived the war he would no doubt have received the brevet of lieutenant colonel.[51] Major Kirby and General Twiggs

[49] Mary Smith to Edmund K. Smith, January 19, 1848.
[50] Edmund Kirby to Mrs. Frances K. Smith, September 23, 1847.
[51] *Id.* to *id.*, April 21, 1848.

were successful, even to securing posthumous recognition of the bravery of the late Captain Ephraim Kirby Smith. His work in Washington completed, Colonel Edmund Kirby, joined by Frances Webster and her children, went to Governor's Island for a short visit with the Russells and thence to Brownsville.[52]

[52] *Ibid.*

## CHAPTER IV

# FROM PROFESSOR TO
# DRAGOON

E<small>DMUND</small> <small>KIRBY</small> <small>SMITH</small> was unable immediately
to secure a leave of absence, although he had just com-
pleted three years of service and was badly needed at
home. Debts, many unknown to the immediate family, had
almost completely wiped out Judge Smith's estate. In April,
1847, Edmund had sent his Uncle Ira a check for $120,
the amount advanced at the time of his graduation. He
had also sent his mother a check for $65.50.[1] He con-
tinued to contribute to her support for the remainder of her
life.

By mid-November, 1848, the Seventh Infantry was stationed at Jefferson Barracks, near St. Louis, Missouri, and
Brevet Captain Smith had settled down to routine garrison
duty—"drill, guard and dress parade; the billiard room
after breakfast, and a visit to the ladies in the evening."
What a life as compared to the war years when even "to
live was to know how to appreciate living." "Now, automa-
ton-like, we involuntarily glide through the same monotonous scene," he wrote his mother, "needing only, like the
works of a watch, to be wound up each twenty-four hours,
when away we spin, tickety-tick, till the stirring notes of

[1] Edmund K. Smith to B. A. Putnam, April 7, 1847.

reveille again wind up our rickety machinery for a repetition of the same daily revolution." There seemed to be no relief from the monotony except to fall in love, and a number of young officers were giving that a fair trial.

There were loud complaints about miserable quarters and even worse weather, but Brevet Captain Smith was not too critical. He expected to remain at Jefferson for probably two or three years and had made himself as comfortable as possible by furnishing his quarters "in a style quite creditable to bachelor apartments." There was a mad scramble for quarters and low ranking officers had little chance. He owed his good fortune to his colonel, William Wing Loring, who by virtue of rank was entitled to two suites. One he used, the other he allowed Brevet Captain Smith to use, thus giving the latter a feeling of considerable independence. "No one now under the rank of Colonel can turn me out of my domicile," he bragged to his mother. "Colonel Loring is an excellent fellow." [2]

Nothing more was heard from Captain Smith until March 1, 1849. He explained his silence with the statement that he had not written, thinking that he would get a leave and beat his letter home. But he had now decided to wait until the following winter to make the trip, even though he was suffering from nostalgia—"visions of deep sands, mosquitoes, fresh mullets . . . and the old place with its air of neglect & decay." A barefooted boy planning the invasion of watermelon patches and orange groves, the fig trees, the bombardment of Deacon Gould's chickens— these memories he would not have erased for "all the gold of California or the bright eyes of Mexico." "But alas! My Bark of life has glided down the Stream of Time, till all that merry crew of childhood which sang so gaily to the

[2] *Id.* to Mother, November 18, 1848.

ripples of the waves, have disappeared before the hard featured sailors of stern reality."

He agreed with the advice in his mother's recent letter relative to the merits of refinement and cultured society. But surely she could not expect much refinement among those whom she styled as "dough boys"; they were never accomplished gentlemen, always ignoramuses. Nevertheless, there was "quite an extensive and agreeable collection of ladies and gentlemen" at the post, and St. Louis was only a few miles away. He seldom visited the city, however, since the "gaieties of fashionable society" held little charm for him.

Now as for matrimony, he would "scorn to be dependent upon the charities of a rich wife—marry a poor one I can't"; therefore, there seemed nothing to do but remain a merry carefree bachelor, "the ne plus ultra of all conditions." Still he must confess that when his mother's recent letter arrived he was in the process of scribbling out his first proposal; but her advice—"as much flirtation, as you please, but no engagements no matrimony"—crushed his "pleasant dreams in the bud." He burned the proposal. " 'Twas cruel in you," he merrily chided, "to have destroyed so unceremoniously the illusion of my fireside future." [3]

Other and apparently more urgent letters arrived from his mother, and Brevet Captain Smith changed his mind about visiting St. Augustine. He resolved to leave for home on June 1. An unthoughtful relative had apparently remarked to Mrs. Smith that both Edmund and St. Augustine had changed so much in the past thirteen years he would not enjoy his visit. Edmund saw worry between the lines of his mother's letters. "When I visit my old haunts, as he [the relative] is pleased to call them," he reassured

[3] *Id.* to *id.*, March 1, 1849.

his mother, "it will not be for present pleasure they may afford me, but for the enjoyment of 'Auld Lang Syne.'"
"But I forgive C. F.," he added, for those unable to enter into the feelings of the small family circle might overlook "one principle implanted in our nature paramount to all others—the love between mother and children." He prayed God daily for forgiveness for his seeming lack of dutiful affection, occasioned by laziness rather than indifference, and asked that he might be able to prove he was "possessed of those feelings which link families together in bonds that neither time, poverty, distance, nor adversities can sever."

Clearly the war years had greatly matured young Edmund. Henceforth he was a more appreciative and dutiful son and a more moral and religious man. When his mother observed that she pitied the delusions of the great throngs rushing to the gold mines of California, he expressed concern for the effects such an inevitable lack of restraint would have upon the morals of society in that area. "I reason from experience, I saw what it was in Mexico, I became convinced then, that not even a reputation for morality & virtue . . . could remain intact when thrown upon our own resources."

He sent his love to Aunt Helen Putnam. She must know little of the influence her prayers had had upon his moral well-being. He would leave St. Louis on June 1, visit with Uncle Edmund Kirby, brother Kirby's widow, sister Frances, and Aunt Kate Russell on the way, and arrive in St. Augustine early in August.[4]

His departure from St. Louis was delayed for several weeks owing to an attack of bilious fever, accompanied by some symptoms of cholera. It probably was cholera, for, as he later related, St. Louis had never experienced such an epidemic. Deaths ran as high as four hundred per day.

[4] *Id.* to *id.,* May 3, 1849.

Hundreds of terror-stricken people, rich and poor, fled for their lives, jamming the streets and roads with their conveyances. When Brevet Captain Smith was finally able to travel he saw scattered cases of the disease along the railroad in Michigan and the Great Lakes. It had not reached as far as Brownsville, New York, but when he arrived there Uncle Edmund was seriously ill. "There seemed some fatality attending my footsteps," he wrote his mother. "It seemed that the doom of the Wandering Jew followed in my track. With a shudder through my veins, I found myself thinking of examining the prints of my footsteps for that mysterious sign of the cross." Learning that a New York newspaper had listed him as among the dead, he hastened to suggest that his mother "be not alarmed for though dead and buried I am alive again." He hoped to be in St. Augustine by the middle of September.[5]

There was further delay at Brownsville while awaiting an extension of his furlough. Uncle Edmund Kirby died while he was there, and before he left New York both his Uncle Ira Smith and Aunt Kate's husband, Dr. Russell, had died. It was with a heavy heart that Brevet Captain Smith prepared to sail southward for the first visit to the place of his birth since, as a boy of twelve, he left for Alexandria thirteen years before. A few hours before sailing he received orders to take charge of a bunch of recruits headed for Florida. "A most precious set they were too," he later sarcastically remarked, "and a most delightful predicament I found myself in—Cmdg Officer, Qr Master, commissioner, and Medical Officer to 54 as raw green specimens from Erins Isle as I almost ever had the felicity of seeing collected together and not an old soldier in the number." He encountered no trouble, however, until they arrived at the St. Johns "when they saw fit to become merry

[5] *Id.* to *id.,* August 7, 1849.

beligerent & insubordinate." For three hours he "had it hot & heavy, knocking down & tying up." Two knives were taken from one "blustering Irishman" who twice vowed he would kill the young captain. Little Kate Russell, who was accompanying her cousin Edmund to St. Augustine, was speechless from fright, and the Reverend Mr. Wright, pastor of the Episcopal Church of St. Augustine, was horrified, especially since it all happened on Sunday.[6] The captain himself might have been frightened at the time, but he thoroughly enjoyed relating the details to his sister.

The visit in St. Augustine was a pleasant one. Mrs. Smith and the Putnams were in good health and spirits, and they showered upon their returning soldier boy all the fine food and affection that doting relatives could provide. And Captain Smith went away happier and better contented than in many years. His visit was cut short by a telegram from his brother-in-law Colonel Webster, informing him of his assignment to duty at West Point, an appointment for which Edmund had made application a few months earlier. His friend Colonel Loring had departed for the West Coast, and no doubt the captain had lost his comfortable quarters. And garrison duty at Jefferson Barracks had proved both unhealthful and monotonous. At West Point he hoped to have time for the cultivation and improvement of his mind through the study of subjects neglected while a student. Should he later decide to resign from the army he would then be better prepared for some other profession.[7]

Captain Edmund Kirby Smith reported at West Point on October 22, 1849, and was immediately put "into the traces . . . and most terribly tight traces" they were. "Up at daybreak, study till 7, breakfast; attend recitation till

[6] *Id.* to Frances Webster, November 7, 1849.
[7] *Id.* to Mother, October 27, 1849; *id.* to Frances Webster, November 7, 1849.

11:30, and then study till 1. Lunch and exercise, thirty minutes; then study till 7 p.m. Dine and indulge in a half-hours luxury of looking at evening parade and hearing superior and skillfully executed music from the cadet band; and finally conclude the *amusements* of the day by studying till bed time—generally 11 p.m." [8]

Professor A. E. Church, head of the mathematics department, assigned the young captain two sections of third-year mathematics, and the instructor had to study harder than the cadets. There would be no relief until he learned what he failed to learn as a student. The first few weeks at the Point were disappointing; he found less opportunity for improvement than when with his regiment. The fine library facilities offered by New York City meant nothing to one who could not even find time to read the daily newspaper.

But after a few weeks the captain-professor was more cheerful. That "abominable mathematics" no longer kept him so busy, and he could get out and ramble in the woods. To him communing with nature could never be idleness. "Ever an admirer of nature," he explained, "I have always considered a love and appreciation of her beauties as forming the true poetry of one's character— She offers the only undying enjoyment upon earth—Ever! Ever appealing to the heart, and uttering with a deep mysterious voice of God's goodness and excellence, she awakens imagination to soar aloft and sing that song of praise which is to be eternal." But his rambles, though scarcely begun, must soon be cut short by winter's icy blast. "Land of sun and flowers!" he exclaimed. "Land of the orange and mocking bird! With all thy swamps and mosquitoes I love thee still." [9]

[8] *Id.* to Mother, October 27, 1849.

[9] *Id.* to Frances Webster, November 7, 1849; *id.* to Mother, December 10, 1849.

With the approach of winter he resolved to look more to his spiritual and intellectual development. "May He who in his infinite wisdom ruleth and directeth all things," he wrote in his diary on November 19, "so govern my actions, so chasten and purify my thoughts, that I may never be called upon to blush for the record of my most secret thoughts and actions." On the following day he began what he hoped would be an intensive study of history. He planned to write brief summaries of great events and developments and accompany them with his own comments. The summary method was adopted with the hope that his memory would be assisted by the reflection required in condensing and transcribing the fuller works. He disagreed with those who argued that he who transcribes "may have his desk full, but his head empty." [10]

Judging from the few pages of notes prepared, Captain Smith failed to get very far in his study of history. He recorded a fear that the people of West Point would think him antisocial, yet his friends knew that his only purpose in returning to the Point was study and reflection. Most so-called pleasures were artificial, anyway, and soon wearied those who participated. "From nature must we seek our most durable pleasure . . . ," he confided to his diary. "Not in the beauty of forms or colors lies the charm alone— Not in the varied woods or shining streams or blue mountains—not in the towering cliff or sloping hill, or wavy valley, or winding river; but in the mysterious sense of God in all, is the deep sublime of nature's loveliness." [11]

While reflecting on the beauties of nature and the mysterious working of the Almighty, Captain Smith was also much concerned over a recent order from the Superin-

[10] West Point Diary of Edmund K. Smith, November 19, 20, 1849, in Kirby-Smith Papers.
[11] *Ibid.*, December 5, 1849.

tendent's office that all officers must attend Sunday morning services in the cadet's chapel. Some officers rebelled.
It is not certain that Smith was among them, but he did
consider joining Simon Bolivar Buckner, George B. Mc-
Clellan, and others in a written protest. Although intensely
religious himself, he disapproved of any attempt to compel others to be so. Pending a decision from the War Department on this contested order, Captain Smith wrote
out a request that should free exercise of his religious
beliefs be "considered incompatible with the interests of
the Academy" he might be immediately relieved from
duty.[12] This request was never submitted, for the order
was not enforced, and the tension was soon relieved.

As winter "glided by rapidly and pleasantly," Captain
Smith reflected that it had been a more enjoyable one than
he had dared expect. A number of bachelor officers, some
of whom had "claim to wit, talent, genius, and scientific
attainments," organized to play chess, read Shakespeare,
and enjoy music. "Our evening gatherings are *recherché*,
entertaining and improving," Smith explained. But all of
his time was not devoted to pleasure, for his mathematics,
particularly differential and integral calculus, demanded
seven to eight hours each day. Furthermore, his health was
not good, and he was giving more thought to the probability of his life being cut short. He reflected more upon
the church and what it meant to him. "We have just entered upon the season of Lent," he wrote his mother in
mid-February, 1850. "How I wish I were with you during this solemn and interesting period. How admirable is
our church system—how beautiful in all its parts—not a
link is wanting in the chain—not an alteration can be
devised. . . . The more I examine it, the more apparent

12 Edmund K. Smith to Mother, December 10, 1849; West Point Diary,
November 29, 1849.

is the peculiar aptness and appropriateness of all its details—and in searching its history I am struck by the careful manner in which all errors of doctrine and practice have been removed whilst the truth and integrity of the whole has remained unimpaired." [13]

The absence of letters from Captain Smith to his mother during the summer of 1850 indicates that they visited together in New York or St. Augustine. The former is the more likely since he remarked on November 24 that he had just heard of his mother's return to St. Augustine. Quite likely they also visited the Websters at Fort Mifflin, Pennsylvania. There had developed between Frances and her mother a coolness that bothered Edmund. Frances explained that she was not aware of any cause for her mother's attitude, but added: "If she *must* have a nightmare, an object of aversion in her family, it may, now poor father is gone, as well be me as any one else— Would to heaven the storm had fallen upon me in his lifetime." [14]

By the fall of 1850 the Websters had moved to Baton Rouge, and Captain Smith had acquired a new dog named "Minna" and settled down for another session at the Academy. The records are silent on what had happened to "Ponto." "Minna sits at my feet whilst I write, or rather lays at my feet," he told his mother, "since she has now *arrived* at that *state* in which it behooves her, if she regards her peace of mind and would preserve an equilibrium of spirits, to be still & keep as quiet as possible. She promises very soon to make me patron of as fine a little family as ever fell to the lot of a Bachelor to support." [15]

Early in 1851 Frances worked out a plan for getting her brother out of the army and established in a civilian

[13] Edmund K. Smith to Mother, February 14, 1850.
[14] Frances Webster to Edmund K. Smith, March 7, 1850.
[15] Edmund K. Smith to Mother, November 24, 1850.

teaching position. Horace Webster, Colonel Webster's brother, had offered to secure for Edmund a teaching position in the New York Free Academy at a salary of $1,500. Frances was elated and pointed out all of the advantages, among which was escape from a life of exposure and the necessity of associating with "coarse minded, unrefined male and female specimens" at army posts, to say nothing of escaping the termination of his "inglorious career, in some ignoble skirmish with the red skins." [16] But Captain Smith was not yet ready to settle down.

During the summer he again enjoyed a visit with his mother. Continued ill health caused him to consider going to some Western resort in the fall of 1851. However, by October he had shown such marked improvement that his doctor recommended cancellation of the Western trip. A month later his weight had increased to 147 pounds, but he was still planning on taking the baths at Brattleboro the following summer. "I cling with strong pertinacity to all my predilections in favor of cold water," he told his mother.[17]

In September, 1852, Captain Smith received orders to rejoin his regiment. Knowing that his mother would be depressed by the probability of his long absence in the West, he wrote her at length, explaining just why it was his duty to report without question. The captain of his company had been made commandant of cadets at West Point; therefore, by virtue of his brevet and seniority Edmund Kirby Smith would now rank as captain. "My military pride, my reputation as a soldier, demand that I should not absent myself under such circumstances," he declared, "and, indeed, my health requires a change of life

---

[16] Frances Webster to Edmund K. Smith, June 2, 1851; *id.* to Mother, August ?, 1851.
[17] Edmund K. Smith to Mother, October 20, November 30, 1851.

and habits, and I am convinced that the active life, which, as commander of a mounted company, I must necessarily lead in Texas, will be the most beneficial change that could have taken place."

His company was now stationed at Ringgold Barracks on the Rio Grande, just opposite Carmargo, Mexico. For two years it had been performing dragoon duty. In anticipation of enjoyable rides over the plains of Texas, Captain Smith wrote his mother: "What pleasure it will be to feel once more like a soldier; to know that I have a profession and am engaged in its legitimate duties. I have chosen the army, or rather the army has been selected for me as a profession, and I see no prospect of its ever being changed. I do not regret it; I am proud of it. But to be contented I must be devoted to it. I must honor my profession and not endeavor to shun or avoid its duties when unpleasant or disagreeable. Should I now remain absent, at a time when the command of my company is offered me, my self-respect would be lowered, my military character endangered, and my companions would, indeed, judge me better fitted for the pedagogue than the soldier."

Colonel Webster had also been ordered to Texas. He would go to Brownsville. All would probably sail on the same boat. Captain Smith was already packing his baggage when he wrote his mother. "There is some advantage in being a bachelor," he remarked. After eliminating all superfluities, the bulk of his baggage would consist of "books, a lamp, bedstead, keg of gun powder, six-shooter, knife and double-barrel shot gun." After observing other officers' families like the Websters attempting to carry complete household furnishings, he felt "somewhat reconciled to an order which, in sending me to Texas, dooms me to old bachelordom." But he would probably not remain long in Texas before securing the twelve to eighteen months leave to which he was entitled. Then he would return East "entirely restored in health & in better spirits." [18]

Captain Smith arrived in the arid land of cactus and outlaws during the winter of 1852–53. He had seen something of this country during Mexican War days, but there had been no opportunity to study its plant and animal life. The almost complete barrenness of the region between Fort Brown and Eagle Pass was oppressive but interesting. Little valuable vegetation was to be found between the Nueces and the Rio Grande, he observed, and the inhabitants were "in keeping with the country and its productions." The most highly regarded man in the region was "a runaway forger from Mississippi." The six-shooter and Bowie knife were common accessories to wearing apparel, and both were used with impunity. Courts were a farce, for officials were "generally professed robbers and smugglers." The foremost magistrate was himself acting under a commission from one Carbajal, an archrobber, disorganizer, and plunderer, who had "completely ingratiated himself with the people along the frontier." "The only persons respected and feared on the frontier (yet cordially hated)," Captain Smith quickly observed, "are the officers and soldiers of the army." [19]

Chasing Indians, filibusterers, and desperadoes was a full-time occupation for these frontier soldiers; consequently, they must live in the saddle for weeks at a time, extending their protection over thousands of square miles down the Rio Grande as far as Fort Brown. The nature-loving captain found the Fort Brown region a delightful relief from the barrenness of Ringgold. Here the luxuriant vegetation had almost hidden the scars of war. He could

18 *Id.* to *id.*, September 28, 1852.    19 *Id.* to *id.*, March 16, 1853.

not refrain from giving his mother a detailed description of its beauty:

A forest of acacias (our Florida popinac) covers a large portion of the ground, and on the very ramparts of the old fort, trees are growing nearly thirty feet high and a foot in diameter. The hibiscus, some dozen species of verbenas and heliotropes, the lantana, our little purple tradescantia and other of our garden and exotic flowers carpet the ground; the rich, scarlet clusters of the coral plant and the yellow, white and pink blossoms of different acacias and mimosas contrast finely among the characteristic yet graceful foliage of the Rio Grande chaparrals; while a thousand creepers, convolvuli, four-o'clocks, etc., festoon the boughs and hang in graceful clusters with rich and variegated blossoms from the highest tops, and cover the river bottom with a dense and almost impenetrable mass of foliage.[20]

How could a man who had devoted his life to being a soldier have acquired so much knowledge of wild flowers?

By the summer of 1853 conversation on the Rio Grande frontier had shifted from filibustering to the rumor of probable war with Mexico. Santa Anna, it was said, was concentrating a hundred thousand regulars and civilian soldiers. American officers on the Rio Grande noted that friendly visits by Mexican officers from across the river had ceased. And Mexicans residing on the American side had been secretly informed that they would soon be reannexed to the old country. Although none of this was verified, Captain Smith expressed a fear that filibustering expeditions into Mexico had given sufficient cause for a renewal of hostilities. Santa Anna might at any time throw twenty to forty thousand men across the river and overrun a great portion of Texas before the Washington authorities learned of his intention.[21]

The War Department became concerned over the Rio Grande frontier and ordered the construction of additional

[20] *Id.* to *id.*, June 1, 1853.     [21] *Ibid.*

fortifications. Captain Smith's company was sent to old Fort Brown to assist in the erection of a four-bastioned fort. "We shall be delightfully employed this winter," he sarcastically remarked, "living in tents and digging mud forts for the amusement of the Mexicans." To him the whole plan for fortifications appeared ridiculous and detrimental to the moral effects of the recent victories over Mexico. Instead of preserving peace the plan would have the opposite effect; for the Mexicans, conscious of American fears, would become bolder and more confident of future victories. If the forts were intended for defense they would be useless; if war came it would be fought on Mexican soil. As for himself, the only benefits he could expect from such a program were further improvement in health and many pleasant visits with Frances and her family.[22]

The semitropical climate which made the lower Rio Grande such a pleasant place to live was also attractive to the mosquito, and in the summer and fall of 1853 yellow fever swept the army camps. Few persons escaped the disease, and more than one fifth died. Captain Smith lay as "helpless as a baby" for a month before his strength proved superior. And Colonel Webster died of the disease on November 4. Three other members of the colonel's family and the servant were also ill at the time of his death. Webster was a highly respected officer of better than average ability. Even the Mexican officers stationed across the river honored his memory by their presence at the burial.[23]

"What a life is an army life!" exclaimed Mrs. Smith when she received Edmund's letter telling of Colonel Webster's death. It would seem that all the sufferings brought upon the family would be a lesson, but she had learned that Kirby's son Joseph Lee had also headed for the career

22 Id. to id., October 19, 1853.
23 Id. to id., November 5, 1853; id. to B. A. Putnam, January 20, 1854.

of his late father. And even Kirby's widow was enthusiastic about it! Of course Frances must now leave the army post, the mother continued, and Edmund must accompany her on "her weary pilgrimage." But where was Frances to go? Her mother would welcome her to St. Augustine, but there was no home to offer. Mrs. Smith now lived with the Putnams, and they were absent from home. Major Putnam was away on business, and Aunt Helen had gone to visit her daughter Kate who had married Dr. John C. Calhoun, Jr., son of the late Senator John C. Calhoun. The old lady was therefore alone except for three or four irresponsible servants and a "troublesome and unsatisfactory child," Fanny Russell.[24]

As soon as Major Putnam returned from his business trip, he wrote Edmund urging that he bring Frances and the children to St. Augustine. Captain Smith secured a three months leave for the purpose of accompanying his sister east, but they went to the home of Colonel Webster's brother at Geneva, New York. Frances had never liked St. Augustine, and she must have known that she and her mother would not be harmonious for a long period of time. Further, there had in recent years been some hard feelings between Colonel Webster and Major Putnam. "Mr. Putnam's violent letter to my husband was never taken notice of . . . ," Frances had written her brother a few years earlier.[25] Colonel Webster left some property in New York which if properly managed would soon pay for itself and give Frances an annual income of probably $2,000.[26]

After seeing Frances safely to the home of Dr. Webster, Captain Smith began his return trip on June 22, traveling by way of the Hudson River and New York Central Rail-

24 Mrs. Frances K. Smith to Edmund K. Smith, November 28, 1853.
25 Frances Webster to id., March 7, 1850.
26 Edmund K. Smith to B. A. Putnam, January 20, 1854.

road. A few days were spent with Mary, Kirby's widow, at Syracuse. Mary had established a private school for small children and had all the students she and her associate could teach. From Syracuse Captain Smith went to Buffalo, Cincinnati, and Louisville. When he wrote his mother on June 30 he was stuck fast in the mud of the Great Portland Canal under a broiling temperature of 98°. The snail-like crawl of his boat at least allowed time to fish for animalculae and to carry on microscopic investigations within the canal.[27] By the time his boat reached Cairo he was sweltering under a 108° temperature while the mosquitoes and kindred pests contended "for the spoils." By July 20 he had reached Fort Smith, Arkansas, after crawling up the Arkansas as far as Little Rock and then traveling the remaining distance by stage. The only excitement had been the spectacle of two Arkansas damsels endeavoring to gouge out each other's eyes. The terrible heat had forced the young Captain to go again and again to the jug containing the claret punch.[28]

Fort Smith was some four hundred miles from Belnap, where Captain Smith was to report. The route led through the Chickasaw and Choctaw country to Fort Washita, thence across a great expanse of sparsely settled territory. He would take an escort, the Captain assured his mother, although he had no fear of the Indians.[29]

Upon arrival at Fort Belnap he was greeted by two West Point friends and "a fine pack of hounds." At daybreak the next morning they were off for the chase. The dogs had scarcely reached the river bottoms when they picked up a trail and soon an immense puma was up a tree. Not expecting to meet such a vicious beast, the hunters had

[27] *Id.* to Mother, June 30, 1854.    [28] *Id.* to *id.*, July 20, 1854.
[29] *Ibid.*

brought along only a revolver with three loads. These were emptied at the beast but did nothing more than enrage him. "Bounding from tree to tree and levelling a dog with every stroke," he seriously threatened the hunters themselves. One man rushed back to camp for a heavier gun while the other two stood guard. The huge beast, finally conquered after a two hours fight, measured almost eight feet.[30]

Plans for additional outings were cut short by an order for Captain Smith and his company to move immediately to San Antonio. They had reached their destination by October 1. "For the benefit of some of my Florida friends, who may be tired of sand and pine barrens, and who still may have energy left to leave the State," Smith wrote his mother, "I will give a brief description of this country." Never had he seen such a beautiful region as that between the Red River and San Antonio. The soil, a limestone base with "a deep layer of rich black vegetable mold," was capable of producing as much as sixty bushels of corn to the acre. Well-watered by numerous streams, "well wooded, with oak, elm, pecan, walnut," and well-covered with a "rich luxuriant growth of mesquite grass," it was capable of becoming the "best stock country on the continent." And with all of this, the land could still be bought for $3.00 to $5.00 per acre.[31]

Captain Smith's company had been designated as escort for the boundary commission which was to undertake the establishment of a permanent line between the United States and Mexico. In recognition of Smith's interest in plant life, Major W. H. Emory, the head of the commission, appointed him botanist. The Captain was delighted; this was more to his liking than any peacetime assignment

[30] *Id.* to *id.,* October 2, 1854.    [31] *Ibid.*

he had ever had. Just before setting out he assured his
mother that every day in the open improved his health and
made him more immune to chills and fever.[32]

The commission, with its forty-wagon supply train, left
San Antonio on October 23, 1854. A week later they were
near Fort Clark, "the last jumping-off place of civilization." Leaving the luxuriant vegetation behind, they entered a region of rocky barren soil cut by rapid streams.
But wild game was even more plentiful. Turkeys by the
"tens of thousands" and "countless covies" of quail roosted
along the way. Much of the country ahead to El Paso was
a trackless wasteland, which until crossed by Smith's West
Point buddies—W. F. "Baldy" Smith, Dick Howard, and
Henry Whiting—who had accompanied another commission through that region in 1849, had probably never been
seen by a white man.[33]

Heavy rains fell while the expedition was at Fort Clark,
making the poor roads almost impassable. Mules had to
be dragged from mud holes by ropes, and men were forced
to put their shoulders to the wagon wheels. At times the
average speed was five miles per day. By dividing his time
between "making roads, playing wagon-master, teamster,
etc.," Captain Smith felt that he was at least broadening
his experiences. No longer, he observed, were there trees
for shade or beauty. Only the scrubby, thorny chaparral
and its friends met the eye. The only thing of beauty was
the streams, "bold, clear, and rapid, abounding in fish,"
as they rushed from the isolated peaks in the distance. The
region was a veritable network of canyons, narrow and
deep. As Captain Smith listened to Devil's River "roaring
and tumbling over the rocks in its narrow channel and
rushing through the dark caverns in the limestone cliffs,"
he imagined himself "entering the portals of Pande-

[32] *Ibid.*        [33] *Id.* to *id.,* October 31, 1854.

monium itself." And the Pecos River was so deep within
its banks and so void of timber along its border that one
might approach to within twenty yards without suspecting
that a river was nearby.[34]

Through Comanche Spring, between the Pecos and the
Limpia, passed the trail followed by marauding Indians
on their way to northern Mexico and return. So great was
their plunder that at times it took them weeks to pass their
stolen livestock by a given point. And so thorough was
their work that little of value was left in their path. Captain
Smith reflected with much concern upon the unhappy
plight of northern Mexico:

The whole northern frontier of that unfortunate country is almost
depopulated; and where countless herds roamed peaceably and se-
curely over the prairie, where flourishing haciendas & rich cathedrals
poured forth their throngs, ruin and desolation have succeeded to
opulence and festivities—the thieving Apache and the prowling
Coyote remain joint masters, the hoarse croak of the raven and the
howl of the wild beast have usurped the lowing of herds and the
merry chimes of the church bell—the ancient remains of Aztec greatness and the massive ruins of the Jesuit stand side by side monu-
mental marks of the two great cycles of change in that now desolated region.[35]

Wild Rose Pass, narrow and studded with jutting rocks,
was the only available route through the Limpia Mountains. Captain Smith chuckled when he thought of how his
friend "Baldy" must have felt traveling this same route
in the dead of night with the Apache close on his heels.[36]
Beyond Wild Rose was observed a prairie dog town, covering some thirty miles and desolating every acre of it. The
dogs fed upon roots of the grama grass and moved as the
supply of food grew short. With the dogs were always two

[34] Id. to id., December 15, 1854.

[35] Journal of Edmund K. Smith Kept while on Service with the Boundary
Commission.

[36] Edmund K. Smith to Mother, December 15, 1854.

quite unwelcome guests—the rattlesnake and the owl.[37]

Beyond the Limpia Mountains the expedition passed into an arid region and was forced to travel as long as thirty-six hours without water, while on all sides "the dried and shrivelled carcasses of animals" gave mute testimony of the "agonies and contortions of death." Descending some twelve hundred feet within a distance of seven miles, the party reached the Rio Grande about "two thousand miles above [the] mouth." The path was then up the river to El Paso, passing San Elizaro and the miserable little settlements of Isleta and Socorro, inhabited by two thousand "dirty specimens of Mexicans." In Spanish days this region was irrigated and the land bore bountifully. But all that now remained were scattered remnants —a few isolated cornfields and unkept vineyards. Captain Smith liked to dream of how this land could again be made to blossom if it should fall into competent hands. The grapes grown there were rivals of those produced in France. And he prophesied that within thirty years "we may see our cellars stocked with wines from these localities, which in delicacy of flavor and variety, will compare with the most famous grape districts of Europe." [38]

Major Emory's boundary commission was now in the area where its work was to begin. Captain Smith was charged with the duty of protecting the commissioners and studying plant life in the area; therefore, he had no direct part in establishing the line. He related to his mother, however, that Colonel Emory was very pleasant and treated him with much consideration, frequently consulting him but leaving him "quite independent" in his command. He accompanied the commission to Janos, the Valley of San

---

[37] Journal of Edmund K. Smith.

[38] Edmund K. Smith to Mother, December 15, 1854; Journal of Edmund K. Smith.

Bernadino, Santa Cruz, and Los Nogales. From the latter point he found opportunities to make repeated trips into the mountains hunting "grizzly bear and big horn." On one occasion he was attacked by a huge bear. "I reserved my fire," he confided to his diary, "and when he reared up within 3 ft of me his huge tusks & formidable claws stared me in the face I believed my last day had come—Providence aided me & I killed the fellow without receiving a scratch." [39]

On August 1, 1855, an order arrived terminating Captain Smith's service with the boundary commission and instructing him to report to the colonel of his regiment. Major Emory wrote to the Secretary of the Interior commending Smith for the manner in which he had performed his duties and asked that it be brought to the attention of the War Department. [40]

The letter from Major Emory must have been well received in Washington. A new regiment of cavalry was in the process of organization and Secretary of War Jefferson Davis intended that it be a model one. Brevet Captain Smith was promoted to a captaincy in this Second Cavalry and ordered to report to Jefferson Barracks. The colonel of the Second was Albert Sidney Johnston; lieutenant colonel, Robert E. Lee; majors, George H. Thomas and William J. Hardee. Among lower ranking officers were John B. Hood, Earl Van Dorn, George Stoneman, and Fitzhugh Lee. These names would soon be known to all Americans.

Captain Edmund Kirby Smith was highly pleased with his new assignment and predicted that the Second would undoubtedly be "*the* Regiment of the Army." Many of the officers were already his friends or acquaintances. Johnston, a classmate of his brother, Kirby, he knew to be "a man of great talents and ability and of good common

[39] *Ibid.*    [40] W. H. Emory to Robert McClelland, August 1, 1855 (copy).

sense." Lee, the superintendent of West Point at the time Smith taught mathematics, was "the most accomplished officer and gentleman in the army." Hardee, "the model drill and duty officer of the mounted service," was an old friend of the family. Thomas, "an old and esteemed friend," had been a lieutenant with Colonel Webster at Buena Vista. Among all of these distinguished officers, Smith told his mother, "your harum scarum boy is the least deserving." [41]

The company to be commanded by Captain Smith had been recruited in the western Virginia mountains by an old friend and classmate Walter Jenifer. "Bud" Wood, a grandson of General Zachary Taylor, had been made second lieutenant in the company. The horses for the whole regiment were the finest that money could buy, costing an average of $150.00 each.

After a few weeks of hard labor, breaking in men and horses, the Second began its long march through the Ozark Mountains and the Indian Territory to Texas. There was no supply train. Carrying their kits and other equipment on their horses, they were to live off of the country through which they rode. By November 28 they had arrived at Fort Gibson, Indian Reserve, after days of exposure to a cutting wind which beat sleet and rain into their faces and made existence a constant misery for man and beast. "Indeed in the whole course of my military experience I have never seen men suffer more," explained Captain Smith. Only Major Hardee had seemed to gain weight as a result of the suffering. [42]

How Captain Smith fared on the remainder of the march through rough Texas weather is not recorded, for several months were to elapse before his family heard from

[41] Edmund K. Smith to Mother, October 20, 1855.
[42] *Id.* to *id.*, November 30, 1855.

him again. Although all his letters were filled with expressions of affection and concern for the welfare of his mother, it was not infrequent that he went for months without writing even a note. Such neglect was inexcusable, and the old lady felt it keenly. To her friends she invented "all sorts of excuses" for not hearing from her soldier son. And the neglect was made even more embarrassing when military friends of the family, such as Major Hardee, kept their own families well-informed.[43] But when Captain Smith did write he usually gave many details of events which had transpired during the period of silence.

He broke his six months of silence on June 17, 1856, but this time with only a short note. He had just arrived at Fort Chadbourne, Texas, and was prepared to leave on an expedition against the Comanches. Colonel Lee would command. Recently about two hundred Comanches, headed by chief Sanico, had committed a number of murders on the frontier and then disappeared toward the upper Red and Canadian river country. Captain Smith, knowing something of that country, was none too hopeful of catching these roving Indians. "A long and tedious march through a barren country at an extremely disagreeable season of the year will probably be the only result of our expedition," he prophesied.

For six weeks the expedition moved about the upper Brazos and Colorado rivers country. Although favored by two good rains, almost a miracle in the dry season, no Indians were caught. "As has been the case with all large expeditions against the nomadic tribes on our western prairies," Smith recorded, "we travelled through the country, broke down our men, killed our horses, and returned as ignorant of the whereabouts of Mr. Sanico as when

[43] Mrs. Frances K. Smith to Edmund K. Smith, August 21, 1855, and June 9, 1856.

we started." The expedition did, however, collect geographical information which he hoped would "prevent the sending of many more expeditions in that direction." [44]

After a few days rest Smith's company was in the saddle again headed for the upper Llano and Guadalupe rivers region where they spent two weeks without even undressing, except for a hasty bath. What a change from the comfortable life of an infantryman, he commented. In the infantry one could accumulate a few comforts such as books to read and could live as a "civilized being and a Christian man." In the cavalry the only luxury was an occasional bear hunt or horse race. And if one should "love books and eschew whiskey" his education would be "sadly neglected." But there was no need to worry about him, he assured his mother. "I shall never become a bear, though I may love the bear hunt. I shall never drink whiskey though I be a dragoon. I may live in a tent but I shall never give up my books nor the refining influence of an intelligent mind."

His life in the cavalry had been truly that of a nomad, sleeping on a horse blanket and using his saddle for a pillow. Horses were dependent upon prairie grass, and the men, except for a little pork, flour, and coffee, relied upon game for subsistence. "I wish you could see me in scouting costume," he wrote his mother.

Mounted on my mule—(the dearest, gentlest, and most intelligent brute,—small but round, fat as a dumpling, with sleek coat, bright eyes and two well developed and expressive ears, actively moving in every direction and speaking as plainly as an alphabet); corduroy pants; a hickory or blue flannel shirt, cut down in front, studded with pockets and worn outside; a slouched hat and long beard, cavalry boots worn over the pants, knife and revolver belted to the

[44] Edmund K. Smith to Mother, June 17, July 31, 1856.

side and a double barrel gun across the pommel, complete the costume as truly serviceable as it is unmilitary.[45]

It seems that the fine horse had now given way to the lowly mule. "Mules we find more intelligent and enduring than horses," Captain Smith remarked.[46]

Only two short notes written by Smith during 1857 have been preserved. He remained in Texas chasing the Indians. "Wild Cat," however, had been substituted for Sanico. Early in the year he was transferred to Fort George, a hotter and more dilapidated post. Letters from his mother arrived regularly, and he enjoyed the family news and St. Augustine gossip. Sister Frances had accepted an invitation from the Putnams to spend the winter of 1856–57 in St. Augustine. Cousin Edmund Kirby, Jr., son of the late Colonel Kirby, had received an appointment to West Point. Aunt Kate Russell was also trying to get an appointment for her son Edmund. Fanny Russell, still visiting in St. Augustine, was much interested in Captain Smith's description of his mule. All wanted him to be certain to bring his uniform when he came home. Cousin Kate Putnam, whose husband, Dr. John C. Calhoun, had died in 1855, was about to marry his younger brother William Lowndes. Would it not be possible for Captain Smith to arrive in St. Augustine in time for the wedding? his mother inquired. It might cause his own "bachelor prepossessions" to give way to "a marrying impulse." She was sure that too long on the frontier without female society was not good for him, for man should never "be left to his own devices." What about Miss Crane, a St. Augustine eligible who had shown interest in Edmund in earlier years? Although not pretty and twenty-five, she was sensible, educated, from a good family, and had a fortune

[45] Id. to id., September 1, 1856.          [46] Ibid.

of probably $30,000. Major Hardee had been casting eyes at her, but with no success; so he had now turned his attention toward Colonel Delafield's daughter at West Point.

Mrs. Smith's plan to move back to the old Segui house. had been abandoned, and she would continue with the Putnams. At one time she had rented the house to the surveyors department, but it was now vacant. No rent, therefore, had been collected for some time. The few remaining servants were hired out, but the income from this source was small. In fact about all the income the old lady had was the money sent by her son. She thanked him for the drafts he sent; they prevented her being a burden on the Putnams, who were very kind to her in spite of her "unequal temper."

Aleck, the Negro boy given Edmund by his father several years earlier, was now about grown and ready to join his master. Previously, Captain Smith had urged his mother to teach Aleck "to cook & make himself useful generally as a bachelor servant." Aleck was now handsome, good-tempered, and genteel, the mother reported, but still had a boyish fondness for play.[47]

On September 1, 1857, Captain Smith wrote his mother that he hoped to see her by December 15. He was about to begin the long furlough to which twelve years of service had entitled him. Presumably he was in St. Augustine for the Christmas holidays and remained there for the duration of the winter. On May 18, 1858, he sailed for Europe on the *S. S. Europa*. His conscience bothered him a bit for leaving home at the only time he could have enjoyed an extended visit with relatives and friends, but he

[47] Mrs. Frances K. Smith to Edmund K. Smith, June 9, October 8, December 18, 1856; March 1, 29, May 21, 1857; Edmund K. Smith to Mother, June 23, September 1, 1857.

was pleased that a lifelong desire to see something of the Old World was about to be realized.[48] From his passport we get our first description of the young Captain's physical appearance—five feet ten inches in height, dark complexion, brown hair, hazel eyes, oval face, large nose and mouth, and a high forehead.[49]

[48] *Id.* to *id.,* May 29, 1858.     [49] See passport in Kirby-Smith Papers.

## CHAPTER V

# ON THE SOUTHWESTERN
# FRONTIER

FROM THE BEGINNING of his trip Captain Smith was seeing the world; no fewer than a dozen nations were represented among the passengers. His mate was a Turkish naval officer. As neighbors he had the Danish minister to the United States and a star of the New York Opera. Also aboard was Madame La Grange, a prima donna and the wife of a Russian count, who in turn was a cousin of Kosciusko.[1]

The *Europa* docked at Liverpool on May 28, and Captain Smith immediately began a pedestrian tour of Wales, where he thoroughly enjoyed the beautiful scenery and the "ivy clad ruins." The beauty of England surpassed all his expectations. By June 5 he was in London. The commoners in England, he observed, liked Americans, but the aristocracy hated them and their institutions "as the cause of all the encroachments which have been made upon their rights & privileges." His love for the English had not been increased by contact. As individuals he found them "rude, surley, disagreeable."

By June 18 he had moved across the Channel to Paris, where, in spite of the so-called despotism in France, he

1 Edmund K. Smith to Mother, May 29, 1858.

found "no marked stages of society—all classes mingle, are affable & obliging & polite." All day he roamed about the streets of Paris, and most of the night he spent writing a detailed account of what he had seen. "Never have I worked so hard," he wrote his mother, "& never have done with so little sleep in my life as since I landed in Liverpool." [2]

The Low Countries were next on the itinerary. He then moved up the Rhine to Frankfort and into the northern German states. He sat and gazed at the Dresden art collection until his "heart fairly throbed with rapture." The gems of the Elector of Saxony were indescribable. He viewed the old home of Goethe, the grave of Schiller, and the battlefield of Waterloo, and traversed the ground made hollow by Martin Luther and Philip Melanchthon. [3] A great musical festival was enjoyed in Prague. Moving on into Austria, he found both the officials and the people helpful and co-operative, even to the extent of permitting him to examine military institutions. Yet with all the interesting and the beautiful, Captain Smith, traveling without a companion, was lonesome and homesick. The more he saw of Europe the prouder and better satisfied he was with being an American. "The English I can't abide & the Germans & French though pleasant & sociable are so different in their habits & peculiar in their tastes that it is an exercise of great self denial to travel with them." [4]

Several days were spent in viewing the scenery of the Alps and then the traveler moved to Italy. Venice with its rich costumes and gondoliers was the most interesting city he had visited. The "mysterious grandeur" of the great monuments at Florence absorbed and entranced him. Rome, with its antiquities and art galleries, was a fit place for weeks of meditation. The artistic perfection of the

Vatican defied all of his efforts at description. "Rome is the quintessence of Italy & Italy I have found to be the concentration of all that is interesting in Europe," Captain Smith explained to his mother.[5]

The loneliness which had stalked him all over Europe proved too much for the traveling Captain while in Italy. He abandoned his plan to visit Spain, returned to Paris and sailed for New York on October 19. After a pleasant Christmas with his mother in St. Augustine, he took Aleck and headed west to join his regiment at Camp Radziminski. Aleck, though delighted with the trip and wishing to be useful, was ill most of the way. Captain Smith feared his servant was "too delicate for rough life on the plains." [6]

Radziminski was situated on the southern slopes of the Wichita Mountains. To the south and west lay a great plain which supported thousands of buffalo. In the rugged mountains to the north were numerous big horn and elk. To no one could this information have been more interesting than to Captain Smith. The climate, however, was not very attractive. Even after Smith arrived in April a hard freeze was recorded.

But wild Comanches, not wild animals, were to be the objects of chase. Major Earl Van Dorn, "a gallant and efficient officer" and a victor over the Indians during the previous year, was ready to lead an expedition of six companies of cavalry and one of infantry to the upper reaches of the Canadian and Arkansas rivers, an unexplored region known only to the Kiowa and Comanche. Captain Smith was made second in command.[7] Carrying no tents and with rations reduced to a minimum of pork, flour, sugar, coffee, and salt, the expedition set out on May 30, accompanied by forty-six friendly Indians from smaller

[5] *Id.* to *id.*, August 15, 20, 1858.     [6] *Id.* to *id.*, March 7, 1859.
[7] *Id.* to *id.*, April 15, 29, 1859.

tribes hostile to the Comanches. Dressed in all their finery, these allies "promised loudly and recounted most heroic deeds of bravery they had in prospect."

For forty-five miles the expedition followed Elk Creek, a tributary of the Red River, and then crossed the divide, traveling "thirty miles through herds of Buffalo to the Washitaw." At that point scouts captured an Indian boy, who was evidently a part of a scouting party on its way to reconnoiter Camp Radziminski. Under intensive questioning the boy told of two large camps of eighteen hundred lodges five days to the north. The Kiowas and Comanches were now in camp discussing war.

The officers consulted and calculated the possible strength of the Indians. It could be as high as ten thousand! Great excitement spread through the companies as Major Van Dorn, taking the boy as a guide and promising to shoot him in case he gave false information, ordered a forward march. All knew that the major "would charge twenty thousand Indians with as much *sang froid* as he would twenty." At the close of another day of hard marching the major announced his plan. By an all night march he would surprise the Indians and fall upon them in camp. The expedition moved on through "almost Egyptian darkness" over hills and bluffs and through ravines in a drenching rain. But morning brought no sight of an Indian camp. The boy said the camps were still three days distance.

The next night camp was pitched on the bank of the South Canadian and a crossing was made on the following morning. The route then lay northward across the North Canadian, Red Fork of the Arkansas, and the Cimarron. Next night a small band of Comanches came near the camp. A minor skirmish resulted in the death of one Indian. The guide now said the camp was nearby, but another thirty miles of marching was necessary before the camp was reached. The Indians had fled. From the signs of recent habitation the number was estimated at about two thousand. Footprints led northward.

Rain and sleet continued to make life miserable as the troops took up the trail. After twenty more miles they halted for food and rest. Soon the alarm was sounded. Indians were on the hill above. Lieutenant Royal and a small mounted force gave chase, and soon sent back for help. Captain Smith and his company raced three miles to the scene of action. The Indians had taken refuge in a wooded ravine through which flowed a small stream. There Lieutenant Royal had surprised them and captured their horses. Instead of trying to escape, these Indians chose "to sell their lives as dearly as possible."

When Captain Smith arrived he ordered his men to dismount, and they "dashed into the thicket after the Florida style of bush-fighting." Smith was shot before he had advanced twenty yards but kept on moving until the battle was over. The shot was at close range, the ball passing "through the upper part of the thigh, just missing the large artery and making a wound about four inches through." Lieutenant Fitzhugh Lee was shot with an arrow which entered under the arm and passed through both lungs. The whites lost thirteen men killed and wounded; the Indians were "literally wiped out."

Captain Smith refused to be taken back to camp on a litter and remained in the saddle for eighteen days. When his company again reached Radziminski on May 31 his wound had almost healed; the "fine bracing air" from the mountains soon restored him to full strength.[8]

Shortly after returning to Radziminski, Major Van Dorn was removed from command and ordered to San Antonio. This transfer left Captain Smith in command

[8] *Id.* to *id.*, June 2, 1859.

of what he later termed the "Wichita Expedition." A threatened clash between reservation Indians and whites in that area brought out five companies of troops from Camp Radziminski. Further difficulties were averted, however, by removal of the Indians northward to a point near the border of Kansas Territory. The "expedition" resulted in nothing more dangerous or exciting than a two month's ride about a country noted for its fresh air and beautiful scenery. Yet this was no grand holiday, for during these months Smith's men tasted no fruits or vegetables, and visions of chickens, eggs, and milk disturbed their sleep and made their days uncomfortable. Aleck no doubt fared better than his master, for he remained at camp and grew "prodigious in stature and laziness." [9]

On September 5, 1859, Captain Smith sat in his tent at Radziminski awaiting the arrival of a wagon train to transfer his company to Camp Cooper. He was pleased with the prospect of moving 150 miles nearer to civilization, yet he dreaded the climate at Cooper where the summers were sultry and the winters bitter cold. He was also reluctant to leave a camp where he himself was in command, especially since his task had been made pleasant by the friendship and assistance of such "high-toned gentlemen" as lieutenants Fitz Lee and Jenifer. Major George H. Thomas commanded the small garrison at Camp Cooper. [10]

While Captain Smith was en route from Radziminski to Cooper, Major Thomas was preparing to lead an expedition against the Comanches. He departed the day before Smith's arrival, leaving to the care of the new commander "some one hundred and fifty brokendown horses, and fifty or sixty broken-down men and women." Fitz Lee had come along to help, but Jenifer, armed with a leave

[9] *Id.* to *id.*, June 12, August 15, 1859.    [10] *Id.* to *id.*, September 5, 1859.

and with matrimonial intentions, had set out for the East. Smith was not at all happy over his new situation. A glance at his description of the location of Camp Cooper explains his discontent: "Fifty miles west of Belknap, and about eighty beyond the line of settlements, is an elevated region of bare, rocky hills, open to the north winds which sweep over the central plateau of the continent three-fourths of the year. Sheltered by a bluff in the bottom of a little stream called the Clear Fork of the Brazos, and in one of the most dreary spots of this dreary section, Camp Cooper is located." The water supply was the Clear Fork which flowed from the gypsum beds to the west, and from the taste of the water, Captain Smith suspected that it might contain samples of "all the drugs in the Medical Department." The one good point about the location was its nearness to the overland mail route which passed within four miles. It was possible for a letter from St. Augustine to reach Camp Cooper within eleven days. "Forgive my complaining strain," Captain Smith requested his mother, "but the wind whistles about my ears and the dust blows around my eyes till I am scarcely responsible for anything I write." He and his new dog "Ugly" condoled with each other on the absence of birds in the area.[11]

Mrs. Smith made good use of the overland mail, relieving a portion of the monotony of camp life by relating facts and rumors in a most interesting manner. Kate Putnam Calhoun, who had just lost her second husband, was very ill and had returned to St. Augustine. Her three boys were terrorizing the entire household. A few weeks later Cousin Kate was reported much improved. She was a "marrying woman," Mrs. Smith remarked, and would no doubt soon be "out" again. Two months later Kate was "fairly in the field."

[11] *Id.* to *id.,* November 1, 1859.

The marble and iron railing for Judge Smith's tomb had arrived from Philadelphia. The Italian marble head slab had cost more than was calculated, but Mrs. Smith was sure her son would be pleased with it.

Emma, Kirby's only daughter, had written to her grandmother. The old lady expressed pleasure with the excellent care Mary had taken of Kirby's children. Frances Webster wanted her mother to visit in New York, but Mrs. Smith doubted that the state of her health would permit. The proposed trip was later called off.

Kate Putnam Calhoun wanted to buy Violet, Aleck's mother. She had been with Kate in South Carolina. Violet had changed much, Mrs. Smith observed. "The strict discipline to which she has been subjected, has subdued her, and she is now a staid faithful servant." Captain Smith replied that, if Kate wished, he would furnish funds for the purchase of Violet in his own name. His old nurse Peg must never be sold except to him. "I will in all probability die an old Bachelor & I am able to support all the old family negroes if necessary."

This and a similar statement made a few months earlier caused Mrs. Smith much concern. "Oh how I wish you had a home of your own and a wife to *look after you,* at least to *sew your buttons* on. . . . And some wee ones to pet in your liesure—we have in this house & to spare of the last. . . ." (These were the children of Kate Calhoun who were about to drive the old lady insane.) "A good true hearted woman," she later added, "would bear up stoutly against even the discomforts of a frontier post— Think of this dear Son and *act wisely*—ere it be too late."

When she heard that her son had been suffering from chills and fever, Mrs. Smith implored him to get out of that "God forsaken country." His father had suffered from the same ailment during the war of 1812. "I have often seen every piece of furniture in the room shaken, when his *stalwart* frame was under the chill," she related.

When the news of John Brown's raid at Harper's Ferry reached St. Augustine, Mrs. Smith temporarily forgot family matters. "The Harpers Ferry revolt has stirred up the South, as it ought to do," she hastily wrote Captain Smith, "and, I dare say will be beneficial in its results." [12]

All the while Captain Smith had remained isolated at Camp Cooper, but monotony and boredom had not been without compensation. In the absence of any place to spend their money, officers and men had no choice but to practice thrift. Smith sent much of his money to his mother. The paymaster had just been around, he wrote, and now he must get rid of "some of the super-abundant cash which is ever troubling me." He enclosed $500. Of that amount, $150.00 was to go to Aunt Kate Russell, if she was in need, and $50.00 to the pastor, but not in his name. His mother was to use the remainder in such ways as she might see fit.[13]

By Christmas, 1859, Captain Smith had been moved to Camp Colorado, "eighty miles south of Belknap, forty from the line of settlements, and two hundred northwest of San Antonio." Situated on a clear stream in the edge of an oak grove which stretched away many miles to the north and west, this was a camp much more to the captain's liking. Deer, geese, duck, and turkey were in abundance. This brought joy to both Ugly and his master. The captain reported the bagging of six fine turkeys within a space of fifteen minutes. But this was not necessarily a sign of superior marksmanship, for he confessed that there were probably a thousand turkeys "within a space

[12] Mrs. Frances K. Smith to Edmund K. Smith, July 28, August 9, September 9, 20, October 20, November 17, December 6, 20, 1859; Edmund K. Smith to Mother, November 10, 1859.

[13] *Id.* to *id.,* November 10, 1859.

of to hundred yards square." Teal and mallard were almost as plentiful, and about the camp kitchen hung numerous hams of venison. "I wish I could stock your larder for the Christmas holidays, and receive in return some butter and eggs," Captain Smith wrote his mother. The prospect for a merry Christmas at camp was slight— not an egg in sight. They were getting some canned goods, but how he would "relish a dish of ripe tomatoes, some old-fashioned boiled potatoes, or a generous pile of smoking roasting-ears!" [14]

The winter at Colorado was severe. Northers struck suddenly and without warning and when accompanied by sleet and snow were "dangerous visitors." One caught Captain Smith and a small force several miles from camp and handled them roughly, but thanks to the protection of a frozen bank and the stimulation from a demijohn of whiskey, they got off with a little frostbite.

Even during the coldest weather, the troops were subject to call at any time and were frequently in the saddle chasing marauding Indians who were stealing thousands of head of livestock annually. Smith described his men as perfect Cossacks, but he admitted that the area to be patrolled was so great they seldom caught any Indians. An illustration of the excitement and danger that might be expected was the experience of Fitz Lee. Lee personally chased an Indian into a cedar brake and found him only when the Indian sprang upon his back. Over and over the two struggled "with doubtful results." The Indian shot a hole through Lee's sleeve. Finally Lee overpowered his opponent and blew out his brains. The victor then paraded the Indian's "shield, head dress and arms with great pride." [15]

In midwinter, 1860, Captain Smith left Colorado for

---

[14] *Id.* to *id.*, December 24, 1859.  [15] *Id.* to *id.*, January 15, 1860.

a thirty day visit in San Antonio. During his absence letters arrived from his mother giving some idea of the growth of sectional feeling back east. "The whole country is in a state of fearful agitation," she declared; "disunion! disunion! . . . is boldly spoken of by the fireside." All were talking of Northern aggression and the insults to the South found in Northern papers. "Southern men and Southern women will not sit down with folded hands if the masses elect a Black Republican President." Uncle Putnam was very much aroused, she said. He loved the Union but he would defend Southern rights to death. "I feel confident that your sword will be offered to the land of *your* birth—Was not the stampede of the Southern Students from the Northern Colleges a beautiful thing— how I honor those youths—I have the blood of a soldier of the Revolution in my veins, and it warms up, as I think how the noble fabric of their building has been desecrated." [16]

A month later the old lady had cooled somewhat. She believed the disunion fever had subsided a bit, still there was "fire burning under the ashes." Many strangers were in St. Augustine for the winter. "These abolition scamps do not hesitate to enjoy our fine climate & hospitalities (when they can get them) hating us inwardly, and out- wardly doing all they dare." She doubted if any of her relatives would be interested in going north of the Mason and Dixon line the next summer.[17]

Captain Smith returned from his leave about the middle of March, 1860. His mother's letters were waiting. He no doubt enjoyed the news and gossip, but one of her statements worried him. She had been very critical of the Beltons for their recent attempt to convert her sister Kate

---

[16] Mrs. Frances K. Smith to Edmund K. Smith, January 11, 1860.
[17] *Id.* to *id.*, February 18, 1860.

Russell to Catholicism. "It grieves me, my dear Mother," he wrote immediately, "to have you speak in such a style, and so bitterly of Uncle Belton and Aunt Harriet—that very bitterness & sectarian prejudice is what disgusts so many with Christianity and is in violence to the true teachings of the Savior & our church—Remember of the three great Christian virtues, the greatest of the three is charity—and that if we have not charity we are nothing. Coln Belton is, I know, a good pure and benevolent Christian, even if he be a Catholic." Aunt Kate had no right to complain. She knew that the Beltons were Catholic before she went to live with them.[18] When Mrs. Smith received this letter she wrote across the top: "I acknowledge the justice of My Sons reproof for want of charity to the Roman Catholics. Am sorry to have been so uncharitable."

For the news relating to the growth of sectionalism, Captain Smith showed concern but not much alarm. The topics of the day must be exciting to cause a "sober staid old Lady of more than 70" to talk as she did, he chided his mother. The waves of sectional excitement had not yet reached the frontier. As for himself, he did not anticipate the dire calamities prophesied by her. The God who had sustained the fathers of the Union would continue to guide in this new crisis. "A war of races is surely not reserved for us—there are too many good and conscientious men in both sections . . . to permit it." [19]

Captain Smith enjoyed his visit in San Antonio. Great changes had taken place since his visit three years earlier, he noted. A more moral and cultured society was in evidence. And no longer did established etiquette require that one go "armed to the teeth." No longer did men go down

18 Edmund K. Smith to Mother, March 20, 1860.
19 *Id.* to *id.*, March ?, 1860.

the street with their wives on one arm and their shotguns on the other. Smith was particularly impressed with the services rendered by the Reverend Mr. Jones, a circuit-riding Episcopal missionary, who was undoubtedly "scattering the seed in ground that had long lain fallow." Surely the harvest would be great and the Master well pleased with the husbandry. "How I envied him his labors! wicked though it be to do so," he confided to his mother. "How willingly would I have changed places with him; how gladly have taken his work and his responsibilities. I have asked and desired for it for twelve years. I am not good enough. . . . I may be too weak to take the final step. At all events my desires are unheeded. An all-wise God has given me work in a different sphere. He wills it not according to my wishes. His will be done. . . ." [20] Ever since he was a baby, his mother replied, she had hoped to see him in the ministry; but she had to say frankly that it was now "too late to embrace this avocation." The greatest service he could render in the future would be in keeping his baptismal vows.[21]

By midsummer talk of disunion had subsided a bit in St. Augustine, even though military companies were holding weekly drills and parades on the plaza. Even Uncle Putnam had sufficiently "conquered his repugnance to crossing the Mason-Dixon line" to agree to accompany his wife and Mrs. Smith on a visit to relatives in New York and Connecticut. Mrs. Smith hesitated, feeling that her strength was not sufficient. She had a horror of becoming ill and being a burden on others, particularly while in the North. She finally yielded, however, when her sister insisted and Putnam agreed that it would do the ladies good to visit old friends. They set sail on July 5, 1860.[22]

[20] *Ibid.*   [21] Mrs. Frances K. Smith to Edmund K. Smith, April 25, 1860.
[22] *Id.* to *id.*, June 2, 23, July 4, 1860.

Captain Smith approved of the Northern trip, hoping both his mother and Aunt Helen would be benefited. But as for himself, he explained, he would "rather remain south of Mason and Dixon's Line and avoid all contact with such atrocities as the Sumnerites and Sewardites of the present day have proved themselves to be." [23]

Life was dull, though comfortable, at Camp Colorado during the spring and summer of 1860. The complete absence of women was partly responsible; the intense heat also assisted. Vegetation parched and the streams dried up. The Comanche Indians continued their raids upon livestock, principally horses, and the troops continued their inability to track them down. There was very little killing, for the Comanches were more thieves than warriors. They seldom killed unless caught where they were compelled to fight. As prairie Indians, they fed upon the buffalo, shifting as the herds did, and were noted for their skill with bow and arrow. The general region of their habitation was the upper Canadian River country. Horses were so essential to their way of life that they were forced to steal an adequate supply. Traveling in small bands and afoot, they would sneak into the stock country and hide until the moon was bright enough to assist in rounding up probably hundreds of horses. Then, riding at top speed, sometimes eighty miles a day, they would head for the buffalo country, often leaving the weaker horses dead along the trail. Once among the buffalo their trail would be blotted out by the tracks of the herd. Here the troops usually gave up the chase and returned to camp empty-handed. [24]

Mrs. Smith and the Putnams had a pleasant visit in the North and returned without serious incident. The nearest approach to hard feelings resulted from a statement by sister Harriet Belton that she intended to convert to Ca-

[23] Edmund K. Smith to Mother, July 5, 1860.   [24] *Ibid.*

tholicism as many of her family as she could. Visits were made to Niagara Falls and to West Point where Mrs. Smith was escorted around by three nephews—Edmund Russell, Edmund Kirby, and Joseph L. Smith Kirby.[25] This Northern tour proved more expensive than expected and Mrs. Smith found herself in debt to Judge Putnam. Captain Smith came to her assistance with a draft for $200, but the postman got drunk and either lost or stole the money. A duplicate was sent. He wished it were within his means to send more, he explained, but he had now gone into the cattle business and was short of cash.[26]

While engaged in camp routine of "hunting, grumbling & chasing small marauding parties of Indians," Smith had decided to establish "a *rancho*." The cattle business might prove both desirable and remunerative, he reasoned, should Abraham Lincoln be elected President and decide to disband the army. "Too old to commence a new profession," he commented, "too honest to try my hand at cattle lifting (the business of the frontier) I'll . . . take to cattle raising." He and the camp sutler, J. M. Hunter, chose a site on a tributary of the Colorado and purchased four hundred head of cattle at eight dollars each. They expected an early and large increase in the size of their herd, for in that area nature was so prolific that "yearlings calve within twelve months from their birth." [27]

Smith had chosen this "beautiful spot" for a rancho either while chasing Indians or wild animals. He much preferred the latter. He had just returned from an exciting bear hunt, he wrote his mother on November 10. "My pack of hounds behaved excellently, and we killed every bear

[25] These were the sons of her sister Kate and brothers Edmund and Reynold Marvin.

[26] Mrs. Frances K. Smith to Edmund K. Smith, July 24, August 5, September 1, 1860; Edmund K. Smith to Mother, September 15, 1860.

[27] *Id.* to *id.*, September 15, October 2, 1860.

started—well mounted I had some thrilling and exciting chases giving Bruin myself the coup de mort in at least one fierce struggle—several of our dogs were hurt but we returned ladened with spoils without accident." [28]

A few weeks later, while returning from a court martial at Chadbourne eighty miles away, he bagged many fine partridges, ducks, and turkeys, and gave a three-mile chase to a bear. "I always travel . . . with my coach and four with outriders," he informed his mother, "and you will smile the more when I tell you that the aforesaid Stylish Conveyance is for the accommodation of my dogs." This old ambulance was about six feet long and had removable seats thus furnishing room for dogs and camp equipment. The captain himself rode a horse. "In the morning I designate the camping ground for the night, my equipage and escort dash off at the rate of seven miles the hour, and when I ride into camp in the afternoon or after dark, I find my tent pitched and blankets spread, a roaring fire, a woodmans feast smoking before it, and a woodmans appetite to add zest to the *Spread*." All of this cost nothing, however, since it was cared for by men around the camp. He now had a nice bunch of dogs—"a pack of stag hounds and four setters Old Ugly heading the list." There were also bear dogs but their "canine respectability" was too much in doubt for him to keep them near. They were housed in the company quarters. [29]

By the time of the Presidential election of 1860 even the soldiers on the frontier had heard and read enough to sense the seriousness of the national crisis. "What does Mr. Putnam think of it," inquired Captain Smith. "I know he is an upright, honest man, conservative and patriotic, and too intelligent to be deceived by scheming politicians." "I am a Southern man in all my feelings," he added, "and

---

[28] *Id.* to *id.*, November 10, 1860.     [29] *Id.* to *id.*, December 6, 1860.

will stand by the fireside whilst the roof tumbles about my ears—and such I fear will be the result in the event of a violent secession." [30]

Two weeks later, before hearing the outcome of the election but expecting a Lincoln victory, Captain Smith urged the use of wisdom and caution: "God grant that *our* people may think wisely and deliberately before acting; else we may act rashly and repent vainly. The seeds of discord have been sown broadcast over the land. Let us earnestly beseech the Great Husbandman lest the weeds of disunion overrun the crop and the whole field be laid waste. I fear the results. God grant that we may weather the storm without dismantling the ship. His will be done." [31]

The stern reality that Lincoln was the President-elect and that South Carolina had seceded shocked even those frontier soldiers who had expected it. Captain Smith counseled caution more than ever. "I fear that our people will act too precipitately," he wrote. "We have grievances and I know they must be redressed, and the slavery question settled definitely and forever." [32] But would it not be better to wait until the entire South could act in unison and "calmly and deliberately and without threats" make their demands? The North would no doubt reject the demands. Then a united South could raise its flag and prepare for "that war which must inevitably follow sooner or later, the rupture of the Union." "Tell Mr. Putnam," he added, "that right or wrong I go with the land of my birth." [33]

[30] *Id.* to *id.*, November 10, 1860.　　　[31] *Id.* to *id.*, November 23, 1860.

[32] A few weeks earlier he had written: "I almost feel like voting for Lincoln when I see families broken up and children so completely separated from their parents." (November 10, 1860.) This statement followed a request that his mother have Peg write Aleck about Violet. Mrs. Smith had transferred the old nurse Peg to Edmund just before going north in 1860. Later in the year she hired her to a man at Fernandina at $6.00 per month.

[33] Edmund K. Smith to Mother, December 24, 1860.

Back in St. Augustine Mrs. Smith did not have her feelings so well under control. South Carolina was out and the Gulf States were probably ripe for a similar move, she wrote her son. "What is to be the end of this great movement God only knows. . . ." Hard times were no doubt ahead but they were preferred to insult, injury, and a loss of property. "Little did or do the Northern Abolitionists —fanatics—Atheists, Socialists devils own (excuse me) know what spirit they have raised in the South." She shared with many others the belief that the South would probably be better off out of the Union. However, she thought Florida would not call for her gallant sons to come home until "Greek meet Greek in the tug of war." They would then no doubt respond quickly and enthusiastically, for she could not conceive of a native-born Southerner serving under Lincoln. Her only advice to her son was to look to the Almighty for guidance.[34]

Important events crowded upon each other and Mrs. Smith, with enthusiasm far greater than would be expected in a lady of her age, rushed the news to her son. "The Secession Ball is rolling and soon there will be a Southern Confederacy," she announced with a mixture of enthusiasm and regret. "A few days now decides the fate of Florida." Major Robert Anderson had evacuated Fort Moultrie at Charleston. She feared the consequences of his action. Many army officers, particularly those from South Carolina, were reported to have resigned. Florida had not yet requested such resignation. Putnam, now a strong secessionist, advised him to be ready but to wait for developments. Colonel William J. Hardee had been in St. Augustine recently. It was rumored that he had just returned from New York where he purchased arms for Georgia.

[34] Mrs. Frances K. Smith to Edmund K. Smith, December 13, 1860.

Another rumor said he might soon go to England for the same purpose. From her window Mrs. Smith could see men putting up a huge flagpole on the plaza. A number of women under the direction of Mrs. Cooper Gibbs were making a flag.[35]

"I never expected to live to see a revolution," she wrote a few days later. But she felt that *"Our Cause* is a *just* one, and I fully believe Providence will smile upon it." The governor of Florida had that day demanded and received a surrender of Fort Marion (San Marcos), including the powder house and barracks. A company of Florida militia witnessed the surrender. A number of guns, it was learned, would be taken to Fernandina. All government property in the South would undoubtedly be taken over, she prophesied. "Carolina has behaved *nobly* in everything —how *beautifully* she took possession of the Arsenal." Both that state and Georgia were asking their gallant men to come home and accept commissions in the state troops. "I wish it had been your good fortune to have been born in one of these States." "Florida poor Florida" would scarcely be able to offer much. But surely her son was "worth something better than a Texan backwoodsman or cattle Driver." He might, if nothing better came his way, accept a commission in Texas, but she hoped that he would not at present give up his commission in the United States army until Florida called.[36]

By mid-January the St. Augustine mails had been seriously interrupted. Steamers which had been in use on the St. Johns River were now engaged in the transportation of guns from Fort Marion to Fernandina. St. Augustine was fast taking on a warlike appearance. An armed company of troops had arrived from Jacksonville and were escorted into town by the St. Augustine "Independent Blues." Mrs.

Smith wondered "if they would *show fight* if a Government steamer should put in and demand or attempt to take the ammunition & muskets, which poor Sergeant Douglas the Ordnance Sergeant had to surrender a few days ago." [37]

The excitement grew more intense daily, Mrs. Smith reported to her son in Texas. Secession and probable war was the one topic of discussion. Older men of military experience had been called upon to man a water battery at the Fort. The ladies were preparing a hospital and collecting supplies. Some persons of means had offered considerable sums of money for equipping troops, but unfortunately there was still no state military organization. She felt certain there would soon be a Southern confederacy and that Jefferson Davis would play a prominent part. Many were reported flocking to Tallahassee seeking commissions. She had no advice to offer Captain Smith, but "Putnam says hold on till *events* make it necessary to leave the *Federal* army." "God grant that we may see you once more," she concluded, "and that the distractions of the times may pass and peace and quiet succeed. May God hold you in the hollow of his hand. May He guide, bless, and preserve you." [38]

Colonel William J. Hardee, a native of Georgia and friend of the Smith family, promised Mrs. Smith that he would also write her son. Hardee had returned to the East several months before the crisis and was in the South during the winter of 1860–61. "Florida and Georgia, our native States, have both seceded and I feel confident that we are destined to have a Southern Confederacy," he wrote Smith. There was little probability that any compromise could reunite the states. Florida had invited her military

[37] *Id.* to *id.,* January 11, 1861. Both this and the previous letter were misdated 1860.
[38] *Id* to *id.,* January 16, 1861.

and naval men to resign from the service of the United States and accept the same rank with state troops. A similar step was being considered in Georgia. The big question, Hardee explained, was "At what time shall we resign?" He had notified the governor of Georgia of his willingness to resign at any moment the governor thought proper.

But Captain Smith's position was different. Florida's resolution had stipulated that the offer must be accepted within thirty days. Smith's distance from home made quick action on his part impossible. "Unless therefore a collision of arms takes place before the Southern Confederacy is organized, I don't think I would resign," advised Hardee. Certainly, Smith was well enough known not to be forgotten by the officials of the proposed Confederacy. In the meantime, there was no probability that he would be called upon to act against the South. Some South Carolina officers, he understood, had refused to resign when their state called. They would wait for the Confederacy. Hardee disapproved of this position, but in Smith's case the time limit could not be met.[39]

Captain Smith had been reading and giving careful study to the events reported; his mind was made up. On the same day that Hardee wrote the above, Smith was explaining his position to his mother and Uncle Putnam. He had been enjoying some more good hunting. On a recent trip he and three others brought back more than seventy turkeys. And already this season he had killed more than two hundred partridges over his setters Ugly and Nell. Owing to the good hunting, his cattle interests, and his many friends, he believed he ought to remain in Texas. "But I long for the sand-hills, I long for the pines, I long for the mullet and hominy of Florida." However, unless the paymaster soon came around, he and a number of

---

[39] William J. Hardee to Edmund K. Smith, January 28, 1861.

others would be compelled to take root in the soil of Texas "from pure inability to get away."

Although far removed from the heated sectional discussions and the secession movement, he felt their effects. He was possessed with "a restless, longing anxiety to know the worst," and was overwhelmed with "a feeling of most indefinable dread." "A fratricidal war looms on the horizon. The course of the Cotton States, the tone of feeling, the messages of their Governors, the acts advocated in their legislatures, are to me most incomprehensible."

"Instead of cultivating a good feeling with, do they wish to alienate the affections of their own brethren of the Border States? Instead of a United South, do they wish a rival power formed between them and the Abolition States on the Canadian frontier? If they do, they will lose Louisiana and Texas, and dwindling down to a fourth-rate power, will find it as hard to maintain themselves at home as it will be difficult to command respect and influence abroad. . . . I can only commit our cause to that Providence who tempers the storm to the afflicted, and pray that we may be spared the horrors of a civil war." [40]

[40] Edmund K. Smith to Mother, January 28, 1860.

*CHAPTER VI*

# "I GO WITH THE LAND OF
# MY BIRTH"

CONSCIOUS OF THE direction in which the current was moving and realizing his inability to check its progress, Captain Edmund Kirby Smith had decided to move with it as quietly and cautiously as possible. Accordingly, he sent to Uncle Putnam a communication which was to be delivered to the governor of Florida at the proper time. He had not been informed as to what action Florida had taken, but should the worst come, his lot would be cast with his native state. Aleck alone seemed pleased with the prospects. To him it meant leaving Texas for St. Augustine, "that Negro paradise." [1]

Another week passed and Captain Smith still had no news on the action taken by the Cotton States, yet he entertained little doubt. They had no doubt acted without calm and deliberation and the attendant evils would soon "try men's souls and test their wisdom." To him the future appeared dark but certain—war, dissension, exhaustion, impoverishment. The one ray of hope was that Kentucky and Virginia might be persuaded to join a Southern confederacy and then use their calmness to hold in check the

[1] Edmund K. Smith to Mother, January 28, 1861. This letter was misdated 1860.

impatient Cotton States. A confederacy composed of the Cotton States alone, he reasoned, would be weak and undesirable. Such a group of states would no doubt attempt to reopen the foreign slave trade, a step "unwise in itself and discreditable to say the least of it." [2]

On February 1 a Texas convention voted in favor of secession. On February 22, Colonel H. E. McCulloch, a commissioner representing the state, accompanied by several companies of state troops, arrived at Camp Colorado and demanded the surrender of all Federal property, including arms, equipment, and livestock. Captain Smith refused to comply, explaining to Colonel McCulloch in person that he could "never, under any circumstances, give up my arms and horses, or negotiate upon terms that would dishonor the troops under my command." Should the colonel persist in his demand, he would mount his troops and "endeavor to cut my way through any force opposed to me."

No fighting took place. After brief negotiations Federal property was surrendered to the State of Texas, and the United States troops, with arms and ten days' rations, rode out. Private property belonging to officers and men, including Captain Smith's bird dogs Nell and Ugly, was left behind. Smith reported that evacuation was hastened out of fear that a collision might at any moment occur between undisciplined state troops and irritated United States soldiers. The Second Cavalry rode to camp near Fort Mason and from that point Captain Smith wrote his report to the assistant adjutant-general, Department of Texas.[3] This report was signed "E. Kirby Smith," the name by which he was henceforth to be known in military annals. In order

2 *Id.* to *id.*, February 3, 1861.
3 *The War of the Rebellion: A Compilation of the Official Records of the Union and Confederate Armies* (Washington, 1880–1901), Ser. I, Vol. I, 559. Hereinafter cited as *Official Records*.

to distinguish him from the numerous other Smiths in the Confederate service, he was commonly referred to as Kirby Smith.

The widow of the late Ephraim Kirby Smith was said to have resented this alleged appropriation of a name which, since the death of her husband, she claimed rightfully belonged to her son. The question was not of sufficient importance to be worth an argument. However, years later a considerable stir was created by the publication of a paper entitled "Our Kirby Smith," and General Edmund Kirby Smith thought an explanation necessary. His brother, he stated, was christened Ephraim Kirby Smith and at West Point and in the army was always registered as Ephraim K. Smith. On the other hand, he himself was christened Edmund Kirby Smith and at West Point, although registered as Edmund K. Smith, was called Kirby by his schoolmates. After the death of his brother he began signing his name "E. Kirby Smith." As for his nephew, he was christened Joseph Lee Smith and was always referred to as "Jo." The boy's mother added the "Kirby" after his father's death.[4]

In this explanation the general made some errors and fell short of giving the full story. In the extant letters from his West Point associates there is not one instance of his being called Kirby. Furthermore, he should have added that in family circles he was always called Edmund or "Ted" while it was his brother who was called Kirby. Nevertheless, to say that Edmund Kirby Smith appropriated the name of his illustrious brother was absurd. Ephraim Kirby Smith never rose above the rank of captain and was scarcely known outside his regiment. Like many other captains who died in battle, he would have remained

4 E. Kirby Smith to John Ruhm, October 18, 1888.

unknown to the world had it not been for the Civil War career of his more famous younger brother.[5]

On March 1, 1861, when E. Kirby Smith made his report he was a captain. Two days later he wrote his mother: "I have been promoted to a Majority and in a few weeks would have been a Lieutenant-Colonel of Cavalry." But he had on that day resigned from the United States army. Rank was no longer a consideration, for he "would rather shoulder a musket in the cause of the South than be Commander-in-Chief under Mr. Lincoln." He would proceed forthwith to Montgomery, Alabama, the capital of the new Confederacy, and place his sword at the disposal of President Jefferson Davis.[6]

Kirby Smith went to Indianola, Texas, to take passage east. Weeks of restless and anxious waiting followed before a steamer arrived. He was very eager to get in the midst of events, he wrote home.

Every tie that connects me with the army has been broken; profession, kin, all the associations of my life have been given up, and not suddenly, impulsively, but conscientiously and after due deliberation—I was the senior Maj of my Regt at the time and the youngest man in the army for my position and am 20 years in advance of my contemporaries. What my future may be I cannot tell. I have no expectations. I only know that I sacrifice to my principles more than any other officer in the army can do & I have the reflection that my conscience upholds me in my course—& that no one can accuse me of mercenary motives.[7]

While waiting in Indianola, Kirby Smith saw his old friend Earl Van Dorn, who had recently been commis-

---

[5] Although the general's family during his lifetime was referred to as the Kirby Smith family and subsequent to his death began using the hyphenated name Kirby-Smith, the general himself never considered Kirby as a part of his family name. Dr. R. M. Kirby-Smith, the only surviving son of the general, states that as a boy he was a Smith. He does not know when he became a Kirby-Smith.

[6] E. Kirby Smith to Mother, March 3, 1861.

[7] *Id.* to *id.*, March 25, 1861.

sioned a colonel in the Confederate army. Colonel Van Dorn immediately wrote Confederate Secretary of War Leroy Pope Walker that Kirby Smith was on his way to Montgomery. Major Smith, he stated, had long been considered one of the "leading spirits" of the United States army. However, the subject was too well known to President Davis to require comment as to his ability and integrity. If it was true, as had been rumored, that Van Dorn had been made colonel of cavalry, he strongly urged that Kirby Smith be made his lieutenant colonel. Furthermore, he was told by this officer that a good portion of the United States troops then camping at Green Lake were pro-Southern and would join the Confederate forces if given the chance.[8]

Kirby Smith paid a brief visit to his aged mother before going to Montgomery. Prior to his arrival Mrs. Smith had sent to President Davis copies of her son's recent letters as evidence of loyalty to the South and his future intention.[9] Adjutant General Samuel Cooper, who himself had recently resigned from the United States service, having seen Van Dorn's letter and probably the one from Mrs. Smith, grew impatient at the delay and wired Kirby Smith at St. Augustine: "Your presence is wanted here. Come at once." [10] Kirby Smith had left St. Augustine before the wire was sent.

The delay in reporting to Montgomery considerably changed the course of his career. Orders had been issued

---

[8] Earl Van Dorn to L. P. Walker, March 26, 1861, *Official Records,* Ser. I, Vol. I, 614–15.

[9] Mrs. Frances K. Smith to Jefferson Davis, April 6, 1861. There was a friendship between Davis and the Smith family. It probably began while Davis and Ephraim Kirby Smith were cadets at West Point. Mrs. Smith was a frequent visitor in New York and quite probably at the Point. Her letters reveal that she was well acquainted with many high-ranking officers. Friendship was a strong influence upon Davis when recommending promotion.

[10] Samuel Cooper to E. Kirby Smith, April 11, 1861, *Official Records,* Ser. IV, Vol. I, 218.

for him to go to New Orleans and take command of the forts on the lower Mississippi River. His own delay in reporting and an urgent demand from New Orleans that an experienced officer be sent at once resulted in a change of plans. Colonel P. O. Hebert was sent instead. As had been suggested by Van Dorn, Kirby Smith was made a lieutenant colonel and ordered to Texas.[11] Before he could leave for his assignment this order was rescinded and he was sent to Lynchburg, Virginia, "to organize, muster into service, and equip" troops as they arrived at that place. Considering his new assignment as one of great responsibility, Colonel Kirby Smith pledged himself to endeavor "by activity and energy, to make up for lack of ability and leave the result with that all-wise Providence who has so far guided and protected me." He urgently requested his mother to look among his books and send the French work on cavalry operations.[12]

Mrs. Smith was unable to find the work on cavalry tactics, but she sent a prayer for the safety of her son and a vitriolic denunciation of the despotism and vandalism of those Northern "fanatics, called troops." How could such things happen among civilized people? No doubt Southern sympathizers like Colonel Belton's family in New York were being spied upon and were afraid to open their mouths. She had quit reading the New York *Herald* and *Times*; their columns were filled with nothing but lies. "I am not a timid cowardly woman as you know," she reminded her son, "but my heart sinks with dread as to what may come." President Davis must take the lead; his "indomitable will . . . tried courage great ability" made him the man of the hour. Surely in him Divine Providence had raised up another George Washington. Confederate troops would soon be pouring into Washington, she hoped, and

11 E. Kirby Smith to Mother, April ?, 1861.    12 *Id.* to *id.*, April 20, 1861.

"you my dear noble brave son will be there." The Confederate cause was "just and righteous." The Yankees
might "pour forth their legions of Vandals, their hearts
(if they have any) are not beating with a sense of the right
and justice of their cause, they are mercenaries & fanatics,
*Cowards.*" [13]

Colonel Kirby Smith left Montgomery for Lynchburg on
April 23, taking with him Major Hugh Lawson Clay, assistant adjutant general, and Captain Thomas G. Williams, commissary. Clay, a brother of Senator Clement C.
Clay of Huntsville, Alabama, was a close friend of both
Secretary of War Leroy Pope Walker and President Davis.
At Lynchburg Kirby Smith and Clay became roommates.
Equally devoted to the Confederate cause and devout
members of the Episcopal Church, they soon became most
intimate friends. He had never known a more agreeable
man than Colonel Smith, Clay confided to his wife. Although young in years, the Colonel had seen "more hard
service probably than any officer of the army." And having
"often preserved the lives of enemies in battle," he believed
his own life "Providentially and specially preserved." [14]

Never one to let excessive enthusiasm cloud his judgment, Kirby Smith saw from the beginning the great problem of organizing and equipping sufficient troops. Neither
did he allow his belief in the justice of the cause to blind
him to the realities of war. When he saw the old and the
young, the statesman, the planter, the minister—the best
blood of the South—marching side by side to the scene of
action, his heart throbbed with anxiety, for he abhorred "a
contest which must be baptized in the blood of all we hold
dear or good in the land." The bitterness and determina-

[13] Mrs. Frances K. Smith to E. Kirby Smith, April 29, May 8, 15, June 18,
1861.
[14] Hugh Lawson Clay to Celeste Clay, May 5, 1861, in C. C. Clay Papers,
Duke University.

tion in evidence on both sides, he prophesied, would make of the conflict one in which principles of humanity would "be cast to the wind." Yet in spite of the horror of it all he envisioned no dearth of Confederate manpower. Virginia alone, he assured his mother, would soon have thirty thousand men in the field. Lack of arms alone was retarding the progress of countless thousands who were eager to move forward. But the greatest weakness was the absence of co-ordination between state and Confederate forces. "Governor Letcher is an incubus," he exclaimed, "and the selection of General Lee to command the Virginia forces is unfortunate." President Davis should take the necessary steps to unify all fighting forces and should either take the field in person or appoint G. T. Beauregard or Joseph E. Johnston to command.[15]

At the request of Confederate authorities, Major General Robert E. Lee, commander of Virginia troops, withdrew the state commander at Lynchburg and left Kirby Smith in complete charge. Eight regiments from Alabama, Mississippi, Arkansas, and Tennessee arrived almost immediately. Others followed and soon regiments were rendezvousing everywhere in the vicinity of Lynchburg, and such an undisciplined lot the colonel had never seen. The Tennesseans, especially, he observed, were "a rough, uncouth, democratic mob from the mountains, good rifle shots at home, but most intractable soldiers abroad." [16]

Among those mustered into Confederate service by Colonel Kirby Smith were several cousins—Reynold, Edmund, and Joseph Lee Kirby, sons of the late Reynold Marvin Kirby, and Winfield Belton, who now called himself Francis. The mother of the Kirby brothers now resided in Richmond. Belton had left his New York home to join Wade

[15] E. Kirby Smith to Mother, May 10, 16, 1861.
[16] Id. to id., May 16, 1861.

Hampton's Legion from South Carolina. Another Edmund
Kirby, son of the late Colonel Edmund Kirby of Brownsville, New York, joined the Federal service. George Geddes Smith, youngest son of the late Captain Ephraim Kirby
Smith, also served the Union. He had gone to sea at the
age of thirteen and was in India at the outbreak of the war.

Down in St. Augustine Mrs. Smith received a "dear
charming letter" from her grandson Joseph Lee Kirby
Smith, Kirby's eldest son, who had graduated from West
Point in 1857. "Oh how I wish you could get him to resign & take his chance with our army," she wrote her son
at Lynchburg; "can you propose it—I think I will try." [17]
Colonel Kirby Smith had also had a letter from his
nephew, even before his own resignation, addressing him
as "my dearest and almost sole relative." "Jo," as the
family always called him, wished advice. Should war come,
what would be the proper course for him? Uncle Edmund
replied that in his own case duty would call him to the
service of Florida. But Jo's position was different. Born of
a Northern mother and at a Northern army post and never
having owed allegiance to any Southern state, his loyalty
should be to the United States. [18]

Joseph Lee Kirby Smith took the advice and became the
first colonel of the Forty-first Ohio Regiment: he was
killed near Corinth in October, 1862. Several years after
the war, friends of the late Joseph Lee claimed that the
young nephew was very hostile toward his "rebel" uncle,
and quoted him as saying: "Years ago he stole my father's
good name, and now he has betrayed his country's flag.
If I could meet him in battle, with force enough to thoroughly beat him, it would do my soul good; and I would

[17] Dwight, *Kirbys of New England*, 180–94; Mrs. Frances K. Smith to
E. Kirby Smith, April 29, May 4, 8, 15, 1861.
[18] E. Kirby Smith to John Ruhm, October 18, 1888.

like to capture him, that I might tell him how his kindred and his former comrades despise him." [19] The statement was probably never made. Its publication brought from the general a vigorous denial of any such hostility. At intervals during the first year of the war, he explained, he received several "kind messages" from his nephew, including a photograph in uniform. [20]

Mustering in, equipping, and dispatching Confederate troops required patience and energy, yet life in Lynchburg was not all hard work. The horrors of war had not yet come and there was still much joy and laughter among those who were preparing—civilians and soldiers chatting and drinking, women and girls cutting and sewing. One day a townsman carrying a bundle of blue flannel walked into one of the sewing circles. A bachelor colonel from Florida wanted two shirts, he announced. And the young lady who made the prettiest shirt might have the colonel himself. There was a mad scramble for the material and Cassie Selden came up with one batch.

Cassie was the daughter of the late Samuel Selden, a man of considerable wealth and prominence. Her father had died when she was about twelve, leaving a widow of twenty-nine and seven children. Cassie and her sister Nina were educated in the Georgetown Seminary near Washington. The widow Selden had later married a Mr. Booker who proved to be a "kind and amiable" stepfather.

The shirts were carried home for the finishing touches. Old colored Mammy worked the buttonholes for Cassie and apparently won the prize. "All's fair in love and war," Cassie later remarked. But the colonel was not aware that he had been won.

[19] John W. Fuller, "Our Kirby Smith," in *Sketches of War History, 1861–1865. Papers Read before the Ohio Commandry of the Military Order of the Loyal Legion of the United States*, 2 vols. (Cincinnati, 1888), II, 163.

[20] E. Kirby Smith to John Ruhm, October 18, 1888.

A few afternoons later John R. McDaniel, banker and railroad president, stopped by the Selden home to announce that he had found just the right man for Cassie. Upon learning the name, Cassie declared that he already belonged to her. She would be highly pleased to come to the McDaniel home to look over the prize. During the course of an evening of festivity, Colonel Kirby Smith heard the story, and Cassie thought he was impressed. But, alas, he walked home with another girl.

Kirby Smith made the McDaniel home his social headquarters and no doubt saw Cassie Selden frequently. She later stated that in thanking her for the shirt he declared it would be a shield of protection against both cold and bullets. But the only bullet that struck him during the war went through this shirt. Cassie also made her soldier friend a dressing case of chamois skin lined with red flannel, which McDaniel sent to him by special messenger. It was this little gift that ripened the "seeds of love," she later related.[21]

On May 22 Colonel Kirby Smith left Lynchburg for Harper's Ferry to join the command of Joseph E. Johnston. He was delighted with this transfer toward the probable theater of action; it would guarantee his participation in the first great battle. Still he was not too confident of victory. His experience at Lynchburg had diminished his confidence in Confederate strength. Spirit, determination, and God's guidance would be responsible if victory came. "Our men are poorly armed and equipped," he sadly confided to his mother. The altered flintlock musket was about the only arm available. "One of the bad phases of States' Rights here exhibits itself. Each State in its sovereign capacity seized the arms, etc. in the forts & arsenals within its limits, instead of turning them over to the Confederate

<hr>

[21] Mrs. Edmund Kirby Smith, *All's Fair in Love and War* (n.p., 1945), 9–15.

government. They appropriated them, at least the efficient ones, to their own use." President Davis was scheduled to arrive in Virginia at an early date, and Kirby Smith hoped it would not be "too late to remedy the blunders of Gov. Letcher and the tardiness of Lee." [22]

Upon arrival at Harper's Ferry, Kirby Smith's gloom increased. From what could be learned, the enemy was preparing to move fifty thousand men against Virginia. About half this force, commanded by his "good friend McClellan," a West Point graduate in the class of 1846, was moving in from Wheeling via the Baltimore and Ohio Railroad. A second force under General Robert Patterson, estimated at thirteen thousand, was moving from Pennsylvania. To meet this formidable advance, Kirby Smith could see nothing stronger than a group of poorly armed, undisciplined volunteers who, although of the best blood of the South, were not worth "one regiment of regulars." The natural consequence of state rights was in evidence everywhere. "We have no army, no concert of action, no proper provision for arming and equipping our men," he complained. "The imbecility and inaction of some of our State governments is and will be almost as disastrous as treachery; and the whole manner in which matters have been ordered and regulated on this frontier can be designated by no better word in the vocabulary of military terms than by the word 'blunder.' " What the outcome would be God alone knew.

He was pleased with the efforts of General Johnston whom he considered "the first military man of the day—active, experienced and intelligent"—still he feared there was not sufficient time remaining to remedy the errors of

[22] E. Kirby Smith to Mother, May 21, 1861. Arthur H. Noll, in his *General Kirby Smith,* tried to explain away this apparent criticism of General Lee. No explanation is needed. Lee was not considered sacrosanct in 1861.

others.[23] He lacked adequate words to picture the deplorable conditions at Harper's Ferry, he wrote Major Clay,
who had remained at Lynchburg. The lack of equipment
and the prevalence of measles had reduced the total effective Confederate strength to not more than 5,000; and the
"utter confusion and ignorance presiding in the councils
of the authorities" was "without a parallel." He agreed
with General Johnston that Harper's Ferry was of little
value for either defense or offense, yet the troops there were
in great danger. The frontier was within a triangle formed
by the Shenandoah and Potomac rivers and Furnace
Ridge. Since the Potomac could be crossed at several
points, an invading force might easily trap the defenders.
This risk was too great, especially when Harper's Ferry
was twenty miles off the main route the enemy would likely
follow in attempting entrance into the valley of Virginia.
Should Winchester fall to a Federal force, the troops at the
Ferry would be sacrificed.[24]

By June 9 the Federal advance under General Patterson,
closing in from Pennsylvania by way of Chambersburg,
had reached Sharpsburg. With Patterson was Colonel
George H. Thomas, Kirby Smith's superior in Second
Cavalry days and now characterized by him as "a Virginia
renegade." McClellan was still said to be advancing by the
Baltimore and Ohio with 15,000 to 20,000 men. To meet
this threat Johnston had an undisciplined force of probably 7,000, including many convalescents and raw recruits.
Kirby Smith, viewing this force through the eyes of a regular army man, thought it "not far removed from an irregular, undisciplined mob," which although full of spirit,

[23] E. Kirby Smith to Mother, June 2, 1861.
[24] *Id.* to H. L. Clay, May 29, 1861; Report of J. E. Johnston, *Official Records,* Ser. I, Vol. II, 470 ff.

would probably "give way in confusion" when heavy resistance was encountered.[25]

Johnston considered striking at either Patterson or McClellan and then moving rapidly to join Beauregard at Manassas Gap. Facing Beauregard was an estimated 30,000 men under General Irvin McDowell. If Johnston could delay the arrival of re-enforcements and then rush to Beauregard's assistance, their combined forces might be able to drive McDowell back across the Potomac and then turn on McClellan. The lack of facilities for rapid transportation was the greatest weakness in the execution of such a plan.

Realizing that at Harper's Ferry his army was "bound to a fixed point" while the activities of his opponents were unrestricted, Johnston continued to occupy it only "in compliance with instructions from an Aulic Council in Richmond."[26] When President Davis arrived in Virginia and learned of the situation, he notified Johnston to use his own judgment. On June 13, having heard that McClellan's advance had reached Romney, Johnston sent A. P. Hill with three regiments to check the Federal's progress while Harper's Ferry was evacuated. Two days later, after destroying bridges, the railroad, and public buildings, the Confederates moved toward Winchester and bivouacked for the night near Charleston. There news was received that Patterson had crossed the Potomac at Williamsport. Johnston decided upon a flanking movement to the Martinsburg turnpike, thus putting himself between Patterson and Winchester, but the Union commander recrossed the river. It was reported that Patterson planned to hold his volunteers with him and rush his regulars to join McDowell.[27]

[25] E. Kirby Smith to Mother, June 9, 1861.    [26] Id. to id., June 24, 1861.
[27] Ibid.; Report of J. E. Johnston, Official Records, Ser. I, Vol. II, 470 ff.

Johnston moved on to Winchester. This town, a commercial center of some importance, was the point of juncture of the principal east-west roads with those from Pennsylvania and Maryland; therefore, it was vital to operations in the valley of Virginia. Johnston's army of the Shenandoah was now in position to check McClellan and Patterson, and, if called upon, to rush to the assistance of Beauregard.

During these days of suspense Colonel Kirby Smith was serving as Johnston's adjutant. Also with this force were his West Point classmates Henry Whiting, Barnard "Barney" Bee, and Dick Howard. Another West Pointer greatly admired by the Florida colonel was the Episcopal minister and commander of a Virginia battery, Captain William Nelson Pendleton. "A good soldier and a good pastor, he is both a temporal and a spiritual leader of his men," Kirby Smith observed. With Patterson's army were also two other West Point classmates—Fitz John Porter and Charles P. Stone.[28]

Kirby Smith estimated the Confederate force at Winchester at about 10,000. Hundreds were ill with the measles. In preparation for rapid movement, all excessive baggage of officers and men was abandoned. The colonel himself was reduced to an extra shirt, an undersuit, two blankets, his servant Aleck, and three horses.[29] A shortage of trained men made the duties of the few officers "onerous and burdensome." Major Whiting and Colonel Kirby Smith took turns sleeping during the night while the other visited regiments and inspected guards.[30]

While at Winchester Kirby Smith was promoted to brigadier general. The only other general officer with Johnston was Brigadier General Barnard Bee. Since the

---

28 E. Kirby Smith to Mother, June 9, 24, 1861.
29 *Id.* to *id.,* June 24, 1861.          30 *Ibid.*

new brigadier was now entitled to a staff, he started a movement to secure the services of his good friend Major H. L.
Clay as adjutant.

Patterson had been instructed to hold Johnston in check
and prevent his going to Beauregard's assistance. "Jeb"
Stuart, observing along the Potomac, reported the Federals
about to recross the river. Colonel Thomas J. Jackson's
brigade was rushed to the assistance of Stuart's cavalry.
Patterson recrossed the Potomac on July 2, and Jackson
began falling back, inflicting the maximum damage yet
protecting his small force. The commands of General Bee
and Colonel Arnold Elzey moved to Darkesville in support
of Jackson. Stuart, a most "active, dashing and untiring
partisan," circled the Federal army, destroying munition
wagons and taking a number of prisoners,[31] and Patterson
called a halt at Martinsburg. Johnston did not choose to
attack him in that town of "solid buildings and inclosures
of masonry."

Here Patterson's army celebrated the Fourth of July
with a several gun salute. The Confederates, according to
Kirby Smith, not choosing to waste powder, had their
bands play "Dixie" from one end of the line to the other,"
and spent the day in eager anticipation of a fight.[32] A few
days later Johnston moved back to Winchester. Patterson
followed as far as Bunker Hill and then turned toward
Smithville as if to attack from the south. Johnston suspected this threat was designed to engage him while Mc-
Dowell moved on Beauregard.

At 1:00 A.M., July 18, Johnston received a wire from
Richmond: Beauregard was hard pressed. The assistance
of the army of the Shenandoah was badly needed. If practicable, he should send the sick and baggage to Culpeper
Courthouse and join Beauregard. "In all the arrangements

[31] *Id.* to H. L. Clay, July 4, 1861.          [32] *Ibid.*

exercise your discretion." [33] Johnston moved immediately.
Passing through Ashby's Gap to Piedmont on the Manassas Gap Railroad, he then ordered the infantry to take the
cars. The cavalry would follow at top speed. He and Bee,
with the Fourth Alabama and Second and Eleventh Mississippi, arrived at Manassas about noon, July 20. Jackson's brigade of Virginia and Georgia troops had preceded
them. Kirby Smith, as second in command, was left behind
to bring up the Tenth Virginia, Third Tennessee, and First
Maryland as soon as transportation could be arranged.

The anxious young brigadier became exasperated at the
frequent stops and starts of the wheezy engines. Suppose
the battle should be fought before he arrived. His men,
most of whom had never experienced the excitement of
battle, were not so concerned. They took advantage of the
frequent stops, appeasing their appetites with ripe black-
berries along the track. "If I had a sword I would cut you
down where you stand," screamed the impatient Kirby
Smith. There was a stampede for the cars.[34]

At Manassas Johnston took command. The Confederates were already deployed along Bull Run for a distance
of some six miles. Brigadier General R. S. Ewell occupied
the extreme right at Union Mills Ford and Colonel N. G.
Evans held the extreme left at Stone Bridge. Protecting the
principal fords between these extremes were, left to right,
the commands of Colonel P. S. G. Cocke, Brigadier Generals M. L. Bonham, James Longstreet, and D. R. Jones.
Brigadier General T. H. Holmes and Colonel J. A. Early
were in reserve on the right. Expecting the arrival of Kirby
Smith during the night and fearing that Patterson might
soon join McDowell, Johnston and Beauregard decided to

[33] S. Cooper to J. E. Johnston, July 17, 1861, *Official Records*, Ser. I, Vol. II,
478.

[34] McHenry Howard, *Recollections of a Maryland Confederate Soldier and
Staff Officer Under Johnston, Jackson and Lee* (Baltimore, 1914), 34.

attack on the morning of July 21. But Kirby Smith did not arrive and some suspicious "early movements of the enemy" caused the plan to be abandoned.

About 6:30 A.M. McDowell began a light attack upon the Confederate left. Bee, Jackson, and Wade Hampton's Legion were ordered to the support of Evans. The attack at the Stone Bridge proved a feint, but a flanking force was thrown across the Run at Sudley Spring about two miles to Evans' left. Leaving a small detachment to defend the Bridge, Evans rushed his riflemen to meet the advance. Bee and F. S. Bartow took up position near the Henry House and then moved in advance to the direct assistance of Evans. The assistance was not sufficient; the combined Confederate forces, faced by an estimated 15,000 Federals under David Hunter and S. P. Heintzleman, gradually fell back. In the meantime, W. T. Sherman's brigade, having failed to force the Stone Bridge, crossed the Run at a ford and threatened the Confederate left flank.

Re-enforced by Hampton's Legion and partially protected by Imboden's battery from Henry Hill, the defending forces were enabled to fall back in fair order. However, a superior Federal battery soon swept the Hill and strong infantry re-enforcements closed in from Stone Bridge. With the battle apparently lost, Confederate discipline weakened and then gave way to confusion and disorderly retreat. "They are beating us back," Bee shouted to Jackson, who was moving into position. "Then, sir, we will give them the bayonet," replied the Virginian as he stood like a "stonewall." "Rally behind the Virginians," cried Bee as his men began reforming their lines.

The Federal offense had halted to reform in the valley between Henry Hill and Young's Branch. Jackson took position in the pines on the east slope of the Hill where he could not be reached by Federal artillery until it came within close range. Johnston and Beauregard had just arrived from the right flank, bringing Pendleton's and Alburtis' batteries. It was now about noon.

The time spent in reforming the Federal command was the savior of the Confederate defenders. The delay gave time for the reorganization of retreating troops and the arrival of other Confederate units from the right flank. And all the while, the cars rattling along the Manassas Gap Railroad were bringing Kirby Smith's regiments nearer to the scene.

The renewed Federal attack begun shortly after noon was directed against both the Confederate front and left flank. There was no mass movement of overwhelming strength. Brigades attacked in succession with bloody results. Bartow rallied his Seventh Georgia and moved into position on Jackson's left. Colonel William Smith swung his Forty-ninth Virginia to the left of Bartow, and Bee's Second Mississippi extended the line to the left of Smith.

At 2:00 P.M. Beauregard, now in command on the scene, ordered a general advance. Temporary gains were made, but massed Federal forces soon halted the drive and began an offensive of their own. Confederate defenses weakened under the onslaught. Bee and Bartow were killed. Hampton was severely wounded. Jackson was shot through the hand. Exhausted men, seized by fear, were thrown into confusion, and mass retreat seemed imminent. But help was near at hand.

Hearing the heavy firing, Kirby Smith stopped the cars and ordered his troops to fall in along the track. Down the line galloped Colonel Elzey, second in command, "his eyes sparkling," followed by Kirby Smith, "the back of his hand raised to the front of his cap." "This is the signal, men," he shouted, "the watchword is 'Sumpter.' " Loud cheers rang out.[35]

At double time these fresh troops rushed toward the scene of action. Pushing through retreating masses, which "fear and exhaustion had entirely demoralized," stepping over entire regiments lying flat on the ground, and refusing to heed cries to turn back lest they too be cut to pieces, Kirby Smith's brigade, joined by J. B. Kershaw's South Carolinians, moved on toward the thick of the fight.

Kirby Smith rode straight to General Johnston and reported, and was ordered to "halt in the rear." But the eager brigadier urged that his men be given a chance. Johnston replied: "It is our left that is driven back—you may move your command forward to its support." "Taking the firing as a guide," Kirby Smith led off in a gallop, but was shot from his horse "as the brigade deployed into line." Colonel Elzey took command.

The heavy fire toward which Kirby Smith was attracted was from "Stonewall" Jackson's Virginia infantry. All of his regiments except the Thirty-third had been lying under protection of the pine woods since the attack began, waiting for the enemy to approach within fifty yards. Just as Kirby Smith's brigade was ready for action the Virginians emerged from their pines, carrying out Jackson's order to "yell like furies." Still other re-enforcements were near at hand. Colonel Jubal A. Early's command had been ordered to report to Beauregard. There was some delay because Beauregard had moved to the left front, but Early continued to move toward the west. On his way he met Johnston and was ordered to the extreme left. He arrived just in time to take part in the final drive. The Federal center fell back, then the wings, as a general Confederate

[35] *Ibid.*, 35–36.

advance developed. Down the slopes of Henry Hill to Young's Branch they hurried, leaving their heavier guns to the Confederates. In vain McDowell tried to rally his men at the Branch, but volunteers, almost void of discipline, would not stand when there was danger of having their retreat cut off. All semblance of organization among them soon disappeared and there were not enough regulars to stop the Confederate advance. Across Bull Run they fled, disregarding frantic appeals from their officers. Soon the roads to Washington were jammed with soldiers, wagons, guns, and Congressmen's carriages. The Confederates themselves, however, had had enough for the day; they called off the chase.[36] Thus ended the first Battle of Bull Run (Manassas), a great moral victory for the Confederacy but one which did no material damage to Union strength.

Johnston pronounced the victory "as complete as one gained by infantry and artillery can be. An adequate force of cavalry would have made it decisive." However, he sadly added that three of his generals were wounded—Jackson and Kirby Smith painfully; Bee mortally.

In after years some of Kirby Smith's friends referred to him as the "Blucher of Manassas," a title no doubt pleasing to him. In 1861 he declared that the victory "was not won by the force of arms, but God in His mercy spread a panic through their hosts and turned them in dismay & ultra confusion at the very moment of their victory." [37] Late in life he was confident that the arrival of his fresh troops upon the enemy's right "caused the panic which so suddenly changed a victory for the Union army into a

[36] Report of J. E. Johnston, *Official Records,* Ser. I, Vol. II, 470 ff.; Howard, *Recollections,* 36; E. Kirby Smith to Mother, July 31, 1861; *id.* to A. L. Long, February 27, 1887; G. F. R. Henderson, *Stonewall Jackson and the American Civil War* (New York, 1949 reprint), 107–17.

[37] E. Kirby Smith to Mother, July 31, 1861.

disgraceful flight." [38] At no time, however, did he attempt to minimize the heroism of "Stonewall" Jackson's Virginia troops. In 1865 President Davis recorded that the Confederacy was "only saved from a fatal defeat at the battle of Manassas by the promptness of General E. Kirby Smith, who, acting without orders, and moving by a change of direction, succeeded in reaching the battlefield in time to avert disaster." [39]

It was reported that Brigadier General Kirby Smith had been killed in battle. However, the first news to reach St. Augustine carried no list of casualties. It must have been the greatest battle ever fought on the continent, exclaimed the general's aged mother. Surely Winfield Scott and his minions had been humbled. "Brave Southerners, go on complete the glorious work!" [40] Then came the news that Kirby Smith was among the dead. Letters of condolence came pouring in. Twelve days of anxiety elapsed before the truth arrived. Aunt Helen Putnam wrote him immediately. The mother was too ill. Two weeks later she confessed that she had "just sense enough left to know and *feel* the decay of my mental powers." [41]

When the news of Kirby Smith's death reached his friend McDaniel in Lynchburg the latter dispatched his nephew to the battlefield to bring the body to that city. Before the nephew arrived the wounded general was being comfortably cared for at Cunningham Manor, the home of Richard H. Cunningham, an uncle of Captain Edward Cunningham, a staff member. "I have indeed had another of my providential escapes," the general wrote his mother. "The ball (a large minnie) entered just back of the colar

[38] *Id.* to A. L. Long, February 27, 1887.
[39] Dunbar Rowland (ed.), *Jefferson Davis, Constitutionalist. His Letters, Papers and Speeches*, 10 vols. (Jackson, 1923), VI, 493.
[40] Mrs. Frances K. Smith to E. Kirby Smith, July 23, 1861.
[41] *Id.* to *id.*, August 24, 1861.

[*sic*] bone on the right shoulder, passing under the muscles of the shoulder blade and the muscles of the spine, missing the artery and the spine and leaving at the left shoulder," leaving a painful and troublesome flesh wound twelve inches in length.[42] After hearing of the many letters of inquiry and condolence and reading his obituary in the newspapers, he laughingly remarked: "It behooves one to be killed occasionally to find out how many friends he has and how anxiously he can be inquired after." [43]

Cunningham Manor was an elegant country place about thirty miles from Manasses. The owners, a childless couple well-advanced in years, showed the general every hospitality. And as a fellow member of the Episcopal Church, he found their whole household pervaded with an "air of true Christian piety" and conducive to spiritual and physical progress.[44] He remained with the Cunninghams until about the middle of August.

Friends at Lynchburg, particularly McDaniel and Cassie Selden, were eager to have Kirby Smith in that city during his convalescence. Cassie was away enjoying the summer at Alleghany Springs when the report of the general's death reached Lynchburg. And before she heard the false news her friend McDaniel had learned the truth and wired her. She cut her visit short and returned home immediately.[45] Kirby Smith arrived at the McDaniel home on August 15.

Recuperation in Lynchburg was a delightful experience. News from the Potomac region that immediate action there was unlikely relieved the general's mind in a military sense. Letters from his mother brought both comfort and amusement. "Did the world ever witness such a spectacle," ex-

[42] E. Kirby Smith to Mother, July 31, 1861.
[43] *Id.* to *id.*, August 16, 1861.  [44] *Ibid.*
[45] Smith, *All's Fair in Love and War*, 15–16.

claimed the old lady in referring to the recent battle. "And then the route, the race! Will it not *grind* the Old Traitor Scott (I have lost all sympathy or respect for him) to have McClellan put *over* him." She thought McDowell, with whom she was well acquainted, "must have puffed and wheezed a little" during the race.[46]

The unexcelled hospitality in the McDaniel home and the privilege of again associating with his good friend Clay made every day a pleasure. And the evening with Cassie rounded out a perfect day. On September 4 Kirby Smith wrote his mother that his wound had healed and he would leave for a trip to Richmond on the following day. A few hours in the Confederate capital would be sufficient to transact this business and pay a visit to Aunt Mary Kirby, who had just lost her son Reynold. He would then return to Lynchburg for his baggage and report to his command at Manassas.[47] He made no mention of matrimonial intentions.

Cassie Selden, young, attractive, vivacious, had already marked him for her own and was concerned over the attention being paid the general by another Lynchburg lady. Since he was a guest in a home where she was treated as a daughter, she came and went with little formality. For hours at a time she pulled from the general stories of army life in peace and war. On Sundays they attended Episcopal services. While returning home from one of the evening services he suddenly asked Cassie if she would be at home at ten o'clock Monday morning. He had a very important question to ask.

Monday was sewing day at the Selden home. Cassie was making a purple skirt "with large palm leaves on it." She sewed the pockets in backward. The general arrived

[46] Mrs. Frances K. Smith to E. Kirby Smith, n.d.; *id.* to *id.*, August ?, 1861.
[47] E. Kirby Smith to Mother, September 4, 1861.

on schedule. He wanted to know if she would marry him at the end of three weeks. The date was set for September 24. In the meantime, he would transact his business at Richmond.

On September 20 Kirby Smith broke the news to his mother. She was soon to have a new daughter, "as good, pure, sincere & true" as ever blessed a man as helpmate. "A truly earnest member of the Episcopal Church, instances of her disinterested charity & good works are known to me—I love her for her goodness & I feel that God has indeed blessed & will prosper & make me a better man by the association." She was from one of Virginia's oldest and finest families, and her qualities would "make her an ornament in the proudest genealogical tree." She must be seen and known to be adequately loved and appreciated.[48]

When Kirby Smith told Aleck of his plans, his servant-friend wept. "Oh, Marse Edmund," he replied, "these are troublesome hard times, bad times to get married. Don't I serve you and take care of you always?" Aleck ever resented "Miss Cassie's" intrusion and his future happiness with the general was always greatest when she was at home with her mother.

By the time Brigadier General Kirby Smith returned from Richmond he had decided upon a honeymoon in Florida. Perhaps his wound was not so completely healed as he had thought! Possibly the authorities at Richmond advised against his returning to his command too soon. The bride later recalled that President Davis granted an extension of leave for the purpose.

The wedding took place as planned midst considerable clanking of officers' swords and the firing of a salute by the militia. Country people about thought the Yankees

[48] *Id.* to *id.*, September 20, 1861.

had come. Aleck had made all traveling arrangements and the newlyweds were soon on their way south. Suddenly Cassie discovered that she had left her trunk keys. Aleck galloped back for them. There were celebrations at Petersburg, Charleston, and other towns along the way; Kirby Smith's name was prominent among the heroes of Bull Run.

The entrance to St. Augustine was blocked by a bridge under repair. The bride and groom set out on foot, hoping to slip into the Putnam home by way of the alley. Aleck disapproved; he wanted a big reception for "Marse Edmund." Furthermore, was not he coming home too! He immediately gave out the news. The militia fired a salute, the band came into action, and the parade was on. Streets, doorways, and windows were thronged with well-wishers. The three little Calhoun boys, feeling the jar of the cannon, rushed into the house and told Mrs. Smith that the cannon were breaking out all the windows. "Oh, I don't care if all are broken in the house," cried the excited mother, "I like it! My soldier son has come!" A reception was held that evening with the general, his wife, and his mother in the receiving line. Cassie soon tired of handshaking and sat down. The old lady kept going. And when the dancing began, mother and son were the center of attraction.

Two weeks were spent in the old home town. The hearty laughs of the dashing young brigadier stirred the memories of friends and servants. Kirby Smith, retiring by nature, would tell little of his experiences but the garrulous Aleck never tired of relating what he and "Marse Edmund" had gone through. And with a feeling of great pride, he presented "Old Miss" with the blood-stained shirt worn by her son during the battle of Manassas.

At the close of their two weeks visit, the general and

his bride, supplied with a trunk full of oranges, began their return trip. "Cassie, make Edmund take care of his money," urged the mother in parting, "all he will ever give you is a good name and plenty of children." [49]

Shortly after the Kirby Smiths left St. Augustine a telegram arrived from Richmond: "General John B. Grayson is seriously ill. You will immediately assume command of the Department of Florida east of Pensacola Harbor and confer with the Governor of Florida." [50] On the following day a special order to this effect was issued from the Adjutant General's Office.[51] Kirby Smith knew nothing of his new assignment until he reached Lynchburg. He hurried to Richmond and was shown "every kindness and consideration" by Davis and the Secretary of War, Judah P. Benjamin. The Florida assignment, it was explained, had been made with the hope that it would be pleasing to the recipient. However, it was well that the notification had not been received, for the situation on the Potomac called for a change of plans. Brigadier General Kirby Smith was to be promoted to major general and assigned one of the divisions in the army on the Potomac.[52]

Major General Kirby Smith approached his new task with humility. He had never expected to be either rich or famous, he confided to his mother, and, in fact, had almost daily prayed that God would preserve him from "riches or exalted position." "I have never claimed distinction and would always willingly have exchanged all

[49] This story of courtship and marriage is taken from Mrs. Kirby Smith's, *All's Fair in Love and War*, 15–29.

[50] S. Cooper to E. Kirby Smith, October 9, 1861, *Official Records*, Ser. I, Vol. LIII, Supplement, 182.

[51] Special Orders, No. 176, October 10, 1861, *Official Records*, Ser. I, Vol. VI, 288–89.

[52] E. Kirby Smith to Mother, October 22, 1861.

the honors of this world for an humble quiet home with those I love around me." [53]

Under the Confederate reorganization plan, a Department of Northern Virginia was created, consisting of the Valley, Potomac, and Aquia districts. Joseph E. Johnston was to command this department. The Potomac District occupied the territory between the Blue Ridge mountains and Powell's River and was flanked by the other two districts. Beauregard, Holmes, and Jackson were made district commanders. To Beauregard's Potomac District was assigned Major Generals Van Dorn, Kirby Smith, G. W. Smith, and Longstreet. Kirby Smith was to command a division of five brigades under W. H. T. Walker, Robert Toombs, Elzey, Evans, and L. T. Wigfall. The men composing these brigades were for the most part from Georgia, Texas, and North Carolina.[54] Upon hearing of Kirby Smith's promotion, Major Clay rushed to Richmond to apply for transfer to his friend's staff.

Major General Kirby Smith immediately took leave of his new wife and left for Centerville, Virginia. She would remain at Lynchburg until he found suitable quarters. He wrote her twice en route, beginning a series of ardent love letters which passed between them during every period of separation for the next thirty years. "I feel your absence dearest wife," he wrote, "as I have never yet felt either Sorrow or Joy . . . not only are you present in my every thought by day and in my dreams by night, but I find myself awaking continuously with the ejaculation, dearest, dearest, darling wife, only to feel my desolation and loneliness the more." [55]

[53] *Ibid.*
[54] General Orders, No. 15, October 22, 1861, *Official Records,* Ser. I, Vol. V, 913–14.
[55] E. Kirby Smith to Wife, October 27, 1861.

Aleck beat "Marse Edmund" to Manassas and had horses and wagon ready for the trip to Centerville. At Centerville the major general pitched his tent beside those of Johnston and G. W. Smith in a lot near the church. His wife's brother, Willie, called that evening. On the following day the generals rode out to examine the army's position, and Kirby Smith stopped by Van Dorn's tent for the evening. "We are all fearful," he wrote his wife, "that M'Clellan can not be induced to make an attack & that the present state of uncertainty & anxiety will continue for an indefinite period." As for himself, he was already impatient; he wished "either to fight or go into winter quarters." In any case, she must have no fear, he urged, for "Providence & our good right arms will vindicate the justice of our cause when the conflict comes." [56]

He felt that the fate of the Confederacy was in the hands of the army in northern Virginia. "If we defeat the enemy here, whatever be their successes elsewhere they will be thrown away. Baltimore will be occupied. Maryland will rise and in all probability the Administration will be overthrown. Should we be routed, however, (which God forbid), the consequences are too awful for contemplation." The big battle, he believed, would take place in November. "The sooner the better," for the Confederate troops were poorly supplied even to live in winter quarters to say nothing of campaigning during the cold weather. Even the officers were living in tents, and in his own tent there was a two foot opening through which the cold November wind was whistling. General Johnston, with worse accommodations than any private, slept on the ground wrapped in the same pair of blankets he used while at Winchester. "I tell him now," remarked Kirby Smith, "that he is too much of a Diogenes for me, that I can no

[56] *Id.* to *id.*, October 28, 29, 1861.

longer keep him company in his contempt for the neces-
saries of life, that I am now a married man with too much
at stake." [57]

Kirby Smith had the greatest admiration for General
Johnston. While stationed at Centerville he confided to
his wife that Johnston was "a true patriot, sensitive and
retiring and with an abnegation of self which ignores all
personal grievances and slights in his great sense of duty
& devotion to his country." [58]

Along with Johnston and staff, Kirby Smith for a time
took his meals at the home of a Dr. Alexander, where there
was always an abundance of butter, eggs, turkeys, duck,
and other fine things. With the arrival of Major Clay in
mid-November the two arranged for a separate mess, for
Clay brought a cook and a number of "domestic necessities." However, visions of the bountiful spread of Dr.
Alexander's table continued to haunt him. "I must confess it," he remarked, "I am somewhat of a gourmet and
enjoy as well as appreciate a good dinner." He also gave
up his tent and he and Clay moved to a shanty which had
been fixed for his headquarters. This was an "extremely
airy" piece of architecture, since on the evening before
they moved in foragers had pulled off the weatherboarding
and used it for firewood. On the next day the stove disappeared but was later recovered. Although this headquarters
was not "exactly of fifth avenue style," it looked mighty
good to one who had envisioned a cold winter with nothing but a piece of canvas between him and the elements.[59]

The cold November wind began to test the enthusiasm
of those Confederates who awaited McClellan's next move.
Kirby Smith retained his enthusiasm for the cause of
"independence," although his confidence was shaken.

---

[57] *Id.* to *id.*, November 1, 1861; *id.* to Mother, November 2, 1861.
[58] *Id.* to Wife, November 4, 1861.    [59] *Id.* to *id.*, November 15, 1861.

After a thorough study of the positions of Confederate troops along with General Johnston and the division commanders, he was not so certain of their ability to defend themselves. Furthermore, all reports from north of the Potomac gave staggering figures on the mighty force being collected there. How could so mighty an army long remain idle in Washington? he queried. Quite likely McClellan would deem it necessary to go into action before Congress convened in December. Only the hand of God could sustain the Confederates in the face of such a mighty host, he confided to his wife.

God has not forsaken us—he will not forsake us—our cause is too righteous and holy a one, our people too earnest and constant in their prayers and entreaties to be deserted from on high. We may be chastened, God in his infinite mercy only knows how long or how severely, but it will not be in his anger—at the right time he will turn his face towards us, and when we have sealed our devotion to our country by the best blood of the land and have carved our title to a nation by the greatest sacrifices he will stamp our new government with the stamp of stability and bless us with the blessings of peace and unity.

And when he heard of the capture of Mason and Slidell on board the *Trent,* he interpreted it as another manifestation of the workings of Providence.[60]

By the time Major General Kirby Smith took command of his division there had been some change in his brigade commanders. Brigadier General Walker, claiming that all the major generals in the district were his juniors, vigorously denounced the higher authorities for failure to promote him and resigned in protest. Kirby Smith, suspecting that his own promotion might have been the source of Walker's dissatisfaction, went to Johnston about the matter. Johnston assured him that it was disregard for seniority, not any individual promotion, that had caused

[60] *Id.* to *id.,* November 11, 19, 1861.

the discontent.[61] Brigadier General George B. Crittenden was assigned to Walker's brigade, but was soon promoted to major general and sent back to his home state of Kentucky. Kirby Smith regretted Walker's action, for he knew him to be a gallant soldier in spite of his habitual discontent. The transfer of Crittenden back to Kentucky, however, pleased the major general; he had found Crittenden to be a very intemperate man whose political connections had been responsible for his promotions. "I trust the influence the Crittenden name is expected to carry in Kentucky will over balance the intemperance of his habits," he confided to his wife. He wanted A. P. Hill promoted to the vacancy, but I. R. Trimble was assigned instead.[62]

Friends had warned Kirby Smith to expect difficulty in handling Brigadier General Robert Toombs, whom they described as "obstinate, ignorant and impracticable." But the major general, who usually looked for the good in everyone he met, soon analyzed the Georgian as "coarse and unrefined verging upon vulgarity," yet at heart a man of good sense and considerable natural intelligence. The "lace and buttons of cavalry" were scarcely able to conceal the "politician and demagogue" that he was. An amusing talker, in spite of his constant murder of the English language, Toombs was to his associates almost the equal of a daily comedy. A "square face coarse features and great breadth of jaws" gave him an appearance "more sensual than intelligent." After thus analyzing the Georgia brigadier, Kirby Smith contemplated no difficulty in dealing with him.[63]

The task of securing efficient staff officers gave Kirby Smith serious concern. Other officers had already picked

[61] Id. to id., November ?, 1861.
[62] Id. to id., November 15, 1861; Official Records, Ser. I, Vol. V, 960–61, 967.
[63] E. Kirby Smith to Wife, November 21, 1861.

over all available men, he complained to his wife. The arrival of Major Clay solved the greatest problem. Captain Edward Cunningham, who had joined the staff at Manassas, remained attached but was ill during the fall of 1861. Captain J. L. Morgan, who voluntarily attached himself, became chief quartermaster and was particularly efficient in providing for the needs of the major general. He added a kitchen to the shanty used as quarters and rounded up chairs, a table, and a desk. And from the backbone of the grey charger from which Bartow fell mortally wounded, he made two unique and serviceable candlesticks.[64]

Late in November Kirby Smith requested that his cousin Francis Belton be assigned to his staff as assistant aide. Belton, a government employee in New York, had escaped from Brooklyn after a threat to hang him for his Southern sympathies. His father, an officer in the old army, had died during the summer of 1861. His mother, Kirby Smith's Aunt Harriet, and young Belton's wife and six children were stranded in the North and had not been heard from in six months.[65] Shortly after Belton's arrival at Kirby Smith's headquarters Cunningham was transferred to New Orleans and he became aid-de-camp.

November, 1861, dragged by slowly. Soldiers and civilians alike speculated on McClellan's possible movements. "Will McClellan not give you a chance to whip him—does he never mean to advance—and must poor Maryland lay down & die in her sorrow?" queried the aged Mrs. Smith from St. Augustine. Florida friends were much concerned over the fall of Port Royal and the threat to Fernandina and Savannah. Most of Judge Putnam's

<hr />

[64] *Id.* to *id.*, November 21, 22, 1861.
[65] *Id.* to Mother, November 23, 1861; J. F. Belton to Mrs. Frances K. Smith, December 23, 1861.

property was in Savannah. The Putnams were ready for a rapid flight into the interior of Florida should the Yankees decide to occupy St. Augustine. "Marrying Kate" Putnam Calhoun had taken great care in packing her "brocade lace dresses," Mrs. Smith observed, but had given little thought to the children's clothes. As for the old lady herself, she wished the Putnams would just leave her behind; she reasoned that neither she nor St. Augustine had anything the Yankees would want. At any rate, she would not *"die of fright,"* at the sight of Yankees.[66]

In Lynchburg Kirby Smith's young wife was nervous to the point of illness. She was bothered with dyspepsia, especially after eating oysters for breakfast, but was afraid to complain of nausea lest her illness be attributed to "other *reasons* . . . which have no foundation." Her husband, greatly disturbed, recommended a grits diet and explained in detail just how to prepare it. Dyspepsia, if allowed to go unchecked, he warned, could have serious consequences. Amiability would be replaced by "discontent and despondency." If on the other hand, she would control her diet, restricting herself to easily digested foods, she would soon reap the reward that accompanied self-denial. One's condition, physical, mental, and spiritual, he explained, might also be improved through participation in worthwhile activities. He suggested charity work and sent funds to be spent in alleviating the suffering of the unfortunate.[67]

In camp near Centerville the condition of the army was as good as limited equipment would permit, still there was dread of the approaching winter. November and December were spent in monotonous drill, reviews, and pres-

---

[66] Mrs. Frances K. Smith to E. Kirby Smith, December 2, 11, 1861.
[67] Mrs. E. Kirby Smith to *id.*, November 3, 1861; E. Kirby Smith to Wife, November 30, December 5, 8, 1861.

entations of battle flags. Impatience, gloom, and disgust became prevalent. Major General Kirby Smith himself grew "more and more impatient of this delay, more and more tired of this war." Would not God soon listen to the prayers of and have mercy on the afflicted South? All about him could be seen the demoralizing effects of idleness. Colonel Pendleton, the fighting parson, solemnly warned that victory was unlikely as long as "much irreligion and profanity characterized our army from the highest in command to the lowest private in the ranks." This observation greatly impressed Kirby Smith. Dissipation among officers had been brought very pointedly to his attention at a party following the review of G. W. Smith's corps. When "apple toddy and champagne became a medium of circulation," he took leave and went to his attic to write his wife. His friend Clay saw the festivities to the end, frequently representing his general in "speechifying." Late in the night when he good-naturedly criticised Kirby Smith for shifting so many duties upon him, the general calmly explained that since he himself did not patronize apple toddy and champagne he "could not be expected to make sober speeches to drunken audiences." [68]

Kirby Smith might have been a light drinker, but he was certainly a heavy eater. And the Kirby Smith-Clay-Belton mess was well supplied. The three celebrated the opening of their lean-to kitchen with a roasted turkey. Richard Cunningham, of Cunningham Manor, sent seven fine Virginia hams, a bag each of hominy and potatoes, two buckets of butter, and some home made pickles. And the general's wife sent articles too numerous to mention.[69]

With the arrival of the chilly winds of December there also came more rumors of a probable attack by McClellan.

[68] *Id.* to *id.*, November 26, December 1, 3, 1861.
[69] *Id.* to *id.*, November 30, 1861.

The general himself, it was said, opposed opening a campaign at that time of the year, but the New York moneyed interests demanded action, and Lincoln and his Cabinet had surrendered to their demand. Therefore, McClellan must move regardless of the disadvantages of the season. Kirby Smith, in daily conference with General Johnston and familiar with all available information on the Union forces, predicted an attack upon Evansport and Dumfries rather than Centerville. The strength of the Centerville position plus almost impassable roads made this a logical decision. What McClellan needed was at least a small victory at not too great a cost, Kirby Smith speculated. To obtain this he might hurl an overwhelming force at some weaker Confederate position. Kirby Smith felt assured, however, that all Yankee hope of reconquering the South had been abandoned. The war had become one of boundary; no doubt Union officials would gladly accept the thirty-sixth parallel. On the contrary, if great battles of conquest or otherwise were contemplated he hoped they would come immediately. The Confederate Army of Northern Virginia was composed principally of "twelve-months men" whose terms would expire in the spring of 1862. Furthermore, army supplies were short within the Confederacy, and should it be necessary to hold troops in readiness for battle during the winter months rather than sending them into winter quarters, more men would probably die from sickness than from bullets. But an immediate attack by McClellan would solve all these problems, for he would be defeated and lose great quantities of supplies to the victorious Confederates. That would no doubt end the fighting, and troops could then go into winter quarters without fear of again being attacked.[70]

Kirby Smith had not been among those who confidently

70 *Id.* to *id.*, November 25, December 3, 4, 1861.

believed that Britain would soon intervene and compel the lifting of the Union blockade of Southern ports, yet the *Trent* affair did give him some hope. Unless the British Lion had been "completely muzzled by the Exeter Hall fanatics," the action of Congress, or the tone of the Northern press, he exclaimed, the Mason and Slidell affair might "bring a roar from the old beast that will scatter the Yankey armadas and lead King Cotton triumphantly into the Port of Liverpool." [71]

On the evening of December 11, 1861, Major General Kirby Smith sat alone in the garret of his shanty. A cold wind whistled through the cracks. "Parades, reviews, the pomp and circumstance of war," he growled, "will now be exchanged for the stern realities of a December campaign." Through a hole he could see his men outside "crouching & shivering about their tattered tents & scanty fires." The hearty laughs and shouts of contentment had died away. For the first time the major general was critical of his superior. General Johnston, "firm & decided almost to obstinacy and impracticality," he complained, would not give up the idea that McClellan just must fight. Consequently, he would permit no troops to go into winter quarters.[72] Only after McClellan proved just as determined not to fight did Johnston finally give in. "I wrung an unwilling consent from Gen Johnston to put my Division in winter quarters," Kirby Smith reported jubilantly. Now he could send for his "Darling Cassie."

His command was shifted to a position along the railroad between Manassas and Union Mills, and there began constructing crude huts to protect themselves from the wintry blasts. The major general and his staff took over the Wilcoxen House, a dilapidated farmhouse a half mile from the railroad. A trusted aide was immediately dis-

---

[71] *Id.* to *id.*, December 11, 1861.          [72] *Ibid.*

patched to bring his wife and "her chattels." After enumerating many household things his wife should bring, the general added: "Bring some books by all manner of means." Could she not borrow from friend McDaniel copies of Prescott's *Phillip II* and Spenser's *Fairy Queen?* She must expect nothing but hardships, inconveniences, and possibly a hasty flight before the advancing enemy, her husband warned.

The eager young wife felt a bit peeved that he would even question her willingness to endure camp life; however, she suggested that it might be better to eat out rather than try to prepare their own meals. She would endeavor to bring along a maid to wait on her.[73]

In spite of uncertainty along the Potomac there was little hustle and bustle in Confederate camps around Manassas during January and February, 1862. The devastation wrought by the recent battle had lost most of its horror, and "the benign influence of crinoline" had "shed an air of peace and quietude" over all. Nina, Mrs. Smith's sister, came for a visit with the Kirby Smiths, and the three spent many pleasant evenings around the fire with their books and sewing.[74] The general himself must have also enjoyed rereading a refreshing communication from J. M. Hunter, his Texas partner in the cattle business. "I do asshore you it is vary grattifying to me to know you are alive & well," wrote the plainsman. "Our cattle are doeing well." One hundred sixty-three new calves had been branded during the past year, and there ought to be two hundred more the next year. The Indians were not "Steeling and Killing mutch." The two stag hounds given him by Kirby Smith had died. Old Ugly

[73] *Id.* to *id.*, December 14, 16, 18, 1861; Mrs. E. Kirby Smith to E. Kirby Smith, December 16, 1861.

[74] E. Kirby Smith to Mother, January 29, 1862.

was all right and would be sent to Virginia the first opportunity. Partridges were more plentiful than ever, and the rivers were alive with ducks and geese. "You may rest asshored," he continued, "that if any misfortune should happen to you that I will account to your mother for every dollar you have in our stock of cattle." He was also taking care of the green chest which contained Kirby Smith's collection of wild flowers. Texans, particularly the Germans, he thought, had not "turned out" for the war as they should. Should it last until next summer, he himself would "take a hand," unless "laid up with rheumatism." [75]

During the winter General Joseph E. Johnston kept his army under marching orders. A concentration of vessels in the vicinity of Hampton Roads was noted, but Kirby Smith, probably thinking along the same lines as Johnston, reasoned that from the nature of the crafts they were not to be used in an extensive Southern campaign. No doubt they were to co-operate with McClellan in an attack at some point in the lower Potomac, probably Evansport. Should this attack be successful, the Federal base would then likely be shifted to the Rappahannock or the vicinity of Fredericksburg, with the hope of cutting off communications with Richmond.[76]

[75] J. M. Hunter to E. Kirby Smith, December 25, 1861.
[76] E. Kirby Smith to Mother, January 29, 1862.

## CHAPTER VII

# AMONG EAST TENNESSEE UNIONISTS

WHILE THE KIRBY SMITHS were enjoying the society of other officers' families at Manassas winter quarters, the War Department was considering him as a successor to Major General Braxton Bragg at Pensacola. Bragg was to be moved west of the Mississippi River.[1] The shift was not made, however, and there is no evidence that Kirby Smith knew he was being considered for the Pensacola post.

Suddenly, on February 15, General Johnston was ordered to relieve Major General Kirby Smith from duty and send him to Richmond for reassignment. Ten days later he was on his way to Knoxville to assume command of the Department of East Tennessee. He would report by letter to General Albert Sydney Johnston at Murfreesboro.[2] His wife returned to Lynchburg and began renovating her wardrobe. She would make an early attempt to tell "Ma" about "my situation," she assured her husband.[3]

Mountainous East Tennessee was a stronghold of Un-

[1] Judah P. Benjamin to Braxton Bragg, December 27, 1861, *Official Records,* Ser. I, Vol. VI, 788–89.
[2] *Id.* to J. E. Johnston, February 15, 1862, *ibid.,* Vol. V, 1073; Special Orders, No. 45, February 25, 1862, *ibid.,* Vol. VII, 908.
[3] Mrs. E. Kirby Smith to E. Kirby Smith, March 8, 1862.

ionism, and the weak Confederate force there had proved utterly incapable of building up Confederate strength. The confidence of Southern sympathizers both in the ranks and at home had been badly shaken. Nothing but physical barriers had thus far prevented the Federals from destroying the valuable railroad, which passed through East Tennessee, connecting Virginia with Georgia. For months Confederate leaders in East Tennessee had been urging President Davis to send an aggressive commander to "restore tone to the army and reinspire the public confidence." [4]

Kirby Smith expressed no pleasure over his transfer. He reluctantly gave up what he considered "the finest command in the army of the Potomac." Later he referred to his days with that army as "the halcyon days of my service." [5] He was even more reluctant to take over a weak command in a region seething with disloyalty to the Confederate cause and constantly threatened by "an overwhelming force flushed with victory and confident of support when they penetrate the country." Yet he realized the importance of the railroad as a lifeline of the Confederacy and felt complimented that the Administration would trust him with such an important task. [6]

The new commander arrived in Knoxville on March 8 and formally assumed his responsibilities on the following day. Headquarters was set up in a large house just across the street from the Bell Hotel. J. G. Meem was "installed as caterer" and Aleck "entered upon his duties as chef and cuisine." The general immediately pronounced the coffee the finest in the Confederacy. [7]

Affairs in East Tennessee were even worse than the new commander had expected. The people were disloyal;

[4] Landon C. Haynes to Jefferson Davis, January 27, 1862, *Official Records,* Ser. I, Vol. VII, 849.
[5] E. Kirby Smith to J. E. Johnston, June 4, 1863, *ibid.,* Vol. XXIV, pt. 3, 948.
[6] *Id.* to Mother, March 1, 1862.    [7] *Id.* to Wife, March 10, 11, 1862.

the troops "a disorganized mob without head or discipline." The only bright ray of hope was the reasonable assurance that the enemy, by directing all its available power toward West Tennessee, would give an opportunity for reorganization in the eastern section.[8] "I find the force in East Tennessee in great disorganization," Kirby Smith reported to President Davis. "All accounts given me were far short of the truth. There has been no one in command since [George B.] Crittenden crossed the Cumberland Mountains. . . . Regiments and detachments were everywhere acting independently, and without military restraint of any kind." There were about 8,000 effective troops in East Tennessee. Half of the force was at Cumberland Gap under the command of Colonel James E. Rains. Another 2,000 were at Knoxville. The others were scattered over the department, guarding bridges and provisions. Except for the Twentieth and Twenty-third Alabama regiments and one Georgia battalion, the entire active force was composed of twelve-months volunteers whose terms were about to expire. And no fewer than 500 men of the Alabama regiments were reported sick with typhoid fever. Six regiments from Virginia had been promised, but only two had arrived. At this rate, the armed forces in East Tennessee would be melted away by the close of the coming summer, even if not destroyed by the enemy before that time.

Opposing the temporary and poorly organized Confederate forces was an enemy of considerable potential strength. At least six regiments with twelve pieces of artillery were threatening Cumberland Gap. Two other regiments were between Somerset and Burkesville, Kentucky, ready to move into Middle Tennessee by way of the Cumberland River. Indications were that the concentration would be toward the Mississippi Valley. If East Tennessee

[8] *Id.* to *id.*, March ?, 1862.

were attacked, Kirby Smith predicted, it would be from Middle Tennessee with the Cumberland as a base and a line of operation by way of "Sparta to Kingston, or possibly Athens." Little assistance could be expected from the East Tennesseans. A few regiments might be enlisted for a short period, but there was nothing available in the way of equipment.[9]

Kirby Smith made rapid preparations for a tour of inspection of his scattered command. An immediate visit to Cumberland Gap was imperative. On the eve of his departure he confided to his wife: "I am overwhelmed with cares & troubles, no one can conceive the actual condition of East Tenn. disloyal to the core, it is more dangerous and difficult to operate in, than the country of an acknowledged enemy." [10] On the same date he reported to the Adjutant General: "I repeat, East Tennessee is an enemy's country. The people are against us, and ready to rise whenever an enemy's column makes its appearance. The very troops raised here cannot always be depended upon. They have gone into service, many of them to escape suspicion, prepared to give information to the enemy, and ready to pass over to him when an opportunity offers." A respectable force in East Tennessee could be of considerable assistance as the enemy continued its movement down the Mississippi. "An army on the plateau of the Cumberland, ready to debouch toward Nashville, threatens their flank, and in its position alone acts offensively." Such an army could not be built of local material. "Would it not be well," the commander asked, "to remove such of the East Tennessee troops as are suspected to a different section of the Confederacy, where in a purer political atmosphere and

---

[9] *Id.* to Jefferson Davis, March 10, 1862, *Official Records,* Ser. I, Vol. X, pt. 2, 308–309.

[10] *Id.* to Wife, March 13, 1862.

removed from their present associations they can do little or no harm and become loyal and good soldiers? In view of the peculiar condition of affairs in this section I believe the public good would be advanced by declaring martial law through the whole District of East Tennessee." [11]

The visit of inspection to Cumberland Gap was postponed. On March 14 a courier dashed into Knoxville with the startling news that the enemy in force was only thirty miles away. During the night the Cumberland range had been crossed in three places and the only opposing force, a regiment of Confederate cavalry, had been captured. Kirby Smith rushed the information to his superior, A. S. Johnston at Decatur, Alabama, and hurriedly ordered General John B. Floyd to bring up his command from Chattanooga, although he "discredited the reports." [12]

Subsequent reports were less alarming. Only one Union regiment had crossed over and only two companies of cavalry had been captured. Still another report placed the number of enemy regiments at four, including Munday's cavalry and the Second Tennessee, Union. A force this large might contemplate a crossing of the Clinch River near the mouth of Powell's River, the commanding general feared. Colonel Danville Leadbetter was directed to rush his brigade to the vicinity of Clinton where by reconnaissance of the main roads he was to ascertain the enemy's strength and probable intentions. All available troops at Knoxville were ordered to Jacksboro, and Kirby Smith and his staff, except for Major Clay, set out for that point via Cumberland Gap. [13]

[11] *Id.* to S. Cooper, March 13, 1862, *Official Records,* Ser. I, Vol. X, pt. 2, 320–21.

[12] *Id.* to A. S. Johnston, March 14, 1862, *ibid.,* 325; *id.* to J. B. Floyd, March 14, 1862, *ibid.,* Vol. LII, pt. 2, 287; E. Kirby Smith to Wife, March 15, 1862.

[13] H. L. Clay to Danville Leadbetter, March 16, 1862, *ibid.,* Ser. I, Vol. X, pt. 2, 333.

Clay was disappointed; he wanted to go too. But Kirby Smith put his arm about the shoulder of his adjutant and persuaded him that he alone could adequately look after affairs at headquarters. Clay was pacified. The Confederate troops would soon know what it meant to be near Yankees, he wrote his sister-in-law. "If our troops run, Smith will turn his powder & ball & steel, in his own right hand, from the enemy upon them. I think he will hunt up a fight and will go into it determined to survive as victor, or fall as a hero." Clay was thoroughly disgusted with East Tennessee. "The people are not worth fighting for & do not want to be defended," he growled, "—they are fit for slavery, not capable of appreciating liberty." General Smith was truly a commander without soldiers or men who could be made into soldiers.[14]

The threatened invasion turned out to be a small-scale operation. A Union force about 1,300 strong, including the First and Second Tennessee regiments, had crossed the Cumberlands and surprised a small body of Confederate troops under Colonel John F. White. The skirmish lasted only five minutes, and the Confederate losses, according to Union estimates, were "5 men killed, 15 wounded, and 15 taken prisoners." The invaders followed the retreating Confederates to Jacksboro and Fincastle and then camped at Woodson's Gap. Before Kirby Smith's re-enforcements arrived, they had recrossed the mountains.[15]

Kirby Smith suspected treachery, and was probably correct. There were too many men of "Union proclivities" among Confederate forces from East Tennessee, he observed. Pickets could not be relied upon, and even officers

[14] Id. to Mrs. Virginia Caroline Clay, March 18, 1862, Clay Papers.

[15] Report of James P. T. Carter, 2nd East Tenn. (Union), March 23, 1862, Official Records, Ser. I, Vol. X, pt. 1, 19–20.

were "not free from suspicion of more fidelity to the Federal than to our service." Again he urged upon the War Department "the propriety, if not the necessity," of removing East Tennessee troops to points where they could not "prove traitors, either by purchase or from love." The successful defense of East Tennessee, he insisted, depended upon the replacement of these undependable troops by men of unquestioned loyalty.[16]

The only strong point within the Department of East Tennessee was Cumberland Gap. Kirby Smith found it defended by 4,000 excellent troops and thought the place almost impregnable. He had scarcely returned to his Knoxville headquarters, however, when a courier arrived with the news that the Gap was under attack by 6,000 Yankees.

Colonel Rains must keep his men under cover, conserve his ammunition, and let the enemy exhaust their artillery, Kirby Smith ordered. The men might take their blankets into the trenches and "sleep" while the heavy firing continued. They would then be fresh should an all-out attack be made. "Trust to your bayonets when the ammunition fails." No re-enforcements could be sent, but the Gap must be held to the "last extremity." [17]

Another courier brought news that an enemy force, thought to be the advance of a larger body of troops from Middle Tennessee, was threatening Kingston by way of Crossville. And General A. S. Johnston telegraphed that enemy forces from Middle Tennessee were also moving toward Chattanooga. To meet this two-pronged advance Kirby Smith had 2,300 men.

Leadbetter was ordered to Kingston with two regiments,

[16] E. Kirby Smith to War Department, March 15, 1862, *ibid.*, 20–21.
[17] H. L. Clay to J. E. Rains, March 23, 1862 (two dispatches), *ibid.*, pt. 2, 356–57.

a battalion, and small units of cavalry and artillery. He was to seize all ferryboats near Kingston and report all information relating to the rumored Federal advance from Crossville One battalion of Maney's brigade was rushed to Chattanooga, which had been defenseless since the departure of General Floyd. Most of Floyd's brigade had now gone home on furlough. Only "260 broken-down men" were still hanging around, and they refused to re-enlist.

In desperation Kirby Smith wired Governor Joseph E. Brown, of Georgia, for men and arms to defend Chattanooga. President Davis also made a personal appeal to Brown. And Secretary of War Benjamin urged Governor J. G. Shorter of Alabama to rush to Chattanooga every available man who could carry a musket. Kirby Smith frankly stated to Richmond authorities that without reenforcements he would be unable to stop the Union advance from either of the threatened points. "The militia will not assemble," he fumed, "and even should they, they are not to be trusted; neither have they arms." On the other hand, at least 20,000 potential Union recruits were awaiting a successful Federal invasion of East Tennessee.[18]

The attack upon Cumberland Gap proved to be nothing more than a demonstration by a portion of S. P. Carter's brigade for the purpose of learning the strength of the Confederate position. The Confederate pickets were driven in on the afternoon of March 21. Light firing continued throughout the following day, but no serious attack developed. The Federals withdrew during the night, convinced that a large force would be required to reduce the Gap. Carter recommended investment for the purpose of starving the Confederates out, unless sufficient forces were

[18] *Id.* to Danville Leadbetter, March 23, 1862, *ibid.*, 356; E. Kirby Smith to S. Cooper, March 23, 1862, *ibid.*, 355–56; Jefferson Davis to J. E. Brown, March 24, 1862, *ibid.*, 358; J. P. Benjamin to J. G. Shorter, March 23, 1862, *ibid.*, 354.

made available for a simultaneous attack from both north and south.[19]

On March 28 George W. Morgan, an old friend of Kirby Smith, was appointed commander of the Union forces in the vicinity of Cumberland Gap. Rushing along the old Wilderness Road as fast as an open buggy could be drawn when horses were frequently required to swim swollen streams, he arrived at Cumberland Ford on April 11. Reorganization of his command, reconnaissance, and study of the probable intentions of Kirby Smith occupied his time for the next few weeks.[20]

At Chattanooga the Union threat did not prove serious and was relieved by the arrival of Georgia troops. But Kirby Smith decided upon additional precautionary measures. The Nashville and Chattanooga Railroad passed through Murfreesboro and Tullahoma and then tunneled through the mountain near Cowan into the Tennessee Valley which led to Chattanooga. From Tullahoma a spur line extended to Manchester, McMinnville, and Sparta. This spur would be the main supply line for any Federal force moving by way of Crossville to Kingston. Brigadier General S. B. Maxey at Chattanooga was instructed to send out details to burn bridges and blow up the tunnel, rendering the railroads unfit for enemy use. A cavalry force was to scout the country in the direction of Sparta. Confederate military stores at Chattanooga were to be moved to Atlanta.[21]

There was little danger of a large scale Union invasion of East Tennessee at that time, and Kirby Smith suspected the truth. Most available Federal troops were being concentrated in the Mississippi Valley where decisive battles

[19] Report of S. P. Carter, March 24, 1862, *ibid.*, pt. 1, 42–44; Report of E. Kirby Smith, March 30, 1862, *ibid.*, 44.
[20] G. W. Morgan to J. B. Fry, June 22, 1862, *ibid.*, 57–62.
[21] H. L. Clay to S. B. Maxey, March 24, 1862, *ibid.*, pt. 2, 358–59.

must soon be fought. Should the Union be victor, East Tennessee would also be lost to the Confederacy. If the fortune of battle favored the Confederates, East Tennessee could not long be held by the enemy, even if successfully invaded.[22]

Federal officials were well informed as to Kirby Smith's weaknesses in East Tennessee; Union sympathizers gladly served as scouts. But Kirby Smith had little knowledge of the strength and position of his opponents. Most reports received at his headquarters were manufactured in East Tennessee and were clearly designed to deceive. Having ordered the destruction of railroad bridges, Kirby Smith then directed Leadbetter at Kingston to send out scouts in the direction of Sparta. If possible, he should get a spy into Nashville. The road from Kentucky by way of Jamestown must be carefully watched. It might be desirable to send a small force into Scott County, for within that county was a militant Union element, which Kirby Smith wished "summarily dealt with." "I give you *carte blanche*," he told Leadbetter, "and will sustain you in any course you may find it necessary to adopt in those counties." Special care must be taken, however, that no marauding be permitted. The actions of the First East Tennessee Cavalry in particular should be watched.[23]

Scouts soon reported that there was no immediate threat from any point. Both Kirby Smith and Clay then sent for their wives to visit them. Mrs. Kirby Smith had been very persistent in her desire to join her husband and had expressed keen disappointment when he canceled such a plan immediately following his return from Cumberland Gap. On March 29 Maxey reported that the enemy force

[22] E. Kirby Smith to Wife, March 26, 1862.
[23] H. L. Clay to Danville Leadbetter, March 26, 1862, *Official Records*, Ser. I, Vol. X, pt. 2, 366; *id.* to S. B. Maxey, March 26, 1862, *ibid.*, 367; E. Kirby Smith to Danville Leadbetter, March 27, 1862, *ibid.*, 369.

recently at Murfreesboro, said to be 10,000 strong, had divided, about one half moving toward Manchester and the other to Shelbyville.[24] Troops at Manchester could use the railroad to Sparta and cross into East Tennessee by way of Crossville. Those at Shelbyville could turn southward by way of Fayetteville and seize the Memphis and Charleston Railroad at Huntsville, Alabama. Should the first group turn from Manchester to Tullahoma, a two-pronged movement could be made upon Chattanooga, each force having the use of a railroad.

Kirby Smith sent the Fifth Georgia, the only armed regiment at Knoxville, to Maxey and instructed him to be ready to receive two other Georgia regiments scheduled to move from Dalton as soon as arms arrived. The only force then with Maxey at Chattanooga was one battalion of Maney's First Tennessee and a few cavalry. Maxey must make sure that the bridge across the Elk River and the Cowan tunnel were destroyed and that the bridge across the Tennessee River at Stevenson, Alabama, was protected against destruction by the enemy.[25] The use of this bridge would be essential in any co-operation with General Albert Sidney Johnston in the Mississippi Valley.

"Until arms arrive from Richmond I can do nothing better for the defense of Chattanooga," Kirby Smith notified Adjutant General Cooper.[26] At this time there was no intention of using the East Tennessee command for offensive operations. General Robert E. Lee explained to Kirby Smith on March 31 that his principal duty was to protect the East Tennessee and Virginia Railroad.[27]

The protection of a railroad running through a hostile country was a difficult task within itself. It required a

[24] S. B. Maxey to E. Kirby Smith, March 29, 1862, *ibid.*, 373.
[25] E. Kirby Smith to S. B. Maxey, March 29, 1862, *ibid.*, 371–72.
[26] *Id.* to S. Cooper, March 31, 1862, *ibid.*, 376.
[27] T. A. Washington to E. Kirby Smith, March 31, 1862, *ibid.*, 376–77.

twenty-four hour watch at every bridge in East Tennessee. Bridge-burning and sabotage in general became Kirby Smith's greatest concern, and severely tested his reputation for patience and forbearance. Only through the arrest and imprisonment of disloyal leaders, he insisted, could the disloyal population be convinced. "They are an ignorant, primitive people, completely in the hands of and under the guidance of their leaders, whose misrepresentations and distortion of facts prevent them viewing matters through an impartial medium." Many of the recently elected public officials were open supporters of the Union, he averred. And when the county courts should convene on April 7 he proposed to administer a Confederate oath of allegiance to newly elected officers. Those refusing to take the oath would be imprisoned.[28]

Under the date of April 2, Adjutant Clay sent out a circular to all commanding officers in counties of doubtful loyalty, instructing each to select "an officer of discretion, coolness, and nerve," to supervise the administering of oaths to elected officials. Each officer, accompanied by twenty-five men, would arrive at the county courthouse at 9:00 A.M., April 7, and see that all officials took the oath. Any who refused were to be arrested and sent to Knoxville.[29]

On this same date Kirby Smith announced the arrest of one David Fry and nineteen associates, all alleged bridge-burners, while attempting to escape to Kentucky. A speedy trial for Fry, "followed by the extreme penalty incurred," he believed, "would have a most salutary effect in this quarter." [30] Furthermore, he insisted that the declaration of martial law throughout the entire Department of East

[28] E. Kirby Smith to S. Cooper, April 2, 1862, *ibid.*, 385–86.
[29] Circular letter, April 2, 1862, *ibid.*, 386.
[30] E. Kirby Smith to S. Cooper, April 2, 1862, *ibid.*, Ser. II, Vol. I, 881.

Tennessee was essential to the success of the Confederate cause. Civil governments in the hands of disloyal officials could scarcely be expected to give justice to supporters of the Confederacy. "But six counties in East Tennessee are friendly to us," he told General Lee; "the others are disloyal; many in open revolt, in which there are organized armed bands that oppress men of Southern principles." [31]

General Lee approved of both the declaration of martial law in East Tennessee and the transfer of troops of doubtful loyalty. Kirby Smith might send these troops to Brigadier General Henry Heth and receive in return three loyal Tennessee regiments from Joseph E. Johnston's army. The terms of the latter would expire in May and it was stated that they would not re-enlist unless permitted to help defend their home state.[32] On April 8, 1862, President Davis suspended civil jurisdiction and the writ of habeas corpus throughout East Tennessee.[33]

The fall of Fort Henry on the Tennessee River and Fort Donelson on the Cumberland in February, 1862, had forced General Albert Sidney Johnston to evacuate western Kentucky and Nashville and fall back to a new position in western Tennessee. Union General U. S. Grant pressed on with confidence. The river route into the heart of the Confederacy lay before him. But suddenly, on April 6, Johnston took the offensive, striking a severe blow at the raw Union forces at Shiloh Church. Grant had been taken by surprise and was several miles away at Savannah. Before he could reach the battlefield, his troops were falling back in great disorder. At the close of the day the Confederates occupied the battlefield, but the temporary victory had cost them the life of their commander. General Beaure-

---

[31] *Id.* to T. A. Washington, April 3, 1862, *ibid.*, Ser. I, Vol. X, pt. 2, 389–90.
[32] R. E. Lee to E. Kirby Smith, April 7, 1862, *ibid.*, 397–98.
[33] General Orders No. 21, April 8, 1862, *ibid.*, 402.

gard took command. The arrival of Federal re-enforcements during the night gave Grant the advantage on the
following day, and Beauregard was forced to fall back
toward Corinth, Mississippi.

Encouraged by the near victory over Grant, Beauregard
was determined to strike again if re-enforcements could be
had. From Corinth he wired General Earl Van Dorn in
Arkansas: "Hurry your forces as rapidly as possible. I
believe we can whip them again." Van Dorn inquired
whether Beauregard could furnish arms. Beauregard replied: "I regret have none; could not remove all I took, but
we will take more. Come on." On the same date Beauregard
also wired for assistance from East Tennessee.

In enumerating to Kirby Smith the troops available at
Chattanooga, General Maxey urged: "If they go, I want to
go. The citizens say they will guard the bridge." Kirby
Smith directed him to leave for Corinth at once, taking
the First and Forty-first Georgia and the Twenty-fourth
Mississippi regiments. He would be joined as quickly as
possible by General Leadbetter with the Twentieth and
Twenty-third Alabama regiments from Kingston and the
Thirty-ninth Georgia from Knoxville. Only the Third
Tennessee, commanded by Colonel John C. Vaughn, would
be left behind at Kingston. One North Carolina battalion
at Clinton, two Georgia regiments at Knoxville, and the
small garrison at Cumberland Gap were the only other
troops to be left in Kirby Smith's department.[34]

Maxey moved immediately and just in time. His troops
passed across north Alabama on the Memphis and Charleston Railroad on April 10. At 6:00 A.M. the following
morning the advance guard of Brigadier General Ormsby

<hr />

[34] G. T. Beauregard to Van Dorn, Earl Van Dorn to Beauregard, G. T.
Beauregard to Van Dorn, and S. B. Maxey to E. Kirby Smith, all April 9, 1862,
*ibid.*, 405–406; E. Kirby Smith to S. Cooper, April 10, 1862, *ibid.*, 409.

M. Mitchell's Federal division moved into Huntsville. This was the force recently reported at Shelbyville. No doubt Mitchell had been informed of Kirby Smith's intention to re-enforce Beauregard. No railroad ran from Shelbyville in the direction of Huntsville, and the bridges were out along the Nashville and Chattanooga Railroad leading to Stevenson, Alabama. Mitchell had made a forced march by way of Fayetteville.

Huntsville was taken by surprise; no resistance was offered. No fewer than twenty-one locomotives and three trains of cars fell into Federal possession. Using these captured cars Mitchell sent troops both east and west along the railroad. Decatur to the west and Stevenson to the east were taken without a struggle. A 100-mile section of the vital Memphis and Charleston Railroad was now in Federal hands. Leadbetter's regiments were cut off in Chattanooga, and, to prevent an immediate Confederate advance upon Huntsville from that point, Mitchell ordered the burning of the bridge over Widden's Creek between Stevenson and Bridgeport.[35]

A few hours before learning of the capture of Huntsville, Kirby Smith received a personal appeal from Beauregard: "Can you not turn over your command and join me at once. I need you." Kirby Smith immediately informed Richmond authorities: "I shall do so. Am I right?"[36] But with the fall of Huntsville went the loss of the use of the Memphis and Charleston Railroad, and further direct assistance to Beauregard at Corinth was impossible. However, two means of indirect aid were still possible. Union commanders were almost certain to attempt to use the Nashville and Chattanooga Railroad to Stevenson and

[35] Two reports of O. M. Mitchell, April 11, 1862, *ibid.*, pt. 1, 641–42; report of E. Kirby Smith, April 13, 1862, *ibid.*, 643.

[36] E. Kirby Smith to S. Cooper, April 11, 1862, *ibid.*, pt. 2, 414.

thence possibly the Memphis and Charleston westward to the Tennessee River. Kirby Smith must, therefore, see that railroad bridges were destroyed as fast as they were rebuilt. In the second place, available forces in East Tennessee might be sent by way of Kingston and Sparta to threaten Nashville, thus checking the aid that might be sent to Federal forces in West Tennessee and northern Mississippi. Kirby Smith decided to make the fullest use of both possibilities.

Colonel Vaughn at Kingston was instructed to send picked companies of cavalry across the mountains into Middle Tennessee to operate at different points in a thorough destruction of bridges. These companies were to be led by "bold but prudent officers" who would keep their men ever on the move, striking quickly and effectively, and then moving away with great speed. Let them "emulate the character [John Hunt] Morgan has already established," Kirby Smith urged. A similar suggestion was sent to Leadbetter at Chattanooga: "Can you not infuse some of Morgan's spirit into the cavalry commanders?" [37]

A few bands of galloping cavalrymen could scarcely be expected to make a serious threat upon Nashville. Kirby Smith outlined his plan to both Lee and Beauregard and asked for sufficient re-enforcements to put it into effect. Four regiments from J. C. Pemberton's army in South Carolina were on their way to join Beauregard. Now that they were cut off by Federal control of the Memphis and Charleston Railroad, Kirby Smith suggested that they be ordered to join Leadbetter at Chattanooga. Beauregard was enthusiastic over the plan to threaten Nashville, but was unwilling to give up his re-enforcements. "Urge War

[37] H. L. Clay to J. C. Vaughn, April 13, 1862, *ibid.*, 417; E. Kirby Smith to Danville Leadbetter, April 13, 1862, *ibid.*, 416.

Department to send you the troops for it by all means and without hesitation," he urged Kirby Smith, "and I will throw a brigade of cavalry across the [Tennessee] river to aid you." But he rerouted the South Carolina regiments to Corinth by way of Mobile.[38]

General Lee also approved the proposed threat against Nashville, which he understood was not defended, but he had no troops to spare. Kirby Smith might use the South Carolina regiments if they came to Chattanooga. When six Georgia regiments were recently ordered to East Tennessee, Lee explained, it was his impression that they were to be used for a demonstration in the direction of Nashville.[39] The tone of these notes indicated some dissatisfaction with either Kirby Smith's delay or the sending of troops to Beauregard.

The proposed invasion of Middle Tennessee did not materialize; Kirby Smith was too cautious to expose the railroad and supplies in East Tennessee to Union sympathizers and Federal forces in nearby Kentucky.

The passage of the Confederate conscription act in mid-April, 1862, further complicated Kirby Smith's problems in East Tennessee. All males between eighteen and thirty-five were made subject to draft. Even before this news arrived a number of Union men had quietly slipped away to the Kentucky mountains to avoid possible punishment under martial law. Federal Brigadier General George W. Morgan at Cumberland Ford, Kentucky, sent scouts and small detachments of troops into Powell's Valley to assist these "refugees." [40] Fear of conscription now increased

[38] *Id.* to G. T. Beauregard, April 13, 1862, *ibid.,* 417; *id.* to S. Cooper, April 15, 1862, *ibid.,* 422.

[39] R. E. Lee to E. Kirby Smith, April 15, 1862, *ibid.,* 422; *id.* to G. T. Beauregard, April 16, 1862, *ibid.,* 424–25.

[40] G. W. Morgan to O. D. Greene, April 19, 1862, *ibid.,* 114.

both the number and fury of those in flight. Many were boisterous and outspoken as they took leave of their homes. They would soon return in blue uniforms, they assured their Rebel neighbors.

With some hope of checking this exodus and of encouraging those who had fled to return to their homes, Kirby Smith announced a policy of leniency. Many misguided citizens, he explained, had through ignorance or misconception of duty committed treason against their state. Designing enemies posing as friends had persuaded a number to join the forces of the enemy. However, if those guilty of treasonable acts would come forward, acknowledge their error, and take an oath of allegiance, they would not be "molested or punished on account of past acts or words." The same leniency would be extended to those who had fled to the enemy, provided they returned and took the oath within thirty days. Having made his generous offer to those who had been "led away from the true path of patriotic duty," the major general commanding declared his determination to protect the lives and property of loyal Confederates in East Tennessee to the fullest of his ability and to suppress treasonable acts of the disloyal. Should the civil courts prove unequal to the task military tribunals would take over.[41]

Arrest orders were issued for those Union sympathizers who circulated exaggerated reports for the purpose of inducing men to flee. All available cavalry was rushed to patrol duty on the line between Clinton and the north valley of Powell's River. If refugees resisted they were to be attacked. The 475 refugees recently captured near Woodson's Gap were to be sent to Milledgeville, Georgia. A special officer was sent to check on the report that a number of them were now desirous of entering the Confederate

[41] Proclamation, April 18, 1862, *ibid.*, 640–41.

service. Those who wished to sign up would be sent to some point outside East Tennessee.[42]

Fear of military courts checked Unionist activities in East Tennessee, but it made no converts to the Confederate cause. A few refugees returned to their homes bringing exaggerated reports of what Union forces in Kentucky were preparing to do. On April 23, 1862, Kirby Smith's provost marshal, W. M. Churchwell, issued a proclamation to the "Disaffected People of East Tennessee" again calling attention to the major general's liberal offer of amnesty and protection to those who would return to their homes and become loyal citizens. After the expiration of the thirty day period those who had failed to return would have their families sent to their care in Kentucky or somewhere beyond the Confederate lines. Likewise, those who should leave their homes after that date would have their families "sent immediately after them." "The women and children must be taken care of by husbands and fathers either in East Tennessee or in the Lincoln Government." [43]

Orders had already been issued to the wife and children of the loquacious William G. ("Parson") Brownlow to prepare to join him. Shortly before Kirby Smith was appointed to command in East Tennessee, Brownlow, refusing to maintain even a semblance of loyalty to Confederate Tennessee, had been thrown into prison. From his cell he wrote Secretary Judah P. Benjamin: "Just give me my passports, and I will do for your Confederacy more than the devil has ever done—I will quit the country." [44] Ben-

---

[42] H. L. Clay to W. L. Eakin, April 19, 1862, *ibid.*, 429–430; *id.* to J. C. Vaughn, April 19, 1862, *ibid.*, 429; *id.* to J. M. Rhett, April 23, 1862, *ibid.*, pt. 1, 649.

[43] "To the disaffected people of East Tennessee," April 23, 1862, *ibid.*, pt. 2, 640–41.

[44] *Ibid.*, Ser. II, Vol. I, 929; W. G. Brownlow, *Sketches of the Rise, Progress, and Decline of Secession* (Philadelphia, 1862), 318.

jamin accepted the proposition, and the "Parson" passed beyond the Confederate lines.

Notices were also sent the wives of Unionist leaders Horace Maynard, Andrew Johnson, and William B. Carter to prepare to join their husbands outside the Confederacy.[45] Loud cries of inhuman treatment came from the ranks of the refugees.

Union Brigadier General S. P. Carter, an East Tennessean, sent a demand that David Fry, the notorious bridge-burner recently captured by the Confederates, be treated as a prisoner of war. Kirby Smith rejected the demand. Fry was wearing civilian clothes when caught; therefore, he was either a spy or a civilian engaged in the "felonious occupation of bridge-burning." If a civilian, he would be amenable to the criminal courts; if a spy, he must answer to the military.[46]

Carter's demand was prompted by General George W. Morgan, who although mildly interested in Fry's welfare, was eager to learn Kirby Smith's present location. "I sent a letter to Kirby Smith, signed by General Carter," Morgan wrote Secretary of War E. M. Stanton, "in order to ascertain his locality, but in reply he simply dated his letter Department of East Tennessee, April 19. I believe he is at Corinth." Morgan was concentrating his forces at Cumberland Ford. "I appreciate the importance of getting into East Tennessee," he explained, "and will soon do so." [47] Naturally he preferred to strike when his old friend Kirby Smith was engaged elsewhere.

Probably in no other region were the commanders on both sides more confused by conflicting reports than in

[45] W. M. Churchwell to Mrs. Andrew Johnson and Mrs. [Horace] Maynard, April 21, 1862 and Mrs. William B. Carter, April 26, 1862, all in *Official Records*, Ser. II, Vol. I, 883–86.

[46] E. Kirby Smith to S. P. Carter, April 19, 1862, *ibid.*, 882–83.

[47] G. W. Morgan to E. M. Stanton, April 29, 1862, *ibid.*, Ser. I, Vol. X, pt. 2, 142.

East Tennessee and Kentucky. Kirby Smith heard that at Salt Lick the Federals had ten regiments ready to march. Further reports claimed that this force was being increased daily by Tennesseans, who in leaving home had sworn to return within two weeks. Kirby Smith was uneasy. He had only 2,000 men at Cumberland Gap and two regiments from that number would not likely be available for service. The term of enlistment of the Eleventh Tennessee Volunteers was about to expire, and the Fourth Tennessee was suspected of having too many disloyal East Tennesseans within its ranks. Brigadier General C. L. Stevenson, the successor to Colonel Rains at the Gap, requested that the Fourth be transferred to some other location. Kirby Smith ordered it to Savannah, Georgia, and sent the Forty-second Georgia as replacement. The conscription law extended the period of service of the Eleventh Tennessee.[48]

Morgan, concentrating his own forces at Cumberland Ford, learned of the removal of the disaffected Fourth Tennessee from the Gap, but figured that it had gone to Kingston. His informants also reported that a number of the estimated twenty-seven guns at the Gap were being sent to Corinth.[49] The Federal general must not have known of the capture of Huntsville on the Memphis and Charleston Railroad.

As of April 26 Kirby Smith's report showed an aggregate of 8,619 men available for duty in his department. Of that number, 1,143 were cavalry. Owing to the many points to be protected it would be impossible to concentrate more than 5,000 for defense at any point. The general was still begging for sufficient re-enforcements to guarantee the security of East Tennessee, although he had little hope of securing them. He notified Beauregard not to expect fur-

[48] E. Kirby Smith to R. E. Lee, April 16, 1862, *ibid.*, 424; H. L. Clay to C. L. Stevenson, April 17, 1862, *ibid.*, 427.

[49] G. W. Morgan to E. M. Stanton, April 29, 1862, *ibid.*, 142.

ther aid from East Tennessee since the enemy was "pressing Cumberland Gap with superior forces." To Brigadier General Humphrey Marshall at Abingdon, Virginia,
he sent an urgent appeal: "Can you not co-operate with me
with the whole or a portion of your force. . . ." Leadbetter at Chattanooga was ordered to hold himself "in readiness to follow the Twenty-third Alabama regiment and
Latrobe's battery to Knoxville at a moments warning."
He had previously been instructed to begin rebuilding the
bridge over Widden's Creek as if an attack upon Huntsville was contemplated. He was now to leave a skeleton
crew to continue the deception. If the enemy attacked and
retreat became necessary, all bridges leading toward Chattanooga were to be destroyed "certainly and beyond all
contingencies." Confederate activities had already caused
Mitchell at Huntsville to call for re-enforcements that he
himself might beat the enemy to offensive movements.[50]

Kirby Smith left for the vicinity of Cumberland Gap by
way of Clinton and Fincastle on April 30. On the following day he wrote back to his wife urging that she "keep of
good cheer" and pray for him, ever remembering that "we
are all in God's hands and that he can effect great results
with small means." [51] Through Bishop Kavanaugh of Versailles, Kentucky, it was reported that 12,000 Federal
troops had passed through Lexington on April 14, headed
for Cumberland Ford. These plus four new regiments of
East Tennessee "renegades" under James G. Spears would
swell Morgan's command to a possible 18,000! And an-

---

[50] E. Kirby Smith to T. A. Washington, April 26, 1862, *ibid.*, 453–54; *id.*
to G. T. Beauregard, April 26, 1862, *ibid.*, 453; *id.* to Humphrey Marshall,
*ibid.*,. 457; H. L. Clay to Danville Leadbetter, April 26, 1862, *ibid.*, 454; E.
Cunningham to Leadbetter, April 30, 1862, *ibid.*, pt. 1, 659; J. F. Belton to
Leadbetter, May 1, 1862, *ibid.*, pt. 2, 478–79; O. M. Mitchell to D. C. Buell,
April 20, 1862, *ibid.*, 618–19.

[51] E. Kirby Smith to Wife, May 1, 1862.

other force estimated at 11,000 was rumored to be moving on East Tennessee by way of Sparta and Kingston.[52]

Kirby Smith concentrated his troops at three points, holding scattered units in position to march to the assistance of any point that was seriously threatened. Brigadier General S. M. Barton was near Jacksboro, observing both Big Creek Gap and the country toward Cumberland Gap. According to enemy estimates, he had seven infantry regiments, 600 cavalry, and eight guns. At Cumberland Gap, Stevenson had an estimated 4,500 infantry, 400 cavalry, and 20 cannon. At Knoxville, ready to move in any direction, was an undisclosed number of regiments. The enemy thought the number to be about ten.[53]

Morgan planned to cut a road through the Cumberland Mountains about equidistant from Jacksboro and Cumberland Gap. Once in Powell's Valley, he could turn upon Barton at Jacksboro or move to the rear of the Gap. He expected his own force to be outnumbered, but he ordered Carter, with four regiments and a battery, to make a feint at the Gap, drive in the pickets, and remain in position before the fortification overnight. Spears, then encamped at the foot of Pine Mountain, would move his three regiments through a specified "narrow defile" and gain Barton's rear. In relating his plans to Secretary of War Stanton, Morgan added that the problem could now be easily solved if Mitchell at Huntsville would "draw Kirby Smith toward Chattanooga." Five days later he reported again. Kirby Smith had withdrawn most of his force from Chattanooga and had himself arrived at Cumberland Gap. An invasion of Kentucky was reported to be his aim.[54]

[52] *Id.* to T. A. Washington, May 5, 1862, *Official Records,* Ser. I, Vol. X, pt. 2, 496; *id.* to S. Cooper, May 8, 1862, *ibid.,* 504.

[53] G. W. Morgan to E. M. Stanton, May 18, 19, 1862, *ibid.,* 201, 204.

[54] *Id.* to *id.,* May 19, 24, 1862, *ibid.,* 204, 213.

Scouts brought to Kirby Smith the important points in Morgan's plan, including the construction of the road through the mountains, which was to be done by East Tennessee refugees. On May 23 the three-pronged movement was said to be under way, but it failed to develop. A few days later the force which had appeared opposite Barton at Big Creek Gap had fallen back. Increased activities among Union partisans in Scott and Morgan counties caused Kirby Smith to suspect an advance by way of Montgomery and Kingston. Additional scouts were sent out to investigate.

Leadbetter, hard-pressed at Chattanooga, had been unable to send any troops to Knoxville. On April 29 Mitchell directed an attack upon the bridge near Chattanooga and threatened the city. Leadbetter, taken by surprise, did a poor job of destroying the bridge. The explosives failed to wreck the west span; so the east span was set on fire. Mitchell reported that his men put out the fire and saved the bridge; Leadbetter reported it destroyed.

The poorly organized Confederate command fell back upon Chattanooga, destroying a few small bridges along roads and the railroad, and waited for the enemy to cross the river. Leadbetter was so poorly informed that he expected an enemy force of 5,000 to attack before the close of the day. His only plan of defense was to observe the enemy "from a favorable point" and await re-enforcements. But Mitchell had gone as far as he had intended. "Holding the main bridge," he reported to Buell, "we can cross to the other shore whenever it be deemed advisable."

Panic seized the residents of Chattanooga and Leadbetter was bitterly denounced for his failure to hold the bridge. "The series of events thus related have excited the upmost indignation of a terrified people," he reported to Kirby Smith, "and no abuse, whether of a personal or official bearing, has been spared me." [55] Kirby Smith sent no official criticism but resolved to get another brigadier. While both Mitchell and Leadbetter waited for re-enforcements, Beauregard, now hard pressed by slow moving Henry W. Halleck, was urging Kirby Smith for a demonstration into Middle Tennessee. Colonel John Adams, commanding a brigade of Beauregard's army on the loose in Middle Tennessee, urged Kirby Smith to send cavalry to help him drive the Yankees from Fayetteville. [56] Leadbetter was instructed to send the cavalry and some small artillery, if it could be spared. The assistance was not sent, however, for the next word from Adams was that the enemy had driven him out of Winchester. Any Federal force moving from Huntsville to Winchester would likely be headed for Chattanooga.

Kirby Smith called for help from the governors of Georgia and Alabama, and sent an urgent request to General J. C. Pemberton at Charleston. Pemberton forwarded the request to General Lee. There were no available re-enforcements, Lee replied, except whatever assistance the governors might furnish and possibly a couple of regiments from Florida.

Alarming information continued to arrive at East Tennessee headquarters. General Mitchell was reported to be receiving re-enforcements along the railroad from Corinth to Huntsville. Heavy columns of Federal infantry and artillery were said to be at McMinnville ready to move upon either Kingston or Chattanooga. Kirby Smith reported his situation to Richmond: "The force from Middle Tennessee, acting in concert with that on the Kentucky line and in communication by telegraph, places me in an

[55] Report of O. M. Mitchell, April 29, 1862, *ibid.*, pt. 1, 655–56; report of Danville Leadbetter, May 4, 1862, *ibid.*, 656–59.

[56] E. Cunningham to Danville Leadbetter, May 21, 1862, *ibid.*, pt. 2, 536.

unfavorable situation, and I fear involves the loss of East Tennessee, and with it the railroad. Cumberland Gap and Chattanooga, the two principal strategic points of this department, separated 180 miles, with a difficult line of communication, are each threatened by a force superior to my whole effective strength. To concentrate at either point involves the abandonment of Cumberland Gap or Chattanooga." [57]

Heavy Federal concentration upon Chattanooga seemed certain. Twelve regiments of infantry and artillery were reported to have passed through Winchester on June 5. Another column, also with artillery, was reported at Jasper. "Remove all the stores to Atlanta and Marietta," Kirby Smith hurriedly instructed Leadbetter. "Make your preparations to destroy whatever cannot be removed in the event the evacuation of Chattanooga becomes necessary. But hold the place as long as possible." When he could no longer hold the town he was to fall back to Cleveland, destroying the railroad toward Dalton, Georgia.[58] As further precaution, the steamer *Lookout* was ordered to move up the Tennessee from Chattanooga, collecting and destroying all boats.[59]

But General Kirby Smith had made his decision. Chattanooga must be held even if its defense entailed the loss of the other extremity of his department. Colonel A. W. Reynolds' Third Brigade was ordered to withdraw from Powell's Valley and report to Chattanooga immediately. General Barton's Fourth Brigade was to move to Clinton and await further orders. Colonel Benjamin Allston's Cavalry Brigade was divided, a part remaining to watch the approaches to Powell's Valley and the other part joining

---

[57] E. Kirby Smith to T. A. Washington, June 6, 1862, *ibid.*, 596–97.

[58] *Id.* to R. E. Lee, June 6, 1862, *ibid.*, 596; H. L. Clay to Danville Leadbetter, June 6, 1862, *ibid.*, Ser. II, Vol. II, 890.

[59] *Id.* to J. B. McLin, June 6, 1862, *ibid.*, Ser. I, Vol. X, pt. 2, 592–93.

forces with McLin at Kingston. From that point scouting expeditions were to be sent out toward both Winchester and Montgomery.

At Cumberland Gap, General Stevenson was left on his own. No longer were there re-enforcements of any strength within reach of him. His position was strong, however, and he had 4,000 men. If he could just hold out until the issue at Chattanooga was settled, help would be rushed to him. But should he be compelled to evacuate the Gap, he was instructed to move toward Abingdon, Virginia.

Although Leadbetter continued to report all quiet at Chattanooga, Kirby Smith urged "the importance of un-relaxing precaution and vigilance." Every mountain pass must be carefully and constantly watched. Mitchell, he explained, had never encountered well-organized opposition, and recent successes might "embolden him to daring and hazardous undertakings." He must not be permitted to make a surprise attack, and in case he left himself open fullest advantage must be taken of his blunder.[60]

Kirby Smith sent his wife to her home at Lynchburg, Virginia, and set out for Chattanooga by special train on the afternoon of June 7. Union guns were shelling the town from across the river when he arrived. While Lead-better had been reporting all quiet, Federal troops under Brigadier General James S. Negley had crossed the mountains from Winchester and surprised Adam's cavalry encamped in Sweeden's Cove near Jasper. According to enemy accounts the Confederates "fled in the wildest disorder, strewing the ground for miles with guns, pistols, and swords."[61]

[60] *Id.* to A. W. Reynolds, June 6, 1862, *ibid.*, 595; *id.* to Benjamin Allston, June 6, 1862, *ibid.*, 596; *id.* to C. L. Stevenson, June 6, 7, 1862, *ibid.*, 592, 598–99; E. Cunningham to Danville Leadbetter, June 6, 1862, *ibid.*, 595.

[61] Reports of J. S. Negley, O. M. Mitchell, and E. Kirby Smith, *ibid.*, pt. 1, 903–905.

Negley moved on to the river opposite Chattanooga and began bombardment on the afternoon of June 7. After witnessing a few hours of noise, smoke, and destruction, Kirby Smith wrote his wife: "The horrors of war—could experiences of those who live in civil wars be extended to succeeding generations we would not have much need or use of armies." [62]

But the general had little time to think of future generations; he was faced by a formidable enemy force that might attempt to cross the Tennessee at any moment. He wired his adjutant to rush Barton's Brigade. Barton was to wire ahead from time to time reporting his progress.[63] General Lee sent the good news that the two Florida regiments were on the way.[64]

The shelling of Chattanooga from across the river was resumed on the morning of June 8. Kirby Smith did not reply but pulled his forces back out of range and waited. Negley made no attempt to cross over. After three hours of bombardment, he began quietly to withdraw his troops. General Mitchell had remained at Huntsville.

Without pontoons, General Negley reported, it would be almost impossible to cross the river. The taking of Chattanooga, however, would not be "very difficult or hazardous," if proper preparations were made. But in view of long and exposed supply and communication lines, the poor condition of the railroad, and the threatened rise of scarcely fordable streams, he had decided to withdraw. He considered the campaign a success; he had captured eighty prisoners, a herd of cattle, and a number of horses bound for Kirby Smith's army.[65] "Our shells did terrible execu-

[62] E. Kirby Smith to Wife, June 8, 1862.

[63] J. F. Belton to S. M. Barton, June 9, 1862, *Official Records,* Ser. I, Vol. X, pt. 2, 603.

[64] W. H. Taylor to E. Kirby Smith, June 7, 1862, *ibid.,* 597–98.

[65] Reports of J. S. Negley, June 8, 12, 1862, *ibid.,* pt. 1, 920.

tion in the town, completely destroying many buildings, among others their commissary depot," reported Colonel H. A. Hambright, who had directed the bombardment.[66] Kirby Smith, however, reported no great damage. He wrote his wife that "there was considerable noise & bursting of shells, but little damage was done." He was sure that the enemy had intended taking Chattanooga by a *coup de main,* but hearing of the arrival of Confederate reenforcements, had abandoned the plan. He knew nothing of the withdrawal until the enemy had recrossed the mountains.[67] He made a very brief report to Richmond: The enemy with an estimated force of 7,000 had withdrawn from before Chattanooga, evacuated Sequatchie Valley and recrossed the mountains into Middle Tennessee. "The enemy buried 8 men and abandoned one 4½ inch rifle brass gun. Our loss 3 wounded." [68]

Negley moved into Middle Tennessee to give chase to J. W. Starnes' cavalry, which had been reported at Sparta, McMinnville, and Altamont. Kirby Smith, tired and ill, rushed back to Knoxville, and to the defense of the other extremity of his department. He found Cunningham ill but still dragging about. Aleck too was sick. Clay was confined to bed at Clinton. The services and advice of these loyal assistants were keenly missed by the general. Only Belton and aide-de-camp J. G. Meem were able to work.

Stopping for only one day at his Knoxville headquarters, Kirby Smith hurried toward the vicinity of Cumberland Gap. He was going forth to battle, he hastily informed his wife, but he had no fear of the results. Should anything happen to him, Aleck would come to her as "a faithful servant." "Tell Mr. Mac [Daniel] that next to

[66] Report, June 8, 1862, *ibid.,* 920–21.
[67] E. Kirby Smith to Wife, June 11 (?), 1862.
[68] *Id.* to W. H. Taylor, June 10, 1862, *Official Records,* Ser. I, Vol. X, pt. 1, 922.

Clay my heart warms toward him with a brother's affection that the remembrance of his kindness & that of his family nerves me to renewed exertions." [69]

During Kirby Smith's absence at Chattanooga, Morgan had "removed the obstructions from roads leading over the Cumberland Mountains," and was now moving the majority of his force into Powell's Valley. Apparently Cumberland Gap was to be attacked from the rear. Morgan had begun moving out of Cumberland Ford on June 8, but was not certain just how far he should go. Scouts had reported that the Confederate force at Cumberland Gap numbered 5,000 and that 8,000 were at Big Creek Gap. These, if combined, Morgan observed, would outnumber him three to one. "What is General Negley doing?" he wired Buell. Negley was "fully employed in Middle Tennessee," Buell answered, and could give no assistance. His stay before Chattanooga was temporary and must not be depended upon. Morgan must rely upon his own resources, and it would probably be well not to risk too much at present.

The Federal commander was already on the march before he received this advice from his superior. He was at Roger's Gap and would reach the valley the next day, he wired Buell on June 10. He would proceed boldly and attempt the destruction of bridges on either side of Knoxville, but he was convinced that the "present fate of East Tennessee depends on Kirby Smith being all occupied at Chattanooga."

Soon Morgan was engaging in wishful thinking that Cumberland Gap had been evacuated. Huge clouds of smoke had been boiling up in that direction. This might be a screen, he thought, behind which a retreat was being carried out. "If the enemy has retreated," he reported to

[69] *Id.* to Wife, June 13, 1862.

Buell, "I shall march at once upon Knoxville, and thence operate upon the rear of the enemy, who has probably gone toward Chattanooga." [70]

Kirby Smith left only two regiments at Chattanooga. The others he ordered to Knoxville. Barton, who had not advanced beyond Loudon, was turned back and sent to Tazewell by way of Clinton. Allston was sent back to Powell's Valley to observe the enemy until hard-pressed. He was then to fall back to the south side of the Clinch River and guard the crossings. Reynolds was ordered to Morristown with instructions to form junction with Barton at Tazewell.

Kirby Smith set up temporary headquarters at Bean's Station. He urged General Humphrey Marshall in southwestern Virginia to co-operate with Stevenson should the latter be compelled to evacuate Cumberland Gap and fall back toward Abingdon. To General Beauregard he sent an urgent call for help in the defense of Chattanooga. "Chattanooga is in danger. If you are not likely to be soon actively occupied can you not send two brigades or a division under an efficient officer to that point? The fall of Chattanooga opens the way into Georgia and exposes our right flank." Leadbetter was temporarily left on his own at Chattanooga. All Kirby Smith could promise him was the two regiments from Florida when they arrived. [71]

On the evening of June 13 a courier rushed into Knoxville headquarters with a message from General Stevenson, who was "in front of the enemy at Wilson's Gap." An effort would be made to hold until re-enforcements could

[70] G. W. Morgan to D. C. Buell, May 22, June 8, 10 (two letters), 1862, *Official Records*, Ser. I, Vol. X, pt. 1, 52, 53, 54; Buell to Morgan, June 9, 1862, *ibid.*, 53; J. B. Fry to Morgan, June 10, 1862 (two letters), *ibid.*, 53, 54.

[71] J. F. Belton to S. M. Barton, June 12, 1862, *ibid.*, Vol. XVI, pt. 2, 677–78; *id.* to B. Allston, June 12, 13, 1862, *ibid.*, 679, 681; E. Kirby Smith to Humphrey Marshall, June 12, 1862, *ibid.*, 680; *id.* to G. T. Beauregard, June 12, 13, 1862, *ibid.*, 680, 681; Belton to Danville Leadbetter, June 12, 1862, *ibid.*, 678.

arrive. Kirby Smith ordered the combined forces of Barton
and Reynolds to move forward from Tazewell, and he himself set out for Bean's Station. When he reached Morristown he received a telegram from Adjutant Cunningham
relaying one from Leadbetter at Chattanooga. Mitchell's
forces were again at Stevenson and Jasper, but as yet no
attempt had been made to cross the Tennessee River.[72]

Again a decision had to be made; again the commanding
general chose to defend Chattanooga. Cumberland Gap
would be evacuated and all available forces sent to Chattanooga. The road to Georgia was more important than the
Gap, he notified Stevenson. Large quantities of Confederate supplies were stored at Dalton, Atlanta, and
Rome. Stevenson was ordered to evacuate the Gap
"promptly and quietly." The best guns were to be removed, if possible, and all others disabled. All camp equipment must be destroyed. His line of withdrawal would
be by Morristown to Cleveland and then either to Chattanooga or Dalton, Georgia. Barton and Allston would use
their full forces to cover the withdrawal. Allston would
cover Powell's Valley, falling back when necessary to
protect the railroad and route to Knoxville.[73]

Kirby Smith hurried back to Knoxville, taking Reynolds' and Thomas H. Taylor's brigades, about 3,500
men, with him. "General Buell seems to be directing the
movement against this department," he reported to Richmond. Since Beauregard's withdrawal from Corinth, a
concerted drive seemed to have been organized against
East Tennessee. "I have striven for an opportunity to
strike a blow; the enemy have invariably retired at my

[72] J. F. Belton to S. M. Barton, June 13, 1862, *ibid.*, 681; E. Cunningham to
E. Kirby Smith, June 14, 1862, *ibid.*, 682–83.

[73] J. F. Belton to C. L. Stevenson, June 15, 1862, *ibid.*, 683–84; *id.* to B.
Allston, June 15, 1862, *ibid.*, 684.

approach, and with every advantage would give me no opportunity. My command has been almost broken down by constantly moving from one end to the other of the line. Communicating by telegraph and acting in concert from behind natural defenses of great strength they have foiled every effort made by me." The concentration that he himself was now attempting for the defense of Chattanooga would give him a maximum of 12,000 men.[74]

Kirby Smith was correct as to Buell's part. On June 11 the Federal commander had ordered Mitchell: "General Morgan is advancing on Cumberland Gap. Endeavor as much as possible to keep your force in an attitude to threaten Chattanooga and occupy the attention of Kirby Smith." [75]

On June 16 it was reported that Union forces were attempting to cross the Tennessee near Chattanooga and a new threat was being made against Kingston. A force of 4,000 infantry and cavalry with 300 wagons had left McMinnville for Pikeville. And three regiments of East Tennessee Unionists were said to be moving upon Loudon for the purpose of destroying the bridge across the Tennessee.

Kirby Smith quickly formulated his plan. He would concentrate his forces along the railroad from Morristown to Loudon. They would then be in position to move against invading columns from any direction. Stevenson was urged to push his withdrawal from the Gap with "all the rapidity you can consistent with order and safety," and retire toward Morristown. Barton, if not hard-pressed, was to fall back to the south side of the Clinch and prepare for forced march to Knoxville. Starne's cavalry, which had recrossed

[74] E. Kirby Smith to S. Cooper, June 15, 1862, *ibid.*, 684–85.
[75] D. C. Buell to Mitchell, June 11, 1862, *ibid.*, Vol. X, pt. 1, 54.

the mountains from Middle Tennessee, was ordered to Cleveland. From that point a careful watch could be kept in the direction of both Pikeville and Kingston.[76]

"My division is concentrated," Morgan wired Buell, on June 16, from Roger's Gap. "I have reliable information that Barton and Kirby Smith, with all their available forces, are marching to attack me. If possible have a serious feint made on Chattanooga." [77]

Morgan's information was not so reliable as he thought. Kirby Smith had no idea of attacking him at a point of his own choice. In fact Kirby Smith had already returned to Knoxville with the intention of moving on to Chattanooga. But the expected push on that point did not develop. The Confederate commander was now convinced that the decisive battle would be fought north of the railroad. He might at any moment leave for Clinch River, he confided to his wife. The approach of the enemy from Powell's Valley was anxiously awaited. If the slightest opportunity should be offered, he would attack.[78]

Surplus arms recently arrived from Richmond were sent to Chattanooga to equip the Florida and Georgia regiments. These re-enforcements would increase Leadbetter's force to about 4,000. He was instructed to prepare one half this force for rapid transfer to the probable battle zone. He must be cautious, however, not to disturb or frighten the residents of Chattanooga. They should be assured that their town would be "defended to the last extremity." [79]

General Stevenson evacuated Cumberland Gap on the

[76] J. F. Belton to C. L. Stevenson, June 16, 1862 (two messages), *ibid.,* Vol. XVI, pt. 2, 686, 687; *id.* to S. M. Barton, June 16, 1862, *ibid.,* 686–87; *id.* to B. Allston, June 17, 1862, *ibid.,* 690.

[77] George W. Morgan to D. C. Buell, June 16, 1862, *ibid.,* pt. 1, 1008.

[78] E. Kirby Smith to Wife, June 19, 1862.

[79] *Id.* to S. Cooper, June 18, 1862, *Official Records,* Ser. I, Vol. XVI, pt. 2, 692; E. Cunningham to Danville Leadbetter, June 18, 1862, *ibid.,* 691–92.

morning of June 18. That afternoon Morgan's men moved in and took possession of the ruins. The Stars and Stripes were raised and "a national salute fired in honor of the capture of this stronghold of treason." "Well, the Gap is ours," Morgan reported to Buell, "and without the loss of a single life." "Had Kirby Smith been personally in command we should have had a battle." To have taken the place by attack, he believed, would have required ten days and a probable loss of two thirds of his command. He was proud to have won the victory by strategy rather than through "storm and hurricane of battle." [80] The Federal general was overrating himself a bit; the strategy was applied at Chattanooga, not Cumberland Gap.

Nothing of value had been left to the Federals in the evacuated fortress. Five siege guns which could not be removed were disabled and thrown off a precipice. Stevenson fell back toward Morristown, as ordered, and prepared to make a stand at Bean's Station and Clinch Mountain.

On the date of evacuation of Cumberland Gap, General Braxton Bragg, who had succeeded the ailing Beauregard, wired that re-enforcements were ready as soon as he could determine the intention of the enemy facing him. Kirby Smith also renewed his appeal to Richmond for more men. Re-enforcements were necessary to victory, he urged. A defeat would mean "the loss of the salines on one side and store-houses and arsenals on the other." [81] Another request was also sent to Governor Brown of Georgia. Could he not send enough men to fill up the ranks of the nine Georgia regiments in East Tennessee? Their average strength had fallen to about 400.[82]

[80] Report of G. W. Morgan, June 22, 1862, *ibid.*, Vol. X, pt. 1, 57–62.

[81] Braxton Bragg to E. Kirby Smith, June 18, 1862, *ibid.*, Vol. XVII, pt. 2, 610; E. Kirby Smith to W. H. Taylor, June 21, 1862, *ibid.*, Vol. XVI, pt. 2, 696–97.

[82] *Id.* to J. E. Brown, June 20, 1862, *ibid.*, 694.

A part of Morgan's force followed Stevenson. The advance guard reached Tazewell on June 20. Kirby Smith thought this was only a foraging party, but, on June 21, Stevenson reported the presence of the enemy in force. An advance upon the Morristown Road was suspected. Clinch Mountain must not be given up without a fight, ordered the commanding general. But in case passage was forced at Bean's Station, the Confederate concentration would be in the vicinity of Rutledge.

Orders went out to all commanding officers on June 22. Barton, at Blair's Cross-Roads, was to await instructions from Stevenson as to when to move up to Rutledge. Reynolds was to set out from Loudon early the next morning, leave the cars at McMillan's Station, and hurry to Blair's. There he would meet Taylor's Brigade and both would await further orders. Starnes, temporarily on the Kingston road, was at first ordered to report to Knoxville, but he too was sent on to Blair's Cross-Roads. Thirty cars and two extra locomotives were rushed to Chattanooga to pick up 2,000 men. They were to arrive at Rutledge by the afternoon of the twenty-fourth. This would bring the concentrated forces up to between 10,000 and 12,000 men. Chief Quartermaster J. L. Morgan was instructed to rush corn and provisions from Morristown to New Market.[83]

This feverish concentration of Confederate forces was in vain. No battle was fought at either Clinch Mountain or Rutledge. Morgan's main force had remained at Cumberland Gap, waiting for Buell to apply more pressure at Chattanooga. While waiting General Morgan sent a dispatch to his old friend Kirby Smith, addressing him

[83] J. F. Belton to J. W. Starnes, June 22, 1862, *ibid.*, 699; E. Walworth to *id.*, June 23, 1862, *ibid.*, 703; Belton to S. M. Barton, June 22, 1862, *ibid.*, 700; *id.* to A. W. Reynolds, June 23, 1862, *ibid.*, 701; *id.* to C. L. Stevenson, June 22, 1862, *ibid.*, 700; *id.* to Danville Leadbetter, June 22, 1862, *ibid.*, 699; *id.* to J. L. Morgan, June 22, 1862, *ibid.*, 701.

as the "Comd. of Opposing Forces." It was returned unopened, marked "not properly addressed." Morgan then sent a personal note. "In memory of 'Auld Lang Syne,' " he said, "accept a couple of bottles of wine, which I brought with me from across the waters. . . . How strange, and how sad it is, that we, and our old comrades should be arrayed in arms against each other. I could not restrain the gush of tears upon hearing of the death of poor Bee. . . ." He was pleased to report that Kirby Smith's nephew, Colonel Kirby Smith, was commanding a brigade under General Halleck. He was eagerly awaiting the day, Morgan concluded, when "we may meet as public, as well as private friends." [84]

At the outbreak of the war Morgan had been in private life, after recently serving as minister to Portugal. The wine bore the date of 1796. Kirby Smith sent both bottles to his wife at Lynchburg. She could keep one for use in case of sickness, he suggested; the other they would "empty to Morgan's health" when peace was declared. The wife, not exactly appreciating the tone of Morgan's letter, replied: "I *hope* you may defeat this *same* Morgan & take him prisoner & I don't care what you do with his army." [85]

During the hot and troublesome days of mid-June, 1862, Kirby Smith, like most of his staff and his servant Aleck, was suffering from typhoid fever. This fact was not made known at Richmond or to his wife. His trusted friend and adjutant, Major Clay, had been so dangerously ill that it was necessary to send him to the care of relatives at Macon, Georgia. He returned to Knoxville on June 24. Anxiety over family affairs further increased General Kirby Smith's burdens. His wife was an expectant mother

[84] G. W. Morgan to E. Kirby Smith, June 26, 1862.

[85] E. Kirby Smith to Wife, June 30, July 2, 1862; Mrs. E. Kirby Smith to E. Kirby Smith, July 4, 1862.

and very unhappy over the physical change and the restraint on activities which had necessarily accompanied such a condition. What a change a year had brought, she wrote half-complaining—from a belle at the Springs with beaux dancing attendance to a matronly looking expectant mother. And when she heard that a relative had given birth to twin girls she remarked: "I trust it will not be the lot of *others* of the family to have them."

Cassie Selden Smith was a proud young lady, reflecting all of the characteristics of her aristocratic background. She had no intense love for the institution of slavery, but she was resentful of what she considered a Negro's war. The little Negro Julia was asleep on the floor by her bed, she wrote her husband late at night. The Negro race was the cause of all the trouble, "and we the sufferers—whilst they revel in happiness and ease." Her hatred for Yankees was exceeded only in her great admiration for her soldier husband.[86]

The threats and counterthreats of Kirby Smith and his opponents in East Tennessee were of minor importance when compared to the great battles being fought on the Virginia front during the summer of 1862. McClellan with 100,000 men on the Peninsula was moving against Lee's 85,000 defenders of Richmond. All military men realized that defeat of Lee would seriously endanger Confederate resistance. Defeat would be "our death warrant," Kirby Smith confided to his wife. "Were our army at Richmond annihilated we would offer but a divided & imperfect opposition elsewhere." Victory, on the other hand, would "seal our nationality." He considered Lee's defense "glorious," but not decisive. In retreat, McClellan had shown "generalship of the highest order." No doubt his army had

[86] See numerous letters from Mrs. E. Kirby Smith to E. Kirby Smith, March–July, 1862.

"reached a degree of discipline rarely acquired." What Lee was able to do before Richmond was all important. "My anxiety is intense," he confided to his wife. "Our fate, our future, our existence hangs upon it." [87]

Kirby Smith was also much concerned about his aged mother, who down in St. Augustine was fighting the battle of her life trying to keep out of trouble with the Yankees. *"Old Bravo"* the mayor, she reported in disgust, and the council, "much like him, all low ignorant Minorcans, puffed up by their devotion to office," had raised the white flag as soon as *two row* boats rounded the point—and afterwards assisted in raising on the Fort *their* flag." But patriotic Sally Hardy and other ladies rushed to the plaza and cut down the Confederate flag pole. They would have no Stars and Stripes waving from that staff!

Putnam, Kate, and the children had left for Palatka, leaving just Mrs. Smith and her sister, Mrs. Putnam, alone in the home except for the two servants Peggy and old August. Mrs. Smith hoped they had enough corn, rice, and bacon to keep from starving. "I would *almost* starve before I would partake of an ounce of the Federal provisions." She was well, however, for her "energies seem to rise as there is occasion for business and resolution."

After two months of Federal occupation the old lady was even more bitter. "We are under the hand of the oppressor—" she exclaimed, "the *cords* are *drawn* upon us, tighter and tighter every day—The object, the avowed object of *the invaders,* is to subjugate us, to *exterminate* us—to *starve* us even into submission." But their only converts were the "Traitors, Unionists & Northern tradesmen," who, like the snake in the fable, had been "warmed in our bosom, nourished, made strong by ill gotten gains & have turned against us—a painful exhibition of the

[87] E. Kirby Smith to Wife, June 25, 29, July 2, 1862.

depravity of Human Nature." The invader's promise that life should go on as usual had been quickly violated. Martial law was proclaimed. No one was to be out at night or leave town without a permit. Houses belonging to secessionists were seized and servants "utterly" demoralized. "Our servants stray about the town without doing any work, perfectly *insubordinate,* they have their own way we have no redress." The window shades were drawn; she and Sister Helen stayed inside. To leave would mean surrender of the house and its contents.[88]

He felt for his old mother, Kirby Smith wrote his wife. A woman of her spirit must be suffering severely "in an atmosphere of Northern boastings and misrepresentations." To his mother he sent advice to be obedient to police regulations or move beyond the lines. As long as victory was in doubt, the invader's policy would appear assured, "the mask will be thrown off, violence & cruelty will be the natural growth of the unholy war which fanaticism and cupidity first inaugurated and now urges to the bitter end."

He too had had experience in a country where much of the population was hostile to his cause. "My policy, while firm has been mild and conciliatory with these people, who when I came were disloyal and disaffected. Success has attended my efforts, and thousands have returned to their homes & to the allegiance of the State & Confederate Government."[89]

Morgan remained at Cumberland Gap, thrusting forth a small column at intervals to keep Kirby Smith worried while Buell advanced toward Chattanooga and a junction with Mitchell. On June 27 Kirby Smith wired Bragg at

---

[88] Mrs. Frances K. Smith to E. Kirby Smith, March 12, 1862; *id.* to Mrs. E. Kirby Smith, May 20, 1862.

[89] E. Kirby Smith to Mother, May 25, 1862; *id.* to Mrs. E. Kirby Smith, June 25, 1862.

Tupelo: "Buell is reported crossing the river at Decatur and daily sending a regiment by rail toward Chattanooga. I have no force to repel such an attack."

Leadbetter reported the arrival of a portion of Buell's army at Bridgeport. At the other end of the department, Stevenson reported the arrival of 6,000 fresh troops to re-enforce Morgan at Cumberland Gap. But President Davis wired that even more re-enforcements than Kirby Smith had requested were being ordered to Chattanooga.[90] Kirby Smith's confidence and enthusiasm registered an increase. "Reenforcements are coming & Bragg is moving up to the Tenn—," he assured his wife, "so that if the attack is not precipitated on me—I shall be prepared to carry the war into Africa." [91]

Brigadier General Henry Heth arrived at Chattanooga on July 1. Kirby Smith reorganized his command into two divisions of four brigades each, Stevenson to command one division and Heth the other. Brigade commanders under Stevenson were Brigadier General S. M. Barton and Colonels James E. Rains, A. W. Reynolds, and T. H. Taylor. Under Heth were Brigadier General Danville Leadbetter and Colonels W. G. M. Davis, Benjamin Allston, and Nathan Bedford Forrest. The last two commanded cavalry brigades.

Shortly after Beauregard was superseded by Bragg, the latter had decided to send Forrest to Kirby Smith's department for the purpose of welding together an effective cavalry unit. Accompanied by ten men, including his brother, Captain Bill Forrest, Colonel Forrest had arrived in Chattanooga about the middle of June. Trouble began immediately. Forrest's fame as a cavalry leader was yet

---

[90] *Id.* to Braxton Bragg, June 27, 1862, *Official Records,* Ser. I, Vol. XVI, pt. 2, 709; *id.* to S. Cooper, June 27, 28, 1862, *ibid.,* 709–10; Jefferson Davis to E. Kirby Smith, June 25, 1862, *ibid.,* 707.

[91] E. Kirby Smith to Wife, July 2, 1862.

to be earned, and there was no great rush at this time to "ride with Forrest." Colonel John S. Scott of the First Louisiana was his senior, and the Louisiana boys objected to the proposed subordination of their leader. Kirby Smith first hoped to solve the problem by giving Scott and Forrest separate commands, but when not enough cavalrymen were available, he decided in favor of Scott.[92] The difficulty was eventually relieved by transferring Scott's cavalry to Kingston. Colonel J. J. Morrison's First Georgia, stationed at Kingston, was ordered to cross the mountains and join Forrest at McMinnville for a raid into Middle Tennessee. With Forrest also went Colonel John A. Wharton's Eighth Texas and W. J. Lawton's Second Georgia.[93]

On July 3 Major General John P. McCown arrived in Chattanooga with a division of 3,000 men from Bragg's army. Kirby Smith could now breathe with some ease. Still weak from typhoid fever, he retired to Montvale Springs near Knoxville to recuperate and to ponder the advisability of carrying the war to the enemy. Clay remained in charge of the Knoxville headquarters and kept in touch with his superior by courier.

Kirby Smith's recovery was rapid. Fresh air, cool nights, a little fishing, and the beautiful mountain scenery were just what he needed. He found the water at the Springs "an infallable cure for dyspepsia & all known ailings." Moving on to the Smokies for a few days, he climbed mountains, stood by great waterfalls, listened to the chase, and shot a fine buck. He returned to "that Knoxville treadmill" bubbling over with enthusiasm for the grandeur of this "Switzerland of America." He dreamed that he was once again on the frontier where nature's beauty eased the

[92] H. L. Clay to Henry Heth, July 5, 1862, *Official Records*, Ser. I, Vol. XVI, pt. 2, 722.

[93] E. Kirby Smith to *id.*, July 6, 1862, *ibid.*, 722; *id.* to J. J. Morrison, July 6, 1862, *ibid.*, 722–23.

anxiety of man. Then he awoke to reality—war, bloodshed, sorrow.[94]

Back at his Knoxville headquarters on July 19, Kirby Smith found the war news encouraging. Forrest had furnished the greatest thrill. Directed by the commanding general to move into Middle Tennessee, he had crossed the mountains by way of Altamont and arrived at McMinnville on July 11. Joined by Morrison, he proceeded by way of Woodbury, galloped into Murfreesboro in the early morning hours of the thirteenth, and played havoc with the entire command of Brigadier General T. L. Crittenden. The railroad and military installations were wrecked, and before nightfall 1,200 prisoners were on the march toward McMinnville.[95] By July 19 the captive officers, including two brigadiers, had arrived in Knoxville.

Again and again Forrest struck with silence and speed, reaching the outskirts of Nashville, cutting telegraph lines and keeping the Nashville and Chattanooga Railroad almost useless to Buell at Stevenson. Isolated Federal garrisons throughout Middle Tennessee were panicky. An attack upon Nashville was feared. Military Governor Andrew Johnson had Capitol Hill fortified, and swore that he would never be taken alive. Time and again, Forrest was reported repulsed, routed, destroyed, but he continued to ride. In relaying to Richmond the news of Forrest's Murfreesboro raid, Kirby Smith added: "This may delay Buell's movement and give General Bragg time to move on Middle Tennessee. The safety of Chattanooga depends upon his co-operation." [96]

[94] *Id.* to Wife, July 9, 11, 15, 19, 1862.

[95] For excellent descriptions of this and other Forrest raids, see Robert S. Henry, *"First With the Most" Forrest* (Indianapolis, 1944).

[96] E. Kirby Smith to S. Cooper, July 19, 1862, *Official Records*, Ser. I, Vol. XVI, pt. 2, 729.

Kirby Smith wired Bragg on July 19 and sent him a letter on the following day, stressing the fact that Buell's forces were being concentrated in the Stevenson-Bridgeport area. An attempt to cross the river was expected at any hour. "The successful holding of Chattanooga depends upon your co-operation," he warned. "It is your time to strike at Middle Tennessee." [97]

More than a month earlier Bragg had promised to move on Buell's rear, but he was still at Tupelo. Although an efficient organizer, Bragg was usually slow to move. To Kirby Smith he now replied that he was unable "to do more than menace and harass the enemy." But on July 22, however, he wired urging that the crossing of the river "be retarded by all means." Strong assistance was being sent to Chattanooga.

Bragg insisted that Kirby Smith go to Chattanooga and take command in person. "The officer I sent you [McCown], I regret to say, cannot be trusted with such a command, and I implore you not to trust him indeed with any important position." McCown had given evidence of a lack of "capacity and nerve for a separate, responsible command." High rank alone was responsible for his being sent to Chattanooga.[98] There was no doubt some justification for Bragg's criticism of McCown, yet one of the general's great weaknesses was failure to trust and to inspire his subordinates. Kirby Smith noted Bragg's advice but did not accept it in its entirety.

The commander of the Department of East Tennessee continued to urge Bragg to act. The nature of the country, the climate, and pressing needs elsewhere, he argued, were insurmountable obstacles to an enemy invasion of Ala-

[97] *Id.* to Braxton Bragg, July 19, July 20, 1862, *ibid.*, 730–31.
[98] Braxton Bragg to E. Kirby Smith, July 20, 1862, *ibid.*, Vol. XVII, pt. 2, 651; *id.* to *id.*, July 22, 1862, *ibid.*, Vol. XVI, pt. 2, 732.

bama or Mississippi during the present summer. Why not leave a small force to watch the Mississippi, "and, shifting the main body to this department, take command in person?" Chattanooga was a good base, supplies would be plentiful, the river could be easily crossed, and Middle Tennessee and possibly Kentucky lay open to advance of their combined commands. "I will not only co-operate with you, but will cheerfully place my command under you subject to your orders." His effective strength Kirby Smith estimated at about 18,000. Half of this number was with Stevenson, watching Morgan in the Cumberland Gap area.[99]

Bragg was in Montgomery when he received Kirby Smith's last appeal. On July 21 he had already started 34,000 troops under General Hardee on their way to Chattanooga. Making the fullest use of the railroads by way of Mobile, Montgomery, and Atlanta, the advance guard was in Chattanooga by July 27. Bragg arrived two days later; he and Kirby Smith went into conference on July 31.

[99] E. Kirby Smith to Braxton Bragg, July 24, 1862, *ibid.*, Vol. XVI, pt. 2, 734–35.

## CHAPTER VIII

# TO KENTUCKY AND BACK

THERE HAD BEEN some changes in the East Tennessee situation since Bragg had first been urged to come to Chattanooga. Morgan had greatly strengthened his position at Cumberland Gap, and, in co-operation with Buell, had been threatening Stevenson. Kirby Smith had ordered that Powell's Valley be "constantly scoured with cavalry" to guard against surprise. He had also gone to Morristown for a conference with his commanders. Then came a report that Buell was moving up Sequatchie Valley to join Morgan. Stevenson was ordered to attack if Morgan made a movement toward Kingston. On July 27 a Federal force was reported at Tazewell. Forrest, Scott, and Colonel John H. Morgan were alerted. John H. Morgan, whose cavalry command was returning from a raid into Kentucky, was ordered to Kingston.[1]

Kirby Smith had long been eager to move against his old friend G. W. Morgan, but now he also had his eyes beyond the Gap. His enthusiasm had been fired by a dispatch recently sent by John H. Morgan while raiding in the vicinity of Georgetown, Kentucky: "I am here with a force sufficient to hold the country outside Lexington and Frank-

[1] H. L. Clay to C. L. Stevenson, July 16, 17, 1862, *Official Records*, Ser. I, Vol. XVI, pt. 2, 728; J. F. Belton to *id.*, July 27, 1862, *ibid.*, 737; *id.* to E. Kirby Smith, July 27, 1862, *ibid.*, 736; *id.* to John H. Morgan, July 28, 1862, *ibid.*, 739.

fort. These places are garrisoned chiefly with Home Guards. The bridges between Cincinnati and Lexington have been destroyed. The whole country can be secured, and 25,000 or 30,000 men will join you at once. I have taken eleven cities and towns with very heavy army stores." [2] On the eve of his departure for Chattanooga to confer with Bragg, Kirby Smith notified Stevenson to prepare for the offensive.[3] To his wife he confided that the enemy would soon have "additional evidences that their scheme of subjugation is absurd and impracticable." [4]

Perfect harmony appears to have existed between Bragg and Kirby Smith in planning their offensives. Kirby Smith reported to his wife that he found Bragg "a grim old fellow, but a true soldier," whom men feared and respected but did not love.[5] Bragg made no show of authority as a result of his superior rank. He explained that he would have been considerably embarrassed entering the Department of East Tennessee had he not received an urgent invitation. "Neither of us have any other object than the success of our cause. I am satisfied no misunderstanding can occur from necessary union of our forces." [6] The sincerity of the two generals was beyond question, but the fact remained that the greatest strength comes from a unified command.

In their Chattanooga conference the two commanders agreed that Bragg should move into Middle Tennessee, with Nashville as his objective. The plan to extend his operations into Kentucky seems to have been of later development. Forrest's cavalry was to be re-enforced and left in Middle Tennessee to pave the way for Bragg's approach.

[2] John H. Morgan to E. Kirby Smith, July 16, 1862, *ibid.*, 733–34.

[3] E. Cunningham to C. L. Stevenson, July 28, 1862, *ibid.*, 738–39.

[4] E. Kirby Smith to Wife, July 28, 1862.   [5] *Id.* to *id.*, August 1, 1862.

[6] Braxton Bragg to E. Kirby Smith, August 8, 1862, *Official Records*, Ser. I, Vol. XVI, pt. 2, 745–46.

Kirby Smith, re-enforced by Brigadier General Pat Cleburne's division, was to assault Cumberland Gap. The responsibility for this decision remains in question. Kirby Smith later stated that the plan to assault was Bragg's idea. And Bragg reported that he advised against assault but withdrew his objection when Kirby Smith persisted. At any rate, should the Gap be taken, the two armies would then jointly invade Middle Tennessee.[7]

Kirby Smith returned to Knoxville and began the movement of his troops toward the Kentucky line. The cavalry forces of Scott and Morrison were ordered to Kingston to watch a Federal force under William Nelson which, in the vicinity of Sparta, was in position to move into East Tennessee. From Kingston, Scott and Morrison could move into Kentucky.

On August 9 Kirby Smith suggested to Bragg that the route by way of Sparta "would seem to be one of your natural lines of operation into Middle Tennessee." By this date Kirby Smith was seriously considering bypassing Morgan at the Gap and moving directly into the Kentucky bluegrass country. If, as was reported, Morgan proved to be well supplied with provisions, reducing the Gap would require much time. "As my move direct to Lexington, Ky., would effectually invest Morgan, and would be attended with other most brilliant results in my judgment," he told Bragg, "I suggest my being allowed to take that course, if I find the speedy reduction of the Gap an impracticable thing."[8]

All was put in readiness at Knoxville headquarters. Dr. S. A. Smith, medical director and staff physician, whom the Kirby Smith family always affectionately called "Old

[7] E. Kirby Smith to J. Stoddard Johnston, October 3, 1866; Braxton Bragg to Samuel Cooper, *Official Records,* Ser. I, Vol. XVI, pt. 2, 741.

[8] E. Kirby Smith to Braxton Bragg, August 9, 1862, *ibid.,* 748.

Doctor," pronounced the general fully recovered from the effects of fever and ready for campaign. Aleck looked after the personal baggage. William R. Boggs, in Kirby Smith's opinion, "one of the most able men in service," and John Pegram, "a man of great merit—a good soldier, a moral man and amicable and accomplished gentleman," had been added to the staff as chief engineer and chief of staff respectively. Boggs had been sent by the governor of Georgia. Kirby Smith had requested the governor to send all the assistance possible; the governor had replied that all he could send was some artillery harness and Boggs.

Of the experienced staff members, Cunningham and Meem, both of whom had spent much time courting Knoxville ladies, the latter to the extent of getting himself engaged, were to go along. Clay was in bed with a double fracture of the thigh, his horse having fallen on him. His wife had come to nurse him. "Cousin Win" Belton, much to his disgust, was to be left behind in charge of headquarters. The general himself, in preparation for the hard days ahead, had his hair cut short and his beard trimmed.[9]

On August 10 Bragg reported that it would be another week before he could begin crossing the river. His troops were still coming in. Kirby Smith need not worry about Nelson at Sparta, he explained, for Forrest would no doubt harass him "out of all ideas of advancing." If not, other forces would be sent to take care of him. Within the next week Bragg expected to make his own decision as to whether or not to march on Nashville or Lexington, Kentucky. "My inclination now is for the latter." It would be inadvisable, he thought, for Kirby Smith to move a great distance into Kentucky, leaving Morgan in the rear, until he himself had engaged Buell. Generals Van Dorn and

[9] *Id.* to Wife, July 28, August 4, 7, 8, 1862; William R. Boggs, *Military Reminiscences of Gen. William R. Boggs* (Durham, 1913), 34.

Price were to move up across West Tennessee simultaneously with the two armies to the east. "I trust we shall all
unite in Ohio." [10]

Kirby Smith pondered but not for long. He would get
to the rear of Morgan, he notified Bragg. If Morgan evacuated and tried to flee, he would give chase. If Morgan held
the fortification, he would wait until Bragg thought it safe
before moving on Lexington. But speed was the essential
thing, he insisted. Each day's delay greatly reduced the
chances of success. [11]

Brigadier General Stevenson, "an officer of worth and
merit" who had been "a treasure" to the Department, had
already moved up closer to Morgan's position and begun
skirmishing with enemy pickets. On August 12 Colonel
Scott's cavalry, 900 strong, and a battery of mountain
howitzers left Kingston for London, Kentucky, to get into
Morgan's rear and fall upon his supply line. Brigadier
General Heth, with the subsistence train and artillery, was
ordered to move through Big Creek Gap on Barboursville.
Kirby Smith himself, with Cleburne's and Churchill's
divisions, was to cross by way of Roger's Gap. If Morgan
allowed himself to be cut off with meager stores, Kirby
Smith remarked in explaining his plans to President Davis,
he must then either starve or surrender. On the other hand,
if Morgan's supplies were ample, then the Confederate
commander must himself decide whether "to invest" Cumberland Gap or "move into Kentucky." He favored the
latter. "It is the boldest and most brilliant in its results."
Morgan would be taken care of, Buell's communications
would be turned, and "if Kentucky be as ripe for the move
as all representations indicate it must involve the abandon-

---

[10] Braxton Bragg to E. Kirby Smith, August 10, 1862, *Official Records*,
Ser. I, Vol. XVI, pt. 2, 748–49.

[11] E. Kirby Smith to Braxton Bragg, August 11, 1862, *ibid.*, 751.

ment of Middle Tennessee by the Federals." Delay would be fatal. He could march on Lexington with 10,000 men and still leave Stevenson strong enough to check Morgan. Could not the popular Kentuckian, General Simon Bolivar Buckner, who had recently been released from Federal military prison, be sent to join him? "His name is a division in any movement on Kentucky." There was not a single Kentuckian of influence in the whole East Tennessee command.

As for the command of the Department of East Tennessee during his absence, Kirby Smith explained to Davis, he would like for McCown to remain in Knoxville. The course to be pursued there should be well marked out: "When the frontier has been disembarrassed of Morgan's command the conscript law should be enforced, and the 10,000 able-bodied men who have been so long protected in their rights by this Government should be made to stand shoulder to shoulder with its defenders. If the leading Union men have the alternative of becoming alien enemies or supporters of the Government and at the same time the conscript law be enforced, I believe a large proportion of the fighting population of East Tennessee will be with us, and those who run away will be a happy riddance." [12] Before leaving on the Kentucky campaign Kirby Smith issued a final appeal to deceived and misguided persons in the United States army to return to their homes, take the oath of allegiance to the Confederacy, and conduct themselves as good citizens. They would be paid a "fair price" for such arms as they brought home. [13]

Kirby Smith left Knoxville at 4 A.M., August 14. A day later he was at Big Creek Gap. Heth, McCown, Churchill, and Cleburne were with him. Morgan hurriedly

[12] *Id.* to Jefferson Davis, August 11, 1862, *ibid.*, 752–53.
[13] August 13, 1862, *ibid.*, 756.

called in his forces from Barboursville and Cumberland Ford. They would only be crushed, he feared, by this huge Confederate army, reported to number 25,000 to 35,000 men. And he had learned that the total Confederate strength in East Tennessee was more than 80,000! But he was determined not to yield, he explained, as long as he had "a pound of meat and an ounce of powder." [14]

Leaving Stevenson, Rains, and Barton with 9,000 men in front of Cumberland Gap, Kirby Smith, with Cleburne's and Churchill's divisions—6,000 strong—passed through Roger's Gap and on August 18 arrived at Barboursville, "a dilapidated village" but "the metropolis of this mountain region." Heth and Leadbetter, with 3,000 men, passing by way of Big Creek Gap, arrived four days later. The advance column of Kirby Smith's army surprised and captured about 50 prisoners and a like number of wagons at Barboursville. Meem, the general's aide-de-camp, personally forced the surrender of about half the number. Meem's spirit was worth a whole regiment, Kirby Smith exclaimed.

Scott's cavalry, moving in from Kingston, fell upon an enemy regiment at London, taking 75 prisoners, 40 wagons, and 175 mules. For all concerned in the Confederate advance, the going had been tough. Marching day and night over rough mountain roads, dragging wagons and artillery by hand, carrying their meager rations on their backs, the men became ragged and footsore, some wearing out their shoes entirely, and marking their bare tracks with blood. But their commander heard no murmur of complaint. The accomplishment of his men, Kirby Smith reported, was "a feat rivaling the passage of the Alps." No fewer than ten regiments were "truly exiles from families and home, with their hearthes desolated, their property de-

---

[14] Report of George W. Morgan, August 19, 1862, *ibid.*, pt. 1, 860.

stroyed and their wives & children at the mercy of a ruthless foe," yet there was no vindictive spirit, no murmur of complaint. Many were veterans of Belmont, Shiloh, Elkhorn, Springfield—"a rough wild ragged looking assemblage," but subordinate, cheerful, and in numerous cases, very religious.[15]

The country around Barboursville was truly enemy territory. "Bushwhackers" immediately began operations on exposed Confederate forces. Barboursville itself was "loaded with most flaming demonstrations of bad taste or patriotism," Kirby Smith wrote his wife. Printed on the paper on which he wrote was "The Spangled Banner is waving over South Carolina." The Confederates were indeed coolly received by the residents.[16]

The country around Barboursville had been drained of its meager supplies, and Kirby Smith realized that he must either move forward into central Kentucky or fall back into East Tennessee. To fall back, he thought would be disastrous to the Confederate cause in Kentucky. "I have therefore decided to advance as soon as possible upon Lexington," he notified Bragg. If he accomplished nothing more than the seizure of quantities of supplies he could fall back to his present position and still be much better off. But he had hope of brilliant results. Kentuckians would be given an opportunity to rally to the Confederate banner. And such a move would also help Bragg in the handling of Buell.[17]

Bragg sent word that he himself would probably start moving within the week, and Kirby Smith decided to move on August 25. Bearers of dispatches from Bragg were Wil-

[15] E. Kirby Smith to Wife, August 19, 21, 23, 1862; *id.* to S. Cooper, April 24, 1862, *Official Records,* Ser. I, Vol. XVI, pt. 2, 777–78; J. S. Scott to John Pegram, August 17, 1862, *ibid.,* pt. 1, 937.

[16] E. Kirby Smith to Wife, August 19, 1862.

[17] *Id.* to Braxton Bragg, August 20, 1862, *Official Records,* Ser. I, Vol. XVI, pt. 2, 766–67; *id.* to Jefferson Davis, August 21, 1862, *ibid.,* 768–69.

liam G. Brent and Paul F. Hammond. They reached Kirby Smith's army while it was still at Barboursville. Hammond, a brother-in-law of Major Clay, who upon Clay's suggestion was to be added to the staff as a volunteer aide, left an interesting description of General Kirby Smith as he stood on the threshold of his first real test as a commander: [18]

> He is thirty-seven. You would not be impressed as by a man of remarkable intellectual endowments, but the phrenologist would say, that his high, receding forehead, narrow at the base, but prominent over the eyes, and widening as it ascends, gives evidence, if not of great mental powers, of uncommon quickness of perception and rapid mental movements. Tall, sinewy, not graceful, every gesture indicates intense physical activity and muscular vigor. In perfect health, black haired, black bearded and mustached, slightly graying, black eyes, penetrating and restless, swarthy complexion; the simple statement of these features might give the idea of only the rude, rough soldier; but on the contrary, with the exception of the gentle Pegram, I have known no officer of the army more habitually under the influence of the kindlier virtues and emotions. An earnest Christian and a gentleman, pleasant manners flow naturally from the goodness of his heart, while an impulsive temper is kept under almost perfect control.

Colonel John H. Morgan, who had been sent by Kirby Smith to destroy the railroad connecting Nashville and Louisville, reported success. Near Gallatin, Tennessee, he captured a freight train loaded with supplies for Buell, emptied the cars of all usable supplies, and pushed the burning train into an 800-foot tunnel. The tunnel supports collapsed.[19] Morgan was ordered to continue his good work, moving on toward Lexington, where Kirby Smith expected to be by early September. General Humphrey Mar-

[18] Paul F. Hammond, "General Kirby Smith's Campaign in Kentucky in 1862," in *Southern Historical Society Papers* (Richmond, 1876–1910), IX (1881), 246–47.

[19] For an interesting account of Morgan's raids see Cecil Holland, *Morgan and His Raiders* (New York, 1942).

shall, operating independently in southwest Virginia, was urged to enter Kentucky through Pound's Gap, and begin co-operative operations in Morgan County. Stevenson was to cling to Morgan until the Federal general either surrendered or evacuated Cumberland Gap. In either case he would then push the majority of his forces forward to join Kirby Smith's main army. McCown, who had expressed grave doubts as to the propriety of advancing further into Kentucky, was ordered to return to Knoxville and take over temporary command of the department. Should Morgan abandon the Gap, McCown was to begin the enforcement of the conscript law, arming and forwarding recruits and convalescents as rapidly as possible. All leading East Tennessee citizens suspected of disloyalty to the Confederacy were to be required to take the oath or leave the state.[20] The return of McCown to Knoxville released "Cousin Win" Belton to join his hero at the front. He was so disgusted with East Tennessee and its people that he never wanted to see them again.[21]

"I have prayed for assistance and counsel from on high, and trust God will direct me on the path of victory and success," Kirby Smith assured his wife. "I have too much confidence in the justness and goodness of God to believe he will let us fail—and but think that like the Egyptians of old he has hardened their hearts & blinded their eyes only to make their destruction the more complete." The step he was about to take was a bold one, and he might be severely censured. "I care not what the world may say, I am not ambitious. . . . I shall conscienciously do my

[20] E. Kirby Smith to Jefferson Davis, August 21, 1862, *Official Records,* Ser. I, Vol. XVI, pt. 2, 768–69; J. F. Belton to C. L. Stevenson, August 22, 1862, *ibid.,* 769; E. Kirby Smith to Humphrey Marshall, August 20, 1862, *ibid.,* 767; John Pegram to J. P. McCown, August 24, 1862, *ibid.,* 776; Boggs, *Reminiscences,* 36.

[21] J. F. Belton to Mrs. Kirby Smith, September 5, 1862.

duty." Like Cortez he was burning his ships behind him; he must move forward into the bluegrass country.[22]

The cavalry forces of Scott, Morrison, and Starnes were instructed to clear the country toward Richmond, Kentucky. Mount Vernon was occupied. The pickets around Crab Orchard were driven in and then the town bypassed. Scott crossed over to the London and Richmond road. Mid-afternoon, August 23, he approached Big Hill, which was occupied by the Seventh Kentucky Cavalry under Colonel Leonidas Metcalfe and a battalion of Houk's Third Tennessee (Union) under Lieutenant Colonel John C. Chiles. Scott ordered a charge, and Metcalfe rushed to meet the attack only to find that he was almost alone on the field. A mere handful of men had made a gesture toward the onrushing Confederates. The remainder, according to Federal accounts, "at the first cannon-shot, turned tail and fled like a pack of cowards," and soon dispersed themselves over several counties, "some fleeing as far as Paris."

Houk's Tennessee Unionists fought well, preventing total destruction, but were forced to fall back toward Richmond. Metcalfe was furious. Never again, he swore, would he lead those cowardly Kentuckians in battle. As Union provost marshals were attempting to carry out General Orders No. 2 to round up and arrest those who had fled, Scott was sending to the rear the spoils of battle, increasing his total to 175 wagons and 650 horses and mules captured since he entered Kentucky. "I have now captured all the trains on both roads to the Gap," he reported, "and do not see how I can subsist many days longer without going down into the blue-grass region, and this I cannot do without being sustained by infantry." He would, therefore, pitch camp on the London-Richmond road between Big

22 E. Kirby Smith to Wife, August 21, 24, 25, 1862.

Hill and Rock Castle River, rest his men, and await further orders.[23]

Kirby Smith's infantry was already on the move before Scott's report was received. Cleburne's division had led the move out of Barboursville on August 25. With his army of 12,000 men, Kirby Smith declared he would "fight everything that presents itself." If Kentuckians in the bluegrass region rallied to the Confederate cause all would be well. Their sentiments would soon be put to the test. Scott, as commander of advance forces, was ordered to insist upon "the most perfect decorum of conduct toward the citizens and their property." [24]

No serious opposition was encountered as the Confederates moved through the narrow passes of the rugged Kentucky mountains. But soon after the advance guard had descended Big Hill into the edge of the bluegrass, an enemy force was reported a short distance ahead. Scott's cavalry, now re-enforced by Starnes's Third Tennessee, galloped off on reconnaissance. It was soon driven back upon Cleburne's infantry. The pursuing Federal cavalry dismounted when Cleburne's infantry opened fire. A lively skirmish continued until darkness and Confederate bullets compelled the Federals to withdraw toward Richmond. It was late afternoon, August 29.[25]

Kirby Smith was pleased with the enemy's apparent decision to give battle at this point. He had feared that the minor opposition encountered in the Big Hill country was a result of an enemy decision to fall back to the natural defenses furnished by the high bluffs of the Kentucky

[23] Report of Lewis Wallace, August 24, 1862, *Official Records*, Ser. I, Vol. XVI, pt. 1, 884; General Orders, No. 2, August 26, 1862, *ibid.*, 885; Reports of J. S. Scott, August 24, 1862, *ibid.*, 885–87.

[24] E. Kirby Smith to Braxton Bragg, August 24, 1862, *Official Records*, Ser. I, Vol. XVI, pt. 2, 775–76; John Pegram to J. S. Scott, August 24, 1862, *ibid.*, 778.

[25] Report of P. R. Cleburne, September 1, 1862, *ibid.*, pt. 1, 944.

River. But if the Federals were now ready to make a stand, Kirby Smith calculated, a severe defeat followed by Confederate pursuit would give the enemy insufficient time to make a strong stand short of Lexington or perhaps the Ohio River.[26]

While Cleburne's men slept on their arms "in line of battle and without any supper," General Kirby Smith was writing his wife: "I am with my advance in the bluegrass region. . . . We have marched 110 miles through a mountain region over almost impassable roads, through a country destitute of supplies of all kinds—ragged bare footed almost starved marching day and night, exhausted from want of water. I have never seen such suffering. . . . Such fortitude, patriotism and self control has never been surpassed by any army that ever existed." His success in entering the Bluegrass he attributed to surprise, otherwise he could never have "forced the passes of the Kentucky mountains." [27]

Regardless of the reasons for success, Kirby Smith's army had left behind that "barren mountain country" with its "ferocious and bitterly hostile population," and was about to enter the "garden of Kentucky, teeming with inexhaustible supplies." [28]

During the evening of August 29, Kirby Smith instructed Cleburne to push ahead early the next morning. Meanwhile a Federal courier was galloping for Lexington. He knocked on the door of Major General William Nelson's Lexington headquarters at 2:30 A.M. He brought a message from Brigadier General Mahlon D. Manson at Richmond. The Confederates in force were before him, he said. What should he do? Nelson advised him not to

[26] Hammond, "Kirby Smith's Campaign in Kentucky in 1862," *loc. cit.*, 250.
[27] E. Kirby Smith to Wife, August 29, 1862.
[28] Hammond, "Kirby Smith's Campaign in Kentucky in 1862," *loc. cit.*, 249.

fight, but to retreat by way of the Lancaster road. But if Manson received this reply at all, it was probably after firing had begun.

August 30 "dawned bright, clear and beautiful." Cleburne's division was on the march by daybreak. Scott's cavalry soon located the enemy in position at Mount Zion near the village of Rogersville, a few miles short of Richmond. Although Churchill's division was some distance to the rear, Cleburne ordered Douglas' battery to open fire, and sent for Martin's battery to hurry forward. A courier galloped up, bringing an order from Kirby Smith not to become involved in a general engagement until Churchill's division was up.

Cleburne slowed down his artillery fire, and a light duel continued for more than an hour. The enemy began an advance. Kirby Smith arrived on the scene about 7:30 A.M. Churchill came up about the same time. He was directed to move to his left, drive in the enemy's right, and cut off retreat toward Richmond. Leaving one brigade in reserve, Churchill took Colonel T. H. McCray's Texans and Arkansans and proceeded through a cornfield and a ravine to the correct position. Simultaneously, the enemy attempted to turn Cleburne's right but was beaten back by Colonel Preston Smith. By this time Churchill had begun his charge. The enemy fell back along the road to a new position on White's farm about two miles distant. In the midst of the engagement Cleburne, described by his immediate superior as "one of the most gallant, zealous, and intelligent" of officers, was wounded in the mouth, rendering him speechless. Colonel Preston Smith took command of the division.

Kirby Smith was determined to move on to Richmond. Giving the enemy little time to reorganize, he again instructed Churchill to drive in the Federal's right flank. The enemy, "concealed by a cornfield and a skirt of timber," opened a terrific musket and artillery fire. Churchill replied with artillery and ordered his infantrymen to hit the ground, protecting themselves by a ditch. Quietly they waited for a "full five minutes" while the enemy advanced to within fifty yards of the ditch. Then came the order to "rise, fire and charge." The Federals stopped, stood their ground momentarily, and then "gave way in every direction." McCray's brigade now being exhausted, Churchill ordered his other brigade, commanded by Colonel Evander McNair to give pursuit. Kirby Smith had directed Preston Smith to drive in the enemy's left, but the battle was over before he could get into position. Churchill's Texans and Arkansans had absorbed the full shock.

In the midst of the excitement, Kirby Smith, momentarily abandoning "the admirable coolness" which he had previously shown, "rushed to the front in the act and perfect spirit of charging with his staff alone, hardly looking even if they followed." But Pegram checked him and persuaded him not to expose himself needlessly.

It was now midafternoon. Major General Nelson had just ridden into Richmond. The Confederates heard the Federals shout as their commander appeared and were confused as to the meaning. Without knowing that a battle was on, Nelson had ridden out from Lexington to supervise withdrawal of troops along the Lancaster road. As he arrived at Lancaster about 9:30 A.M. he heard the firing. Procuring a fresh horse, he and a single staff member, traveling byroads to avoid Confederate cavalry, rode for Richmond at top speed. He found the Federal forces "in a disorganized retreat or rather rout." Manson reported for instructions. A stand would be made at the cemetery on the edge of the town.

From a wounded Federal soldier Kirby Smith learned

of Nelson's arrival. Night was fast approaching. The Confederate commander resolved to give the enemy the chance neither to bring up re-enforcements nor to withdraw under the cover of darkness. The town was about two miles away.

Nelson hastily threw up fortifications on a ridge just outside of town, making use of stone fences and the cemetery. For the third time, Kirby Smith directed Churchill to drive in the enemy's right. Preston Smith's division "at a double-quick" charged the center and left. Nelson's forces fell back, both sides suffering heavy casualties. In Nelson's words: "Our troops stood about three rounds, when struck by a panic, they fled in utter disorder." Through the town and a mile beyond the Yankees fled; tired Rebel infantry could pursue them no farther. It was now the cavalry's turn.

Colonel Scott with 850 men had been sent around the town to take position on the Lexington and Lancaster roads and make ready to catch the fleeing Federals. Setting up his batteries so as to cover both routes of escape, he began to pick up stragglers about 4 o'clock. About 6 o'clock the great mass of "poor, discomfited fugitives rushed pell-mell into the ambuscade." The catch was good but many slipped through and escaped into cornfields and woods. Darkness finally ended the chase. General Manson attempted escape but his horse was shot and fell on him. He was made prisoner. General Nelson was wounded and captured, but later escaped into a cornfield. Far into the night, companies of weary Confederates continued to bring in their prisoners of war.

Meanwhile, their commander was busy dictating orders of congratulation and appreciation. "The country shall know of your sufferings on the march," he assured his tired army, "as well as the bold, pressing charges of this day."

The following day being Sunday, it was his desire that troops assemble with their chaplains and "return thanks to Almighty God, to whose mercy and goodness these victories are due." [29]

The battle of Richmond was over. A full day of marching and fighting had given Kirby Smith's army a complete victory. Cleburne's and Churchill's veterans were too much for the raw recruits from Kentucky and Indiana. The Confederate losses: 78 killed, 372 wounded, one missing. The Confederate gain: more than 4,000 prisoners, the enemy's entire wagon train and stores of supplies, 10,000 stands of arms, and nine pieces of artillery. Nelson reported 206 killed, 844 wounded, 4,303 captured or missing. [30]

"The battle was fought in direct disobedience to my orders and those of General Nelson," declared Major General Horatio G. Wright, commander of the Department of Ohio, on the day following the humiliating defeat. It was "brought on" by Manson. In reviewing the events, Manson himself made no mention of Nelson's order not to fight, but he gave some significant information as to why the rout was so complete. He had arrived in Richmond only three days before the battle. The troops he found there were for the most part men of ten to twenty-five days service. "Some of the regiments never had had a battalion drill and knew not what a line of battle was. They were undisciplined, inexperienced, and had never been taught in the manual of

[29] *Ibid.*, 251; Reports of E. Kirby Smith, August 30, September 3, 6, 16, 1862, *Official Records*, Ser. I, Vol. XVI, pt. 1, 931–35; Report of P. R. Cleburne, September 1, 1862, *ibid.*, 944; J. S. Scott, September 11, 1862, *ibid.*, 938–39; T. J. Churchill, September 8, 1862, *ibid.*, 940–41; Preston Smith, September 16, 1862, *ibid.*, 946–49; William Nelson, August 31, 1862, *ibid.*, 908–909; M. D. Manson, September 10, 1862, *ibid.*, 910–16; General Orders, No. 10, September 30, 1862, *ibid.*, 936.

[30] Return of Casualties in Union Forces, *Official Records*, Ser. I, Vol. XVI, pt. 1, 909; Table of Casualties [Confederate], *ibid.*, 936.

arms." [31] This did not explain, however, why he led such raw troops into battle instead of retreating. Kirby Smith was probably correct in his belief that the surprise was complete. Manson probably thought he was opposed by a small force come down to forage in the bluegrass region.

Sunday, August 31, was spent in burying the dead, caring for the sick, and making preparations for a forward movement. In the evening Scott was ordered to move his cavalry forward to the Kentucky River. The next day he chased scattered bands of Federal cavalry around Lexington and as far as Georgetown. On September 3 he entered Frankfort. Having no suitable Confederate flag with him, he raised the flag of the First Louisiana Cavalry over the Capitol.

On September 1 Kirby Smith started his infantry toward Lexington. Scattered bands of Federals offered slight resistance and then fell back. A few miles beyond the Kentucky River the troops were halted for rest and food. The men were beginning "to feel fully the effects of their arduous labors for the past fortnight, and straggled badly." A Mr. Todhunter, an elderly gentleman of wealth and Confederate sympathy, insisted that Kirby Smith accept the hospitality of his mansion nearby. While eating dinner, the general was interrupted by the exciting news that a Yankee cavalry force was approaching. While other staff members buckled on their swords and pistols, Pegram rushed out to reconnoiter. The "Yankees" were only Scott's cavalry clad in blue uniforms captured at Richmond. Kirby Smith, not wishing any more such excitement, ordered that henceforth only Yankees should wear blue.[32]

[31] H. G. Wright to H. W. Halleck, August 31, 1862, *ibid.*, 907; Report of M. D. Manson, September 10, 1862, *ibid.*, 910–916.

[32] Hammond, "Kirby Smith's Campaign in Kentucky in 1862," *loc. cit.*, 290–91.

Kirby Smith was uneasy. If Lexington should be strongly defended, his straggling troops would not be equal to the task before them. It was doubtful whether more than 2,500 effective men could be thrown into an immediate attack. Instructions were rushed to Heth at Richmond to unload his provision wagons, reload them with men, and hurry toward Lexington. By 8:00 A.M. the following day no fewer than 2,000 new troops had come up.

In the meantime, Pegram had been sent boldly forward to demand the surrender of Lexington. He met no pickets and soon learned that the town had been evacuated the previous day. After some delay the mayor was finally located, and he formally surrendered the town. Kirby Smith rode into town the following day, September 2. John H. Morgan made his dramatic entrance into his home town on September 3. "As we rode forward in the morning," a member of Kirby Smith's staff later recalled, "the scene was lovely beyond description—a brilliant river and fresh sweet atmosphere; a long rolling landscape, mellowing under the early Autumn rays, but still covered with luxuriant blue grass, intersected with numerous low stone fences crossing each other at right angles, and studded with brick mansions and little whitened outhouses also of brick, with gray plastered chimneys, flocks of sheep, the fine bred horses and immense cattle browsing on the pastures or lying under the stately trees, the air of quiet and of order, the evidences of neat substantial comfort and wealth reminded us of English rural scenery." Indeed from the time they crossed the Kentucky River, "where the lovely blue grass country burst upon our sight, we were astonished and enchanted." Again, the Confederate officers reasoned, they were among people of culture, among friends. Townspeople in large numbers turned out to greet the Confederates, but it was noted that very few men were among them. It was explained that Union men had run away and Confederate sympathizers, still not convinced, were afraid to leave their houses. The ladies of Lexington presented Kirby Smith with a flag, which continued to wave at his headquarters for the duration of the war.[33]

"The Army of the Confederate States has again entered your territory under my command," Kirby Smith proclaimed throughout the bluegrass region.[34]

Let no one make you believe we come as invaders, to coerce your will, or to exercise control over your soil. Far from it. The principle we maintain is that government derives its just power from the consent of the governed.

I shall enforce the strictest discipline in order that the property of citizens and non-combatants may be protected. I shall be compelled to procure subsistence for my troops among you, and this shall be paid for.

Kentuckians: We come not as invaders but as liberators. We come in the spirit of your resolutions of 1798. We come to arouse you from the lethargy which enshrouds your free thought, and forbodes the political death of your state.

We come to test the truth of what we believe to be a foul aspersion, that Kentuckians willingly join the attempt to subjugate us, and to deprive us of our prosperity, our liberty, and our dearest rights.

We come to strike off the chains which are rivited [sic] upon you. We call upon you to unite your arms and join with us in hurling back from our fair and sunny plains the Northern hordes who would deprive us of our liberty, that they may enjoy our substance.

Are we deceived? Can you treat us as enemies? Our hearts answer, "No!"

"My entrance into the blue grass region of Kentucky has been a perfect ovation," the general wrote his wife. "Old and young have flocked to me, and with tears in their eyes have thanked God for their deliverance from persecu-

---

[33] Ibid., 291–92; E. Kirby Smith to Mrs. C. C. Clay, May 8, 1890, Clay Papers.
[34] Undated copy in Kirby Smith Papers.

tion. . . . I wish you were with me to share the honors which have been heaped upon me and to witness the heart felt thanks with which I have been greeted." Recruits were coming in by the thousands.[35]

A courier was hurriedly dispatched to Knoxville to carry the details of victory and urge General McCown to rush forward all available arms. "Kentucky is rising *en masse*," Chief of Staff Pegram joyfully told McCown. "If the arms were here we could arm 20,000 men in a few days." [36] But Kirby Smith confided to Confederate authorities at Richmond, that, although it "would be impossible for me to exaggerate the enthusiasm of the people here," continued success depended upon Bragg's action against Buell and the policy of the Confederate government in defending loyal Kentuckians against the armed hordes collecting at Cincinnati and Louisville.[37]

Speculation was rife in Kirby Smith's camp. If Bragg would now play his part by defeating Buell, Kentucky would be rescued. Grant must then evacuate Mississippi and move up to the Ohio line of defense. Van Dorn would then be free to cross into Arkansas and move against the Federals in Missouri. In short, Kirby Smith's invasion could easily be the beginning of the expulsion of all Yankees from Southern soil.[38]

Many Union sympathizers themselves thought this might well be true. Excitement in Louisville and Cincinnati became intense. "To arms!" cried the Cincinnati *Gazette*.[39] "The time for playing war has passed. The enemy is now rapidly approaching our doors." General Lew Wallace declared martial law within the city, closed

[35] E. Kirby Smith to Wife, September 4, 6, 1862.

[36] John Pegram to J. P. McCown, September 5, 1862, *Official Records*, Ser. I, Vol. XVI, pt. 2, 797.

[37] E. Kirby Smith to S. Cooper, September 6, 1862, *ibid.*, pt. 1, 933.

[38] Hammond, "Kirby Smith's Campaign in Kentucky in 1862," *loc. cit.*, 293.

[39] September 2, 1862.

all business houses, and ordered citizens to assemble for work on fortifications.[40]

Kirby Smith himself was enthusiastic, but he was conscious of difficulties and dangers. He now occupied a very advanced position. He must be vigorous in collecting all the fruits of his victories, yet sufficiently cautious to avoid being trapped by the enemy. Colonel Scott, "active, efficient, and daring," was given the multiple assignment of scouting the country, especially toward Louisville, distributing copies of the Proclamation wherever he went, preventing citizens from sending off their cattle and hogs to Ohio, and giving protection to volunteers who wished to enlist in the Confederate service. He was to watch the race between Buell and Bragg, and if the former got into the lead, to destroy the bridges along the Louisville and Nashville Railroad.

Leadbetter was dispatched to Lebanon to drive off the small enemy force there and collect the stores before they could be carted off to Louisville. Heth was pushed forward near Covington, and in conjunction with Preston Smith, was to occupy Cynthiana, Georgetown, and Paris. John H. Morgan would report to him and the two might discuss a possible cavalry raid into Ohio. Four companies of cavalry under Captain Robert McFarland, were rushed back to Somerset to check upon the rumor that General Morgan was evacuating Cumberland Gap. If no definite news could be had at that point, McFarland was to "push on toward the Gap" until reliable information could be had.

All commanders were enjoined to observe three important principles of policy—require their troops to "behave in an orderly manner, as otherwise the people cannot

[40] Cincinnati *Gazette*, September 3, 1862; New York *Herald*, September 3, 1862.

be favorably impressed"; compel Home Guards to surrender their arms and accept parole, pledging to give no further assistance to the Union cause; and risk no engagement unless sure of success. A reverse at this critical time, the commanding general warned, would seriously affect the attitude of citizens, retarding the progress of recruiting.[41]

On September 7 and 8 Kirby Smith sent urgent appeals to General Humphrey Marshall, enclosing copies of the Proclamation. Could he not "hasten as rapidly" as possible his "march toward Cynthiana and Falmouth, in order to support General Heth, who [might] attack the enemy at any moment"? Would he not also see to it that his troops conduct themselves as friends of the citizens, giving particular attention to "the order relative to horse thieving"? [42]

Marshall was a hard commander from whom to get even a semblance of co-operation. He was excessively eager to preserve his own independence. Early in March, 1862, he had conceived the idea of penetrating Kentucky from southwestern Virginià. General Lee passed the proposal on to Kirby Smith, who had just taken command in East Tennessee, adding: "General Marshall has been directed to place himself in communication with you and to regulate his movements by any instructions he may receive from you; though it is not the wish of the President that you withdraw him from that section of country or control his operations, unless you find it feasible to unite with him in an advance into the State of Kentucky." [43]

---

[41] John Pegram to J. S. Scott, September 8, 15, 1862, *Official Records,* Ser. I, Vol. XVI, pt. 2, 803, 829; H. P. Pratt to *id.,* September 9, 1862, *ibid.,* 804; E. Cunningham to *id.,* September 11, 1862, *ibid.,* 811–12; John Pegram to Henry Heth, September 10, 17, 1862, *ibid.,* 807, 838; *id.* to Danville Leadbetter, September 6, 1862, *ibid.,* 799; *id.* to John H. Morgan, September 11, 1862, *ibid.,* 813; *id.* to Robert McFarland, September 10, 1862, *ibid.,* 807.

[42] E. Kirby Smith to Humphrey Marshall, September 7, 10, 1862, *ibid.,* 801, 807.

[43] R. E. Lee to E. Kirby Smith, March 15, 1862, *ibid.,* Vol. X, pt. 2, 330.

It would seem from these instructions that Kirby Smith was not exceeding his authority in sending appeals to Marshall. A third appeal was sent on September 12. Would Marshall hurry to Paris "as rapidly as possible"? A formidable enemy concentration had been reported at Louisville and Covington.[44]

On this same date, Marshall was writing a reply to Kirby Smith's note of September 7. It had always been the intention of the President that he "raise a separate army to be commanded by myself," Marshall explained. However, he was willing to co-operate in all movements for the good of the cause, and he hoped that Kirby Smith would place no barrier in the way of his securing recruits for his command.[45] Kirby Smith sent this note to Bragg and requested that Bragg set Marshall right.[46]

By this time Bragg had moved his army into Kentucky. The concentration of his forces at Chattanooga had been delayed far beyond expectations. Buell had made the fullest use of this delay in bringing up his own troops, which opposed Bragg in half-moon formation extending from Stevenson, Alabama, to McMinnville, Tennessee, the river and the mountains separating the two armies. Bragg had finally moved on August 28, two days before the battle of Richmond. Marching up the Sequatchie Valley to Pikeville and across the mountains to Sparta, he passed around Buell's left wing. Near Sparta he received a dispatch from Kirby Smith, telling of his success and urging Bragg to move into Kentucky and effect "a junction with my command and holding Buell's communications, to give battle to him with superior forces and with certainty of success."

44 E. Kirby Smith to Humphrey Marshall, September 12, 1862, *ibid.*, Vol. XVI, pt. 2, 814–15.

45 Humphrey Marshall to E. Kirby Smith, September 12, 1862, *ibid.*, Vol. LII, pt. 2, 349.

46 E. Kirby Smith to Braxton Bragg, September 16, 1862, *ibid.*, Vol. XVI, pt. 2, 833–34.

Bragg abandoned whatever intentions he had toward Middle Tennessee and continued his march to Carthage, Gainesboro, and the Cumberland River. Hearing of Nelson's defeat at Richmond, Buell fell back to Nashville and made ready to be attacked. Andrew Johnson strengthened the fortifications around Capitol Hill. Bragg kept on marching.[47]

From Red Sulphur Springs he notified Cooper: "My advance will be in Glasgow to-day and I shall be with them to-morrow. My whole force will be there on the 14th." He would then be between Buell and Kirby Smith, the position for which he had been struggling. Buell was following and his advance was now at Bowling Green. "From Glasgow we can examine him and decide on the future." [48]

Kirby Smith was impatient. Daily reports brought rumors of large concentrations of Federal troops at Cincinnati. A portion of Grant's army was said to be moving up the river to Louisville. Should a large force move from the Ohio, the advanced Confederate force at Lexington would be threatened so seriously that Kirby Smith would be forced to fall back, losing most of the supplies accumulated there. Furthermore, a withdrawal would greatly retard the recruiting he had undertaken. "Unless, however," he wrote Bragg, "you can either speedily move your column in this direction or make with me a combined attack upon Louisville before all of Grant's army arrives there I shall be compelled to fall back upon you for support. Louisville is in my opinion the great point to be arrived at, and the destruction of the force now there, can, I think, be accomplished without difficulty." [49]

[47] See manuscript article by Kirby Smith on the Kentucky campaign in Kirby Smith Papers; Stanley Horn, *The Army of Tennessee* (Indianapolis, 1941), 167.

[48] Braxton Bragg to S. Cooper, September 12, 1862, *Official Records,* Ser. I, Vol. XVI, pt. 2, 815.

[49] E. Kirby Smith to Braxton Bragg, September 15, 1862, *ibid.,* 830.

Kirby Smith found recruiting in the bluegrass country a difficult task. Most young men who favored the Confederacy had already signed up. Those who had been undecided were still not convinced. Response was much slower than he had anticipated, he wrote his wife, "but when I see their magnificent estates their fat cattle & fine stock I can understand their fears & hesitancy—they have so much to lose." [50]

He still had 10,000 stands of arms which had been captured at Richmond, Kirby Smith informed Bragg. "The Kentuckians are slow and backward in rallying to our standard. Their hearts are evidently with us, but their blue-grass and fat cattle are against us." However, a number of regiments were in the process of organization, and if time permitted, the arms ought to be taken up. If General Breckinridge were only present in the bluegrass country, regiments would be more easily filled. [51]

Bragg moved steadily onward. Kirby Smith had expected him to give battle to Buell at Horse Cave, but he did not. On September 16 he threw full strength upon the Federal garrison at Mumfordville, which surrendered without firing a shot. "My junction with Kirby Smith is complete," he notified General Cooper. "My position must be exceedingly embarrassing to Buell and his army. They dare not attack me, and yet no other escape seems open to them." [52]

Bragg was indeed in an enviable position. Squarely across Buell's communications with Louisville and destroying the railroad as he went, he could move on to Louisville or fight, whichever he pleased. Ample supplies

---

[50] *Id.* to Wife, September 16, 1862.

[51] *Id.* to Braxton Bragg, September 18, 1862, *Official Records,* Ser. I, Vol. XVI, pt. 2, 845–46. There is an error in the printed copy of this dispatch where "fat grass" is used in the place of "fat cattle." This error has been corrected.

[52] Braxton Bragg to S. Cooper, September 17, 1862, *ibid.,* pt. 1, 968.

could be had in central Kentucky, and re-enforcements from Kirby Smith and Humphrey Marshall were within reach. Had the general wanted to fight, he could scarcely have chosen a better position than the line of the Green River.

Kirby Smith sent congratulations, thirty wagons of "flour and hard bread," and placed himself subject to Bragg's command. He ordered Cleburne's and Preston Smith's brigades to Shelbyville, a position from which they could readily join in a march on Louisville. The remainder of his command he withdrew to Paris, Georgetown, and Frankfort, from which points movement could be made in either direction. Since the defenses at Louisville appeared to be so weak that Bragg's force alone could take them, Kirby Smith urged Bragg not to call up so many troops as to leave central Kentucky unnecessarily exposed. He particularly desired to keep a portion of Scott's cavalry for scouting duty. "A descent unexpectedly upon Richmond by the old troops of Morgan would at this time greatly embarrass me." [53]

Kirby Smith was much concerned about his old friend Morgan. Spies sent to the vicinity of Cumberland Gap were unanimous in reporting Federal preparations for evacuation. For two months Morgan had sparred with the Confederate force under Stevenson, with no important results. It was feared that the Federals might come out of the Gap still eager for a fight. Little did outsiders, not even the War Department at Washington, suspect the serious plight of the garrison. When supplies ran dangerously low, Morgan had sent out a foraging party. McCown reported this from Knoxville, stating that the foragers had 500 wagons. He doubted, however, if Morgan intended to evacuate.[54] What

[53] E. Kirby Smith to Braxton Bragg, September 18, 19, 1862, *ibid.*, pt. 2, 845–46; John Pegram to Henry Heth, September 18, 1862, *ibid.*, 844.

[54] J. P. McCown to E. Kirby Smith, September 16, 1862, *ibid.*, 836.

McCown did not know was that instead of hauling in adequate supplies the foraging party itself almost starved in the barren wilds of Clay County.

After September 6 Morgan's men had no bread; after September 12, there was no forage for animals. The choice must be surrender, starvation, or evacuation. But so effective was General Stevenson's investment, evacuation seemed almost impossible. A Kentucky surveyor who was present thought there was a chance. He pointed out to Morgan a line of retreat along an old trail known as Warrior's Path, which led through eastern Kentucky to the Ohio River. Few supplies and little water could be expected along the route.

Morgan called a council of his three fellow brigadiers, and they decided to try the route of escape. There were many East Tennessee Unionists in the garrison. To them almost anything would be preferable to the humiliation of surrender. Evacuation began on September 16 and by September 19 the advanced guard had reached Manchester, Kentucky. After two days of rest and reorganization at Manchester, the march was resumed.

Kirby Smith suspected that Morgan might attempt escape by way of Manchester, Booneville, and Mount Sterling. He urged grouchy, slow-moving Marshall to hurry to the vicinity of Mount Sterling and intercept Morgan's exhausted force. Speed and co-operation were most essential, for Bragg had ordered Kirby Smith to be ready for a joint movement on Louisville on September 23. Colonel John H. Morgan was placed in charge of the cavalry units and ordered to the vicinity of Irvine, where he could scour the country around Booneville and toward Manchester.[55]

Occupying a position from which he could move in any

55 Report of G. W. Morgan, October 3, 1862, *ibid.*, pt. 1, 992–96; E. Kirby Smith to Humphrey Marshall, September 18, 1862, *ibid.*, pt. 2, 846; E. Cunningham to J. H. Morgan, September 19, 1862, *ibid.*, 851.

of three directions, Kirby Smith was enthusiastic, even happy. A defeat of Buell he felt would furnish that "complete assurance" that was necessary to cause Kentuckians openly to espouse the Confederate cause; for "the hearts of the people are with us." They had suffered too much oppression in their complete Union subjugation to be aroused instantaneously. And if Buell's defeat could be accompanied by victory in Maryland, peace "on an honorable basis" might also be expected.[56]

Central Kentuckians and even Union soldiers had been much impressed by the bearded young general. When a Union relief group came from Cincinnati under a flag of truce to take care of the wounded, Kirby Smith treated the members with great kindness. One member inquired if there was anything he could do for the general in repayment for this kindness. There was. Kirby Smith would like a note written to his sister Frances.

Upon returning to Cincinnati, A. B. Coleman wrote the note. The general looked remarkably well, was "in fine spirits & apparently happy," he told Frances. The people were much attached to him. "You will readily perceive that there are very many (too many) here who do not give proper credit to those *in the service* of the opposition to us, but my experience causes me to wish that more of our people might be brought in contact with your brother & the other officers whom we met, and there would be less rancour & ill feeling; as an intimate knowledge of their kindness (such as extended to us) would gratify any reasonable person." [57]

Kirby Smith waited impatiently for Bragg's order to march on Louisville. It did not come; Bragg had decided neither to fight Buell immediately nor to attack Louisville.

[56] E. Kirby Smith to Wife, September 20, 1862.
[57] A. B. Coleman to Frances Webster, September 23, 1862.

Bearing to his right, he marched on Bardstown, permitting Buell to move to Louisville unmolested, except for a few stings from Joe Wheeler's cavalry. In an attempt to justify his course, Bragg later reported: [58]

With my effective force present, reduced by sickness, exhaustion, and the recent affair before the intrenchments at Mumfordville, to half that of the enemy, I could not prudently afford to attack him there in his selected position. Should I pursue him farther toward Bowling Green he might fall back to that place and behind his fortifications. Reduced at the end of four days to three days' rations, and in a hostile country, utterly destitute of supplies, a serious engagement brought on anywhere in that direction could not fail (whatever its results) to materially cripple me. The loss of a battle would be eminently disastrous. I was well aware also that he had a practicable route by way of Morgantown or Brownsville to the Ohio River and thence to Louisville. We were therefore compelled to give up the object and seek for subsistence.

Did Bragg expect a battle to last more than three days! There is no truth that his effective strength was not more than half that of Buell. Had he ordered Kirby Smith to join him, their combined strength probably would have exceeded that of Buell. No amount of explaining can remove the guilt of incompetence.

On September 21, from near Hodgenville, Bragg wrote Kirby Smith presumably apprising him of the decision to get out of Buell's path. The letter has been lost, but Kirby Smith's reply indicates disappointment if not criticism: "I regard the defeat of Buell before he effects a junction with the force at Louisville as a military necessity, for Buell's army has always been the great bugbear to these people, and until defeated we cannot hope for much addition to our ranks from Kentucky." His infantry and artillery, about 11,000, he assured Bragg were ready. General Marshall, he hoped, could be depended upon to watch

[58] Report of Braxton Bragg, May 20, 1863, *Official Records*, Ser. I, Vol. XVI, pt. 1, 1088 ff.

any advance from Covington and assist John H. Morgan in checking on the forces from Cumberland Gap. "With regard to supplies, I have large quantities at Danville and am also collecting them at Frankfort." [59] Two days earlier he had written Bragg that available wagons had been loaded at Frankfort and Danville and were on their way to Bardstown.[60]

Kirby Smith was willing to join Bragg in a move on Louisville if the commanding general so ordered, but he had a feeling that his services would be more valuable in other places. He felt "every confidence in the ability of General Bragg to take Louisville" without assistance; therefore, he represented to him "the exposed condition in which I shall have to leave this rich section, with an enemy toward Cincinnati and another toward the Gap." Had it not been for Bragg's order to hold himself in readiness, Kirby Smith would have threatened Covington and Cincinnati. He feared that a junction with Bragg anywhere below Louisville "both loses us the valuable stores and supplies captured here and checks the organization of new levies now in fair progress." [61]

John H. Morgan sent in the report that the Union forces from Cumberland Gap had passed through Booneville and were on the way to Proctor. Morgan had first encountered this escaping Union force at Manchester. He continued to harass them as they moved on toward Proctor,

[59] E. Kirby Smith to Braxton Bragg, September 23, 1862, *ibid.,* pt. 2, 866.
[60] *Id.* to *id.,* September 21, 1862, *ibid.,* 861.
[61] *Id.* to *id.,* September 21, 1862, *ibid.,* 861; *id.* to Humphrey Marshall, September 21, 1862, *ibid.,* 859. Years later, after he had developed a considerable dislike for Dr. S. A. Smith, Boggs, later Kirby Smith's chief of staff, "inferred" that the Doctor persuaded Kirby Smith not to attack Cincinnati. But he gave no reason why Dr. Smith wished no such attack (Boggs, *Reminiscences,* 41). President Davis later stated that Kirby Smith probably could and would have taken Cincinnati had he not felt it his duty to remain in position to co-operate with Bragg (Jefferson Davis, *The Rise and Fall of the Confederate Government,* 2 vols. [New York, 1881], II, 382–83).

attacking on the flank and scattering a herd of cattle, then riding to the front and placing obstructions in the road. Union General Morgan later related that "it several times happened that while the one Morgan was clearing out the obstructions at the entrance to a defile, the other Morgan was blocking the exit from the same defile with enormous rocks and felled trees." [62]

Kirby Smith alerted Marshall at Mount Sterling, and then decided to move his own entire force to join Marshall. If General Morgan continued his present course, he would be met at Mount Sterling. Should he abandon his artillery and move into the mountains, he would be pursued by cavalry. General Stevenson, whose force of between 6,000 and 8,000 men had been following Morgan at a distance since the evacuation of Cumberland Gap, was ordered to give up the chase and report to Bragg at Harrodsburg.

Kirby Smith went in person to Mount Sterling on September 25, but he notified Bragg that both his and Marshall's troops would be held in readiness to co-operate with Bragg's army.[63] He confided to his wife that Morgan's evacuation of the Gap was the "finishing touch to our brilliant little campaign," for the Federal general must either suffer defeat or be driven into the mountains toward the Big Sandy, a wild region destitute of supplies. In either case, Kirby Smith would then be ready to co-operate with Bragg "to decide the fate of Kentucky." [64] There was certainly no good reason for Kirby Smith's not trying to intercept Morgan, for by the time the former arrived at

[62] George W. Morgan, "Cumberland Gap," in R. U. Johnson and C. C. Buell (eds.) Battles and Leaders of the Civil War, 4 vols. (New York, 1884, 1888), III, 62–69 (hereinafter cited as Battles and Leaders) ; Report of G. W. Morgan, October 12, 1862, Official Records, Ser. I, Vol. XVI, pt. 1, 992–96.

[63] E. Kirby Smith to Humphrey Marshall, September 24, 1862, ibid., pt. 2, 869–70; id. to Braxton Bragg, September 25, 1862, ibid., 873; G. W. Brent to G. G. Garner, September 25, 1862, ibid., 874–75.

[64] E. Kirby Smith to Wife, September 27, 1862.

Mount Sterling Buell's army was entering Louisville. Bragg was resting.

Morgan did not move into the trap set for him at Mount Sterling but chose the mountain route to safety. Bearing to his right, he crossed Licking River at West Liberty and continued by way of Grayson to Greenup and on to the Ohio. John H. Morgan's Confederate cavalry continued delaying tactics until the Federal force reached Grayson and then gave up the fight. General Morgan made good his escape, but he was in neither condition nor position to help Buell. Bragg later very weakly claimed that Kirby Smith's chase to intercept Morgan "prevented a junction of our forces, and enabled General Buell to reach Louisville before the assault could be made upon that city." [65] Was not Bragg in command of all troops? If he had not approved of Kirby Smith's efforts he could have ordered otherwise. The fact that Bragg did not interfere, however, places upon Kirby Smith the responsibility for allowing Morgan to escape.

By September 30 Kirby Smith was back at his Lexington headquarters. Two days later Bragg, leaving his own force under command of General Leonidas Polk at Bardstown, ordered Kirby Smith's forces to concentrate at Frankfort for the gala celebration that was to accompany the inauguration of a Confederate governor of Kentucky. In theory Kentucky was now a Confederate state, and the fact must be impressed upon the people. Bragg thought a Confederate state administration would be a great boost to morale, although it was supported by troops. A logical candidate for the office of governor was Richard Hawes, who had been chosen lieutenant governor in the Confederate government set up at Russellville in 1861.

[65] Report of Braxton Bragg, May 20, 1863, *Official Records,* Ser. I, Vol. XVI, pt. 1, 1088 ff.

Kirby Smith later related that he tried to persuade Bragg to give up the inauguration and begin concentrating his troops for a showdown with Buell. But Bragg replied that his command at Bardstown alone could handle Buell. The inauguration would go on. Kirby Smith then prevailed upon General Simon B. Buckner, as a Kentuckian, to try to dissuade Bragg. Buckner also failed.[66]

The approach of Federal troops broke up the inaugural ceremony, and the Confederates were forced to "skedaddle," Kirby Smith wrote his wife. Buell, his supplies replenished, had begun moving out of Louisville on October 1. His left wing, commanded by General A. M. McCook, divided—one division under J. W. Sill moving toward Frankfort by way of Shelbyville and the other two under McCook himself moving on Taylorsville. The remaining two corps of Buell's army under T. L. Crittenden and C. C. Gilbert began closing in on Bardstown. Bragg had made poor use of his cavalry for scouting purposes and was left with the mistaken idea that Sill's division was the main body of Buell's army. Accordingly, on October 2, he ordered Polk to move toward Frankfort and strike the enemy's flank while Kirby Smith struck from the front.[67]

Kirby Smith later severely criticized Bragg for not knowing that Buell's full force was in his own front.[68] The criticism is just, but there is no evidence that Kirby Smith himself was any better informed. If this was Buell's advance, he hurriedly wrote Polk at Bardstown, then their two commands were "too far apart and beyond supporting distance." On the same day Bragg notified Kirby Smith

---

[66] E. Kirby Smith to J. Stoddard Johnston, October 31, 1866. See also Kirby Smith article in Kirby Smith Papers.

[67] Braxton Bragg to Leonidas Polk, October 2, 1862, *Official Records*, Ser. I, Vol. XVI, pt. 2, 896–97.

[68] E. Kirby Smith to J. Stoddard Johnston, October 31, 1866.

that "our whole force must be brought to bear at the same time." [69] But no one knew where to concentrate.

Polk hesitated in carrying out Bragg's order of October 2 to move toward Frankfort. On the following day he received another, stating that since the Federal move on Frankfort appeared to be a feint he might use his own judgment.[70]

Bragg was still badly confused. On October 4 he ordered Polk to draw up in front of Harrodsburg and to send J. M. Withers' division to re-enforce Kirby Smith. And Kirby Smith was instructed to move forward toward Versailles. On October 7 Kirby Smith received word from Stevenson that Colonel Scott reported the enemy, 20,000 strong, crossing the river at Frankfort. The news was rushed on to Bragg, and Kirby Smith, without waiting for further orders, notified his commanders to concentrate in the vicinity of Versailles. From that point he hoped either to strike the force that crossed at Frankfort, or, in case that move was only a feint, to "cover the Kentucky River with my whole command at Lawrenceburg" and move up on Bragg's right. And should Bragg decide to concentrate to the rear of Harrodsburg, Kirby Smith could retreat toward Nicholasville.

Kirby Smith himself hurried to Versailles ahead of his main force. General Withers, recently arrived from Bragg's army, was directed to hold Lawrenceburg in order to protect the crossing of Stevenson's and Heth's commands, which Kirby Smith stated numbered 18,000 men. John H. Morgan was sent to cross the river at or above Frankfort to destroy the enemy's supply train and harass his rear.[71]

[69] *Id.* to Leonidas Polk, October 3, 1862, *Official Records,* Ser. I, Vol. XVI, pt. 2, 901; Braxton Bragg to E. Kirby Smith, October 3, 1862, *ibid.*
[70] *Id.* to Leonidas Polk, October 3, 1862, *ibid.,* 903–904.
[71] C. L. Stevenson to John Pegram, October 7, 1862, *ibid.,* 920; Pegram

On October 8 Kirby Smith learned that the enemy had moved out of Frankfort. He then ordered his concentration at Lawrenceburg. At 9:30 P.M. he informed Bragg that Sill, 10,000 strong, was encamped on the Lawrenceburg-Bardstown road, about five miles from Lawrenceburg. His own advance was less than two miles from town. He was sending Withers and Churchill to cross Salt River and attack the enemy in front, while he himself led an attack on the rear. The time for attack was set at dawn, October 9. If the information received were correct, he prophesied that the "victory will be most complete." Should the enemy retreat before the attack was made, Kirby Smith would then "move for Buell's rear or flank," unless Bragg directed otherwise.[72]

Kirby Smith entered Lawrenceburg at 3:30 A.M., October 9, only to learn that the enemy was ten miles away, "too far for us to overtake them." He then issued orders for his entire force to move to the support of Bragg, "who is between Harrodsburg and Perryville." To Bragg he wrote, "If I had had rations I should have pushed after Sill and got in Buell's rear; as it is, I am hurrying rapidly to your assistance."[73]

Bragg's battle had already been fought without the assistance of Kirby Smith. The latter later stated that he got the news of the battle of Perryville on the evening of October 9. On October 7 Hardee's corps of Bragg's army reached the village of Perryville and took up a strong position defending the water holes of Doctor's Creek. Continued dry weather had made such water holes precious.

---

to J. M. Withers, October 8, 1862, *ibid.*, 924; *id.* to J. H. Morgan, October 8, 1862, *ibid.*, 925–26; E. Kirby Smith to Braxton Bragg, October 7, 1862, *ibid.*, 920.

[72] *Id.* to *id.*, October 8, 1862, *ibid.*, 925; John Pegram to *id.*, October 8, 1862, *ibid.*

[73] E. Cunningham to J. M. Withers, October 9, 1862, *ibid.*, 928; E. Kirby Smith to Braxton Bragg, October 9 (2 dispatches), 1862, *ibid.*, 927–28.

Close on Hardee's heels was the center of Buell's army under Gilbert. The two forces were soon engaged in a struggle for drinking water. Hardee called for re-enforcements; Bragg directed Polk to take Cheatham's division to the rescue. But still not knowing that it was the main portion of Buell's army now engaging Hardee, Bragg did not recall Withers from Kirby Smith. And he further informed Polk that as soon as the enemy was routed near Perryville, he should move to the support of Kirby Smith in the vicinity of Versailles.

Hardee rushed to Bragg a polite but urgent request to reconsider his order dividing his forces, insisting that wherever the enemy was met it should be with full force. "If it is your policy to strike the enemy at Versailles," Hardee implored, "take your whole force with you and make the blow effective." On the other hand, if Buell was to be met at Perryville then all available forces should be rushed to that point.[74] Bragg did not heed the advice; consequently, when Polk arrived at Perryville and took command he had only about 12,000 men. Buell's potential strength was some 58,000, although only about 22,000 men became engaged.[75] Buell himself was so ignorant of Bragg's blunder that he failed to strike a crushing blow.

The morning of October 8 was spent in light skirmishing and "shelling the woods," while Polk sent Joe Wheeler's cavalry to ride around the Federal flanks and report both position and numbers. Bragg had ordered Polk to open battle immediately, but Polk, receiving additional information as to the enemy's superiority in numbers, called a council of war and decided to await developments. When Bragg heard no firing and failed to receive explana-

---

[74] W. J. Hardee to Braxton Bragg, October 7, 1862, *ibid.*, pt. 1, 1099.
[75] D. C. Buell, "East Tennessee and the Campaign of Perryville," in *Battles and Leaders*, III, 31 ff.

tion of the delay, he rode from Harrodsburg to Perryville, arriving about 10:00 A.M. At 1:00 P.M. the Confederates opened attack upon McCook's corps on the Federal left. Bloody fighting continued for the remainder of the day, the Federals falling back more than a mile, leaving the Confederates in possession of the battlefield.[76] There was no decisive victory. Fighting men on both sides assumed that the battle would be resumed on the following day.

But Bragg again decided to surrender the initiative. Instead of calling Kirby Smith and Marshall to his assistance, he first ordered a return to the position held before the battle, but by the following morning he had his entire force on the march towards Harrodsburg. And by the time Kirby Smith reached this point on October 10, Bragg's army was moving out toward Camp Dick Robertson.

Kirby Smith rushed to Bragg and urged him to do an about face and throw their combined force of 60,000 veterans against Buell.[77] "For God's sake, General, let us fight Buell here," he begged. "I believe that without a command even, our men would run over Buell's army composed, as it more than half is, of new levies." Bragg felt encouraged and resolved to give battle. "I will do it, sir," he replied. "Select your position, put your men in line of battle and I will countermarch my column." A loud shout went up from Kirby Smith's veterans.

A position just outside Harrodsburg was selected, and the remainder of the day was spent in preparing fortifications. Bragg inspected the position during the afternoon and ordered a few alterations. He returned to Harrodsburg for the night, and Kirby Smith pitched his tent near the

[76] Reports of Braxton Bragg, October 20, 1862, and May 20, 1863, *Official Records,* Ser. I, Vol. XVI, pt. 1, 1088 ff; Reports of D. C. Buell, October 9, November 4, 1862, *ibid.,* 1022 ff.

[77] Basil W. Duke later estimated Bragg's potential strength at 68,000. See Duke to Kirby Smith, October 20, 1866.

field. By midnight the enemy was reported less than a mile away. At 3:00 A.M. Bragg sent for Kirby Smith. They remained in conference until almost dawn, the time for battle. Kirby Smith slowly returned to the field. There would be no battle, he informed his officers. Instead, a rapid retreat would begin immediately. "I disagreed with him & combatted his objections," he later explained, "contending that we had supplies & provisions and should risk an engagement before evacuating the country. But Bragg replied that he could not afford to risk the destruction of his army." [78]

Bragg reported to Richmond that he again offered battle at Harrodsburg but the enemy declined; so he withdrew toward his base of supplies at Bryantsville. He halted for two days at Camp Dick Robertson as if he intended to offer battle. But soon the combined forces were ordered to begin the long retreat to Cumberland Gap. Again Bragg assigned a shortage of supplies as the cause for his decision. Had he remained in central Kentucky until the fall rains, he explained, bad roads and a shortage of supplies would probably have resulted in the loss of his entire army. To Kirby Smith, however, this retreat remained the most humiliating incident in his military career. In after years he wrote that the campaign "ended most ingloriously, and for the first time in the history of the Confederacy, an army of veterans retreated before an inferior force largely made up of new levies." [79]

No doubt an opportunity for a Confederate victory had slipped away. The dangers of which Bragg seemed to have been overconscious were more apparent than real. None

[78] Hammond, "Kirby Smith's Campaign in Kentucky in 1862," *loc. cit.,* X, 73; E. Kirby Smith to J. Stoddard Johnston, October 31, 1866; Kirby Smith article in Kirby Smith Papers.

[79] Report of Braxton Bragg, May 20, 1863, *Official Records,* Ser. I, Vol. XVI, pt. 1, 1088 ff; E. Kirby Smith to J. Stoddard Johnston, October 31, 1866; Kirby Smith article.

were so great that they could not have been overcome by
a competent general. And if Buell had been an aggressive
fighter he would have capitalized on Bragg's timidity and
indecision and crushed his divided command. How much
advice Kirby Smith gave Bragg cannot be determined;
therefore, his responsibility for the humiliation to Confederate arms cannot be assessed. There is no indication that
he was better informed than Bragg, yet in his recent invasion of central Kentucky he had shown aggressiveness
and a strong desire to fight. It is clear, however, that after
Bragg's arrival, Kirby Smith definitely considered himself
in a subordinate position. As Sill was approaching Frankfort on October 5, he had written his wife from Versailles:
"Gen. Bragg is in command—I am no longer at head of
affairs but have only to obey orders." But he was convinced
that if Bragg expected to "maintain his position in Kentucky he must fight Buell." [80]

The way back was long and hard; there was no spirit
or enthusiasm to alleviate the suffering. Buell was content
to see the Confederates leave and had no intention of attempting a crushing blow. Bragg moved by way of Mount
Vernon and Crab Orchard, Kirby Smith by Big Hill, and
Marshall left by way of Richmond for Pound's Gap and
southwestern Virginia.

Bragg placed Wheeler in charge of all cavalry and
directed him to report to Kirby Smith. The latter, before
leaving Bryantsville, ordered Wheeler to cover the river
crossings and protect the flanks of both retreating columns.[81] Kirby Smith's advance reached Lancaster about
midnight October 13–14. At 1:30 A.M. he reported to
Bragg at Crab Orchard: "My command from loss of sleep
for five nights, is completely exhausted. The straggling

[80] E. Kirby Smith to Wife, October 5, 1862.
[81] John Pegram to Joseph Wheeler, October 13, 1862, *Official Records*,
Ser. I, Vol. XVI, pt. 2, 939–940.

has been unusually great. The rear of the column will not reach here before daybreak. I have no hope of saving the whole of my train, as I shall be obliged to double teams in going up Big Hill, and will be necessarily delayed there two or three days. There is quite a strong position in front of Big Hill, which I will hold as long as possible." [82]

A day later Kirby Smith was engaged in getting his and much of Bragg's train up Big Hill while an enemy advance was threatening Stevenson, who was bringing up the rear. "I have little hope of saving any of the train, and fear much of the artillery will be lost. I shall push forward the ordnance and provision trains first." [83] But Kirby Smith was irritated and unduly pessimistic, for his men, who lined the hill from foot to summit, when "starved and tired mules faltered and fell, seized the wagons and lifted them by sheer force over the worst places." All day, all night, and until noon of the following day, "the trains, in one unbroken stream, continued to pour over Big Hill, and then the troops followed." [84]

The Confederates were again in the land of Unionists. Bushwhackers were more aggressive than ever, firing upon soldiers in both the line of march and in camp. This, however, encouraged stragglers to keep up. By October 17 Kirby Smith was at Big Rockcastle River; his command extended back to Big Hill. He was growing more resentful of alleged mistreatment by Bragg. He thought Bragg had chosen the direct route and sent him the hard way, he complained to Polk. "His trains have been turned off on my line, delaying me two days, my command working day and night pulling them up Big Hill. I gave his wagons the

[82] E. Kirby Smith to Braxton Bragg, October 14, 1862, *ibid.*, 943.

[83] *Id.* to *id.*, October 15, 1862, *ibid.*, 949.

[84] Hammond, "Kirby Smith's Campaign in Kentucky in 1862," *loc. cit.*, X, 75.

preference, when I would have secured the safety of my columns had I not been encumbered with them and might have done it by moving on with my train alone. My train is now turned off by a circuitous route and one that is almost impassable, and on which they must be delayed a long time, if not abandoned." And now Kirby Smith was informed that Bragg intended moving his army off and leaving his own flanks exposed. "Cannot we unite and end this disastrous retreat by a glorious victory?" he inquired of Polk.[85]

There was no junction of Kirby Smith and Polk's commands for the purpose of giving battle; thanks to the effectiveness of Wheeler's cavalry operations no enemy force made a serious threat. The Army of Kentucky crawled slowly through London, Barboursville, and Cumberland Gap into East Tennessee. From Flat Lick, Kentucky, on October 20, Kirby Smith formally resumed command of the Department of East Tennessee. It was hoped that the shortage of supplies would be relieved when the army reached the Gap; Kirby Smith had sent advance orders for the collection of food for soldiers and animals at posts along the way beyond the Gap. But he was soon complaining that "all along my route reports reach me of the provisions left for my men being seized by the Army of the Mississippi." And from Cumberland Gap he reported that at least 10,000 of his command were scattered over the country "trying to find something upon which to live." Another 6,000 would probably soon be forced to join in the search.[86]

Bragg had already reached Knoxville, and while Kirby Smith was writing his discouraging report a courier from

[85] E. Kirby Smith to Leonidas Polk, October 17, 1862, *Official Records*, Ser. I, Vol. XVI, pt. 2, 959.
[86] *Id.* to Braxton Bragg, October 22, 1862, *ibid.*, 975.

Bragg's headquarters was on his way bearing new orders. Kirby Smith would leave 3,000 men at Cumberland Gap and rush the remainder of his command to Kingston preparatory to an invasion of Middle Tennessee. Kirby Smith was astounded and enraged. After failing to give battle to Buell when their combined armies were in excellent fighting condition, why should Bragg now wish to undertake a new campaign when the men were worn out and half-starved? His reply was short and to the point: "The condition of my command now is such as to render any immediate operations with it impossible. The men are worn down from exposure and want of food. They are much in want of shoes, clothing, and blankets. There cannot now be more than 6,000 effective men left in my whole force. Having resumed the command of my department I am directly responsible to the Government for the condition and safety of my army. As soon as my command can be perfectly fitted out I will take the field with it. In its present condition it is impossible to move it." [87]

Before receiving Kirby Smith's reply Bragg had left for Richmond to report to President Davis on the conduct of the Kentucky campaign. And Kirby Smith had dispatched his trusted friend "Old Doctor" Smith to Richmond with a personal letter to President Davis. While passing through Knoxville, Dr. Smith dashed off a letter to Mrs. Kirby Smith at Lynchburg. The general was in excellent health, he reported. All were mortified over the retreat from Kentucky. Lexington would have been a wonderful town in which to spend the winter. The ladies in Kentucky were "very enthusiastic in our cause, but the men lack spirit." Very few joined the army and most of them went into the cavalry. Since Bragg assumed com-

[87] *Id.* to *id.,* October 23, 1862, *ibid.*

mand in Kentucky he must bear the responsibility for failure. Possibly before another winter Kirby Smith's army would be back in Kentucky.[88]

Kirby Smith arrived in Knoxville on October 24 a tired and discouraged man. He avoided a rousing public reception by slipping into town at night. When his arrival became known a group of ardent admirers demanded that he sit for a full length portrait for the State Gallery. In his quiet and "elegantly furnished" rooms in the home of "Little Jimmy" Cowan, the young general meditated upon the futility of war. Again he was seized with a desire to resign and enter the ministry. But, as had previously been the case, a thorough searching of his soul convinced him that he was not good enough for holy orders. All was not gloom, however, for at Flat Lick, near Barboursville, he had received the glad tidings that he was the father of a baby girl. They named her Catherine Selden. He resolved to visit his family at Lynchburg at an early date.

"You are astonished at our exodus from Kentucky no doubt," he wrote his wife. "No one could have anticipated it—Bragg's movements since taking command in Ky have been most singular and unfortunate." But it was now done, and he was looking forward to seeing "that little blue eyed prodigy of ours." [89]

Kirby Smith found affairs in East Tennessee in an uncertain and deplorable condition. Without his knowledge Major General Sam Jones had been placed in command of the department. He wired Richmond for instructions. Secretary of War G. W. Randolph replied on October 26. Kirby Smith had been promoted to lieutenant general. By virtue of his rank he would command in East

[88] S. A. Smith to Mrs. Kirby Smith, October 22, 1862.
[89] E. Kirby Smith to Wife, October 20, 25, and October ?, 1862.

Tennessee, but Jones would remain within the department until further plans were developed.[90]

A few days later a long personal letter from Davis was received. The letter sent to Davis by Dr. Smith has apparently been lost; therefore, its contents can be determined only by Davis' reply. Davis agreed that the Kentucky campaign had been "a bitter disappointment," but he felt that events should not be judged by "knowledge acquired after they transpired." He had talked at length with Bragg, he told Kirby Smith, and the general "spoke of you in the most complimentary terms, and does not seem to imagine your dissatisfaction." Davis felt that Bragg had proved his administrative capacity and demonstrated an intimate knowledge of his troops. Although some other commander of greater ability might "excite more enthusiasm," he would in all probability not be "equally useful."

Having disposed of Bragg by expressing considerable confidence in him, Davis launched a discussion of possible military movements in several theaters. Back to Bragg again, he told Kirby Smith, "Genl Bragg cannot move into Middle Tenn. with prospect of success without your cooperation. You are now second in rank and possess to an eminent degree the confidence of the country. Your own corps could not be so useful led by another commander. How then can I withdraw you or withhold your troops?"

If he could be certain that Bragg could get 30,000 recruits in Middle Tennessee, the President continued, "I would not hesitate upon your request to assign you to the duty of covering Mobile Columbus and Vicksburg, by placing your army at Selma and Meridian to act as might be necessary." But promises of recruits could not be relied

<hr />

[90] G. W. Randolph to E. Kirby Smith, October 26, 1862, *Official Records,* Ser. I, Vol. XVI, pt. 2, 979.

upon. "When you wrote [me] your wounds were fresh, your lame and exhausted troops were before you, I hope time may have mollified your pain and that future operations may restore the confidence essential to cheerfulness and security in campaign." Again he wished to thank Kirby Smith and his brave troops for their "patient fortitude and heroic daring" during the recent campaign.[91] Nothing more needed to be said; Kirby Smith had great confidence in Jefferson Davis, and would co-operate with Bragg, even follow his leadership, if the President requested it. But Davis was still not certain that his trusted friends would be reconciled. He wired Kirby Smith to come to Richmond. The general was pleased with the opportunity to talk with the President and to visit his family at Lynchburg. Davis' appeal to Kirby Smith's patriotism was very effective; neither Kirby Smith nor any member of his staff uttered a recorded word of criticism of Bragg's Kentucky campaign for the duration of the war.[92]

On his return trip from Richmond and Lynchburg, Kirby Smith apparently met Bragg on the cars. "I saw Gen. Bragg," he wrote his wife; "every one prognosticated a stormy meeting—I told him what I had written to Mr. Davis but he spoke kindly to me & in the highest terms of praise and admiration of 'my personal character and soldierly qualities'—I was astonished but believe he is honest & means well." Bragg's army would soon begin moving out of Knoxville, headed for Murfreesboro by way of Bridgeport. Kirby Smith's forces would follow immediately, and he would join them as soon as conditions permitted. They hoped to take such portions of Middle Tennessee "as the Yankeys *will let us.*" [93]

[91] Jefferson Davis to E. Kirby Smith, October 29, 1862, Kirby Smith Papers.
[92] E. Kirby Smith to J. Stoddard Johnston, October 31, 1866.
[93] *Id.* to Wife, November 8, 1862.

While Kirby Smith was away from Knoxville, Adjutant General Cooper had written that an invasion of Middle Tennessee by Bragg had been decided upon. A portion of the troops from the East Tennessee department were to assist. Kirby Smith himself would decide which troops could be spared. He would also decide whether to accompany these troops in person or to remain in East Tennessee.[94]

Although resolved to assist Bragg to the extent of his strength, Kirby Smith saw little hope of victory. He and Bragg would have in Middle Tennessee not more than one half their effective strength in Kentucky. Marshall's command was back in Virginia, an estimated one tenth of those who had gone into Kentucky had remained there, and one fourth of those who had returned were on the sick list. And "Old Doctor" Smith was grumbling and prophesying misfortune. Yet in the face of all this, Kirby Smith was resolved to go in person to Bragg's assistance; he feared mutiny among his men should they be placed directly under Bragg.[95]

On November 9 C. L. Stevenson, who had been promoted to major general, was directed to move forward his batteries and wagon train "via Sparta and McMinnville, to Winchester." If upon reaching Crossville the route by way of McMinnville appeared too dangerous, he would turn his train by way of Pikeville and the Sequatchie Valley. Two days later the route by way of Sparta was definitely abandoned in favor of Pikeville.[96]

Suffering from a pain in the leg and a severe head cold, Kirby Smith planned to remain in Knoxville for a few

[94] S. Cooper to E. Kirby Smith, November 1, 1862, *Official Records,* Ser. I, Vol. XX, pt. 2, 384; *id.* to Braxton Bragg, November 1, 1862, *ibid.,* 384–85; Special Orders, No. 255, October 31, 1862, *ibid.,* 385.

[95] E. Kirby Smith to Wife, November 8, 1862.

[96] J. F. Belton to C. L. Stevenson, November 9, 11, 1862, *Official Records,* Ser. I, Vol. XX, pt. 2, 396–97, 398.

days, putting his department in order and sitting for the portrait he had agreed to have painted. After his first sitting he wrote his wife that, although the artist claimed to have "caught the expression," the result was "one of the most frightful brigand looking figures" he had ever seen. But perhaps the artist was all right; he had produced wonderful portraits of other generals.[97] When the portrait was finished, Kirby Smith thought it "a queer looking thing." [98]

Bragg left Knoxville on November 11. The advance of his army had already reached Tullahoma. The Union army, now under the command of General W. S. Rosecrans, was reported at Lebanon and Nashville. Kirby Smith supected that instead of taking Nashville his and Bragg's armies would probably be "skedadling back across the Cumberlands" before winter began. He showed little eagerness to rush ahead with his own troops, explaining that the affairs of his department needed his attention. He continued despondent, complaining bitterly against the horrors of war and longing for a quiet secluded life with his little family. He urged his wife not to starve little Carrie. She was too thin when he saw her. The bottle should be brought in if necessary. If she were not properly cared for "those long attenuated little arms will rise up in judgment against you." Being so well-fed himself, he hated the thoughts of others being hungry. Nothing had revived his own spirits quite so much as the big platter of "smoking hot" partridges on his breakfast table. "Little Jimmie" Cowan, with whom he boarded, was quite a sportsman and always kept the larder well-stocked.[99]

Kirby Smith's military hopes were somewhat revived by news that his former superior Joseph E. Johnston had

[97] E. Kirby Smith to Wife, November 10, 1862.
[98] *Id.* to *id.*, November 12, 1862.
[99] *Id.* to *id.*, November 11, 14, 16, 20, 1862.

been appointed to command in the West. Under Johnston's supervision would be the armies of Bragg, Kirby Smith, and Pemberton in Mississippi. Kirby Smith secretly hoped to see Johnston succeed Bragg and was probably partly responsible for such a suggestion by General Polk. The conversation with President Davis, however, had dispelled all such hope. On November 11 Kirby Smith received a personal letter from Johnston. At the time of writing, Johnston was in Richmond recuperating from a wound and wondering about his next assignment. He would like to have Kirby Smith with him again but realized that the latter's high rank now entitled him to a separate command. However, it would be a kind stroke of fortune if the two could be near each other.[100] Kirby Smith sent both Davis' and Johnston's letters to Cassie with instructions to file them with his private papers. "I value them as expressions of friendship & esteem." [101]

"I am indeed rejoiced that Jo Johnston is to take command in the West," he wrote his wife on November 20. "I can serve under and with him in earnestness of purpose and devotion of heart." In his opinion, East and Middle Tennessee and the Mobile area would soon be attacked simultaneously and a co-ordinator such as Johnston was needed to direct the activities of the three principal Confederate armies. The activities of the coming winter and spring would be most eventful and "on the result of those campaigns will our future in a great measure depend." [102]

Still trusting in God, Kirby Smith remained hopeful of eventual victory, although he had lost much of his confidence in a glorious future for the Confederacy. The war had reached such gigantic proportions and the expense

---

[100] J. E. Johnston to E. Kirby Smith, November 4, 1862.
[101] E. Kirby Smith to Wife, November 11, 1862.
[102] *Id.* to *id.*, November 20, 23, 1862.

was so staggering, he explained to his wife, that the Richmond authorities dared not announce figures to the public. Should the war continue another year, and he saw no other prospect, the debt would be so great that it could never be paid. Confederate notes and bonds would then be valueless. He suggested that Cassie consult her stepfather, Mr. Booker, about possibilities for the investment of money. To him real estate seemed the safest. It would fluctuate in value but would always remain. "A loan secured by a *first* mortgage on property would be a safe and good investment." Although he wished to provide for the future as much as possible, he had no fear of it: with the energy and talents God had given him he could certainly provide for his wife and baby even under the darkest misfortunes.

In the midst of the terrible suffering brought on by the war, Kirby Smith was constantly reminded of his duties as a Christian. Never before in our history had there been such "a wide field for the quiet and unostentatious exercise of true charity." He urged Cassie to resume her work at the Sunday School and to minister to the unfortunates. "My whole salary is at your disposal, and I do believe every dollar rightly and secretly expended in true charity, will be returned ten fold openly." [103]

Leaving General Heth in charge of the Department of East Tennessee, Kirby Smith joined his troops at Murfreesboro early in December, 1862. At Murfreesboro he conferred with Bragg and also President Davis, who had come in person to look over the Middle Tennessee situation. Kirby Smith returned to Knoxville and resumed command of his department on December 23. There was really no need of his remaining in Middle Tennessee, for under the new plan insisted upon by Davis, few of his troops would be left there. Over the protest of Johnston and

[103] *Id.* to *id.,* November 23, 1862.

Bragg, Davis decided to send Stevenson's division to the assistance of Pemberton in Mississippi, thus seriously weakening Bragg as he stood face to face with Rosecrans thirty miles away. This left only McCown's division of Kirby Smith's army with Bragg.

The army in Middle Tennessee was in "fine fighting condition," Kirby Smith thought. There should be no doubt of a Confederate victory when Bragg and Rosecrans should meet. He was even more enthusiastic over possible developments in Mississippi, where Johnston had gone in person. "Should you determine upon operations in person," he wrote Johnston, "I trust you will send for McCown's division, and let me join you." [104]

Rosecrans moved on Bragg in late December. Simultaneously an estimated 4,000 Federal troops threatened Cumberland Gap and moved on toward Bristol. Another force was rumored at Big Creek Gap ready to march on Knoxville. Having no cavalry and not more than 6,000 men in the whole department, Kirby Smith was practically helpless. He frantically urged Sam Jones in southwest Virginia to send General Marshall in pursuit. The invaders proved to be about 1,000 strong, under Brigadier General Samuel P. Carter, interested principally in bridge-burning. They destroyed important bridges over the Watauga and Holston and disappeared into the Kentucky mountains before the slow-moving Marshall could catch up.[105]

[104] *Id.* to J. E. Johnston, December 26, 1862.
[105] *Id.* to S. Cooper, December 30, 1862, *Official Records,* Ser. I, Vol. XX, pt. 2, 470; *id.* to Samuel Jones, December 29, 1862, *ibid.,* 468; Jones to S. Cooper, January 8, 1862, *ibid.,* 490–91.

## CHAPTER IX

# TO THE TRANS-MISSISSIPPI

EARLY IN JANUARY, 1863, Kirby Smith was suddenly called to Richmond, and on January 14 was officially appointed to command of the Southwestern Army, "embracing the Department of West Louisiana and Texas." While the new commander was arranging for the transfer of his baggage, this order was rescinded, and he was assigned to command in North Carolina. But not wishing to replace his friend G. W. Smith, Kirby Smith insisted on a return to the first order, and was soon on his way to Louisiana. Before reaching his destination, he received still another order, dated February 9, 1863: "The command of Lieut. Gen. E. Kirby Smith is extended so as to embrace the Trans-Mississippi Department."

Kirby Smith's advance in command had been unusually rapid, even in a new army. The dash he had shown at Manassas and in his recent invasion of Kentucky had popularized his name. Both President Davis and General Lee were much impressed. When Davis asked Lee for an opinion on those generals then commanding corps, Lee gave the highest rating to Jackson and Longstreet. D. H. Hill was placed third. Then he added: "I need not remind you of the merits of General E. K. Smith whom I consider one of our best officers." But the combination of influences that sent Kirby Smith to command the Trans-Mississippi

Department was the strained relations between him and Bragg, the need for a competent general west of the river, and Davis' personal admiration.[1]

Kirby Smith, his wife and baby, his trusted staff members, including Meem, Belton, Cunningham, Boggs, and "Old Doctor" Smith, and his faithful servant Aleck and old nurse Mahala left for Louisiana late in January. Major H. L. Clay, still handicapped by his injury, remained in Richmond. He had expected to accompany his general and was eager to go, for he could think of no other duty "so acceptable as that upon Gen Smith's staff." Yet he was not very happy over the transfer, fearing that it placed the general "upon the shelf, tho' it is not so intended." No great battles could be fought west of the Mississippi, he explained to his brother, Senator C. C. Clay, for there could be no great concentration of forces anywhere in that extensive area. Yet Kirby Smith would be held "responsible for the inroads which the enemy may make." Major Clay's only reservation about going to the Trans-Mississippi region was that he almost refused to serve any longer under General Boggs as chief of staff. His friend Kirby Smith assured him, however, that Boggs would have no authority over him.[2]

By February 15 the Kirby Smith party was in Mobile waiting for transportation of horses and baggage. All expected considerable difficulty in crossing the Mississippi River, the general wrote his mother, since two Federal gunboats were reported between Vicksburg and Port Hudson. His wife added a note that she was determined to go on with her husband, even if it should be necessary

---

[1] Special Orders, Nos. 11, 33, January 14, February 9, 1863, *Official Records,* Ser. I, Vol. XV, 948, and Vol. XXII, pt. 2, 787; E. Kirby Smith to Mother, February 15, 1863; R. E. Lee to Jefferson Davis, October 2, 1862, *Official Records,* Ser. I, Vol. XIX, pt. 2, 643.

[2] H. L. Clay to C. C. Clay, January 8, 1863, Clay Papers.

to travel for "a month in the ambulance." [3] From Mobile the general's party moved to the Mississippi, crossing at Port Hudson. Major General Richard ("Dick") Taylor had a boat waiting to take them up the Red River to Alexandria.[4]

Kirby Smith's first act as commander of the Trans-Mississippi Department was to arrange with General Pemberton at Vicksburg for the transfer of General Sterling Price west of the river. Such a transfer had already been approved by the War Department. In Arkansas and particularly among Missouri troops both east and west of the river, there was a feeling that Price was the man to defend the Arkansas valley and eventually carry the war into Missouri. There was also some feeling that it was unjust to require Trans-Mississippi troops to fight east of the river when they were so badly needed at home. The Missouri troops were eager to accompany Price in the transfer until they learned that no immediate invasion of their home state was contemplated. They then changed their minds; they wanted none of the mountains of Arkansas.[5]

On March 7, 1863, Lieutenant General Kirby Smith issued General Orders No. 1, assuming command of the department. Two days later he announced his staff:[6]

Personal staff: Capt. J. G. Meem, Jr., aide-de-camp; First Lieut. E. Cunningham, aide-de-camp; First Lieut. E. Walworth, volunteer aide-de-camp.

Department staff: Brig. Gen. W. R. Boggs, chief of staff; Capt. J. F. Belton, assistant adjutant-general; Capt. H. P. Pratt, assist-

[3] E. Kirby Smith to Mother, February 15, 1863.

[4] Boggs, *Reminiscences*, 54.

[5] J. A. Seddon to E. Kirby Smith, February 3, 5, 1863, *Official Records*, Ser. I, Vol. XXII, pt. 2, 781–82; T. C. Reynolds to Seddon, February 5, 1863, *ibid.*, 782; *id.* to W. P. Johnston, May 26, 1863, Thomas C. Reynolds Papers, Manuscript Division, Library of Congress.

[6] General Orders No. 1, March 7, 1863, *Official Records*, Ser. I, Vol. XXII, pt. 2, 798; General Orders No. 3, March 10, 1863, *ibid.*, 799.

ant adjutant-general; Col. B. Allston, inspector-general; Maj. J. F. Minter, chief quartermaster; Maj. W. H. Thomas, chief of subsistence; Lieut. Col. John A. Brown, chief of ordnance and artillery; Surgeon S. A. Smith, medical director.

At the time Kirby Smith assumed command the Confederate force in the Trans-Mississippi Department was composed of a number of scattered commands under the inefficient leadership of Major General Theophilus H. Holmes. Holmes had arrived in Arkansas early in August, 1862, and established headquarters at Little Rock. He dispatched Major General T. C. Hindman to northwestern Arkansas to take command of some 9,000 men, including about 3,000 Indians, commanded by Colonel Douglas H. Cooper, and prepare for an invasion of Missouri. The invasion was not attempted; increasing Federal pressure in the direction of Vicksburg brought an urgent request that Holmes do what he could for the defense of that stronghold. Consequently, Holmes was unable to send sufficient re-enforcements to Hindman. The latter lost the battle of Prairie Grove to Generals James G. Blunt and F. J. Herron on December 7, 1862, and shortly began a retreat to Little Rock, arriving there in mid-January, 1863, with his force greatly reduced by sickness and desertion.

Meanwhile Holmes had been able to do little along the Mississippi. Arkansas Post, about fifty miles from the mouth of the Arkansas River, had been strongly fortified by the Confederates. Holmes had stationed there a garrison of about 5,000 men under the command of Brigadier General Thomas J. Churchill. On January 9 a Federal force, estimated at 32,000, under the command of Major General John A. McClernand and supported by Rear Admiral W. D. Porter's fleet, appeared before the Post. After a five hour bombardment, Churchill surrendered the entire garrison on January 11.[7] Arkansas was now open for Federal invasion.

There had been little Confederate activity in the Louisiana district since the fall of New Orleans. Major General "Dick" Taylor was sent back to his home state to weld together the scattered Confederate units and such state troops as could be furnished by Governor Thomas O. Moore. Upon arrival he found that the "Confederate Government had no soldiers, no arms or ammunition, and no money, within the limits of the district."[8] The next few months were spent in an effort to bring together a Confederate force sufficient to menace the Federal advance on Port Hudson and Vicksburg. Taylor received no assistance or directions from the departmental commander at Little Rock.

Since late in 1862 Confederate forces in Texas had been under the command of Major General John Bankhead Magruder. Action had been limited to the recapture of Galveston on Christmas Eve. This brief survey makes it clear that very little attention had been given to the military organization of the Trans-Mississippi region.

Before Kirby Smith left Richmond both the President and the Secretary of War had stressed that his most important duty west of the Mississippi "would be directed to aiding in the defense of the Lower Mississippi, and keeping that great artery of the West effectually closed to Northern occupation or trade." As long as his assistance was demanded along this line he would not be expected to give much time to the northern portion of his department. Soon after assuming command he received a notice from the Secretary of War, reiterating the previous

---

[7] Thomas L. Snead, "The Conquest of Arkansas," in *Battles and Leaders*, III, 441 ff.

[8] Richard Taylor, *Destruction and Reconstruction* (New York, 1879), 102.

opinion but adding, "but, unfortunately, I fear an even more pressing necessity requires your personal presence and influence at an early day in the State of Arkansas." From many reliable sources had come "the most deplorable accounts . . . of the disorder, confusion, and demoralization everywhere prevalent, both with the armies and people of that State. The commanding general seems, while esteemed for his virtues, to have lost the confidence and attachment of all; and his next in command, General Hindman, who is admitted to have shown energy and ability, has rendered himself, by alleged acts of violence and tyranny, perfectly odious." Consequently, the army formerly between 40,000 and 50,000 had "dwindled, by desertion, sickness and death," to between 15,000 and 18,000, and those remaining were "disaffected and hopeless and . . . threatened with positive starvation. . . ." Furthermore, the civilian population was reported "in a state of consternation," exposed to "lawless marauders and deserters" who were plundering citizens of their meager means.

Kirby Smith was further instructed that before going in person to Arkansas he should plan operations on the Lower Mississippi, looking to the defense of the districts along smaller rivers and bayous back from the river. This could be done with comparatively small means by placing sharpshooters and a few light guns at strategic points along the bayous. "From the nature of the country and the few narrow routes that exist, as well as the little breadth of the streams," the Secretary of War concluded, "I am satisfied that the whole country is among the most defensible in the world, and that comparatively few resolute, experienced men could repel hosts of invaders." [9]

[9] J. A. Seddon to E. Kirby Smith, March 18, 1863, *Official Records,* Ser. I, Vol. XXII, pt. 2, 802–803.

Several days before Seddon wrote the above, Kirby Smith had set out for a three weeks tour of inspection in Arkansas. Traveling by way of Camden, he arrived in Little Rock on March 17. Conditions there were not nearly so bad as had been reported. Morale among the troops was good, deserters were returning daily, and the regiments, which had become skeletons after the defeat at Prairie Grove, were rapidly filling to their normal numbers. This improvement Kirby Smith attributed to the energetic methods used by General Holmes in rounding up absentees and providing every possible comfort for his troops, the dismissal of Hindman, and the transfer of General Price west of the Mississippi.

Kirby Smith found that the strength of the forces in Arkansas had been greatly exaggerated. Two divisions of infantry totaling less than 10,000 effectives, a very small force under William Steele, and J. S. Marmaduke's cavalry constituted the total force in Arkansas. The Indians had gone home. The new commanding general soon complained to President Davis of the shortage of troops throughout the entire department. The fighting population had gone east of the Mississippi, he observed. "The male population remaining are old men, or have furnished substitutes, are lukewarm, or are wrapped up in speculations and money-making." [10]

General Holmes was made commander of the Arkansas District, including Missouri, and the Indian Territory. In fact this was the only position he had previously filled, for as Kirby Smith reported to Davis, Holmes had remained at Little Rock and given his entire attention to the defense of Arkansas and a possible invasion of Missouri. "There was no general system, no common head; each district was acting independently." Consequently, it was nec-

[10] E. Kirby Smith to Jefferson Davis, June 16, 1863, *ibid.*, 871–73.

essary for the new department commander to "begin *de novo* in any attempt at a general systematizing and development of the department resources." [11]

Holmes expressed pleasure at being relieved of his "elephant," and strongly urged Kirby Smith to make Little Rock his headquarters. Thomas C. Reynolds, "Confederate Governor" of Missouri, also urged the selection of Little Rock, but for a different reason. He had no confidence in Holmes, even as a district commander. In view of Holmes' "tendency to despondency," he urged Kirby Smith to "reserve *entirely* for your *exclusive* decision, the question of abandoning any portion of the Arkansas Valley." Then Governor Reynolds was much interested in an invasion of Missouri and felt that Kirby Smith, rather than Holmes or Price, should lead it. Price was popular with Missouri troops and with Confederate sympathizers in that border state, but the leadership of a regular military man was needed. And since the Kentucky campaign, Reynolds observed, Kirby Smith's name had been "a household word in Mo. & the North West." Should the new department commander now fail to lead the expedition, Missourians would suspect that the Confederate government was "not in earnest." According to Reynolds, Kirby Smith realized the political importance of such an invasion and agreed to lead it in person.

On a recent trip from Shreveport to Washington, Arkansas, Reynolds had learned that Arkansans were also interested in the proposed invasion of Missouri; they wanted to get Missouri troops out of Arkansas. They hoped that with extra troops gone the price of provisions would decline. Besides, Arkansans considered Missouri and Texas troops "great depredators."

The Missouri governor was well pleased with the new

[11] *Ibid.*

commander of the Trans-Mississippi Department. "Do not feel much anxiety about us over here," he wrote W. Preston Johnston at Richmond. "There have been great blunders & great deficiencies, but croakers have exaggerated them. Kirby Smith is emphatically the right man in the right place." [12]

Kirby Smith selected Shreveport for his permanent headquarters because of its central location, even though he thought it "a miserable place with a miserable population." Located at the head of navigation on the Red River, this town was on a direct route between Texas and Richmond. He began immediately to make it the "center of communication, as well as the geographical center." Work was begun on a telegraph line connecting Shreveport with Monroe, Louisiana, and Little Rock. Soon he planned to connect with Alexandria and the Texas lines.[13]

In spite of several days of rough weather, Kirby Smith was encouraged by his tour of inspection in Arkansas. Conditions were not as bad as he had expected, and he met with friendly greetings from many associates of former years. One friend brought sad news, however. "Old Ugly," his favorite bird dog of happier prewar days in Texas, was now deaf and blind. The poor creature had "pined away" after being deserted by his master. Friendly greetings were most pleasing, the general confided to his wife, but he knew his troubles would soon begin. Yet regardless of his trials, he would be constantly encouraged by the presence of his little family. Had Carrie cut the tooth that had been expected? [14]

On April 14, 1863, Kirby Smith received the news that

---

[12] T. C. Reynolds to E. Kirby Smith, May 13, 1863, Reynolds Papers; id. to W. P. Johnston, May 26, July 18, 1863, ibid.

[13] E. Kirby Smith to Wife, March 19, 1863, Kirby Smith Papers; id. to Jefferson Davis, June 16, 1863, Official Records, Ser. I, Vol. XXII, pt. 2, 871–73.

[14] Id. to Wife, March 19, 1863.

Union General Nathaniel Banks had evacuated Baton Rouge and was moving his troops west of the Mississippi to Berwick Bay. Already, it was reported, no fewer than 15,000 men had been concentrated there. No doubt the Federal general intended to occupy western Louisiana. Another force of equal strength, commanded by General McClernand, was reported at Richmond, Louisiana, ready to operate along Bayou Macon.

Kirby Smith immediately ordered Holmes to rush a division from Little Rock to Camden to be held there in readiness to move toward Monroe. This division would be commanded by Brigadier General J. G. Walker, who had recently arrived from the east.[15] A day later Holmes was instructed to send Walker's division on to Monroe so that it would be in position to move to the assistance of Taylor, should the latter be compelled to fall back to Alexandria.[16]

Major General Magruder, commanding the Texas District, was apprised of the situation in Louisiana and directed to move all available forces toward Opelousas. Taylor, who had fewer than 4,000 men,[17] could not hold back indefinitely the advance of so superior a Federal force, Magruder was informed, and unless he was reenforced, western Louisiana would be lost and Texas cut off from the remainder of the Confederacy.[18]

As the Federals advanced from Berwick Bay along Bayou Teche, Taylor fought a succession of delaying en-

[15] *Id.* to T. H. Holmes, April 14, 1863, *Official Records,* Ser. I, Vol. XV, 1041.

[16] *Id.* to *id.,* April 15, 1863, *ibid.,* 1042–43.

[17] On two other occasions Kirby Smith gave Taylor's strength at 4,000 and 5,000. Taylor himself later stated that he had no more than 3,000 men. *Official Records,* Ser. I, Vol. XV, 391.

[18] J. F. Belton to J. B. Magruder, April 16, 1863, *Official Records,* Ser. I, Vol. XV, 1043.

gagements and fell back to Opelousas by way of New Iberia and Vermilionville. The Federal commanders did not press hard, and it was April 20 before their advance reached Opelousas, leaving ample time for the removal of Confederate stores to Alexandria.[19]

Kirby Smith called for help from Pemberton, commanding east of the Mississippi. Taylor was being "driven back by overwhelming numbers," he explained. Banks's evacuation of Baton Rouge and subsequent movements west of the river indicated that his plan was to occupy western Louisiana rather than attack Port Hudson. Could not Pemberton transfer some of his troops from Port Hudson to Taylor's command? If this was not practical, could Pemberton relieve some of the pressure on Taylor by threatening New Orleans? "Unless we are re-enforced or some counter-movement is made on the other side of the river the enemy must succeed in their occupation of West Louisiana, and thus effectually close up the only channel by which supplies can be passed east of the Mississippi." [20]

The want of adequate transportation, Pemberton replied, made it impossible for him to operate effectually west of the river. He wished also to call attention to enemy operations at New Carthage and Richmond.[21] A day later Pemberton reported that the enemy was engaged in cutting a passage from Young's Point through to the Mississippi near New Carthage. "Without co-operation it is impossible to oppose him. Inform me what action you intend to take." [22] Before receiving the above notes, Kirby Smith was again urging Pemberton to send re-enforcements from

[19] Taylor, *Destruction and Reconstruction*, 129 ff.

[20] E. Kirby Smith to J. C. Pemberton, April 15, 1863, *Official Records*, Ser. I, Vol. XV, 1042.

[21] J. C. Pemberton to E. Kirby Smith or Richard Taylor, April 17, 1863, *ibid.*, 1044.

[22] *Id.* to *id.*, April 18, 1863, *ibid.*, 1045.

Port Hudson. He also wrote Confederate authorities at Richmond, urging that since the expected attack on Vicksburg and Port Hudson were apparently not to be made at present, Taylor should be re-enforced by troops from east of the river.[23]

Then came a message from General Stevenson at Vicksburg. Eight gunboats had attempted to pass the bend. Two were disabled, a third one was sunk, but the other five got by. Kirby Smith rushed a note to Holmes. He must hasten the departure of Walker's division and wire ahead for transports to be collected at Camden and Monroe.[24]

Taylor continued to fight and fall back in good order. By April 20 he was beyond Opelousas moving toward Alexandria. Kirby Smith sent an expression of "gratification at the conduct of the troops under your command" and appreciation of the energy and skill exercised by their commander "in extricating them from a position of great peril." It was hoped that the enemy would for the present be content with the occupation of the lower Red River and not push for control of the entire valley. However, Taylor was assured that the departmental commander was doing all that he could to secure re-enforcements. An urgent request had been sent east of the river; Walker's division was on its way; and three Texas regiments were now near Mill Creek on the Red River and had been instructed to move to Alexandria.[25]

There was little at that to justify Kirby Smith's wishful thinking that the Federals would not continue their push. For Rear Admiral Porter's small fleet was about to enter the Red River, and Banks's forces were moving in from the south. Kirby Smith called for the concentration of all

[23] E. Kirby Smith to J. C. Pemberton, April 19, 1863, *ibid.*, 1046; *id.* to S. Cooper, April 18, 1863, *ibid.*, 1045.

[24] *Id.* to T. H. Holmes, April 19, 1863, *ibid.*, Vol. XXII, pt. 2, 828.

[25] J. F. Belton to Richard Taylor, April 20, 1863, *ibid.*, Vol. XV, 1047.

The Segui House in St. Augustine, Florida, now held in trust by the St. Augustine Historical Society (from a photograph in possession of Dr. R. M. Kirby-Smith, Sewanee, Tennessee).

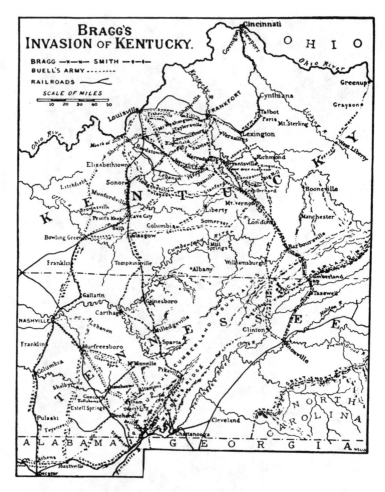

The Kentucky Campaign (from Robert U. Johnson and Clarence C. Buel
[eds.], *Battles and Leaders of the Civil War* . . .
[New York, 1887–88], III, 6).

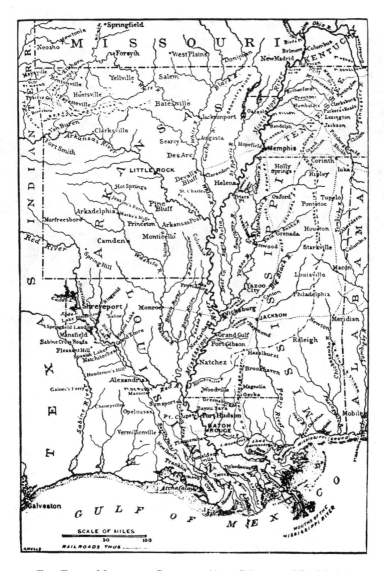

The Trans-Mississippi Command (from Johnson and Buel [eds.],
*Battles and Leaders*, IV, 348).

THE KIRBY SMITH FAMILY AT SEWANEE, SHOWING TEN OF THE ELEVEN CHILDREN
(from a photograph in possession of Dr. R. M. Kirby-Smith, Sewanee, Tennessee).

available forces in eastern Texas at Niblett's Bluff and dispatched an officer to that vicinity "to collect the stragglers and deserters from General Taylor's army," who were reported making their way to Texas in large numbers.[26] The only Confederate fortification on the lower Red River was Fort De Russy, and it could be easily taken if approached simultaneously by water and land. With the approach of the enemy it was dismantled and evacuated.

With no gunboats on the rivers and a greatly inferior force on land the Confederates could do nothing but continue their retreat. He did not possess the means to resist occupation, Kirby Smith notified Pemberton. Pemberton still felt unable to assist, for the enemy had reoccupied Baton Rouge and was again threatening Port Hudson. The whole Red River country seemed to be lost, Kirby Smith wrote Holmes. Taylor would continue to fall back until he reached Shreveport. Holmes must protect his own supplies at Camden, send his boats up the river out of reach, and make his own arrangements "for the defense of the Ouachita and Upper Black Rivers." Walker would move his command to Shreveport, not Alexandria. With these final instructions, Kirby Smith and his staff moved up the Red River from Alexandria to Shreveport. They had been preceded by boats carrying all movable public property.[27]

The day before leaving Alexandria Kirby Smith reported to the War Department, giving General Taylor full credit for the brilliant movement of troops, materials, and stores. "Could General Taylor have drawn upon Port Hudson for re-enforcements, or had the troops in East and

---

[26] W. R. Boggs to W. R. Scurry, April 20, 21, 1863, *ibid.*, 1047–49.

[27] *Id.* to Richard Taylor, April 22, 1863, *ibid.*, 1051; *id.* to J. G. Walker, April 22, 1863, *ibid.; id.* to T. H. Holmes, April 22, 24, *ibid.*, 1050, 1054.

West Louisiana been under one control, the force at Port Hudson might have been marched across to the Atchafalaya and rapidly transported to the scene of action in time to have defeated General Banks." It was now Kirby Smith's plan to concentrate his forces at Natchitoches and Shreveport and "take the offensive, with strong hopes of recovering the country when the waters fall." [28]

General Banks was well pleased with his campaign. Conquest of the Teche country had placed in his possession quantities of lumber and an estimated 20,000 head of cattle, mules, and horses. Shipment of Confederate supplies east of the river had been interrupted. And Banks estimated that from two to five million dollars worth of Confederate supplies had been seized for use of the Union armies.[29]

Porter's gunboats were at Alexandria by May 8. Taylor's retreating forces had now reached Natchitoches. Walker's division from Arkansas had still not arrived on the Red River. Swollen streams resulting from heavy spring rains had greatly retarded its progress. The Federal force, estimated at 28,000, continued to push on up the Red River, and Taylor began preparations for the evacuation of Natchitoches. If further retreat became necessary, Kirby Smith instructed, then Taylor was to obstruct the narrows of Red River by felling trees and sinking boats in the channel.[30]

To Kirby Smith the loss of the Red River Valley as far up as Jefferson appeared inevitable. A Federal invasion of east Texas was quite likely. Magruder was instructed to concentrate his forces near Nacogdoches and take command in person. Texans were warned of their danger and

[28] E. Kirby Smith to S. Cooper, April 23, 1863, *ibid.*, 386–87.
[29] N. P. Banks to H. W. Halleck, April 29, 1863, *ibid.*, 1117–18.
[30] E. Kirby Smith to Richard Taylor, May 11, 1863, *ibid.*, 1081–82.

urged to raise local companies for home defense. General Alfred Mouton, commanding the cavalry force which had fallen back toward Niblett's Bluff, was ordered "to attack the enemy's flank and rear in the direction of Opelousas, and to harass him continually." [31] Kirby Smith was considering abandoning the Arkansas Valley and ordering Holmes to the defense of Shreveport.[32] The loss of Shreveport would mean the sacrifice of an immense quantity of supplies and would leave no base to which to retreat.

Although hard-pressed and in danger of losing temporarily the possession of the Red River Valley, Kirby Smith was pleased with Banks's advance with so large a force. "The decisive battle of the West must soon be fought near Vicksburg," he wrote Holmes. "The fate of the Trans-Mississippi Department in a great measure depends on it, and Banks, by operating here, is thrown out of the campaign on the Mississippi." [33]

Banks too was conscious of the fact that he was about to miss the main attraction near Vicksburg. He called a halt several miles short of Natchitoches. On the evening of May 15 Kirby Smith was informed that the Federal forces were falling back toward Alexandria. Grant had written Banks on May 10 concerning the possibility of co-operation of their armies at Vicksburg. Although most enthusiastic about such a possibility, Banks reluctantly notified Grant: "But I must say, without qualifications, that the means at my disposal do not leave me a shadow of a chance to accomplish it." The best he could hope to do would be to cross over and join a movement against Port Hudson. But after spending a night in meditation, he notified

[31] W. R. Boggs to W. R. Scurry, May 14, 1863, *ibid.*, 1084; *id.* to Alfred Mouton, May 14, 1863, *ibid.*, Vol. XVI, pt. 2, 4.

[32] E. Kirby Smith to T. H. Holmes, May 9, 1863, *ibid.*, Vol. XXII, pt. 2, 835.

[33] *Id.* to *id.*, May 16, 1863, *ibid.*, 839–40.

Halleck that he would "make every sacrifice and hazard everything" to join Grant.[34]

Banks began his withdrawal on May 13, "taking off negroes, waggons, teams, and every thing valuable that could be carried off in *2,000 waggons*—bearing down fences & destroying crops, the latter being as he stated his principal object." [35] Ten days later Banks's army was on the east side of the Mississippi. Taylor and his command had followed at a safe distance, Taylor himself going by steamer to Alexandria and his infantry moving overland to the Teche, where junction was to be made with Mouton's cavalry. Before the forces could be united, however, Banks had crossed to the east side of Berwick Bay. Taylor wanted to continue pursuit, but Kirby Smith had other plans.

Loyal western Louisianians were shocked and frightened at the apparent ease with which their country had been invaded and the frightful toll of slaves and other property taken by the enemy. Governor Moore was even more shocked at the great amount of disloyalty among the citizens. The swamps were full of "runaway conscripts," he wrote the governor of Texas. The "demoralization of the people at home from various causes is very great." He urged Governor Francis R. Lubbock to visit Shreveport where the two of them could confer with General Kirby Smith. With the assistance of the general's experience and military skill, probably some plans for mutual protection of their states could be worked out.[36]

Guy M. Bryan of Texas, recently appointed assistant adjutant general on Kirby Smith's staff, relayed to his friend Governor Lubbock the seriousness of conditions

[34] N. P. Banks to U. S. Grant, May 12, 1863, *ibid.*, Vol. XV, 317–18; *id.* to H. W. Halleck, May 13, 1863, *ibid.*, 318.
[35] Thomas O. Moore to Francis R. Lubbock, May 25, 1863, in Francis R. Lubbock Papers, Texas State Archives.
[36] *Ibid.*

within the department, especially if Grant should be successful at Vicksburg. He had conferred with Governor Moore and Kirby Smith. They were considering calling a conference of governors and other officials at either Shreveport or Marshall, Texas. Governor Moore was greatly alarmed at the "lukewarmness & disloyalty of citizens" of Louisiana. On the top of these worries Bryan added another. He had learned that the aged Sam Houston might run again for governor of Texas. If so, he would almost certainly be elected. "The consequences would be calamitous indeed," Bryan exclaimed. "This, taken in connection with state of affairs in this State [Louisiana] would place us at the mercy of the enemy, or a purely military rule— God forbid such a state of things—Gen Smith is certainly a most agreeable and sensible gentleman, & his reputation is high as a soldier." [37]

Louisiana planters not only feared the loss of their slaves but also that these Negroes would be sent against their former masters as soldiers. During the recent campaign the Trans-Mississippi forces had first encountered Negroes in arms, and Taylor's troops had captured some. Kirby Smith was displeased with the capture. No quarter should be given armed Negroes, he quickly admonished Taylor. "In this way we may be relieved from a disagreeable dilemma." However, since Negroes in insurrection had been captured they should be turned over to state authorities "to be tried for crimes against the State." Should Negroes be executed by Confederate military order, "it would certainly provoke retaliation." But if executions were by state authority, then "no exception can be taken." [38]

[37] Guy M. Bryan to F. R. Lubbock, May 22, 1863, *ibid.*
[38] E. Kirby Smith to Richard Taylor, June 13, 1863, *Official Records,* Ser. II, Vol. VI, 21–22; S. S. Anderson to *id.,* June 13, 1863, *ibid.,* 22.

The Adjutant General's office at Richmond disapproved of Kirby Smith's proposed treatment of armed Negroes and recommended that they be considered as "deluded victims." If captured, they should "be treated with mercy and returned to their owners." [39] The War Office also recommended mercy for these "deluded victims of the hypocrisy and malignity of the enemy," but advised that their leaders "be dealt with red-handed on the field or immediately thereafter." [40]

Kirby Smith altered his original instructions so as to conform with recommendations from Richmond, and redoubled his efforts to prevent Negroes from falling into the hands of the enemy. Every exposed plantation became a recruiting center for Negroes, he complained to his district commanders; therefore, as Confederate troops fell back before the approaching enemy all able-bodied male Negroes should be carried with them. Planters should be notified of the approaching danger and urged to move their Negroes to safer localities. "Every sound male black left for the enemy becomes a soldier, whom we have afterward to fight." [41]

Even while Banks was moving up the Red River, driving Taylor's small force before him, Pemberton was frantically calling upon Kirby Smith for co-operation with the Confederate armies east of the river. "My force is insufficient for offensive operations," he explained. "I must stand on the defensive, at all events until re-enforcements reach me. You can contribute materially to the defense of Vicksburg and the navigation of the Mississippi River by a movement upon the line of communications of the enemy

[39] H. L. Clay to E. Kirby Smith, July 13, 1863, *ibid.*, 115.

[40] J. A. Seddon to E. Kirby Smith, August 12, 1863, *ibid.*, Ser. I, Vol. XXII, pt. 2, 964–65.

[41] E. Kirby Smith to Sterling Price and Richard Taylor, September 4, 1863, *ibid.*, 990.

on the western side of the river. He derives supplies and re-enforcements for the most part by a route which leads from Milliken's Bend to New Carthage, La., a distance of some 35 to 40 miles. To break this would render a most important service." [42]

Since Banks had now crossed to Grant's assistance Kirby Smith felt compelled to do what he could for Pemberton. Accordingly, on May 20, he suggested to Taylor the expediency of destroying Grant's line of communication west of the Mississippi. If Taylor, re-enforced by Walker's division, could move up the Tensas and hit the Federal line of communication, Grant might be effectively checked, "if not frustrated." He was conscious of Taylor's desire to recover lower Louisiana and threaten New Orleans, Kirby Smith said, "but the stake contended for near Vicksburg is the Valley of the Mississippi and the Trans-Mississippi Department; the defeat of General Grant is the *terminus ad quem* of all operations in the west this summer; to its attainment all minor advantages should be sacrificed." If Bayou Vidal could be seized and held for a ten-day period Grant's whole army would be endangered. Should Grant have already been defeated before Vicksburg, it would "insure his destruction." [43]

Taylor later stated that he remonstrated vigorously against being sent on such a campaign, pointing out the impossibility of approaching Vicksburg from the west. The way to relieve the Confederate forces east of the River, he insisted, was to capture the Berwick Bay fortifications, overrun the Lafourche, interrupt Banks's communications with New Orleans, and threaten the city itself. Banks would then be compelled to rush from Port Hudson down

[42] J. C. Pemberton to E. Kirby Smith, May 9, 1863, *ibid.*, Vol. XXIV, pt. 3, 846.

[43] E. Kirby Smith to Richard Taylor, May 20, 21, 1863, *ibid.*, Vol. XXVI, pt. 2, 12–13, 15.

the east bank of the river to the defense of New Orleans. But Kirby Smith, Taylor explained, was under too much pressure to give this plan serious consideration. To Taylor he remarked that "Confederate authorities in the east were urgent for some effort on our part in behalf of Vicksburg, and that public opinion would condemn us if we did not *try to do something.*" [44] Taylor's account was no doubt colored by subsequent events, but Kirby Smith was definitely under pressure. His duty with regard to the lower Mississippi had been stressed upon him from the time he was appointed to his new post.

Walker's division from Arkansas did not arrive on the Red River until May 24. It immediately joined Taylor in the movement toward New Carthage by way of New River and the Tensas. Embarking at Catahoula Lake on May 29, the combined forces were expected to reach their destination opposite Vicksburg by June 2. This movement "cuts off Grant's retreat, and completes the destruction of his command, I hope," Kirby Smith informed Governor Thomas C. Reynolds of Missouri.[45]

Still growling a dozen years after the War, Taylor said he entertained no high hopes for this two-hundred-mile excursion "away from the proper theatre of action in search of an indefinite *something.*" But he reluctantly obeyed orders. Taking a chance on escaping the notice of Federal gunboats, he moved his forces up the Tensas to a position opposite Vicksburg. In order to protect his own boats from the enemy's reach he sent them back down the Tensas and up the Ouachita.

The expedition was disappointing in results. Walker attacked and captured a small Federal force near the

[44] Taylor, *Destruction and Reconstruction*, 137–38.
[45] E. Kirby Smith to T. C. Reynolds, June 4, 1863, *Official Records*, Ser. I, Vol. XXII, pt. 2, 855–56.

village of Richmond, midway between the Tensas and the Mississippi. Then moving to the vicinity of Young's Point he fell upon two other fortified camps, garrisoned mostly by Negro troops, and drove the garrisons to the protection of Federal gunboats on the Mississippi. But all stores collected in that area had been removed, and Grant, having shifted position, was now getting his supplies by way of the Yazoo. In reporting to Kirby Smith, Taylor admitted that a much greater loss should have been inflicted upon the enemy and placed the responsibility for failure upon his subordinate commanders and the common soldier's great fear of gunboats.

Disgusted with apparent failure and eager to get back to lower Louisiana, Taylor prepared to abandon the campaign for the relief of Vicksburg and to transfer Walker's division south of the Red River. Kirby Smith's headquarters was notified to this effect on June 8, but three days later Taylor reported that he had decided not to withdraw Walker "until the enemy's developments and the condition of affairs around Vicksburg are more fully developed." Kirby Smith replied that he thought the decision a wise one. And in forwarding Taylor's reports to Richmond he called special attention "to the ability and energy displayed by that gallant officer in the discharge of his duties as district commander." [46]

As Kirby Smith complimented the services of Taylor he was aware of the rumor of strained relations between them. Taylor had opposed the campaign to relieve Vicksburg, and someone at his headquarters had remarked that it might be well for the departmental commander to take the field in person. There is no evidence that Taylor contrib-

[46] Taylor, *Destruction and Reconstruction,* 138; Richard Taylor to W. R. Boggs, June 8, 1863, *Official Records,* Ser. I, Vol. XXIV, pt. 2, 457–62; H. P. Pratt to Taylor, June 15, 1863, *ibid.,* Vol. XXII, pt. 2, 868; E. Kirby Smith to S. Cooper, June 17, 1863, *ibid.,* Vol. XXVI, pt. 2, 71.

uted to this dissension beyond an open and vigorous criticism of the commanding general's plan. Rumors soon reached headquarters at Shreveport. Kirby Smith hastily informed Taylor's headquarters that certain rumors emanating from that source were "calculated to injure me," and requested that steps be taken to counteract such false impressions. He had had General Taylor's "interests at heart," he explained, and wished to give him an opportunity to prove "how greatly he has been misappreciated" in Louisiana. Taylor had been told that he would be left in command "unless it became necessary to send an officer senior to him with the re-enforcements ordered to Louisiana, in which event I would myself take the field in person." But for the present he considered it important that he himself remain at headquarters "till the bureaus and departments have been organized and some general system has been introduced throughout the Trans-Mississippi Department." [47]

General Holmes, the district commander in Arkansas, was also concerned over the campaign for the relief of Vicksburg. To support Taylor in this movement Kirby Smith had ordered Brigadier General J. C. Tappan to move his division from Camden to Monroe. Holmes feared this would so weaken the forces under his command as to make the long awaited invasion of Missouri impossible. Kirby Smith assured him that Tappan's transfer to Louisiana was only temporary. As for the invasion of Missouri, however, it must wait until Grant was defeated east of the Mississippi. Neither was he favorable to the organization of guerrilla bands in Missouri, a plan being particularly urged by Marmaduke. No good could result from such a plan of warfare, he reasoned; "it only entails additional

[47] E. Kirby Smith to E. Surget, June 3, 1863, *ibid.*, 29–30.

persecution and distress upon our friends, without advancing our cause in that State." The greatest contribution Holmes could make at that time would be to send a brigade of cavalry to operate along the west bank of the Mississippi as low as Lake Providence. And, if possible, a battery of artillery should be sent to destroy Federal transportation on the river. Many plantations on the Arkansas side of the Mississippi were being cultivated by Negroes for Federal benefit. This practice should be broken up and the Negroes captured.[48] Holmes immediately sent two brigades of cavalry with artillery to the Mississippi area.

While Taylor was operating opposite the vicinity of Vicksburg, Kirby Smith received a note from Joseph E. Johnston, at Canton, Mississippi. Port Hudson was invested by Banks, he said, and Grant was before Vicksburg. Johnston was preparing to go to the assistance of Vicksburg, but could do nothing for Port Hudson. "If you can do anything to succor Port Hudson, I beg you to do it." [49] So great was the mutual admiration between Johnston and Kirby Smith that a request from one was considered by the other as forceful as a command. A few weeks earlier Johnston had written Kirby Smith from Tullahoma, Tennessee, where Bragg's army was awaiting another attack by Rosecrans. How different it would have been, he remarked, if Kirby Smith had been assigned to the Trans-Mississippi immediately after returning from the Kentucky campaign. "You would have cooperated with Pemberton—fought the Federal army east of the Mississippi, if your troops were not fully employed west of it. Then Bragg would not have been weakened & Rosecrans

---

[48] S. S. Anderson to T. H. Holmes, June 4, 1863, *ibid.*, Vol. XXII, pt. 2, 856–57; E. Kirby Smith to *id.*, June 4, 5, 1863, *ibid.*, 856, 857.

[49] J. E. Johnston to E. Kirby Smith, May 31, 1863, *ibid.*, Vol. XXVI, pt. 2, 26.

would have been routed as well as Grant—You would now be in Mississippi and we in Kentucky." [50]

Kirby Smith had little hope of furnishing much relief for Port Hudson. General Mouton's cavalry was already in lower Louisiana, but no important results had been reported. Banks was no doubt getting his supplies along a line east of the Mississippi leading from Baton Rouge. However, Kirby Smith promised to "spare no exertions" in co-operating in defense of both Vicksburg and Port Hudson.[51] He passed Johnston's urgent request on to Taylor at Alexandria, adding that he had confidence Taylor would do all he could to relieve both garrisons and to throw in supplies whenever possible.[52]

Taylor was pleased with the suggestion that he operate opposite Port Hudson. He had arrived at his Alexandria headquarters on June 10, leaving Walker in command in the Tensas country, and had found the news from south of the Red River most unsatisfactory. General Mouton had proved himself "unequal to the task of handling and disposing of any large body of troops." From Mouton's reports, Taylor complained, one was "quite in the dark" as to his location, accomplishments, and "the condition of affairs on the Lower Teche." [53]

Taylor dispatched a staff officer, Brigadier General C. L. Elgee, to discuss with General Johnston plans for co-operation in the vicinity of Port Hudson; ordered three regiments of Texas cavalry under Colonel J. P. Major to Morgan's Ferry on the Atchafalaya; and hurried to take personal command in the Teche country. There he joined

[50] *Id.* to *id.*, April 18, 1863, Kirby Smith Papers.

[51] E. Kirby Smith to J. E. Johnston, June 10, 1863, *Official Records,* Ser. I, Vol. XXVI, pt. 2, 43.

[52] H. P. Pratt to Richard Taylor, June 15, 1863, *ibid.,* Vol. XXII, pt. 2, 868.

[53] Richard Taylor to W. R. Boggs, June 11, 1863, *ibid.,* Vol. XXIV, pt. 2, 461–62.

Mouton and Thomas Green. After charging these officers with the responsibility of collecting all kinds of vessels for transportation on the Teche, he returned to Morgan's Ferry, crossed the Atchafalaya with Major, and moved down the Fordoche to within hearing of the firing at Port Hudson. Major was instructed to push on and join Mouton below Bisland, passing Plaquemine in the night to avoid detection. This movement was completed on June 22.

Meanwhile, more than fifty craft had been collected on the Teche, and during the night of June 22 they were "paddled down the Teche to the Atchafalaya and Grand Lake." Brashear City (Berwick's) was surprised and quickly captured at dawn June 23.[54] A thousand prisoners and considerable quantities of ordnance and stores were taken. A day later Taylor reported the capture of stores and his intention to transport them to safety, and added: "I push on to the La Fourche this evening." [55]

In the meantime Elgee had returned from east of the Mississippi and reported the almost hopeless situation at Vicksburg. General Johnston proposed no plan of cooperation other than the one being attempted. Taylor, feeling a great need for Walker's assistance in lower Louisiana and despairing of any results from the campaign opposite Vicksburg, ordered him to move to Monroe where he could take steamers for Alexandria. But Kirby Smith, now on his way toward Walker's headquarters, countermanded the order and sent Walker back east of the Tensas.[56] Kirby Smith had received another urgent request from General Johnston: "Our only hope of saving Vicksburg now depends on the operations of your troops on the other side

---

[54] Taylor, *Destruction and Reconstruction*, 139–41.

[55] Richard Taylor to W. R. Boggs, June 23, 24, 1863, *Official Records*, Ser. I, Vol. XXVI, pt. 1, 210–11.

[56] Taylor, *Destruction and Reconstruction*, 139; Guy M. Bryan to P. O. Hebert, June 30, 1863, *Official Records*, Ser. I, Vol. XXVI, pt. 2, 97.

of the river. . . . Now, if you can contrive either to plant
artillery on the Mississippi banks, drive beef into Vicksburg, or join the garrison, should it be practicable or ex-
pedient, we may be able to save the city." Pemberton was
quoted as saying Vicksburg could probably be saved if
Kirby Smith could send in an "abundance of cattle" and
8,000 men.[57]

Kirby Smith might find an abundance of cattle, but he
had no 8,000 men to add to the garrison. But he was determined to do all he could. On June 20 he left for Monroe, sending in advance 300,000 percussion caps which he
hoped could be transported to Pemberton.[58] He inquired
of General Walker what could be done about throwing men
and supplies into Vicksburg. Walker replied: "I consider
it utterly impracticable." At no time since he had arrived
opposite Vicksburg had he had more than 4,700 effective
men, and at the present, even with Tappan's brigade from
Arkansas, he had not more than 4,200. To get to Vicksburg would require more than twenty miles of marching
down a narrow peninsula with overwhelming enemy forces
ready to move into his rear and render his defeat and capture inevitable. And as for the proposed batteries on the
banks of the Mississippi, Walker declared that there was
not a single point from Young's to Lake Providence that
could be held by his small force for more than a few
hours.[59]

After visiting Walker's headquarters, Kirby Smith gave
up all hope of relieving Vicksburg other than sending in
the caps. He notified Johnston to that effect on July 4. On

[57] J. E. Johnston to E. Kirby Smith, June 26, 1863, *ibid.*, Vol. XXIV, pt. 3, 979.

[58] E. Kirby Smith to P. O. Hebert, June 29, 1863, *ibid.*, Vol. XXVI, pt. 2, 97.

[59] J. G. Walker to E. Kirby Smith, July 3, 1863, *ibid.*, Vol. XXII, pt. 2, 915–16.

that same day Vicksburg was surrendered. Two days earlier President Davis had written from Richmond: "I am convinced that the safety of Vicksburg depends on your prompt and efficient co-operation. As far as practicable, I desire you to move your forces to the Mississippi River, and command in person operations for the relief of the besieged city." [60] The message arrived too late.

Back at his Shreveport headquarters again, Kirby Smith congratulated Taylor on his "brilliant successes at Berwick Bay" and urged him to transport captured supplies, especially ordnance, to places of security such as Natchitoches or Niblett's Bluff. Walker's force would be ordered to join him as soon as the Vicksburg situation was settled.[61] Two days later he instructed Walker that as soon as the fall of Vicksburg was verified he should move his division to Alexandria and await orders from Taylor.

The fall of Vicksburg would no doubt be followed by the loss of Port Hudson, Kirby Smith informed Taylor, thus giving to the enemy complete control of the Mississippi River. Consequently, any Confederate occupation of New Orleans would be only temporary. A considerable quantity of supplies might be seized, but the invading force would be caught in "a cul-de-sac" from which it could not escape. Even though the Federals gained complete control of the Mississippi, Kirby Smith did not expect an immediate attempt to occupy Louisiana. Nevertheless, Taylor was urged to make adequate preparations for the defense of the upper Red River valley. "Its occupation in force by the enemy loses us its supplies, and endangers the wheat-growing region of Texas; it cuts the department in two,

---

[60] Jefferson Davis to *id.*, July 2, 1863, *ibid.*, 902.
[61] E. Kirby Smith to Richard Taylor, July 9, 1863, *ibid.*, Vol. XXVI, pt. 2, 106–107.

and renders the concentration of the troops from Arkansas difficult, if not impracticable." [62]

Meanwhile, Taylor had followed his success at Brashear City by immediately dispatching Green and Major to Donaldsonville and Mouton to Thibodaux, from which point pickets were thrown out to within twenty-five miles of New Orleans. Green made an ill-advised and disastrous attack upon Fort Butler at the junction of the Lafourche and the Mississippi. The best Taylor could do for Port Hudson was to station a half dozen guns on the Mississippi near Donaldsonville and disrupt Federal commerce for a few days. Port Hudson surrendered on July 9. Taylor later complained: "The unwise movement toward Vicksburg retarded operations at Berwick's and on the river, and Port Hudson fell." [63]

Attempts at diversion along the Mississippi in Arkansas had failed even more completely than those in Louisiana. Late in May, 1863, Secretary of War Seddon had suggested to General Johnston that the seizure of Helena would be of assistance in relieving the pressure on Vicksburg. Johnston passed the suggestion on to Kirby Smith, and the latter forwarded it to General Holmes with instructions "to act as circumstances may justify." Holmes replied by telegraph: "I believe we can take Helena. Please let me attack it." "Most certainly do it," answered Kirby Smith.[64]

On this same day Kirby Smith explained to President Davis: "The district commanders are officers of merit and

[62] *Id.* to J. G. Walker, July 11, 1863, *ibid.*, 108; *id.* to Richard Taylor, July 12, 1863, *ibid.*, 109.

[63] Taylor, *Destruction and Reconstruction*, 143–45; Richard Taylor to W. R. Boggs, July 4, 1863, *Official Records*, Ser. I, Vol. XXVI, pt. 1, 212–14.

[64] E. Kirby Smith to S. Cooper, July 10, 1863; J. A. Seddon to Joseph E. Johnston, May 25 [23], 1863; T. H. Holmes to E. Kirby Smith, June 15, 1863; and E. Kirby Smith to T. H. Holmes, June 16, 1863, all in *Official Records*, Ser. I, Vol. XXII, pt. 1, 406–408.

ability, and while they have my confidence I shall not take the field in person within their district commands, unless a large concentration of troops becomes necessary, when I shall certainly place myself where both inclination and duty call me." [65] Such a decision was not easily reached; Kirby Smith liked to be in the midst of action. But he realized that for the present at least his duties must be principally administrative.

Holmes was eager to attack Helena. He had received numerous reports of heavy movement of troops to Grant's aid at Vicksburg, leaving other fortified points almost deserted. The capture of Helena would check this transfer, and, if reports were accurate, it could be easily accomplished. Before requesting Kirby Smith's permission to make the attack, Holmes had set out for a conference with General Price at Jacksport. While on the road he wrote ahead inquiring whether he and Price could "with propriety attack Helena" and whether the condition of Price's troops would "justify the attempt." Price was enthusiastic. His troops were "fully rested and in excellent spirits," he answered. And Marmaduke had reported only 4,000 or 5,000 Federals at Helena. If the movement should be "conducted with celerity and secrecy," Price entertained "no doubt of your being able to crush the foe at that point." [66]

Receiving Kirby Smith's approval, Holmes hastened to the attack. On June 18 he issued marching orders. Although seriously retarded by swollen streams the combined forces of Price, L. M. Walker, J. F. Fagan, and Marmaduke were before Helena by July 3. Holmes assumed command in person. The attack was ordered for daybreak

[65] E. Kirby Smith to Jefferson Davis, June 16, 1863, *ibid.*, pt. 2, 871–73.

[66] T. H. Holmes to W. R. Boggs, August 14, 1863, *ibid.*, pt. 1, 408–11; *id.* to Sterling Price, June 8, 1863, *ibid.*, pt. 2, 863; Price to Holmes, June 9, 1863, *ibid.*

July 4. Nature had protected the river town of Helena with a ring of hills, and Holmes knew little of the strength of Federal positions there. According to orders, Price was to strike Graveyard Hill, Fagan attack Hindman Hill, and Marmaduke move against Rightor Hill. Walker was to hold his troops in position along Sterling Road north of town and be ready to carry the fight into the town as soon as these hills were in Confederate hands.

The whole plan was badly managed. There was little co-ordination. Fagan and Marmaduke had attacked their objectives and been repulsed before Price began moving. Price succeeded in taking Graveyard Hill, but was soon forced to fall back. Losses were heavy.[67] On this same day Pemberton surrendered Vicksburg. Holmes fell back to White River, returned to his sick bed, and left Price in active command.

The Mississippi River was now in Federal possession; the Trans-Mississippi region was isolated. Henceforth, Kirby Smith must assume authority and responsibilities for which he had no training. On July 25, 1863, he issued General Orders No. 31: Communications with Richmond having been interrupted, henceforth, "all officers and agents connected with the army" in the Trans-Mississippi Department would "receive their instructions from the department commander." Such officers would report immediately to Shreveport headquarters, stating the nature of their duties and "the authority under which they are acting." [68]

Realizing the seriousness of his isolation, Kirby Smith turned his attention to possible foreign assistance. A. Superviele was dispatched to France with a letter to Confederate representative John Slidell. France must be impressed

---

[67] T. H. Holmes to W. R. Boggs, August 14, 1863, *ibid.*, pt. 1, 408–11.
[68] General Orders No. 31, *Official Records*, Ser. I, Vol. XXII, pt. 2, 948.

with the plight of the Trans-Mississippi region and urged to intervene in its behalf, Kirby Smith insisted. "This succor must come speedily, or it will be too late. Without assistance from abroad or an extraordinary interposition of Providence, less than twelve months will see this fair country irretrievably lost." With the cream of the Trans-Mississippi manpower with Confederate armies east of the River, "the aged, the infirm, and the lukewarm constitute the mass of the population that remains."

The French must be made to see that Federal conquest of the Trans-Mississippi region would bring their protectorate in Mexico face to face with a hostile United States "of exhaustless resources and great military strength, impelled by revenge and the traditional policy of its Government to overthrow all foreign influences on the American continent." If the French intended to intervene, Kirby Smith suggested, they should seize the east bank of the Rio Grande River and make that river secure for the importation of supplies for the Confederacy. "The whole cotton trade west of the Mississippi will thus be secured to the French market, and the enemy will be anticipated in making a lodgment on the Rio Grande, from which he could not be driven without great difficulty." [69]

The Trans-Mississippi Department would soon "be thrown entirely upon its own resources," Kirby Smith advised Adjutant General Cooper. "Without the assumption of extraordinary powers, my usefulness as department commander will be lost. If possible, instructions and orders to meet this emergency should be sent by special messengers. . . . Whilst my whole course as a military commander has hitherto been to keep within the limits of the laws, and to refrain from the exercise of power not strictly granted me, I feel that I shall now be compelled to assume

[69] E. Kirby Smith to John Slidell, September 2, 1863, ibid., 993–94.

great responsibilities, and to exercise powers with which I am not legally vested." He would, however, always act "with caution and forebearance," and trust that the President would sustain him in any necessary assumption of authority.[70]

This important announcement was referred to the Secretary of War and the President, and Davis indorsed thereon: "My confidence in the discretion and ability of General Smith assures me that I shall have no difficulty in sustaining any assumption of authority which may be necessary." He believed in selecting able heads of departments and then allowing them large discretion.[71]

[70] *Id.* to S. Cooper, July 28, 1863, *ibid.*, 949–50.    [71] *Ibid.*

## CHAPTER X

# COTTON AND CONFUSION

THE MOST PRESSING problem now confronting Kirby Smith was that of securing adequate military supplies, particularly arms. And to this problem there were two phases—importation and payment. The only practical route for importation was the Rio Grande and the only source of money supply was cotton. In keeping the Rio Grande open for both the importation of supplies and the exportation of cotton, the French could be of greatest assistance.

In 1861 Great Britain, France, and Spain had agreed jointly to intervene in Mexico to compel recognition and payment of foreign debts. A combined force was sent to Mexican waters to apply necessary pressure. Spain and Great Britain soon became suspicious of the intentions of Napoleon III of France and withdrew. The French remained, and in the summer of 1863 French troops occupied Mexico City. A hand-picked assembly of Mexican notables declared the old government headed by Juarez abolished, and called for the establishment of a limited monarchy with a Catholic prince to be known as Emperor. The crown was offered to Prince Ferdinand Maximilian of Austria. French troops remained to protect the throne of the new Emperor. This meant a French protectorate over

the occupied portions of Mexico. The United States protested vigorously but could do no more.

With hope of assistance for its cause, the Confederacy
showed sympathy for the French regime in Mexico. Yet
friendly relations between the Confederacy and Mexico
were constantly threatened by border incidents.[1] And even
when all was quiet along the border incoming cargoes of
arms were in danger of being seized by both the French
and the United States blockading squadrons.

When Kirby Smith took command west of the Mississippi, cotton in the vicinity of the Rio Grande was selling
at fifty to sixty cents per pound. Speculators, unrestricted
in their exports, had run the price of cotton out of the reach
of Confederate purchasing agents. Major Simeon Hart,
quartermaster for the purchase of supplies with cotton, was
without funds to acquire cotton at such inflated prices;
therefore, he had little of the staple with which to meet his
contracts for supplies.

When Hart was appointed to this position it was understood that he was to be "intrusted with the exclusive power
of purchasing cotton for the Department in all the upper
and western parts of Texas, and should be looked to for
the supply of munitions and quartermaster's stores for the
army in the Trans-Mississippi District." Long "experience
in the Mexican trade" plus a reputation for "great energy,
and practical judgment" had been responsible for his
appointment.[2]

Hart appealed to General Magruder for funds or an
order to impress a sufficient amount of cotton. Magruder
passed the request on to the new commanding general.
Kirby Smith declined to draw on the depositories without

---

[1] For details of these incidents see J. A. Quintero to J. P. Benjamin, April
20, 1863, and inclosures, *Official Records*, Ser. I, Vol. XXVI, pt. 2, 48 ff.

[2] J. A. Seddon to E. Kirby Smith, October 29, 1863, *ibid.*, Vol. LIII, Supplement, 904–905.

warrants from the Treasury Department at Richmond but called Magruder's attention to the impressment act passed by Congress. Magruder might control the shipment of cotton by speculators by impressing transportation facilities. Furthermore, he might control the government supply of cotton by "impressing so much as you need, giving purchase vouchers for it." [3]

On June 4, 1863, Kirby Smith dispatched a letter to C. G. Memminger, Secretary of the Treasury, calling attention to the great difficulty in getting funds into the Trans-Mississippi Department. Should Vicksburg and Port Hudson be lost, further transfer of funds would be almost impossible. Therefore, Kirby Smith recommended that an experienced Treasury official be sent west of the river and "invested with full authority and instructions to regulate the operations of your department on this side of the river." He further suggested that "notes paid into the hands of receivers, collectors, and depositors be reissued . . . as a part of the monthly issue of $50,000,000 authorized by the last Congress." Pending a reply from Memminger, Kirby Smith ordered the depositories not to cancel any more notes until further notice.[4]

The critical financial situation, Kirby Smith reasoned, might be somewhat relieved by tax money. He appointed tax collectors and charged them vigorously to collect all revenue due the Confederate government.[5] A vigorous collection of taxes, he hoped, would increase circulation and tend to retard the decline in value of Confederate currency. Already, he pointed out, many citizens, "demoralized by speculation and the love of gain," were refusing to accept

[3] J. B. Magruder to S. Cooper, June 8, 1863, *ibid.*, Vol. XXVI, pt. 2, 57–65; W. R. Boggs to Magruder, May 29, 1863, *ibid.*, 20.
[4] E. Kirby Smith to C. G. Memminger, June 4, 1863, *ibid.*, Vol. XXII, pt. 2, 854–55.
[5] Circular, September 4, 1863, *ibid.*, 990.

Confederate notes in payment for supplies or debts. "Any person persisting in this course," he warned, "can be declared an alien enemy, his property sequestered, and himself sent without our lines." Before going to this extreme, however, district commanders were ordered to impress property whenever needed, paying prices fixed by the state commissioners.[6]

In reporting to Adjutant General Cooper, Kirby Smith explained his hesitation to draw upon the depositories without warrants from Richmond and again insisted that a Treasury agent be sent west of the Mississippi with full authority to issue warrants on the depositories "upon estimates made and approved at department headquarters."[7] President Davis endorsed on this letter: "The difficulty of communicating with General Smith renders it necessary to perfect the organization so as to require few references to or orders from this place."

The cotton-trade situation along the Rio Grande continued to grow worse. Hart had made contracts for supplies, such as that with King, Kennedy and Stillman of Brownsville, which obligated him to furnish several hundred bales of cotton each month. But even with Magruder's assistance, Hart got little cotton. Furthermore, cargoes contracted for by the War Department at Richmond were arriving; still more cotton was needed to pay for them. Kirby Smith had urged Hart to make every effort to collect sufficient cotton at Matamoras. On May 20 the *Sea Queen* arrived off the mouth of the Rio Grande. This powerful steamer, said to be heavily loaded with war supplies under a contract with Bellot and Company, would need 1,800 to 2,000 bales of cotton for its return voyage.[8]

[6] General Orders, No. 45, September 16, 1863, *ibid.,* Vol. XXVI, pt. 2, 580.
[7] E. Kirby Smith to S. Cooper, June 16, 1863, *ibid.,* 55–57.
[8] James J. Bennett to Simeon Hart, May 30, 1863, *ibid.,* 78.

Magruder, although stressing the seriousness of a probable failure of the Confederate government to fulfill its
obligations, notified Kirby Smith that he had decided not
to impress cotton on his own responsibility. However, if
Kirby Smith would issue a direct order for impressment
he would execute it faithfully. Hart made a direct appeal
to Richmond for an impressment order, but both Davis
and Seddon endorsed thereon that they favored such a step
only as a last resort. Kirby Smith, however, did not hesitate. Without waiting for further instructions from Richmond, he ordered Magruder: "In all cases where the exi-
gencies of the service make it necessary . . . you will
make impressments in accordance with the act, without
first referring the matter to these headquarters." [9]

Almost as serious as the shortage of funds with which
to buy cotton was the difficulty in transporting it from the
interior to the Rio Grande. There were no railroads in
western Texas; consequently, the wagon train was the only
means of transportation. Kirby Smith found a number of
soldiers detailed as teamsters in this transportation service.
These he ordered Magruder to return to active service as
soon as their places could be taken by slaves hired from
planters. He realized the delicacy in meddling with the
slavery question, and sought to put the matter on a patriotic basis. Magruder was instructed to send a few loyal
planters among the other planters in the slave counties
"to induce the owner to hire as many as he can spare from
his plantation." As a last resort, Magruder was to make
a *pro rata* assessment, and impress the number needed.
This action, however, was to be taken with great precaution "so as to wound the sensibilities of the people as little

⁹ J. B. Magruder to W. R. Boggs, June 23, 1863, *ibid.*, 77; Simeon Hart to
J. A. Seddon, June 20, 1863, *ibid.*, Vol. LIII, Suppl., 873–74; E. Kirby Smith
to J. B. Magruder, June 23, 1863, *ibid.*, Vol. XXVI, pt. 2, 78.

as possible." For it was equally as important to secure "loyal and zealous" support among those at home as to increase the ranks. Precaution was doubly important in Texas at that time in order not to damage the chances of loyal Confederates in the state election in August. It would be advisable, Kirby Smith suggested to Magruder, not to resort to impressment of slaves until after the state election. Even in the impressment of cotton to pay for the military supplies on the *Sea Queen,* it would be wise to limit it to the area along the Rio Grande until after the election. The important point was to avoid any unnecessary excitement which might "influence the minds of voters." [10]

Even should an adequate number of slaves be secured as teamsters, this would not solve the problem of transportation. Kirby Smith estimated that government-owned cotton in the vicinity of Shreveport alone amounted to 20,000 bales. To move such an amount to the Rio Grande by wagon would require months. Yet the military supplies that were to be purchased with it were needed immediately. A possible solution was offered in a proposal by one S. Simpson, who claimed to represent a number of English firms, that he would buy government cotton where it was stored and pay in sterling exchange, which could be used in the immediate purchase of supplies. Kirby Smith was impressed by the proposal. "This will relieve you from the difficulty of transportation to Matamoras," he wrote Hart. He advised Hart to enter into some such arrangement with Simpson or others. [11]

All connected with the cotton problem realized that unless some better method of delivery could be devised foreign confidence in the Confederacy's ability to meet its obligations would be seriously shaken. For weeks there had been

[10] S. S. Anderson to J. B. Magruder, June 26, 1863, *ibid.,* 85–86.
[11] E. Kirby Smith to Simeon Hart, June 24, 1863, *ibid.,* 80–81.

vessels lying at anchor at the mouth of the Rio Grande while their captains tried in vain to secure cotton in exchange for valuable military cargoes. As late as June 11 only seventy-five bales of government cotton had arrived while speculators brought in thousands daily. Furthermore, loyal merchants at Brownsville and Matamoras, who had furnished large quantities of supplies on Hart's promise to pay in cotton, were growing impatient. Their patriotism could scarcely be expected to endure forever.[12]

Senator William S. Oldham of Texas later reported to Davis that privileges granted to cotton speculators in Texas had greatly demoralized the people. Some thirty to forty persons, "mostly Jews, Yankees, and foreigners," had secured contracts to import military supplies and export cotton to pay for them. "The privilege to speculate in cotton was the real subject of the contract; the furnishing of supplies was but an incident." Few supplies were brought in while cotton was taken to the Rio Grande and sold for gold. "The planters and small traders carried Treasury notes there to purchase supplies and replenish their stocks of goods, and were forced to submit to its depreciation in selling it for gold to men who had obtained the gold for Texas cotton bought of the planters with Confederate notes." Oldham further charged that no fewer than 5,000 conscripts had been detailed by the conscript bureau to haul this cotton for speculators. Those persons thus favored in the cotton business had made great profits, but there was "a deep feeling of dissatisfaction" among the victims. Oldham was severe in his denunciation of military orders which he claimed had "tested both the patience and patriotism of the people of Texas." The military authorities, he declared, had no respect for agents of the

[12] Charles Russell to B. Bloomfield, June 11, 1863, *ibid.*, 93–94.

War or Treasury departments. Many quartermasters had themselves turned speculators.[13] Davis referred this letter to Kirby Smith.

The urgent needs of the Trans-Mississippi Department, the necessity for preserving Confederate credit, and the complete failure of Hart to deliver cotton drove Kirby Smith to order Brigadier General H. P. Bee, commanding in western Texas, to impress sufficient cotton to meet the needs of the government. A few exemptions from impressment were to be allowed, particularly to those who were collecting cotton to pay for the importation of machinery. Since impressment was certain to be unpopular and those officers commanding in Texas needed to preserve their popularity as long as possible, Magruder and Bee were directed to make all impressments in the name of Kirby Smith and by his order.[14] Bee soon complained that the order to impress cotton was almost nullified by the lack of transportation. He had two hundred wild mules and no one to work them. His teamsters had deserted. They would not work for Confederate currency worth a few cents on the dollar when they could get five or ten dollars per day in specie elsewhere.[15]

The need for arms was so great that General Kirby Smith was willing to incur considerable unpopularity in order to secure them. Before the fall of Vicksburg he had consistently urged Pemberton to forward at least 10,000 stands of arms. Those promised him from Richmond had not arrived, and he figured that they had been stopped at Vicksburg. Unable to get any action from the hard-pressed Pemberton, he appealed to Richmond for application of

[13] W. S. Oldham to Jefferson Davis, January 4, 1864, *ibid.*, XXXIV, pt. 2, 820–21.

[14] E. Kirby Smith to J. B. Magruder, June 27, 1863, *ibid.*, Vol. XXVI, pt. 2, 94–95.

[15] H. P. Bee to Edmund P. Turner, August 24, 1863, *ibid.*, 181.

pressure upon the Vicksburg commander.[16] When Vicksburg fell, the arms intended for Kirby Smith were seized by the enemy.

The situation now grew worse, yet from Richmond there came encouragement. General Josiah Gorgas, chief of ordnance, wrote that unless "some unseen contingency intervenes," he would have 8,000 to 12,000 arms on the coast of Texas within the next three months. This was welcome news, for in Arkansas alone one third of the organized troops were without arms. Governor Flanagin proposed to call up 5,000 to 8,000 state troops whenever arms were available. And the principal chief of the Choctaws was complaining of not receiving arms promised by the Confederacy. Kirby Smith tried to pacify the Indians by explaining how their arms were lost at Vicksburg. Others would be forwarded to the Indians as soon as they arrived.[17]

Magruder was directed to rush to Shreveport headquarters the first 6,000 arms landed in Texas. What about his own 7,000 unarmed men, Magruder replied. Might he not keep such arms as he needed or at least his *pro rata* share of them? He might keep 3,000 Kirby Smith agreed; the remainder must be forwarded immediately. There had arrived within the Department many men recently prisoners from Vicksburg. The department now had within its limits an estimated 10,000 "old and tried soldiers" who were without arms.[18]

[16] E. Kirby Smith to J. C. Pemberton, June 6, 1863, *ibid.,* Vol. XXII, pt. 2, 859; *id.* to S. Cooper, June 9, 1863, *ibid.,* Vol. XXVI, pt. 2, 41–42.

[17] Josiah Gorgas to E. Kirby Smith, July 22, 1863, *ibid.,* 118–19; W. R. Boggs to J. B. Magruder, August 13, 30, 1863, *ibid.,* 164; E. Kirby Smith to *id.,* August 30, 1863, *ibid.,* 189; *id.* to Principal Chief of Choctaw Nation, August 13, 1863, *ibid.,* Vol. XXII, pt. 2, 967.

[18] Special Orders, No. 134, September 10, 1863, *ibid.,* 1003; S. S. Anderson to J. B. Magruder, September 10, 1863, *ibid.,* 1003; Magruder to W. R. Boggs, October 12, 1863, *ibid.,* Vol. XXVI, pt. 2, 304; Boggs to Magruder, November 6, 1863, *ibid.,* 393.

There was truly little cause to argue over arms until they arrived and cotton could be collected in sufficient quantities to pay for them. Magruder and Bee attempted impressment. A "tremendous uproar" resulted; little cotton was made available. Hart claimed that all impressed cotton as well as that purchased by Magruder's quartermaster should be turned over to him. Magruder refused. No definite system was worked out. Confusion prevailed.

Kirby Smith hoped to relieve some of this confusion by centralization of administration. On August 3, 1863, he announced the appointment of Lieutenant Colonel W. A. Broadwell as chief of the Cotton Bureau for the Trans-Mississippi Department. Henceforth all government agents engaged in buying or disposing of cotton would report to and receive instructions through him.[19]

With the Federals in control of the Mississippi they would no doubt attempt to make it an artery of through trade to New Orleans. Secretary of War Seddon urged Kirby Smith to mount sufficient guns along the west bank seriously to disrupt if not completely destroy that trade. Furthermore, the Federals would likely attempt to seize all cotton within reach of the west bank and even begin to contract for the growing of cotton on plantations near the river. Kirby Smith was urged to burn all cotton within Federal reach that could not be moved to safety. Owners themselves could not be depended upon to destroy their own cotton. Hoping against hope that it would not be seized by the enemy, they would postpone destruction until too late. Seddon urged special efforts to prevent the cultivation of river plantations under Federal auspices. It might even be wise, he suggested, to withdraw all planters and their property a distance of eight or ten miles from the river,

---

[19] General Orders, No. 35, August 3, 1863, *ibid.*, Vol. XXII, pt. 2, 953.

thus rendering the border area useless to the enemy.[20]

Magruder made a vigorous effort to enforce Kirby Smith's impressment order. When he learned that Bee was exempting cotton belonging to persons to whom the Confederacy was indebted, he bluntly informed him that such was not in accord with orders. "Individuals can wait for their money or their cotton," Magruder exclaimed; "delay, though it may result in loss to them, is not death—the death of credit abroad—as it is to us." The immediate problem was to fulfill the contracts for the cargoes arriving from abroad. No cotton belonging to the state was to be impressed, but no contractors were to be exempted. Neither was a planter to be allowed more cotton than was needed "to purchase a reasonable amount of supplies." To allow him more would be to class him as a speculator. These were orders, specific and binding, until Kirby Smith should say otherwise.[21]

News of the intention to burn all cotton in danger of falling into enemy hands brought vigorous protests from both planters and speculators. What a pity to destroy cotton that would be of such great value in European markets. One John A. Stevenson proposed to Broadwell that he would exchange 11,549 bales of cotton located at specified unexposed points for a like number belonging to the Confederate government and in danger of falling into Federal possession. The only additional requirement that he made was that Kirby Smith issue an order not to burn the cotton thus exchanged. Stevenson in turn proposed to dispose of the cotton to citizens of foreign nations friendly to the Confederacy. The purchasers were to be given pos-

---

[20] J. A. Seddon to E. Kirby Smith, August 3, 1863, *ibid.,* 952–53.

[21] J. B. Magruder to H. P. Bee, August 4, 1863, *ibid.,* Vol. XXVI, pt. 2, 137–39.

session of the cotton where located and were to be given permission to transport it beyond the Confederate lines.

Kirby Smith approved the proposition and authorized Broadwell to enter into such an agreement.[22]

The cotton controversy, especially in Texas, brought charge and countercharge against those who were in any way connected with cotton trade. Kirby Smith lamented that "the state of the public mind and the tone of public feeling is such that every man jealous of his reputation hesitates about having his name associated with any Government transaction in cotton."

Broadwell gave a more detailed description of the situation in his report to Memminger.

"The policy pursued [in Texas] has been vacillating, and the general management exceedingly bad; a variety of agents and numberless contractors appearing in the market at one time brought the Government in competition with itself, and prices were in consequence rapidly advanced; speculation was rife, and great eagerness manifested to invest the currency in an article by which the money could be converted into a sounder character of funds. Selling cotton for gold, buying up Confederate paper at its depreciation, and reinvesting in our cotton, which could be again sent to Mexico, was ascertained to be a profitable business, and led to swindling and bad faith. A system of bogus Government contracts was inaugurated, by which the fortunate few obtained permits giving them freedom from molestation. The cotton was invariably carried out, frequently with the use of conscripts as teamsters, and other assistance from the Government, the contracts rarely ever filled. The bonds that had been given for their faithful performance had no validity in law, and would have been forfeited if this were not the case. The public service was embarrassed by a failure to receive what the officers were led to expect, and the necessities of the Government compelled the impressment of the cotton of those who appeared on the Rio Grande without military protection. A species of favoritism was established, which created great dissatisfaction, and continued conflict

---

[22] J. A. Stevenson to W. A. Broadwell, August 24, 1863, Kirby Smith Papers; E. Kirby Smith to *id.*, August 29, 1863, *ibid.;* Copy of agreement, dated August 24, 1863, *ibid.*

grew out of the various military orders, which appeared necessary from time to time." [23]

Kirby Smith tried to persuade Colonel A. W. Terrell to head a special cotton bureau for Texas, but he declined, giving among other reasons a distrust of Broadwell. The offer was then made to P. W. Gray, who was assured that if he would consent a definite policy would be adopted. The sole duty of the Texas bureau, Kirby Smith explained, would be "to get possession of and collect cotton at depots" where it would be available and safe. The greatest difficulty would be in securing transportation of cotton "without exciting the opposition of the people." He planned to issue cotton certificates on the cotton collected in depots. A trusted agent would then be sent abroad to purchase supplies with these certificates and ship them to the Trans-Mississippi Department "without the intermedium of contracting parties." [24]

Gray apparently also declined the appointment, and Kirby Smith sent Guy M. Bryan from Shreveport headquarters to Houston to organize the bureau and select personnel, giving him full authority to act. Four "good men" from planting and mercantile groups were chosen. William J. Hutchins was made chief and W. P. Ballinger attorney.[25]

On November 22, 1863, Kirby Smith formally assigned Hutchins to his new post with the rank and pay of lieutenant colonel. He was to "obtain from the planters, by

[23] W. A. Broadwell to C. G. Memminger, December 26, 1863, *Official Records,* Ser. I, Vol. XXVI, pt. 2, 535–38.

[24] E. Kirby Smith to P. W. Gray, October 13, 1863, *ibid.,* 310–12.

[25] The other members were James Sorley, W. J. Kyle, B. A. Shepherd, and George Bell. E. Kirby Smith to W. A. Broadwell, November 1, 1863, Kirby Smith Papers; Guy M. Bryan to Pryor Lea, October 8, 1864, Austin *Weekly State Gazette,* October 26, 1864.

sale or agreement, and, if necessary, by impressment, all cotton that the Government may require for the purchase of army stores of all kinds, and to meet existing liabilities heretofore accrued." All Confederate agents, officials, and contractors "engaged in the purchase or removal of cotton" were to report to him the nature and extent of their business and be governed by his instructions. Future applications for contracts were to be first submitted to him. Military commanders were instructed not to make any cotton contracts without Hutchins' approval. Hutchins himself would report to department headquarters through Broadwell.[26]

The Texas cotton bureau immediately announced its plan. Without a specific censure of any person or group the previous confused modes of handling the cotton question were pronounced failures. A new plan was necessary, one that would "secure uniformity, efficiency, and permanency"; preserve faith in the Confederate government; and supply the army with the necessary "arms, clothing, medicines, etc." As old citizens of Texas who had been interested in cotton for many years, the members of the bureau had accepted their offices "not as a matter of choice, but from a sense of duty." For the success of their efforts they would rely upon "the frank co-operation of the planters." "Our plan is to purchase one half of the cotton of the planter, or other holder, and, on delivery at a Government depot or other place agreed upon, to give an exemption against military impressment for a like quantity. Under this exemption, cotton can be held or exported at the pleasure of the owner, and teams engaged in its transportation will also be free from impressment. For cotton sold to us we will give certificates at its specie value, to be

[26] Special Orders, No. 198, November 22, 1863, *Official Records*, Ser. I, Vol. XXVI, pt. 2, 437–38.

paid for in cotton bonds or such other equivalent as Congress may provide."

This plan was announced in the form of an appeal to the people and was designed to be permanent. It had been worked out after conferences with Kirby Smith, Magruder, Senator Oldham, and other legislators who promised to seek such Congressional action as was needed.[27] "Planters of Texas," the appeal concluded, ". . . [your] cotton is contraband to the enemy; every bale falling into his hands is seized for his Government. We appeal to you, shall there not be united, harmonious, active, efficient co-operation, by devoting a portion of your cotton to the great duties of the crisis—the successful defense of Texas from enslavement and devastation?"[28]

The great confusion could scarcely be eliminated immediately by the appointment of a cotton bureau. Magruder was never a man to permit law or orders from a superior to interfere with what he considered military necessity. He and Major Hart had previously made contracts with Nelson Clements and E. B. Nichols for the importation of supplies from Europe. The supplies were to be delivered at Brownsville and paid for in cotton. Some of the supplies, including a number of Enfield rifles, had arrived, but Hart had failed to provide the necessary cotton. Magruder ordered his chief quartermaster, Major B. Bloomfield, to purchase the required amount of cotton. More than fifteen hundred bales had been purchased and were in the process of shipment when Kirby Smith intervened. All cotton in Magruder's possession would be surrendered to designated persons, he ordered. Magruder,

[27] Broadwell later stated that the plan was not approved by him. He thought the "Government should control all cotton, and allow none exported, except . . . to supply the military necessities of the country and preserve our credit." Broadwell to C. G. Memminger, December 26, 1863, *ibid.,* 535–38.

[28] "To the Cotton Planters of Texas," December 4, 1863, *ibid.,* 480–82.

much irritated, asked that he be "relieved from all connection with the cotton business." [29]

Special Order No. 198, issued a week earlier, had already clearly relieved Magruder of all authority over cotton. However, he did not cease issuing orders. On December 20 he ordered Hutchins to provide cotton for payment "of all contracts for arms and ammunition" contracted for by him. If he could get 30,000 stands of arms, Magruder insisted, they would be worth all of the cotton in Texas. Two contracts were specified. These contractors had been granted permission to take cotton out of the country. One of them, T. W. House, had been sent to Vera Cruz to arrange for bringing in 16,000 Enfields recently released by the French. These rifles were to be paid for in cotton at the rate of thirty cents per pound, and the rifles might cost as much as sixty dollars each. In confidence, Magruder stated to the cotton bureau that at least one fourth of his troops were without arms.[30]

The cotton bureau protested against Magruder's violation of departmental orders. The general replied that he knew the military situation, and it was his duty, if the need arose, to disregard orders of his superior "until he can be heard from." [31]

His superior was not long in being "heard from." By Special Order No. 198, Kirby Smith informed Magruder, "the operations of the cotton office are independent of your control, and were so intended by that order to be. You have no further connection with that subject other than to render such military assistance as may be needed by Colonel Hutchins for carrying out the objects for which that office was created. . . . You will, therefore, issue no or-

[29] J. B. Magruder to W. R. Boggs, November 29, 1863, *Official Records,* Ser. I, Vol. XXVI, pt. 2, 457.

[30] E. P. Turner to W. J. Hutchins, December 20, 1863, *ibid.,* 517–18.

[31] J. B. Magruder to James Sorley, December 21, 1863, *ibid.,* 520–22.

ders interfering with the cotton office in any manner, except
. . . for military reasons." Interference for military reasons must be temporary and a copy of the order forwarded
to headquarters immediately. Colonel Hutchins was not
subject to orders from Major Bloomfield and Major Hart
was subordinate to Colonel Hutchins.[32]

This communication stung Magruder hard, although he
must have expected something like it. He could not have
been ignorant of the intention of Order No. 198. Since he
had apparently lost the confidence of the lieutenant general commanding, he replied, a request to be relieved from
duty was in order. He was restrained from making such
a request only by "the generous confidence placed in me
by the army and people of Texas." Under existing conditions, he felt that his knowledge of affairs in that state
made him the only person capable of rendering efficient
service there. He would cheerfully comply with all Kirby
Smith's instructions except the one requiring him to confer with Lieutenant Colonel Hutchins in times of military
necessity. He could not "consent to consult with my inferior officers as to the exercise of the highest powers with
which the law clothes the general in cases of emergency."
He was "therefore under the painful necessity of declining, respectfully but firmly, to consult with Lieutenant
Colonel Hutchins as to the course I should pursue in any
case of military necessity."

At great length, Magruder sought to defend his action
as being in the best interest of his district. His orders which
appeared to run counter to those from headquarters, he
explained, were either a military necessity or issued before
he had knowledge of those powers assigned to the Texas
cotton-bureau. His sole aim was to supply his troops with
badly needed arms. The use of cotton was necessary in

[32] C. S. West to J. B. Magruder, December 26, 1863, *ibid.*, 538–39.

securing those arms; military necessity demanded that he secure that cotton.

For future guidance he wished specific instructions: First. Was he to fulfill the arms agreement with House? Second. Should he cancel the instructions to Colonel Benavides? Third. Was he or the cotton bureau to grant exemptions of slaves from impressment? [33]

If the contract with House was on the most favorable terms, Kirby Smith replied, then it should be carried out. The cotton bureau would no doubt be able to furnish the required amount of cotton. Since the instructions to Benavides had probably already been carried out, there would be no point in canceling them. As for the exemption of slaves from impressment, the cotton bureau possessed no such power. However, if it was necessary to exempt slaves, the bureau must first consult the military commander. But it "would prevent confusion for all future impressments of cotton to be made through" the cotton office. [34]

It was Kirby Smith's plan to make the Texas cotton bureau the purchasing agent for the department, canceling all unfilled contracts already in existence, but leaving military authorities to determine the quality and quantity of supplies required. [35] Hutchins was to select as his assistants experts in the purchase of ordnance, quartermaster, and commissary supplies. Lists of supplies needed would be furnished through the adjutant general's office at headquarters. The need for ordnance stores was particularly pressing. "One large battle or the loss of our army supply trains to either the Army of Arkansas or Louisiana," Kirby

[33] J. B. Magruder to W. R. Boggs, January 6, 1864, *ibid.*, Vol. XXXIV, pt. 2, 830–37.

[34] C. S. West to J. B. Magruder, January 16, 1864, *ibid.*, 881–82.

[35] A part of the credit for the military disaster in Arkansas during the previous year was attributed to inferior powder secured from Mexico.

Smith revealed to Hutchins, "would leave us without powder and but little lead." [36]

By the close of 1863 there had been some improvement of the cotton situation, but it was still far from efficient. No figures on the work of the Texas bureau were yet available, but Broadwell was able to report on other purchases. His own cotton office had made no purchases, sold no cotton, nor made a contract. He had spent his time collecting "data as to what had been done, what ought to be done, and saving the property liable to loss." His data revealed that about 100,000 bales of cotton had been purchased by other agents—14,000 in Arkansas, 20,000 in the Ouachita country, 45,000 in the Red River parishes of Louisiana, and about 16,000 in Texas through Major Hart's office. Two very efficient quartermasters—Captain W. W. Barrett and Captain N. A. Birge—had collected 350 wagons and transported 7,000 bales from Louisiana to the banks of the Sabine River, from which point they could be sent to Houston by railroad. And Major A. W. McKee, quartermaster at Alexandria, had sent 1,600 bales to Niblett's Bluff for the use of Major Bloomfield, Magruder's quartermaster. [37]

Attempts to bring in money and arms via the Texas coast had been equally as unsuccessful as the acquisition of cotton. The *Love Bird,* an English schooner loaded by Nelson Clements of London and consigned to Hale & Company, carrying "10,000 Enfields, 156 revolvers, 2,000,000 cartridges, and 5,000,000 caps," dropped anchor in Mexican waters and began unloading by lighters at Point Isabel, Texas. When 4,200 Enfields had been unloaded, the

[36] E. Kirby Smith to W. J. Hutchins, March 4, 1864, *Official Records,* Ser. I, Vol. XXXIV, pt. 2, 1019–20.

[37] W. A. Broadwell to C. G. Memminger, December 26, 1863, *ibid.,* Vol. XXVI, pt. 2, 535–38.

French frigate *Magellan* seized the *Love Bird* and the remaining arms, although General Bee, commanding in west Texas, had notified the French consul of the expected arrival of the *Love Bird* and that its cargo was exclusively for Confederate use. The commander of the *Magellan* claimed to have information that these arms were destined for use by the Mexican forces of Juarez.[38]

"You have in many respects done your duty faithfully to your country," Bee wrote Clements, "but you have lacked foresight and prudence." Those Enfields seized by the French might have won the war for the Confederacy during the coming winter, he suggested. Clements had blundered by placing incompetent persons in charge. The *Love Bird* should have been anchored in Confederate waters. "I am disheartened and annoyed," Bee concluded.[39]

Kirby Smith was also annoyed. Brigadier General James E. Slaughter was soon on his way to relieve Bee in west Texas. It was hoped that Slaughter possessed "the faculty of controlling the Mexican population and accommodating the differences which are continually arising on that frontier." [40]

While the French and the Federals were seizing arms bound for the Confederacy, Mexicans were seizing funds. High waters and Federal operations on the Mississippi had made the transfer of funds hazardous. Since the fall of Vicksburg Kirby Smith had been sending urgent pleas to Richmond for financial assistance. Months passed and nothing was heard from the Secretary of the Treasury. Finally Kirby Smith learned through the Secretary of War that financial plans were in the making. But for this in-

[38] Statement by French Consul I. I. Buzon, September 30, 1863, *ibid.*, 273–74; H. P. Bee to Nelson Clements, October 3, 1863, *ibid.*, 286–87.

[39] *Ibid.* Although Slidell later secured the release of these arms, they were not on the coast of Texas.

[40] E. Kirby Smith to S. Cooper, June 10, 1863, *ibid.*, 43.

direct information, he wrote President Davis, "I should ere this have taken the matter into my own hands." If relief did not come soon he would be compelled to establish branches of both the Treasury and Post Office departments, and "raise a loan from the people on certificates, pledging the faith of the Government to redeem them in interest-bearing bonds." In addition to the lack of funds for purchasing supplies, there was a lack of money to pay troops.[41] "Bonds in large quantities and of small denomination should be sent," Kirby Smith urged. "The redundant currency should be called in by loans on the people. This could be accomplished successfully with bonds, or interest-bearing certificates, made payable by Congress for Government dues." [42]

Six weeks later Kirby Smith was again pleading with Davis for financial relief. Faith in the Confederate government was being greatly reduced by failure to settle the accounts of deceased soldiers whose families were in need. Only the establishment of a branch of the Treasury Department west of the Mississippi could furnish the relief demanded. And if it was the plan to appoint someone west of the river to that position, "I know no one who, from his standing in the community, his financial and administrative abilities, and his integrity of character, would be better fitted than Dr. S. A. Smith, of Alexandria, Louisiana." [43]

The Treasury Department at Richmond attempted to send relief by way of Mexico. A special representative

---

[41] District commanders were quarreling among themselves over what little money was available. Magruder claimed to have been required to purchase large quantities of supplies for Taylor in Louisiana and William Steele in the Indian Territory, paying for them out of his allotment. Neither, he stated, had repaid him. Magruder to W. R. Boggs, *Official Records,* September 29, 1863, Ser. I, Vol. XXVI, pt. 2, 269–70.

[42] E. Kirby Smith to Jefferson Davis, September 28, 1863, *ibid.,* Vol. XXII, pt. 2, 1028–29.

[43] *Id.* to *id.,* November 15, 1863, *ibid.,* 1069–70.

carrying $16,000,000 arrived in Monterey. Upon advice of friends he placed his money boxes in temporary custody of Patricio Milmo of Milmo and Company, a supposedly friendly house with which the Confederacy had done much business. Milmo later refused to surrender the funds and notified Confederate authorities they were being held as security for unpaid obligations. Kirby Smith, after considerable correspondence in protest against such a step, notified Governor Vidaurri: "In view of the action of Messrs. P. Milmo & Co. I have been constrained reluctantly, to prohibit for the present the exportation of cotton, and also the egress of all Mexican property." [44]

Santiago Vidaurri, governor of the border states of Nuevo León and Coahuila and sometime in control of Tamaulipas with its important port of Matamoras, was the father-in-law of Milmo. From the beginning of the war Vidaurri had professed friendship for the Confederacy. Through the effective services of Confederate agent Juan A. Quintero he had been made to see the importance of Confederate trade. Large quantities of Mexican goods for which there was no other market could be sold to the Confederacy at a tremendous profit. And by permitting the passage of European goods through Mexican border states into the Confederacy, substantial income from tariffs would replenish Vidaurri's almost empty treasury.

Before Kirby Smith assumed command west of the Mississippi a number of contracts had been made between Confederate agents and border state trading firms. In most cases cotton was promised in payment for Mexican and European supplies. As previously noted, the difficulty in procuring cotton had left Confederate agents unable to pay. Milmo and others were clamoring for payment. In seizing the Confederate funds Milmo claimed to be taking

[44] For the lengthy correspondence see *ibid.*, Vol. LIII, Suppl., 930 ff.

the only course that would guarantee payments to Mexican creditors.

When informed of the seizure of Confederate funds by Milmo and Company, Vidaurri at first refused to take any part in the controversy. But Kirby Smith's order closing border trade changed his mind. He could not afford to lose his only important source of revenue. Kirby Smith appointed three commissioners to join Quintero in putting pressure on Vidaurri. An agreement was soon reached. Debts due to Milmo and his associates would be paid. Other claims would be investigated. The Confederate funds would be released. Good relations between Vidaurri and the Confederacy were thus re-established.[45]

[45] The best study of Mexican-Confederate relations is found in Frank L. Owsley, *King Cotton Diplomacy: Foreign Relations of the Confederate States of America* (Chicago, 1931).

## CHAPTER XI

# THE GENERAL AND THE GOVERNORS

W<small>HILE AWAITING THE</small> outcome at Vicksburg and Port Hudson, Kirby Smith had urged Magruder to concentrate all disposable troops in East Texas in the vicinity of Niblett's Bluff. Regardless of the outcome of the struggle for control of the Mississippi, Kirby Smith expected Banks to renew his attack upon the Red River Valley, which he would use as a base of operation against Texas. The presence of a considerable force at Niblett's Bluff would embarrass Banks in such an attempt. Should the Federals fail before Vicksburg and Port Hudson, troops would probably be pulled from Missouri to assist the Army of Mississippi, relieving the pressure on Arkansas, and making possible a Confederate concentration in Lower Louisiana sufficient to protect that "rich and beautiful region." In any case, Niblett's Bluff had great advantages as a place of rendezvous; from that point troops could be moved to the defense of Red River Valley, Lower Louisiana, or Galveston.[1]

Magruder began moving his troops toward Niblett's Bluff, called upon the governor of Texas to raise a defense

[1] E. Kirby Smith to J. B. Magruder, June 11, 1863, *Official Records*, Ser. I, Vol. XXVI, pt. 2, 47–48.

force of 10,000 men, and requested that Kirby Smith meet him at Rusk, Cherokee County, for a conference on defensive strategy.[2] Before the proposed conference could be held both Vicksburg and Port Hudson had surrendered and the problem of defense had been made more serious. Federal control of the Mississippi made co-operation between Confederate forces east and west of the river almost impossible. Not only was Kirby Smith left on his own resources but his department lay open to invasion from many sides. Soon each district commander and the governor of the state, fearing that theirs would be the region invaded, began calling for re-enforcements and military supplies. Following the defeat at Helena, civil and military leaders in Arkansas lost all feeling of security. Kirby Smith thought them unduly alarmed, and stated to Holmes that serious enemy operations against Arkansas at that time were unlikely.[3]

Governor Flanagin of Arkansas had already complained to President Davis that Arkansas' defenses had been greatly weakened and he feared there was a plan to abandon the state.[4] Kirby Smith assured Flanagin that no such abandonment had ever been contemplated. The recent removal of some troops from Arkansas had been a military necessity. Yet even after the removals, troops left to the Arkansas district were almost equal to the total strength in the remaining portions of the department. As for the removal of machinery from Camden, an act for which he had been criticized, this was but a precaution. Camden was within easy reach of the enemy operating from the Mississippi. "Machinery and material of vital importance to it must be removed to safe points in the in-

2 J. B. Magruder to E. Kirby Smith, June 29, 1863, *ibid.*, 96–97.
3 E. Kirby Smith to T. H. Holmes, July 10, 1863, *ibid.*, Vol. XXII, pt. 2, 916.
4 Jefferson Davis to H. Flanagin, July 15, 1863, *ibid.*, 931–33.

terior. Disregard of this principle has already seriously impaired our resources."

Although the abandonment of Arkansas was not contemplated, Kirby Smith did warn that should the Federals mass a formidable force for a push up the Red River, the Arkansas valley might of necessity have to be temporarily abandoned and all available forces concentrated on Red River. The governor was urged to prepare for such an eventuality by organizing a local defense force of either militia or persons outside the conscript ages. "In conclusion, I would assure the Governor of Arkansas that I have the interests of his State at heart; that I am not biased by local influence, but shall labor faithfully with the limited means at my disposal to preserve the integrity of this department." [5]

President Davis was much concerned over the discontent in Arkansas. "You now have not merely a military, but also a political problem involved in your command," he explained to Kirby Smith. There were rumors of a movement to detach the Trans-Mississippi states from the other portion of the Confederacy. "Unreasonable men think they have been neglected, and timid men may hope that they can make better terms for themselves if their cause is not combined with that of the Confederacy," Davis observed. He realized that Kirby Smith could not satisfy the wants of each section, yet he thought much discontent might be avoided and misconstruction prevented by explanation to the governors of the states. "Men are sometimes made valuable coadjutors by conferring with them without surrendering any portion of that control which is essential for a commander to retain." Even in the establishment of war plants it might be necessary "to defer to the wishes of the people of the different States to have such

[5] E. Kirby Smith to id., July 11, 1863, ibid., 919-20.

establishments within their limits." At any rate, establishments should be so scattered that "not more than one could be destroyed in a single expedition of the enemy." These, however, were problems that the Trans-Mississippi commander alone could solve. His success in this field would greatly influence military success, for "in proportion as the country exhibits a power to sustain itself, so will the men able to bear arms be inspired with a determination to repel invasion."

"We are now in the darkest hour of our political existence," the President concluded. "I am happy in the confidence I feel in your ability, zeal, and discretion. . . . May God guide and preserve you, and grant to us a future in which we may congratulate each other on the achievements of the independence of our country." [6]

Discontent and excitement in Arkansas were real, although founded on false rumors. General Price relayed to department headquarters information, which he believed reliable, that the enemy was massing 60,000 men for a three-pronged movement into Arkansas—"One army from Northwestern Arkansas, another down the White River Valley, and the third from the Mississippi." Since forces available for defense were quite inadequate, Price strongly urged Kirby Smith to order concentration of all troops within Arkansas along "some line of defense at least as far south as the Arkansas River." [7]

A few days later Price reported a large enemy force moving down Crowley's Ridge in northeastern Arkansas, constructing fortifications and building telegraph lines as they went, and carrying with them pontoon trains. He was convinced that this force was entering the state with the intention of staying. He felt that the Arkansas valley

[6] Jefferson Davis to E. Kirby Smith, July 14, 1863, *ibid.*, 925–27.
[7] Sterling Price to *id.*, July 23, 1863, *ibid.*, 941–42.

must be defended. "The abandonment of it would surrender their State, the Indian Territory, and Missouri
to the enemy, and to that great extent diminish the resources of the Confederacy." Accordingly, he was concentrating his forces in the vicinity of Little Rock with
the intention of making a stand there. There was no hope
for re-enforcements unless Kirby Smith could send them,
for Steele could not be moved from the western part of
the state without deserting the Indians and probably losing
their friendship.[8]

Kirby Smith was able to promise little assistance to
Price. He ordered J. C. Tappan, who a few weeks earlier
had been called to the support of Walker in northeast
Louisiana, to move his brigade back to Arkansas. Magruder was directed to send Brigadier General S. P. Bankhead's brigade from Bonham to re-enforce Steele at Fort
Smith. And Kirby Smith entered into an agreement with
Governor Flanagin under which the latter would undertake to raise a volunteer force, consisting of men between
45 and 50, to be officered by State appointed brigadiers,
but subject to the orders of the district and department
commanders. Kirby Smith, on his part, would supply the
force with arms, ammunition, and quartermaster supplies
and not call it to duty outside the state.[9]

Magruder complied with the order to send Bankhead
to Arkansas, but he did so with much misgiving. The
number of men under his own command, he reported, was
unequal to the task of defending the long coastline of
Texas. To him the threat to the coast was greater than
that to the wheat-growing region to the north. Convinced
of his inability to defend the Texas coast, Magruder urged

[8] *Id.* to W. R. Boggs, July 27, 1863, *ibid.,* Vol. LIII, Suppl., 884.
[9] S. S. Anderson to J. C. Tappan, August 1, 1863, *ibid.,* Vol. XXII, pt. 2,
951; W. R. Boggs to J. B. Magruder, August 6, 1863, *ibid.,* 955; Note of
agreement between Kirby Smith and H. Flanagin, August 10, 1863, *ibid.,* 962.

that Taylor be instructed to return to Texas those troops furnished him for the repulse of Banks. He was particularly eager for the return of the three batteries of light artillery.[10]

Taylor returned the batteries, and Kirby Smith ordered Colonel Major to move his command back to Texas, joining that of Brigadier General H. E. McCulloch, who had succeeded Bankhead as commander of the northern Subdistrict of Texas.[11] Unlike Magruder, Kirby Smith thought the wheat fields of northern Texas the most vulnerable section of the state. Taylor was further instructed to send his "spare arms and accouterments" to Little Rock.[12]

Meanwhile, Kirby Smith, in anticipation of the increase in the problems confronting him as department commander, requested a conference with the governors of the Trans-Mississippi states. Since Vicksburg had fallen, he explained, the keys to the department were now in the hands of the enemy. Time alone would reveal where and when the enemy would strike. Furthermore, the loss of the Mississippi had severed connections with Richmond; consequently, the Trans-Mississippi Confederacy "must be self-sustaining and self-reliant in every respect." To accomplish this, the commanding general must have the confidence and co-operation of the "leading spirits and judicial minds" of the several states. Accordingly, it was his desire that the governors and members of the supreme courts meet him in conference at Marshall, Texas, on August 15.[13]

The proposed conference of governors, justices, and

[10] J. B. Magruder to W. R. Boggs, August 11, 12, 1863, *ibid.*, Vol. XXVI, pt. 2, 158, and Vol. XXII, pt. 2, 963–64.

[11] Guy M. Bryan to J. B. Magruder, August 20, 1863, *ibid.*, Vol. XXVI, pt. 2, 174; *id.* to Richard Taylor, August 25, 1863, *ibid.*, 182.

[12] W. R. Boggs to *id.*, August 6, 1863, *ibid.*, Vol. XXII, pt. 2, 954–55.

[13] E. Kirby Smith to Govs. Thomas C. Reynolds, F. R. Lubbock, H. Flanagin, and Thomas O. Moore, July 13, 1863, *ibid.*, 935–36.

other leading men assembled at Marshall on August 15, 1863. Kirby Smith offered six topics for discussion and investigation. Heading the list was an inquiry into the condition and temper of the states and the people since the fall of Vicksburg. By what means could the people be induced to do their utmost in the protection of their homes? Cognizant of the despondency and the growing spirit of disloyalty to the Confederate cause, Kirby Smith wished a discussion of how to restore confidence and hope of ultimate victory. The remaining topics were more definite in nature, covering the subjects of currency, methods of securing and disposing of cotton, appointment of commissioners to confer with French and Mexican authorities, and the production and purchase of military supplies. These topics were referred to four committees headed by Judge W. Merrick, of Louisiana, Governor Thomas C. Reynolds, of Missouri, Governor-elect Pendleton Murrah of Texas, and Senator W. S. Oldham, of Texas.

The question of greatest immediate concern to the civil governors was the extent to which the general commanding should exercise civil authority. It was the opinion of the committee headed by Judge Merrick that the general should exercise only those civil powers exercised by the Confederate authorities at Richmond which were "absolutely necessary" to military success. If, as suggested by the Secretary of War, the general commanding was authorized from Richmond to exercise powers not granted to other commanders but exercised by civil officials, the general must exercise these powers in accordance with existing law. "The respective States composing the department have organized governments," the committee advised, "and it could not have been the intention of the Secretary of War to advise the commanding general to exercise authority which belongs to the States, they still having officers present ready to perform their respective duties and functions."

The questions of disloyalty, resources, and military stores were referred to the committee headed by Governor Reynolds. The committee felt compelled to admit that some disloyalty and much more despondency existed among the people, yet it believed the mass of the people were loyal to the Confederacy and had complete confidence in the ability and integrity of the commanding general. As the best means of obtaining the maximum support from the whole population in the protection of their homes, the committee urged "the execution of the conscription law, with the privilege of volunteering, the calling out of the militia by the Governor, the enrollment of volunteers for the same term of service most agreeable to persons not liable to military duty, and the development of some system for recruiting volunteers in areas occupied by the enemy." And "by every consideration of public safety and necessity we urge the impressment of negro teamsters to take the place of soldiers in all Government trains."

While agreeing that a more accurate report on resources could be secured through agents appointed by the general commanding, the committee estimated "that Texas can and will put into the field from 15,000 to 20,000 men; has grain, bacon, and beef enough to feed the army and her people for at least two years; has four gun factories, making eight hundred guns per month; has metal (copper and tin) to make one hundred cannon, and gun wagons for like number completed and in course of construction; is making percussion caps; has two powder mills; has 30,703 pounds cannon powder, 28,635 pounds lead, 90,000 rounds fixed ammunition, and 6,232 pounds buckshot. Has distributed to counties a limited quantity of powder and caps; has forwarded great numbers of cotton-cards to her people; is manufacturing cotton-cards, and has material to keep in good repair the factories in the penitentiary. Arkansas can furnish 8,000 to 10,000 men; has immense quantities of provision and forage. Louisiana can furnish 5,000 to 6,000 troops; has an excess of corn, sugar, and molasses." Missouri's value to the Confederacy would be limited to being a recruiting ground.

A subcommittee headed by Colonel Pendleton Murrah, governor-elect of Texas, to which was referred the question of the "appointment of commissioner to confer with French and Mexican authorities in Mexico" reported in favor of such an appointment. The dependence of the Trans-Mississippi Department upon the ports of Mexico for valuable imports made an understanding with authorities there of great importance. Since the Confederate Government was not in position to carry on regular diplomatic correspondence and since such correspondence would be directed almost entirely to the interest of the Trans-Mississippi Department, the matter ought "to be left to the discretion of the commander." Accordingly, the commander was urged to select competent and trustworthy men to sound out both French and Mexican leaders to "ascertain their disposition toward our Government and people, and what we may expect from them in the way of favor or opposition; what credits, etc., may be founded upon the resources and productions now taken up in our own territory." "The condition of the Trans-Mississippi Department, her wants, what is believed and understood of the disposition of the French authorities toward us, it is believed fully authorizes the commanding general, who is not, and cannot be, instructed from Richmond, to assume and act upon all civil matters pertaining to this agency, questions of mere irregularity or even of doubtful authority in instituting and conducting this correspondence, letting the interest of the country and necessities under which it labors be the laws to guide his discretion and action."

The committee for the study of the questions of cotton and currency headed by Senator Oldham expressed the opinion that owing to the position in which the department now found itself, cotton was "the only safe and reliable means for carrying on efficient military operations for the defense of the country west of the Mississippi." Under the circumstances, the commanding general had authority in accordance with the "impressment act" to make use of cotton in acquiring needed military supplies. Since it would be impossible to secure Confederate Treasury notes in sufficient quantities to pay for this cotton and since even if it were possible the increase in the "already redundant currency" would result in further depreciation of Confederate notes, the committee recommended that cotton be paid for in certificates which the Government must redeem in bonds bearing 6 per cent interest payable in specie. Planters, it was believed, would prefer such certificates to depreciated Treasury notes, for these certificates would increase the circulating medium without a corresponding increase in depreciation. Furthermore, should the commanding general take over the entire supply of cotton, with such modification as he himself deemed advisable, the cotton trade would be taken from the hands of the speculators, and the depreciation of Confederate notes would be decreased. Public demoralization resulting from "the greed of gain and avaricious desire," which had already infected the country, might be considerably reduced.

The reports of all committees, except for the bond provision, were approved by the conference. Governor Reynolds then proposed that in order to "harmonize and infuse vigor into the patriotic efforts of the people, obtain and diffuse correct information, and discourage disloyalty," the governors should form themselves into an unofficial committee of public safety. Committees of correspondence should be organized in each county and parish for the purpose of communicating with the committee and with governors of other states. The patriotic people of each county and parish should organize themselves into Confederate associations of co-operation. The resolution was unanimously adopted.

Having received the thanks of General Kirby Smith for their loyalty and advice, the conference adopted a resolution of confidence in the commanding general and adjourned.[14]

Kirby Smith immediately forwarded to President Davis a copy of the proceedings of the Marshall conference. He felt "great hesitancy and repugnance," he explained, "in assuming any powers not clearly expressed or implied by my position" and would do so "only when impelled by necessity." In the absence of necessary powers, he would endeavor to meet his difficulties "boldly, yet conscientiously, and trust my acts will be reviewed with leniency." He had not sought the position he now held and hoped that the President would not hesitate to remove him whenever the public interest might require it. Until then he would devote all of his energy in support of the "cause which is holy and righteous, and which, under God's providence, I believe will ultimately triumph." Yet he confessed that he would "hail with pleasure the day which relieves me from cares and responsibilities, never coveted, which are wear-

---

[14] *Ibid.*, 1004–10; W. S. Oldham, "Memoirs" (manuscript in University of Texas Library), 369–70; Shreveport *Semi-Weekly News*, September 4, 1863.

ing out my constitution and making me prematurely old." [15]

On the following day Kirby Smith wrote to Seddon urging that the "appointing power in cases provided by law should be delegated to the commander of this department," subject to presidential approval. Seddon referred this letter to Davis who endorsed thereon: "The power to appoint cannot be delegated." Assignments and promotions, however, "could be acted on for the time." [16] Kirby Smith was already exercising this power to a limited extent. What he desired, but never got, was definite assurance that those appointments, assignments, or promotions made by him would be approved by the President. The best Davis would ever do was to assure the Commander of the Trans-Mississippi Department that "as far as the Constitution permits, full authority has been given to you to administer to the wants of your department, civil as well as military." [17]

While Kirby Smith conferred with state officials at Marshall, military pressure on the department was increasing. A five-pronged Federal attack appeared probable. A column from the north was reported about to enter the Indian country; a second, estimated at 20,000, was moving from Helena upon Little Rock and had reached a point only twelve miles from that city; a third, said to number 10,000, had left Vicksburg for the vicinity of Monroe; and a fourth was moving from Natchez toward Harrisonburg. It was also expected that Banks would soon move upon Lower Louisiana.[18] Should these threats develop into ac-

15 E. Kirby Smith to Jefferson Davis, September 11, 1863, *Official Records*, Ser. I, Vol. XXII, pt. 2, 1003–1004.

16 *Id.* to J. A. Seddon, September 12, 1863, *ibid.*, Vol. LIII, Suppl., 895–96.

17 Jefferson Davis to E. Kirby Smith, April 28, 1864, *ibid.*, 985–86.

18 W. R. Boggs to J. B. Magruder, August 28, 1863, *ibid.*, Vol. XXII, pt. 2, 982.

tual invasions, the weak and scattered forces in the Trans-Mississippi Department would be unequal to its defense.

"Your homes are now in peril," the general commanding announced to the people of Arkansas, Louisiana, and Texas. "Vigorous efforts on your part can alone save portions of your States from invasion." The advance of the enemy must be contested "at every thicket, gully, and stream." He must be harassed from all sides and his supplies cut off. Only by most determined efforts could the people of the Trans-Mississippi region defend their property and independence; consequently, they must organize promptly for their own defense. "Time is our best friend. Endure awhile longer; victory and peace must crown our efforts." [19]

Along with this appeal was sent instructions for the organization of local defense units composed of men not falling within the conscription ages of eighteen to forty-five. Arms and supplies would be furnished by the Confederate Government. Field officers would be appointed by the department commander; company officers elected by the members. "These organizations will not be called into actual service until necessity arises," the people were assured, "and will not be required to go beyond the limits of the State to which they belong. They are expected to serve, when called out, as long as the emergency exists, then to return to their ordinary pursuits until again needed." [20]

Already efforts were being made to implement the conscription laws, calling into service men between eighteen

---

[19] *Ibid.*, Vol. XXVI, pt. 2, 581; Shreveport *Semi-Weekly News*, October 2, 1863.

[20] General Orders, No. 42, September 5, 1863, *Official Records*, Ser. I, Vol. XXII, pt. 2, 996. Kirby Smith later reported that this appeal resulted in raising 8,000 troops in Texas, a few companies in Arkansas, but "little or nothing was effected in Louisiana." Kirby Smith to S. Cooper, November 14, 1863, *ibid.*, pt. 1, 25.

and forty-five. On June 3 Brigadier General E. Greer had been officially assigned to duty as commandant of conscripts, with headquarters at Shreveport, and camps of instruction had been ordered established in each district "for the collecting and thorough drill of the conscripts." [21]

Early in June Kirby Smith had also inaugurated a plan to round up recruits in Missouri, assigning Colonel Waldo P. Johnson the duty of accomplishing the task. Johnson had insisted that many guerrilla bands there would prefer signing up as regulars. Kirby Smith had a definite dislike for guerrilla activities and reasoned that if these men could be signed up as volunteers for one year, they would be so located at the expiration of their terms that they could then be conscripted. [22]

Efforts were also made to check the number of desertions from regiments already in service. In accordance with instructions from President Davis, Kirby Smith offered pardons to those who would return to their commands by September 30. And preparations were made to send cavalry to arrest those who failed to return. [23] There had been an "unparalleled number" of desertions among Texas troops serving under Taylor in Louisiana. The only way to stop such a "disgraceful abandonment of colors," Kirby Smith advised Taylor, was to use "the most summary punishment." [24]

Within the subdistrict of northern Texas commanded by Brigadier General H. E. McCulloch desertions were wholesale. Those deserters must be brought back or exterminated

[21] General Orders, No. 15, June 3, 1863, *ibid.*, pt. 2, 853; S. S. Anderson to J. B. Magruder, June 11, 1863, *ibid.*, Vol. XXVI, pt. 2, 47.

[22] S. S. Anderson to W. P. Johnson, June 13, 1863, *ibid.*, Vol. XXII, pt. 2, 865–66; *id.* to T. H. Holmes, June 13, 1863, *ibid.*, 865.

[23] General Orders, No. 38, August 26, 1863, *ibid.*, 980; E. Cunningham to Sterling Price, September 7, 1863, *ibid.*, 997.

[24] S. S. Anderson to Richard Taylor, September 19, 1863, *ibid.*, Vol. XXVI, pt. 2, 241.

Kirby Smith ordered. "Where clemency and persuasion fail, force must be resorted to." And when these deserters, estimated to number as high as 3,000, were reported to be armed and organized, Kirby Smith ordered Bankhead's brigade to Bonham to assist in breaking up this organized resistance. McCulloch was further authorized to use "Quantrell's Missourians" in the round up. But Quantrell's men proved a greater menace than the deserters. McCulloch continued to urge still more drastic action: "Establish a court here, try and execute some of these fellows for desertion, and send some of these disloyal men who harbor deserters and spout treason to some safe place in heavy irons." But Kirby Smith, always wishing to temper justice with mercy, hoped that a spirit of patriotism would eventually prevail.[25]

Magruder attributed the great number of desertions in Texas to the unjust practice of detailing some soldiers for civilian duties and denying the applications of others. Discouraged and disgusted, many not so favored either walked off or claimed to be sick. Magruder insisted that the good of the service demanded that there be no more details except for strictly military purposes.[26]

And from the conscript bureau Brigadier General Greer complained that he could not fill up regiments as long as Texas judges nullified the conscript laws by the manner in which they interpreted the exemption provisions. The only solution to his problem, he urged, was for the general commanding to suspend the writ of habeas corpus and substitute martial for civil law.[27]

[25] E. Kirby Smith, to H. E. McCulloch, September 25, October 2, November 2, 1863, *ibid.*, 258, 285, 382–83; *id.* to T. H. Holmes, October 2, 1863, *ibid.*, Vol. XXII, pt. 2, 1030; McCulloch to Kirby Smith, February 5, 1864, *ibid.*, Vol. XXXIV, pt. 2, 945.

[26] J. B. Magruder to W. R. Boggs, October 26, 1863, *ibid.*, Vol. XXVI, pt. 2, 354–56.

[27] E. Greer to *id.*, December 7, 1863, *ibid.*, 493–95.

Kirby Smith had no power to declare martial law and was not inclined to force a test decision on the constitutionality of the conscript law, but there was still another source of military strength yet untapped. Many planters in exposed areas, fearing widespread disloyalty among their slaves, preferred hiring them to the government as laborers, particularly teamsters. This would release numbers of white laborers for military duty. There was also some sentiment in favor of enrolling Negroes as soldiers. Early in the summer of 1863 Kirby Smith ordered his district commanders to survey their labor needs and then determine the *"pro rata* call in each county."* Should the patriotism of planters not be sufficient to induce them to hire their slaves to the government, impressment must be resorted to. In all cases, however, the general urged, great precaution should be observed; it was as important to preserve the loyalty and zealous support of those at home as to increase the fighting force.[28]

On September 21, 1863, Kirby Smith permitted his chief quartermaster to call for 3,000 Negroes to be organized under white superintendents. "This is as near a military organization as I dare venture upon," the general explained.[29]

With the enemy threatening from many points, Magruder's Texas troops alone appeared safe from immediate attack. Kirby Smith ordered him to complete his organization of state troops as quickly as possible, call up all available companies of minute men, and move his forces near

[28] S. S. Anderson to T. H. Holmes, July 7, 1863, *ibid.*, Vol. XXII, pt. 2, 907; E. Kirby Smith to Sterling Price, J. B. Magruder, and Richard Taylor, September 5, 1863, *ibid.*, 994–95.

[29] *Id.* to E. H. Cushing, September 21, 1863, Kirby Smith Papers. It was not until July, 1864, that Kirby Smith, in accordance with a recent act of Congress, declared all male Negroes between 18 and 45 subject to conscription. One fifth of those affected were to be immediately enrolled. General Orders, No. 55, *Official Records*, Ser. 1, Vol. XLI, pt. 2, 1014.

the Red River.[30] By the time Magruder received this order he also had information from Brigadier General Bee on the Rio Grande that Federal invasions by Lavaca and the Sabine Pass were contemplated. The aim no doubt was the possession of Houston, "the center of all the railroads and in the heart of the most valuable portion" of Texas. Magruder reluctantly continued his preparation for movement toward the Red River, but he warned the department commander that should the defense of northern Texas and western Louisiana drain the troops from the coast of Texas the enemy would most certainly possess it, including large quantities of cotton and sugar. Yet he agreed that through concentration only was there hope of decisively defeating the enemy at any point.[31]

Three days later Magruder wrote again. The wheat region of northern Texas was important, but he did not believe its defense was worth the risk of losing the more important corn and cattle region of the state plus the cotton trade with Mexico. With about 11,000 men he must aid in the defense of northern Texas and Louisiana, and defend 400 miles of coast.[32]

Meanwhile, Brigadier General William Steele, not having yet been joined by Bankhead and receiving no help from the Creeks or Choctaws, was falling back before a Federal force estimated at 6,000. And Price, in preparation for the evacuation of Little Rock, was ordered to exert every effort to remove valuable stores to Washington and Arkadelphia.[33]

---

[30] W. R. Boggs to J. B. Magruder, August 28, 1863, *ibid.*, Vol. XXII, pt. 2, 982.

[31] J. B. Magruder to W. R. Boggs, September 1, 1863, *ibid.*, Vol. XXVI, pt. 2, 195–96.

[32] *Id.* to *id.*, September 4, 1863, *ibid.*, 203–205.

[33] J. F. Crosby to Guy M. Bryan, August 30, 1863, *ibid.*, Vol. XXII, pt. 2, 983–84; William Steele to W. R. Boggs, August 30, 1863, *ibid.*, 984; S. S. Anderson to Sterling Price, August 30, 1863, *ibid.*, 983.

With Steele and Price calling for help and falling back toward the Red River, Magruder moving slowly to the defense of northern Texas but prophesying major Federal attacks upon the exposed coast of Texas, and Taylor, fearful that Banks would soon be on the move again, complaining over a possible return of Walker to Arkansas and of the desertion of Texas troops who preferred to fight in their home state, General Kirby Smith's position was not an enviable one. "The difficulties of my position are well known to you," he wrote Taylor, "—a vast extent of country to defend; a force utterly inadequate for the purpose; a lukewarm people, the touchstone to whose patriotism seems beyond my grasp, and who appear more intent upon the means of evading the enemy and saving their property than of defending their firesides." His difficulties were multiplied tenfold by the fact that in adopting plans of operation he must combine the viewpoints of both soldier and statesman. "The President impresses it upon me, the representative and the leading men of the States urge upon me, that the States must be defended; that, once in the hands of the enemy, they will be irretrievably lost to the Confederacy. But for these considerations, I would long since have followed the military principle of abandoning a part to save the whole, and, concentrating in advance, been ready to strike decisively and boldly when the campaign would have been materially influenced." In the case of Arkansas he feared that if the Valley should be abandoned, there would be much defection of Arkansas and Indian troops. By calling up state troops under order of the governor he hoped for more loyalty than would otherwise be manifested.[34]

Kirby Smith considered time the most important element of success. There should be no engagements unless the

[34] E. Kirby Smith to Richard Taylor, September 3, 1863, *ibid.*, 988–90.

chances for success were good. Only delaying actions should be resorted to, weakening the enemy by lengthening his supply line. Eventually the Confederate forces must be concentrated in the Red River Valley where a definite stand would be made.[35]

To President Davis, Kirby Smith painted a gloomy picture of conditions in the Trans-Mississippi Department. With Federal forces, including a "large portion of Grant's army," poised ready to strike from many points, there were scarcely 30,000 effective men available to meet the attacks. Holmes and Price in Arkansas with about 8,000 armed and 2,000 unarmed troops were facing 20,-000; Steele had less than 5,000 poorly armed men with which to meet Blunt; Taylor with about 10,000 effectives was waiting for a superior army under Banks; and Magruder could muster fewer than 6,000 troops for the defense of Texas. These forces could probably be doubled by the addition of state troops if arms could be had. But since Kirby Smith's arrival in the department the only arms received from outside were 1,800 "broken and unserviceable muskets" brought across by way of Natchez. Large quantities of arms destined for the department had been lost at Vicksburg. There was not even the usual number of shotguns and rifles in private hands, for these had been collected and sent east of the Mississippi during the early months of the war. Consequently, state troops, who could be raised by the thousands, knowing there was little chance of being armed, were despondent and disheartened.[36]

Kirby Smith's trouble continued to multiply. A Federal force was reported to be concentrating at Brashear City. On September 6 a message came from Taylor's headquarters that a large force was moving from Trinity toward

[35] *Ibid.*     [36] *Id.* to Jefferson Davis, September 5, 1863, *ibid.*, 992–93.

Alexandria. Kirby Smith thought it more likely a plundering expedition than a serious attempt, but he had already ordered Major to halt his movement toward north Texas and await developments.[37] The attack upon Alexandria did not materialize.

Then came news from Magruder's headquarters that an enemy fleet had appeared off Sabine Pass and bombarded the works on September 8. On August 31 General Banks had ordered Major General William B. Franklin to embark his troops on transports in the vicinity of New Orleans in preparation for a landing at Sabine Pass and the seizure of the railroad at Beaumont. If successful, further plans for the invasion of Texas would be put into operation. Franklin was to contact Lieutenant Frederick Crocker, who was to command a supporting naval force.[38]

The transports, accompanied by the gunboat *Arizona,* left New Orleans on September 4. Off Berwick Bay they were joined by the gunboats *Clifton* and *Sachem.* The *Granite City* had been sent in advance to place signal lights to mark the entrance to the channel of the Pass so that the other vessels could pass in before dawn on September 7. The *Granite City* did not arrive in time, and the flotilla missed the pass. The entrance had to be postponed another day and thus the secrecy of the planned attack was lost.

On the Texas channel of the Pass stood Confederate Fort Grigsby manned by forty-four men under the command of Lieutenant R. W. Dowling. By midmorning September 8 the four gunboats and transports carrying several hundred men had passed inside the bar. The *Sachem* and *Arizona* were to follow the Louisiana channel and the

[37] W. R. Boggs to E. Surget, September 5, 1863, *ibid.,* Vol. XXVI, pt. 2, 209; E. Kirby Smith to *id.,* September 6, 1863, *ibid.,* 210.

[38] N. P. Banks to W. B. Franklin, August 31, 1863, *ibid.,* pt. 1, 287–88.

*Clifton* the Texas channel. The *Granite City* was held in reserve. The *Clifton,* first to draw the fire of Fort Grigsby's six guns, received a direct hit and surrendered within a few minutes. The *Sachem* met a similar fate, and the *Arizona* and *Granite City,* accompanied by the transports, hurriedly recrossed the bar. Three days later General Franklin was back at the mouth of the Mississippi.

The expedition failed completely. But for the misfortune to the gunboats and the impossibility of managing such boats in shallow water, Banks reported, a Federal army would have been placed "between Taylor, Magruder, and Kirby Smith, and given us with certainty the immediate control of Texas." For within ten days after the initial landing he could have had 20,000 men in Houston.[39]

After receiving first news of the Federal attack at the Pass and in expectation of further news that Fort Grigsby had fallen, Magruder halted the movement of his troops toward north Texas, and rushed all available forces toward Beaumont and Orange, where they could impede if not prevent the progress of the victorious enemy up the Sabine River. But upon his own arrival in Beaumont, Magruder received word of the "brilliant victory." He felt, however, that so large a force, which he estimated at 15,000, would certainly attack again, probably up the Calcasieu toward Niblett's Bluff. He rushed a dispatch to Taylor. The Federals had probably gone to the Calcasieu, he said. Could Taylor concentrate his forces at Niblett's Bluff? If so, the two Confederate armies might crush the enemy. Failure to do so would enable the enemy to ascend the Calcasieu and destroy communications between the two armies. Lower Louisiana would then be lost and Texas would be invaded.

---

[39] *Id.* to H. W. Halleck, September 13, 1863, *ibid.,* pt. 1, 288–90; *id.* to President Lincoln, October 22, 1863, *ibid.,* 290–92; W. B. Franklin to N. P. Banks, September 11, 1863, *ibid.,* 294–97.

Taylor was in no position to concentrate with the speed requested, he replied. The Red River Valley, "of first importance to both Texas and Louisiana," must not be neglected. Besides, if the Calcasieu was the enemy's objective, the Federals would be established there before his own force could arrive. He suspected, however, that some point farther west than the Calcasieu was to be attacked and that the activities at Sabine Pass were only a cover up.[40]

In the meantime, Magruder had reported to Kirby Smith: "I can, I hope, fortify against him on the Texas side, at the mouth of the Sabine but cannot do so on the Louisiana side." If the enemy gained possession of Niblett's Bluff, Taylor would have some difficulty in extricating his army. Consequently he urged Kirby Smith to order Taylor to concentrate near the Bluff where the two armies could co-operate in preventing the invasion of Texas from Louisiana. Owing to low water in the Red River, he calculated that the enemy would not risk an invasion into Louisiana.

Magruder's request came at a time when Kirby Smith was already engaged in explaining to Governor Thomas O. Moore that there was no intention of abandoning Louisiana. The governor had complained of the return of Tappan's brigade to Arkansas and expressed a fear that Walker's division might also be ordered back. Even with Walker's division, he insisted, Taylor's force was inadequate for the defense of Louisiana. Furthermore, it was reported that Kirby Smith had sent his family into Texas as if in preparation to abandon even Shreveport, which had been well fortified.

It was now necessary that the general commanding con-

---

[40] J. B. Magruder to Richard Taylor, September 10, 1863, *ibid.*, pt. 2, 218; Taylor to Magruder, September 15, 1863, *ibid.*, 231.

vince another distressed governor of his good intentions. There was no intention of sending Walker back to Arkansas, he replied. That command had been formally joined to Taylor's forces. However, had Walker's troops been left in Arkansas, Holmes "would probably now be in possession of the Arkansas Valley, instead of being forced back to the line of the Washita." As for Tappan's command, it had never been ordered to join Taylor. It had merely been sent to co-operate with him in northern Louisiana opposite Vicksburg. Taylor's forces might be inadequate for the defense of Louisiana, but, even so, they were half again larger than Holmes's in Arkansas and twice the strength of Magruder's in Texas. Further, Taylor's troops were mostly Texans who really preferred to be defending their home state.

The only practical means of bolstering the defense of Louisiana, Kirby Smith explained to Governor Moore, was for the governor himself "to bring out every able-bodied man in the State for the defense of his fireside." If Shreveport was better fortified than other points in Louisiana then it was the fault of the district commander, for when the fortifications were being constructed at Shreveport, Taylor was instructed to erect such other fortifications as he saw fit. As for the commanding general's family being sent out of Shreveport, his wife and baby had merely gone to the home of Senator Louis T. Wigfall at Marshall, Texas, to escape the yellow fever that was raging.[41]

Kirby Smith was sensitive to criticism. Showered with complaints and urgent requests from the four corners of his department, he confided to his absent wife: "I have walked up & down, gone out & come back—restless, dissatisfied—everything (officially) has gone wrong—I am miserable, discontented, unhappy." But he wrote more

[41] E. Kirby Smith to T. O. Moore, September 12, 1863, *ibid.*, 221–22.

optimistically to his aged mother. When he learned of her expulsion from St. Augustine he assured her that there would be a day of retribution when God had sufficiently scourged the South. She must not believe rumors; all would end well. "A righteous and just cause is in the hands of a holy Judge who will ultimately crown it with success." [42]

The Federal attack at Sabine Pass and the ease with which it was repulsed were confusing. When the fleet first appeared off the Pass, Magruder reported its presence, giving the strength as twenty-seven vessels with a land force of probably ten thousand men. Kirby Smith, correctly supposing the enemy's intention to be the capture of the Pass and Bay and then an invasion of east Texas, had urged Taylor to prepare for co-operation with Magruder. The size of the enemy force indicated that it had been drawn from New Orleans and the Berwick Bay region. If this were true, then the pressure on Taylor in Louisiana would be relieved and he could hasten to Magruder's support. Taylor was reminded that his command contained many Texas regiments and if not actively employed they would become restive and desert should their home state be invaded.[43]

When Magruder reported the failure of the Federal attack upon Fort Grigsby and the withdrawal of the fleet, the enemy's intentions became a puzzle. That so large a force under so capable a commander as Franklin should be so easily repulsed, Kirby Smith was unable to believe. It must be, as Taylor suggested, that the attack was designed to cover up a more serious effort elsewhere. Certainly as long as the enemy's plans were undeveloped Taylor should not move any portion of his command to

[42] *Id.* to Wife, September 10, 1863; *id.* to Mother, September 10, 1863.
[43] *Id.* to Richard Taylor, September 12, 1863, *Official Records*, Ser. I, Vol. XXVI, pt. 2, 220–21.

Niblett's Bluff. Pending further developments, Kirby Smith directed, Taylor and Magruder would hold themselves in readiness to rush to each other's assistance.[44]

At the same time that Franklin was attacking Sabine Pass two other Federal armies under Generals Frederick Steele and J. W. Davidson were closing in on Little Rock. On September 10 Davidson crossed to the south of the Arkansas, and Price, both faced and flanked by superior forces, evacuated Little Rock late in the same day, falling back toward Arkadelphia. He "did wisely in saving and keeping together" his small army, Kirby Smith reassured Price. The line of the Ouachita should be strengthened and held if possible. As he fell back toward this line, all means of transportation should be taken over. Telegraph wires should be removed and taken away. No immediate relief could be expected from either Taylor or Magruder; "both have their hands full." Kirby Smith reasoned, however, that the enemy, estimated at more than 20,000 men, would not soon be ready to advance beyond the Arkansas.[45]

But the enemy kept advancing, pushing the Confederate rear guard through Benton and threatening Arkadelphia. Kirby Smith ordered Taylor to send Walker's division and Major's brigade to Natchitoches. Taylor he believed safe for the time being in Lower Louisiana; he expected Franklin to strike at the Lavaca or the Rio Grande, and he had information that Grant would attack Mobile. If the invasion from Little Rock became still more threatening, Taylor's full strength would be concentrated on the Red River. The general commanding still doubted that the Federals intended pushing a large force beyond Little Rock, for by November roads would be almost impassable.[46]

[44] *Id.* to *id.*, September 17, 1863, *ibid.*, 233.
[45] *Id.* to Sterling Price, September 12, 1863, *ibid.*, Vol. XXII, pt. 2, 1014.
[46] *Id.* to Richard Taylor, September 19, 1863, *ibid.*, Vol. XXVI, pt. 2, 242.

Although Price continued hard pressed in Arkansas, neither Walker nor Major came within supporting distance. On September 18 Taylor reported heavy enemy concentration at Berwick's Bay. Kirby Smith authorized him to hold Walker but let Major's cavalry move toward Natchitoches.[47] Taylor also retained Major, pending further instructions from Shreveport.

The commander of the Trans-Mississippi Department was now convinced that "the intention of the enemy is clearly to overrun and possess this side of the river, controlling the Mississippi. It may then be their policy to accept intervention, acknowledging the independence of the States east of the river." In this process of conquest Kirby Smith expected an attack either along the Red River or at Sabine Pass. Should the capture of Louisiana be the first objective, the logical line of operation would be Simmesport, Marksville, and Alexandria. He thought the route recently followed by Banks "the longest most difficult one by which the State can be invaded." In any case, in view of the enemy's superiority in numbers, Taylor could do no more than check the progress. Taylor's troops would no doubt do well, for they had the "utmost confidence" in him. And Taylor's skill and sound judgment would enable him "to take advantage of the least fault of his enemy." [48] Kirby Smith advised Taylor to be governed by circumstances and his own judgment but not to risk a general engagement unless there was a "reasonable chance of success." [49]

Uncertainty continued. The Federal forces concentrated at Berwick Bay made no attempt to advance up the Teche. Kirby Smith made a hurried trip to Holmes's headquarters to look over the situation in Arkansas. The abandonment

---

[47] *Id.* to *id.*, September 20, 1863, *ibid.*, 244.
[48] *Id.* to T. H. Holmes, September 21, 1863, *ibid.*, Vol. XXII, pt. 2, 1023–24.
[49] *Id.* to Richard Taylor, September 23, 1863, *ibid.*, Vol. XXVI, pt. 2, 250.

of either Lower Louisiana or Arkansas seemed necessary. Only by concentration in a single district could the Confederates hope to strike a decisive blow. Should the Federals advance in force from Little Rock, Kirby Smith informed Taylor, a major portion of the troops in Louisiana must be rushed to Arkansas. "A success there clears the Indian country, whilst it redeems the Arkansas Valley. The despondency is greater in that State than elsewhere, and the Indians are preparing to change their allegiance." [50] Kirby Smith, in preparation for a probable movement of Taylor's troops toward Arkansas, ordered that supplies for 6,000 men be immediately collected at Minden.[51]

Upon arrival at Arkadelphia, Kirby Smith found that bad feeling existed between Holmes and Price, "beyond the healing power of any physician but separation." While he recognized Holmes's superior military ability, he found that Price had "more the confidence and love of the troops." In view of this fact, he thought the interest of the service would be promoted by the removal of Holmes to some command east of the Mississippi. As his successor, Kirby Smith preferred Buckner or Cleburne. The latter, being from Arkansas, would be a "valuable addition."

Reduced by desertion and sickness, Holmes had not more than 7,000 troops. Kirby Smith instructed him to prepare to fall back toward Shreveport. The major portion of his supplies should be immediately removed from Washington, Arkansas, to Shreveport. And since Holmes's position at Arkadelphia was strong only for protecting supplies at Washington he should move toward Camden. The best route for the enemy in an advance upon Shreveport would be from Little Rock and Pine Bluff by way of

[50] *Id.* to *id.,* September 25, 1863, *ibid.,* 255–56.
[51] S. S. Anderson to W. H. Thomas, September 26, 1863, *ibid.,* 259.

Camden. Should Holmes remain at Arkadelphia, he would then be cut off and prevented from joining forces with Taylor. The Little Missouri, Kirby Smith thought, would be a stronger line of defense than the Ouachita, for "its bottoms in winter are impassable." As Holmes fell back from Camden toward Shreveport, destroying all supplies that could not be carried off, Taylor would be concentrating his troops in the Red River Valley ready for a showdown. Kirby Smith himself would then take personal command of the concentrated forces. But the execution of all such plans must await the development of the enemy's plans.[52]

From Holmes's headquarters at Arkadelphia Kirby Smith wrote Jefferson Davis, presenting a gloomy picture of affairs in the Trans-Mississippi Department. "Events, as they crowd upon us, are fast realizing my worst anticipations," he explained. "The despondency of our people, their listlessness, their deafness to the call of both the civil and military authorities, the desertions from our ranks, checked neither by vigor nor clemency, all indicate despair and abandonment. Unless a great change takes place, unless succor comes to us from abroad, or unless the providence of God is strikingly exhibited in our favor, this department will soon have but a nominal existence. Without men, without arms, with a people so demoralized by speculation that submission is preferred to resistance, the immense efforts being made by the enemy must be crowned with success."

At Little Rock, poised for the attack and awaiting only the bringing up of supplies before moving, Frederick Steele commanded an estimated 25,000 men. To oppose him Holmes's army, now reduced by sickness and desertion, numbered not more than 7,000. What aid Taylor could

<hr>

[52] E. Kirby Smith to R. W. Johnson, October 8, 1863, *ibid.*, Vol. XXII, pt. 2, 1035–36; *id.* to T. H. Holmes, October 7, 1863, *ibid.*, 1034–35.

furnish was a question, for he, with only 10,000 men, was opposed by a Federal concentration at Berwick's Bay, including Banks's army plus the corps of E. O. C. Ord and J. B. McPherson from Grant's army. Indeed, Kirby Smith feared, Union commanders were about to hurl "fully 80,000 men" at the scattered Confederates, who would be unable to concentrate more than 15,000 at any point.[53]

Upon his return to Shreveport, Kirby Smith found a long communication from Magruder. The Texas commander was convinced that the 15,000 Federals which Taylor reported at Berwick Bay were not the same troops that attacked Sabine Pass. The latter group he felt certain was off the coast of Texas ready to renew the attack while the force at Berwick's moved across Lower Louisiana and advanced on Houston by way of Niblett's Bluff. To meet this threat, he had less than 5,000 available men. Last May, he explained complainingly, he possessed a fine army of 16,000 men. But when Taylor was hard-pressed Kirby Smith had ordered him to send 5,000 men to Louisiana. "He [Taylor] declines coming to my assistance now, and I desire the return, with the least possible delay, of the troops sent him by me, in accordance with your orders."

Magruder had already ordered Bankhead to return from the Indian Territory to Houston. Would Kirby Smith not immediately order Major's brigade to Beaumont? Without this assistance the heart of Texas would probably be invaded and the Confederate cause in the West lost. "In a word, in my judgment, Texas is virtually the Trans-Mississippi Department, and the railroads of Galveston and Houston are virtually Texas." Should the enemy gain control of these railroads and also occupy the Teche and Lafourche region, no Confederate army could operate below Niblett's Bluff and Alexandria. Therefore, he begged

[53] *Id.* to Jefferson Davis, September 28, 1863, *ibid.*, 1028–29.

not only for the return of his Texas troops but also that Kirby Smith would order Taylor in the direction of Niblett's Bluff.[54]

Kirby Smith supported Taylor. It would be foolish, he thought, for the latter to move to Niblett's Bluff when Banks had still not revealed his intentions. Yet Taylor must stay on the enemy's flank, and if Niblett's Bluff and Texas were definitely the objectives, then he must make every effort to co-operate with Magruder. To Magruder, however, Kirby Smith replied that the Texas commander must rely upon his own resources.[55]

Magruder's alarm increased. He was convinced that the enemy force, the advance of which was at Vermilionville, was bound for Texas, 30,000 to 40,000 strong. There might still be time, he urged, for Taylor to reach Niblett's Bluff via the Alexandria road. Such assistance was the only hope. Otherwise the enemy's progress could only be checked by the 8,000 troops available in Texas. Houston would inevitably fall and with it probably Galveston and the railroads, "and the heart of the Trans-Mississippi is irretrievably gone." [56]

Kirby Smith attributed the slowness with which Federal forces were moving in Lower Louisiana to the news of Bragg's victory at Chickamauga and the apparent necessity of Grant's weakening his forces on the lower Mississippi in order to re-enforce Rosecrans. Taylor must observe this weakening process but take no chances, he advised. "Difficult as you may find it, you must exercise great caution in your operations. You must restrain your own impulses as well as the desires of your men. The

[54] J. B. Magruder to E. Kirby Smith, September 26, 1863, *ibid.*, Vol. XXVI, pt. 2, 260–62.

[55] E. Kirby Smith to Richard Taylor, October 15, 1863, *ibid.*, 323; *id.* to J. B. Magruder, October 15, 1863, *ibid.*, 323–24.

[56] J. B. Magruder to W. R. Boggs, October 18, 1863, *ibid.*, 335.

Fabian policy is now our true policy. In the present state of the public mind, a defeat to your little army would be ruinous in its effects. When you strike, you must do so only with strong hopes of success." [57]

Still uncertain as to the enemy's intentions, Kirby Smith alerted both Holmes and Magruder. Should the movement be on the Red River, Holmes must be ready for rapid movement to the south, leaving in Arkansas one brigade of infantry and Marmaduke's cavalry. He would move either "direct to Shreveport or by Minden to Campti, crossing the river at Grand Ecore." Magruder was instructed to push his available force as near to Niblett's Bluff as practicable, sending mounted men and light artillery as far as the Calcasieu. From that point they could then co-operate with Taylor, should the move be against Texas, or rush to form a junction with troops from Arkansas and Louisiana in the Red River Valley above Natchitoches. Should his state troops refuse to go beyond the borders of Texas, they should be left behind but reminded that such battles as were contemplated on the border of Texas would, if lost, leave the state open to invasion. Definite marching orders would be sent as soon as a Red River campaign became a certainty; however, should Magruder receive conclusive information that the valley was about to be invaded he would move toward Natchitoches without awaiting further orders. The general commanding expressed confidence that the concentration of Confederate forces would prove sufficient not only to "destroy the column venturing up Red River, but will decide the fate of the department for the next twelve months." [58]

Further reports from Taylor indicated that the enemy's objective was the Red River rather than Texas. Kirby

[57] E. Kirby Smith to Richard Taylor, October 20, 1863, *ibid.*, 341–42.

[58] *Id.* to T. H. Holmes, October 25, 1863, *ibid.*, Vol. XXII, pt. 2, 1049; *id.* to J. B. Magruder, October 25, 1863, *ibid.*, Vol. XXVI, pt. 2, 353–54.

Smith spurred Magruder to make rapid plans for co-operation. The military road from Niblett's Bluff to Alexandria crossed the Calcasieu about thirty miles from Alexandria. From this crossing roads led to Cotile and Natchitoches. Magruder could make junction with Taylor at Cotile "or possibly lower down." All available troops must be brought to oppose the invaders of the valley for the "fate of the department" depended upon the outcome.[59]

Magruder, although not convinced that Red River rather than Texas was the enemy's objective, began moving his force toward Niblett's Bluff. The Texas state troops refused to leave Texas, but this was of no great concern to Magruder since he thought their services demanded at home. Upon hearing that General A. J. Hamilton and staff had arrived at New Orleans, he was more than ever convinced that Texas was the objective. With the Confederate forces away co-operating with Taylor, he pessimistically prophesied, the state troops would be unable to protect Galveston, Houston, and the system of railroads, and "at one blow" the conquest of Texas would be complete.

Since the enemy was making no aggressive movements in western Arkansas and the Indian Territory, Magruder insisted that Kirby Smith order Bankhead's brigade back to Texas. And since the wheat fields of northern Texas were, he believed, of less importance than the coast of Texas, he wished Bankhead's brigade ordered to Nacogdoches. From that point it could be sent to Natchitoches to co-operate with Taylor and Holmes or to Houston, in the event of a coastal attack. Furthermore, he wished McCulloch, commanding in north Texas, to send all state troops to the south.[60]

On October 31 Holmes wired Kirby Smith that the

[59] *Id.* to *id.*, October 26, 1863, *ibid.*, 356.

[60] J. B. Magruder to W. R. Boggs, October 27, 1863, *ibid.*, 359–360; *id.* to E. Kirby Smith, October 29, 1863, *ibid.*, 368–70.

enemy was again advancing in Arkansas. Kirby Smith replied: "You must oppose the enemy with all the means at your disposal." If greatly outnumbered he should avoid a general engagement and fall back, but "contesting every defensible point, and destroying as far as possible all supplies that might be made available," to the enemy. Kirby Smith was not too much worried about this advance. "The first heavy rains," he reasoned, "will arrest any movement, and make their position critical." [61]

In Lower Louisiana, the enemy who had moved with caution as far as the junction of the Courtableau and the Teche and to the vicinity of Opelousas, began falling back toward Berwick Bay about November 1. Green's cavalry continued to play upon the Federal flanks just as it had during the advance, fighting small-scale battles almost every day. The advance on both Texas and the Red River was temporarily abandoned, and Taylor, ever on the watch, attributed the withdrawal to the necessity of recalling troops from the Mississippi area to furnish re-enforcements for Rosecrans.[62]

Kirby Smith gave Taylor and his staff full credit for the successful manner in which they had parried the blows of a superior force. "I would respectfully call attention of the Department to General Taylor's operations in Lower Louisiana," he wrote Richmond. "Cautious, yet bold; always prepared for and anticipating the enemy; concentrating skillfully upon his main force, holding it in check, and crippling its movements; promptly striking his detached columns, routing and destroying them, the enemy have been completely foiled in the objects of their campaign,

[61] E. Kirby Smith to T. H. Holmes, November 1, 1863, *ibid.*, Vol. XXII, pt. 2, 1054–55.

[62] Richard Taylor to W. R. Boggs, November 2, 1863, *ibid.*, Vol. XXVI, pt. 2, 392.

and have fallen back for a new plan and a new line of operations." Brigadier General Thomas Green and four other of Taylor's associates were recommended for promotion.[63]

Taylor toyed with the idea of following up the enemy's withdrawal with an expedition into the Lafourche district, but Kirby Smith advised against it as being too hazardous. Such an occupation would have little military importance, and should the Atchafalaya rise the force would be trapped and have great difficulty in extricating itself. Taylor was advised to settle down to a winter of observing the Federal forces in Lower Louisiana, striking at exposed detachments when opportunity presented itself. All idea of transferring any portion of Taylor's force to Arkansas had been abandoned. The distance was too great and the winter weather would make extensive operations there almost impossible. Kirby Smith was still convinced that if the enemy planned any extensive operations during the winter it would be in the Red River Valley while the high waters could be helpful. Kirby Smith planned to go in person to look over the situation in Arkansas. If he only had a man like Green in command of Holmes's cavalry, he explained, much could be done to destroy the enemy's supply line.[64]

Disturbing reports from Texas delayed Kirby Smith's visit to Holmes's headquarters; he sent a courier with a note of suggestions. Why not throw Marmaduke's cavalry of 5,000 to 6,000 men across the Arkansas and hit the railroad which brought Federal supplies from the White River? Holmes might co-operate with Marmaduke by sending an infantry force to threaten Little Rock. This plan Kirby Smith thought to be the "only feasible plan of

---

[63] E. Kirby Smith to S. Cooper, November 8, 1863, *ibid.*, pt. 1, 384–85.
[64] E. Kirby Smith to Richard Taylor, November 23, 1863, *ibid.*, 439.

operation" unless the Federals had been greatly weakened in the plan to re-enforce Rosecrans. In case such a weakening had occurred, Holmes might occupy Pine Bluff with his entire force and throw a part of his cavalry against enemy communications. The enemy would then be compelled either to evacuate Little Rock or to attack Holmes. If retreat became necessary, Holmes could move "by Monticello, along Bayou Bartholomew to Monroe, through a country abundant in supplies." [65]

Having no great fear of enemy advancement in Arkansas during the winter months, Kirby Smith turned his attention toward Texas. The attack so long expected by Magruder had occurred. On November 2 a Federal force had landed at Brazos Santiago and marched on Brownsville, which place was evacuated by General Bee on November 4. Magruder felt certain that this force had come from the mouth of the Mississippi.[66] Kirby Smith received news of the Federal landing on November 13. He immediately ordered Magruder to have Bee retreat up the Rio Grande Valley, use his cavalry to prevent Federal raids toward San Antonio, and protect the roads from Eagle Pass and Laredo to San Antonio.[67]

Upon hearing from Taylor and reading in Northern newspapers that Franklin remained in Louisiana with two corps, Kirby Smith concluded that Banks's attack in Texas must of necessity be a small-scale operation. Banks's "occupation of Brownsville and the Rio Grande with any considerable force would be placing it out of position without obtaining control of the Mexican trade." Should Banks command a force as large as that reported [68] then Magruder

---

[65] *Id.* to T. H. Holmes, November 30, 1863, *ibid.,* Vol. XXII, pt. 2, 1081–82.

[66] J. B. Magruder to W. R. Boggs, November 10, 1863, *ibid.,* Vol. XXVI, pt. 2, 403.

[67] C. S. West to J. B. Magruder, November 14, 1863, *ibid.,* 413–14.

[68] Bee reported 12,000.

should expect an attack at Matagorda Bay with San Antonio as the objective.[69]

On November 27 Magruder reported a Federal movement against Saluria and urged Kirby Smith to send reenforcements. Green's and Major's brigades should be detached from Taylor and sent back to Texas, "as all these troops are Texans." [70] Kirby Smith replied that Green's cavalry division was being sent by way of Niblett's Bluff and that he himself would leave immediately for Taylor's headquarters to confer on other possible re-enforcements.[71]

After conferring with Taylor, Kirby Smith concluded that the situation in Texas was not so desperate as pictured by Magruder, especially since there was no reliable information that more than 6,000 troops had left Louisiana for the coast of Texas. No further re-enforcements would be sent to Magruder at that time, and the Texas commander was instructed to make no change in the organization of Green's cavalry division, as it might be necessary to recall it from Texas on short notice.

Kirby Smith, apparently with Taylor's approval, had decided that, in spite of winter conditions in Arkansas, something must be done to relieve that state. General Frederick Steele, the Federal commander there, was in control of the "wealthy and populous" part of the state, including the capital. Through the adoption of a moderate and conciliatory course, he was "fast reconciling if not winning over the people." He was reported already to have organized four Arkansas regiments, and although commanding a weakened force, if allowed to remain in possession undisturbed during the winter he would be greatly strengthened both physically and politically. Military loss of

[69] E. Kirby Smith to J. B. Magruder, November 26, 1863, *Official Records,* Ser. I, Vol. XXVI, pt. 2, 444.

[70] J. B. Magruder to E. Kirby Smith, November 27, 1863, *ibid.,* 448–49.

[71] E. Cunningham to J. B. Magruder, December 2, 1863, *ibid.,* 468.

Arkansas also would mean its political loss, and with Arkansas would go the Indian Territory and northern Texas.

Steele's force was reported to be weak and there was little chance that he could be re-enforced from east of the Mississippi. "This time," Kirby Smith concluded, "if not propitious, offers the only opportunity that will ever present [itself] for striking a blow for the recovery of the Arkansas Valley." He would withdraw General Mouton with two brigades from Taylor and move them quietly and quickly to the support of Holmes before the enemy learned of the transfer. He hoped that Steele, knowing Holmes's weakness, could be drawn out of Little Rock for a general engagement and then be met by the combined force. "A success on the Arkansas River would bring back the absentees, give an *esprit* to the troops, and leave a respectable force disposable for operations without the District of Arkansas." [72]

Kirby Smith himself left for Camden, Arkansas, on December 12. The following week was spent in inspecting the forces stationed between Camden and Washington. Holmes was found to be in possession of very little information about the enemy, and even that had not been passed on to department headquarters. Kirby Smith made every effort to accumulate necessary data and was greatly surprised at what he learned. It was found that Steele had been working a large force in strengthening his position and that now both Pine Bluff and Little Rock were heavily fortified and well manned. By drawing in smaller detachments from outposts, Steele could concentrate at least 12,000 men. With the brigades sent by Taylor the combined Confederate force still would not exceed that number. Pine Bluff might be taken by assault, but would not be

[72] E. Kirby Smith to J. B. Magruder, December 15, 1863, *ibid.*, 508.

worth the price. So many supplies had been accumulated at Little Rock that Steele's troops there were independent of communications; therefore, it would be folly to attack the fortifications there. "Great as is the magnitude of the stake, and deeply as I feel the necessity, not only for my personal reputation, but for the interests of the district and the department, of striking a blow for the Arkansas Valley, had I been in possession of these facts, and been furnished with the information I now have obtained, I should never have thought of undertaking at this season an expedition so Quixotic and impracticable." [73]

Holmes was directed to go into winter quarters along the line of the Ouachita and to endeavor to discipline and improve the morale of his troops preparatory to spring operations. Mouton was ordered to stop in northern Louisiana and give protection to a large cargo of arms to be crossed over the Mississippi.[74] Kirby Smith returned to Shreveport the day after Christmas.

On October 28, 1863, he had made urgent appeals to Generals Johnston and Bragg to send arms across the Mississippi. To Gorgas he sent detailed instructions for getting vessels into the Brazos River. All attempts to import arms by the Rio Grande, he explained, had been blocked by either the Federals or the French.[75]

News soon came from Johnston that arms were on their way and information from Richmond indicated the quantity as 26,000 stands. These arms were in charge of Major Thomas H. Price. Kirby Smith directed Colonel Isaac F. Harrison to take his cavalry force and one hundred wagons to the Mississippi to assist in the crossing below Catfish Point in Chicot County, and to transport the arms to Mon-

[73] *Id.* to Richard Taylor, December 23, 1863, *ibid.,* Vol. XXII, pt. 2, 1110–11.
[74] *Ibid.*
[75] *Id.* to Joseph E. Johnston and Braxton Bragg, October 28, 1863, *ibid.,* Vol. XXVI, pt. 2, 365; *id.* to Josiah Gorgas, November 5, 1863, *ibid.,* 391.

roe. Strictest secrecy was ordered. Not even loyal Confederates were to be allowed knowledge of what was being attempted. As wagons were being collected, the people were to be led to believe that they were for the use of General Holmes. Fearing that Harrison's force would be inadequate, Kirby Smith directed Brigadier General Mouton to go to his assistance.[76]

[76] E. Cunningham to I. F. Harrison, December 10, 1863, *ibid.*, Vol. XXII, pt. 2, 1092; E. Kirby Smith to Alfred Mouton, December 23, 1863, *ibid.*, 1110.

## CHAPTER XII

# "NO BED OF ROSES"

THE DAWN OF the new year 1864 offered little hope to the Confederate cause either east or west of the Mississippi. In the Trans-Mississippi Department the pressure had been somewhat relieved, except in Texas where it had never been so great as pictured by Magruder. General Kirby Smith still expressed confidence in ultimate victory; he still had "faith in the goodness of God." His "hopeful spirit, cheering words & merry joyous laugh" inspired confidence among his close associates and helped to overcome the despondency which had followed the fall of Vicksburg. He was growing gray under the strain of responsibility, still his young wife imagined she could detect some new hair on his bald head. Except for a few weeks spent in the home of Senator Wigfall in Marshall, Texas, to escape from the sickly season in Shreveport, his wife remained with him at headquarters. To her, "What Edmund does is *exactly right.*" Little Carrie, bright and cheerful, was the light of the house and the hope of hearts. A new addition to the family was expected next June. Aleck, ever faithful, had become reconciled to the general's marriage, yet could not refrain from comparing Cassie with the "Old Missus" back in St. Augustine. Back in Florida aged Mrs. Smith was praying to live until she could see her children again. Her health was good, although her eyesight was failing. She and the Putnams now resided at the inland town of Madison, some distance removed from St. Augustine. Patriotism there, the old lady complained, was at a low ebb. "Every man is engaged in speculations great and small." And the women, never having had an opportunity "to *compare themselves with others*," were "full of pretentions" and thought they were "at the top of the *Tree* of gentility and accomplishments." Their chief desire was to array themselves in fine clothes run in through the blockade. It mattered not to them that they were paying $150 for a $15 dress, Mrs. Smith remarked. Still there were a few kind and sensible persons in Madison.

Mrs. Smith could get little news from St. Augustine. She had heard that Putnam's house had been confiscated and sold for $4,000. What had happened to the contents of the old Smith home on Hospital Street she did not know. It was not the probable destruction of the furniture over which she grieved but the books, some of which had been in the family for more than a hundred years. There was no kind of destruction, she exclaimed, at which "those Yankee devils" would hesitate.

At headquarters Kirby Smith still missed the services and friendship of Major Clay. "Old Doctor" Smith, who had been with the general since Manassas days, continued the idol of the family, although Mrs. Kirby Smith also thought very highly of Major Guy Bryan. Cunningham and Meems continued efficient and loyal. "Cousin Win" Belton had been promoted to colonel and sent to Arkansas to become adjutant to General Holmes.[1] Only Brigadier General Boggs, chief of staff, seems not to have enjoyed the full confidence of the commanding general. Kirby Smith felt that Boggs was not capable of handling affairs at head-

[1] E. Kirby Smith and Wife to Mother, September 22, 1863, January 11, 1864; Mrs. Frances K. Smith to E. Kirby Smith, January 25, 1864.

quarters when he himself was away. He requested President Davis to promote Dr. Smith to brigadier and make him chief of staff. Years of intimate association had convinced him of Dr. Smith's "merits and abilities." "A citizen of this department, of spotless integrity, of large fortune and influence, a man of enlarged and comprehensive ideas, with capacity, head, and administrative abilities of a high order, he is qualified for the position of chief of staff or Assistant Secretary of War," should Congress create such a position.[2]

Of his three district commanders, Kirby Smith thought Taylor the only one upon whom he could rely. A "good soldier" and a "man of ability," Taylor would be all that could be desired, if he could "only forget his habits and training as a politician." As for Holmes, Kirby Smith thought him a true and faithful patriot worthy of being loved for his virtues, but under troubles and responsibilities his mind had weakened and he was now lacking in self-confidence and fixity of purpose. He should be replaced by a younger man of energy, boldness, and prudence. Price could not fill this need.

Kirby Smith thought Magruder a man of ability and energy, although he was impulsive, frequently committed follies, and had "an utter disregard for law." Furthermore, he had no faculty for selecting capable assistants. He was a hard worker but lacking in administrative ability. He might do well as the commander of a corps, yet "no reliance could be placed upon his obedience to an order unless it chimed in with his own plans and fancies."

Better support in the form of high-ranking officers was necessary, Kirby Smith complained, if the Trans-Mississippi Department was to "weather the storm" then threat-

---

[2] *Id.* to Jefferson Davis, January 20, 1864, *Official Records,* Ser. I, Vol. XXXIV, pt. 2, 897.

ening. "The Government must not send me any more cast-off material. I want support, and able support." The Trans-Mississippi was neither a "bed of roses" nor a field in which laurels could be won or an outstanding reputation made, for the Confederate government would continue to center its strength and resources in the armies of Virginia and Tennessee, leaving other departments to do the best they can with limited resources. The only recompense the commander of the Trans-Mississippi Department could expect would be "the consciousness of having discharged his duty with purity and rectitude of purpose." [3]

Financially embarrassed, short of men and supplies, and with a large-scale Federal spring offensive certain, General Kirby Smith was justified in his pessimism. The Treasury Department was attempting some relief, but it proved too little. Two Treasury officials arrived in the Trans-Mississippi Department in January, 1864, with instructions "to stamp and reissue the notes funded by the depositories." This would give little relief, Kirby Smith observed, since the depositories had funded only $7,000,000 to $8,000,-000. With the enemy threatening to cut off connections both by way of the Mississippi and Mexico, what was then to be done? "In debt, with no supplies from Richmond, no authority to pledge the credit of the Government," Kirby Smith feared the effect this financial embarrassment was having on both civilian and military morale. "Ought not Congress to take some steps to enable this department to become self-sustaining financially, as it has been for some time, and must be hereafter, militarily?" he inquired of President Davis. [4]

Supplies remained scarce. Kirby Smith sent Major J. F. Minter abroad to supervise the fulfillment of a special con-

[3] *Id.* to R. W. Johnson, January 15, 1864, *ibid.*, 868–70.
[4] *Id.* to Jefferson Davis, January 28, 1864, *ibid.*, 920–21.

tract with Messrs. Bouldin and Newell, and requested that President Davis place him on the "same footing as other purchasing agents abroad." As chief quartermaster for the Trans-Mississippi Department, Minter had shown himself to be a man of "great integrity" and "business capacity." [5] For those supplies that might be received through the Gulf ports or via the Rio Grande, Kirby Smith set up a scale of apportionment among districts. [6] For supplies to be purchased locally an unsuccessful attempt was made at price fixing.

General Taylor reported in January, 1864, that his troops were short of corn. This commodity was worth $3.00 per barrel on the market. The government price was about half that amount; consequently, planters were insisting that they had no corn for sale. It proved necessary to impress even enough corn for bread. "This practice alienates the affections of the people, debauches the troops, and ultimately destroys its own capacity to produce results," Taylor observed. Planters would either hide their produce or ship it beyond reach. Many would refuse to plant more than they required for their own needs. And the leather situation, Taylor said, was equally as bad. The government price was not more than one half the market price. Tanners, fearing seizure of their leather, were refusing to put more hides in their vats. "I know of no law to compel a man to tan against his will," Taylor commented. [7]

The meat supply in the department was ample, but most of it was in Texas. During recent months little had been

[5] *Id.* to *id.*, November 21, 1863, *ibid.*, Vol. XXII, pt. 2, 1074.

[6] Arkansas, Indian Territory, and North Texas 4/10, with depots at Bonham and Jefferson, Texas; Texas, New Mexico, and Arizona 2/10, with depots at San Antonio and Houston; Western Louisiana 3/10, with depot at Shreveport; Department-at-large 1/10, with depot at Shreveport in charge of Major W. H. Haynes. General Orders, No. 56, November 16, 1863, *ibid.*, 1071.

[7] Richard Taylor to W. R. Boggs, January 21, 1864, *ibid.*, Vol. XXXIV, pt. 2, 902–903.

received in Louisiana. The purchasing officers had failed, Taylor complained, and the beef impressed was scarcely fit to be eaten during the winter months. And the fear of impressment had resulted in many discontented owners delivering their cattle to the enemy.[8] In hope of relieving the meat shortage, Major William H. Thomas, chief commissary of subsistence, had entered into a contract with J. B. Dunn at Jefferson, Texas. Dunn was to slaughter and pack 4,000 beeves and 10,000 hogs, but failure to secure the needed animals reduced the prospects to 3,000 and 6,000. Many hogs in the process of fattening had died of cholera. And much of the meat packed by Dunn was later reported unfit for consumption.

Other arrangements were made for slaughtering hogs at Bonham and Tyler, Texas, and Fulton, Arkansas. An effort was made to acquire these hogs in localities exposed to the enemy, leaving others in the hands of farmers who were encouraged to produce bacon for military use.

Wheat was plentiful in Texas, but the lack of transportation facilities limited the supply in other districts. The conscription of farm laborers in areas where slaves were few was seriously affecting production.[9]

Under the able management of Major W. H. Haynes, the clothing bureau was expected soon to be capable of supplying all demands upon it. Shoe factories at Shreveport and Jefferson, Tyler, Houston, and Austin, Texas, and Washington, Arkansas, were turning out 10,000 pairs of shoes monthly. Hats were being made at these same places to the number of 9,000 to 13,000 monthly. From the

---

[8] *Ibid.*

[9] Thomas-Dunn contract, September 19, 1863, Confederate States Army Collection, B, Louisiana State Archives; W. H. Thomas to John Reid, January 11, 1865, *ibid.; id.* to J. B. Magruder, January 11, 1865, *ibid.; id.* to J. P. Johnson, January 20, 1864, *Official Records,* Ser. I, Vol. XXII, pt. 2, 1137–39.

penitentiary at Huntsville, Texas, 1,200,000 yards of cotton and woolen cloth were received each month. A plant under construction at Tyler would have a monthly capacity of 200,000 yards of woolen jeans. Major Haynes was optimistic about greatly increased overall production of clothing during the coming year.[10]

Major Thomas G. Rhett, chief of ordnance and artillery on Kirby Smith's staff, reported that upon the approach of the enemy the ordnance works at Little Rock, Arkadelphia, and Camden had been moved to Tyler, Marshall, and Shreveport. At Tyler had been established a "laboratory for fabricating battery and small-arms ammunition" and also a shop for the repair of arms. Gun and machine shops, foundries, and a powder mill and magazine were soon to be in full operation at Marshall. Large supplies of saltpeter, sulphur, lead and iron were being collected there. At Shreveport were foundries, shops, and laboratories for the production of ammunition. Still other ordnance works were in production at Houston and San Antonio, and powder, sulphur, and lead were also being acquired from Mexico." [11]

Under the direction of Thomas G. Clemson, the Niter and Mining Corporation was operating a furnace in Marion County, Texas, where pig iron and castings were being produced. Another furnace was in the process of construction in Davis County, and a third was proposed for Anderson County. Major Isaac Reed and associates had been working the niter caves in northern Arkansas and the lead mines in Sevier County until chased off by the enemy. They now had transferred their work to the caves of west-

[10] W. H. Haynes to W. R. Boggs, January 18, 1864, *ibid.*, 1134–35.

[11] T. H. Rhett to J. P. Johnson, October 22, 1863, January 19, 1864, *ibid.*, 1141–42, 1140–41.

ern Texas. Lead and niter were also being purchased at San Antonio by Captain R. H. Temple. There was a definite shortage of iron.[12]

There was still a shortage of arms within the Trans-Mississippi Department, and there was little hope of relief from east of the Mississippi. On February 7, 1864, General Leonidas Polk notified Kirby Smith that he was too completely occupied with other duties to supervise any effort to cross arms over the Mississippi. He suggested that a capable supervisor and a cavalry escort be sent east of the river for that purpose. Polk would provide a train of wagons so constructed that the beds could be used as ferry boats in crossing the river. Kirby Smith, however, must furnish the teamsters; Polk had no men to spare.[13]

Confederate agents abroad were trying desperately to get badly needed arms to the coast of Texas, but only a trickle was getting through. On February 3, 1864, Charles J. Helm, acting under orders from General Gorgas, reported from Havana that he had just shipped aboard the steamer *Alice* some 2,000 Enfields and muskets. Other arms in small quantities were shipped by sailing vessels. On April 2 Helm reported 6,000 more Enfields ready for shipment as soon as sufficient cotton was on hand to pay for them. Gorgas was trying to get cotton out of Mobile. Could not some cotton be sent from Texas, Helm inquired of Magruder? Should a few hundred bales be received in Havana, "I could then send you such a return cargo as will delight your gallant army." [14]

On January 15, 1864, Kirby Smith explained to Taylor that "The interruption of the Rio Grande trade makes

[12] Benjamin Huger to J. P. Johnson, January 15, 1864, *ibid.*, 1139–1140.

[13] Leonidas Polk to E. Kirby Smith, February 7, 1864, *ibid.*, Vol. XXXIV, pt. 2, 947–48.

[14] C. J. Helm to J. B. Magruder, February 3, 1864, *ibid.*, 941; *id.* to *id.*, April 2, 30, 1864, *ibid.*, pt. 3, 727–28, 798.

the introduction of supplies through the enemy lines the *sine qua non.*" Such trade had been suggested, if not encouraged, by the War Department. Shortly after Kirby Smith took command west of the Mississippi, Secretary Seddon had referred to him the application of John T. Chidister of Arkansas for a contract to furnish supplies "obtained from the United States in exchange for cotton." Seddon pointed out that, although undesirable, such trade was preferable to allowing either the armies or the people to suffer from lack of supplies. It should be specified, however, he said, that cotton was to be delivered only after supplies were received, and, if possible, that the cotton should be sold abroad.[15] Nothing is known of the success of the Chidister proposal.

With the situation becoming more desperate, Kirby Smith again turned to the possibility of securing supplies through enemy lines. He sent representatives to New Orleans and Washington to secure "the tacit consent of the Federal authorities" for "the exchange, through foreign houses, of cotton for gold, sterling, or army supplies." His plan was to take over, "by purchase or impressment," the private cotton in sections where supplies were to be delivered. An agent of the cotton bureau would be furnished to work with Taylor's quartermaster, if necessary. Already a considerable amount of cotton had been sold by the cotton bureau to Messrs. Menard and Stevenson. Taylor was requested to give all practicable aid to this firm in the exportation of its cotton.[16]

After "testing the practicability" of securing supplies from the enemy, Taylor concluded that little could be ex-

[15] J. A. Seddon to E. Kirby Smith, March 12, 1863, *ibid.,* Vol. LIII, Suppl., 850–51.

[16] E. Kirby Smith to Richard Taylor, January 15, 1864, *ibid.,* Vol. XXXIV, pt. 2, 871. In the Ouachita area 24,357 bales had been sold to Menard and Stevenson. Richard Taylor to W. R. Boggs, January 16, 1864, *ibid.,* 877–78.

pected from that source other than medicines and a few light articles which could be smuggled through. He had had the assistance of high-ranking Federal officials in New Orleans, but they had been unable to secure even the tacit consent of the military authorities for the passage of quartermaster and commissary stores. Consequently, Taylor recommended that no more Confederate cotton be allowed to pass through the lines except in payment for supplies already received. He felt certain that Federal authorities would never permit Stevenson to carry out his contract. Furthermore, he had changed his mind on the question of destroying private cotton in danger of falling into Federal possession.

A month earlier he had expressed opposition to cotton burning: "It is at the very moment we are withdrawing all protection from the citizen, leaving him to the enemy's mercy, that we destroy the only means he has of supporting his family." A month more of experience and thought caused him to conclude: "So long as the Federals can receive cotton from our lines or have any prospect of procuring it by occupation of any portion of our territory, they will observe their existing policy and regulations prohibiting the shipment of supplies to us." Although warmly sympathetic with those destined to have their property destroyed, he was convinced that every pound likely to reach the enemy should be burned.[17] Taylor's proposal was in keeping with Kirby Smith's views on cotton burning.

On March 14, 1864, Kirby Smith estimated that there were about 150,000 bales of cotton in Louisiana. As the enemy moved in, Taylor was directed to burn all cotton east of the Ouachita. That south of Alexandria was also to be burned except that exempted by special order and

[17] *Id.* to *id.*, January 11, February 16, 21, 23, 1864, *ibid.*, 852–53, 971–72, 977–78, 982–83.

so much as might be necessary for the subsistence of loyal people. Families having no other source of income might be left from five to twenty bales.[18]

Governor Murrah, "a self-made, strong-headed man," who was ambitious to the extent of wishing "credit for everything" he did, further complicated the cotton situation in Texas, practically nullifying the efforts of the cotton office and Kirby Smith. By acts of December 10 and 16, 1863, the Texas legislature authorized the governor "to sell $2,000,000 of 6 per cent bonds, the proceeds to be paid into the Treasury, these bonds to be paid primarily in cotton." The money was to be used "to provide for defense of the State and to repel invasion, and for the purchase of machinery for manufacturing purposes." Acting under the authority of these acts, Governor Murrah sent his agents out to buy cotton in competition with the Texas cotton office established by Kirby Smith, offering prices far in advance of what the Confederacy could pay. The disgruntled public quickly abandoned practically all sales to the cotton office.[19] Hutchins and Broadwell protested in vain. Murrah insisted that he was not interfering with Confederate authorities but merely seeking to acquire supplies for defense.

Broadwell, much irritated, denounced the governor's actions as illegal. But the question of legality, he realized, was of little concern to people "sorely irritated by military impressments and profoundly disgusted with the former system of exporting cotton." These people were eager to adopt the state plan "which virtually offers to the citizen who ranges himself on the side of the Governor support against Confederate authorities, thus leading, in case of actual collision, to open resistance." The result was "specu-

18 E. Cunningham to Richard Taylor, March 14, 1864, *ibid.*, pt. 1, 495.
19 W. A. Broadwell to E. Kirby Smith, April 4, 1864, *ibid.*, pt. 3, 730–32.

lation, rascality, and swindling without any parallel in the history of this war." Broadwell recommended that in case Murrah refused to permit Confederate control of cotton Kirby Smith should either take military steps to impress all cotton in Texas or withdraw Confederate troops, leaving defense of the state in the hands of the governor.[20] Prominent Texas newspapers also joined the protest against state competition with the Confederacy under the guise of giving assistance.[21]

"I am much pleased to hear that you design no interference with the plans of the Government for the acquisition of cotton in your State," Kirby Smith wrote Murrah. "But, my dear sir, without intending it, the system inaugurated by your agents has already completely paralyzed the efforts of my officers to purchase." He had no desire to discuss the legality of Murrah's action, but he was convinced that the results could be nothing short of disastrous. Cotton and cotton alone could be the means of paying Confederate debts to the people of Texas and of acquiring supplies through Mexico. "I am perfectly well aware that the former management of the Government business on the Rio Grande was properly and severely criticised; that the great want of system and efficiency disordered our relations with Mexico and destroyed the credit of the Government." It was to correct these evils that the cotton office was established and placed in the hands of highly qualified merchants which appointments were approved by the general public and even the governor himself. "If their course has been injudicious I appeal to you to suggest changes or to co-operate with them."[22]

Owing to the pressure of military duty Kirby Smith had

[20] *Ibid.*    [21] Houston *Daily Telegraph*, July 6, 1864.

[22] E. Kirby Smith to Pendleton Murrah, April 5, 1864, *Official Records*, Ser. I, Vol. XXXIV, pt. 3, 734.

no time to analyze thoroughly the cotton problem. Guy M. Bryan was sent to confer with Governor Murrah, and on April 11 a published notice from the governor's office announced that the State of Texas would buy no more cotton. All cotton contracts already made, however, were to be fulfilled. This would absorb about all the marketable cotton in Texas, Hutchins reported to Kirby Smith. But there was still a way by which the great exportation under the governor's plan could be thwarted, Hutchins suggested. Under the law of Congress a state could export only cotton actually owned. The state could not "exempt" or "protect" that half left in the hands of the people. A strict enforcement of overland trade regulations would prevent the governor from withdrawing such a large amount of cotton from the country. How far the commanding general was willing to go in the matter must be decided by himself.

Hutchins had about despaired of the cotton office's being of much further use. There was little cotton in its possession and less chance of acquiring any considerable quantity. The certificates issued in payment for cotton thus far had not been legalized by Congress, and further issues would scarcely be acceptable by those persons with cotton for sale. Could not Congress be persuaded to do something, Hutchins begged. Could Congress be induced to fund these certificates in 6 per cent specie bonds and authorize the cotton office to sell enough cotton for specie to pay the interest thereon? Would Congress agree for the Treasury Department to accept these certificates in payment of public dues?

Hutchins' gloom increased. Under a recent act of Congress anyone could ship out cotton by sea on condition that one half of the cargo belonged to the government. Bond was also required of the shipper to insure that one half of the return cargo would be government supplies.

Presumably a similar regulation would be adopted for overland traffic. The cotton office would then be unable to secure any cotton at all. If the numerous private exporters did not bring back adequate government supplies, how then could supplies be secured?

Was it General Kirby Smith's plan, Hutchins inquired, that, as a last resort, extensive impressment would be ordered? "I am aware," he explained, "that the cotton office is based upon the assertion of your power to impress cotton, and that its efficiency has been derived from a compliance with its requirements to avoid impressment." The power to impress was still seriously questioned and a court decision could likely be expected. The exercise of such a power would involve "personal liability" and "much odium"; consequently, the Texas cotton office would be unwilling to execute such an order. Impressment being a military power, it should be executed by military authorities only.[23]

This new controversy over cotton caused Kirby Smith to wish more than ever to be rid of the whole problem. On May 12 and June 6, 1864, he wrote President Davis, urging that steps be taken to legalize the Texas cotton office. After reviewing the conditions which made the establishment of such an office mandatory, he insisted that its promises be legally redeemed: "The ratification of its acts and the redemption of its obligations appear indispensable, not only for the preservation of good faith, but as an act of justice to the gentlemen who have transacted the business."

Kirby Smith further urged more consideration for the Trans-Mississippi Department. Judge Gray, who had recently been appointed assistant secretary of the treasury for the department, should be clothed with all the power

[23] W. J. Hutchins to E. Kirby Smith, April 18, 1864, *ibid.*, pt. 4, 646–50.

allowed by law. "In all legislation," he begged, "the isolated condition of this department must be borne in mind, and as far as is consistent with safety in delegating great powers, it should be made independent and self-sustaining."

In the absence of specific instructions, Judge Gray would have no connection with cotton, yet Kirby Smith believed the whole cotton problem, as it involved finances, should be handled by the Treasury Department. "I earnestly desire to be relieved from the embarrassment attending its direction, and request that legislative enactments may definitely declare the powers and determine the mode by which this staple is to be made the medium for supplying the department." [24]

No immediate relief could be expected from Richmond and the demand for supplies was great; therefore, Kirby Smith gave notice on June 1, 1864, that the government must have half the cottton within the Trans-Mississippi Department. This cotton would be secured by purchase wherever possible, but in case owners refused to sell the necessary amount would be impressed. Six commissioned officers were designated to execute the order. All cotton acquired in Texas was to be turned over to Hutchins, but the cotton office was not mentioned in the order. District commanders were instructed to furnish such military assistance as was necessary. In case impressment had to be resorted to, state-owned cotton was to be exempted. Three days later another order was issued. Cotton, tobacco, sugar, molasses, rice, or military and naval stores could be shipped overland to Mexico only after paying export duties. Permits would be granted to those who furnished certificates that their exports were "sole and exclusive"

[24] E. Kirby Smith to Jefferson Davis, May 12, 1864, *ibid.*, pt. 3, 821–22; *id.* to *id.*, June 6, 1864, *ibid.*, pt. 4, 645–46.

property of a state or the Confederacy. Permits would be granted to individuals only where goods had been acquired from the Confederate government in payment for supplies.

This curtailment of the transportation of privately owned goods still did not make available a sufficient number of wagons to transport military supplies. One half of all wagons now engaged in overland trade were needed by the government to supply armies in the field, Kirby Smith announced on July 12. Those freely offered would be paid for at fair prices. Should this number not meet the requirements, other wagons would be impressed during the emergency. Those hauling exempted cotton would not be impressed.[25]

Realizing that the steps he felt compelled to take were drastic ones and were certain to result in vigorous protest from those adversely affected, Kirby Smith sent his trusted representative Major Guy M. Bryan to Richmond in the spring of 1864 to explain matters to President Davis. Bryan was instructed to insist upon the necessity of more vigorous support by Richmond authorities. After conferring with Bryan, Davis wrote: "In reply to your request urging the necessity of better sustaining you in the administration of your department, I can only say that it has been my earnest endeavor not only to comply with your expressed wishes, but to extend your power to the utmost limit consistent with law and the nature of our Government. . . . Nothing on my part has been left untried to invest you with the requisite authority for effectively administering your department."[26]

The new orders produced considerable protest, the most

[25] General Orders, Nos. 34, 35, June 1, 4, 1864, *ibid.*, 639, 643–44; Order No. 52, July 12, 1864, *ibid.*, Vol. XLI, pt. 2, 1005; E. Kirby Smith to W. A. Broadwell, June 11, 1864, *ibid.*, Vol. XXXIV, pt. 4, 666–67.

[26] *Id.* to Jefferson Davis, May 5, 1864, Kirby Smith Papers; Davis to Kirby Smith, June 14, 1864, *Official Records*, Ser. I, Vol. XXXIV, pt. 4, 671.

prominent of which came from Judge Pryor Lea of Austin. In a series of open letters to the commanding general the judge attributed most of the errors to "multiplicity of your engagements, your military training and pursuits without mercantile experience, and your consequent reliance on the judgment of others." The acts of Congress and the orders from the Secretary of War, Lea asserted, "entirely preclude and absolutely forbid" those regulations recently issued by Kirby Smith.[27]

Guy M. Bryan of Kirby Smith's staff replied. He wrote, he said, both as a loyal Texan and as one closely connected with military headquarters at Shreveport. "Gen. Smith is an unostentatious, conscientious Christian gentleman, as well as a skillful and gallant soldier." The general was often embarrassed from "want of law"; consequently, had he always waited for instructions from Richmond "the enemy would now be in possession of this Department." In every case when an order had been found in conflict with regulations from Richmond the order had been revoked. The military earnestly desired to be relieved of all connections with cotton. In fact Bryan himself had recently been sent to Richmond to put the matter clearly before authorities there. He had also previously served as Kirby Smith's representative in establishing the Texas cotton office.

What was needed, Bryan explained, was "complete branches of the Government on this side of the Mississippi." He had no patience with those weaklings who feared that such an establishment would result in separation from the eastern part of the Confederacy. "Separation is a phantom," he asserted, "that can only frighten the ignorant; we have too much to do now, struggling for

[27] Pryor Lea to E. Kirby Smith, August 24, 1864, Austin *Weekly State Gazette*, August 24, 1864.

existence, to think about anything else than that which will enable us to defeat the vandals who are desolating our land, and threatening us with extermination." [28]

Judge Lea denied any prejudice against General Kirby Smith, yet insisted that great grievances had resulted from official errors. Regardless of the general's "good qualities," public confidence had decreased and dissatisfaction increased. The belief was widespread, the judge insisted, that the commanding general was not qualified; that he had a tendency constantly to disregard the law and assert arbitrary powers. The people were not convinced that military usurpation was necessary to the defense of the department.[29]

Judge G. W. Smith of LaGrange joined Lea in protest, charging that Kirby Smith's Mexican trade regulations were not only unauthorized by law but also in direct violation of the law.[30]

Not all Texans, however, agreed with the judges. A number of newspapers came to the general's defense. He had no desire to debate technical points with Judge Lea, explained the editor of the Houston *Daily Telegraph,* but he thought Kirby Smith had "acted the part of a good citizen and a good General," especially in issuing his recent cotton order. The army must be supplied.[31] If Kirby Smith's cotton policy pleased the government, exclaimed the editor of the Washington (Arkansas) *Telegraph,* "certainly no citizen has a right to complain." He thought the policy "not only lawful" and consistent with President Davis' orders but also "eminently wise." [32]

After abandoning the Texas cotton plan, Governor

---

[28] Guy M. Bryan to Pryor Lea, October 8, 1864, *ibid.,* October 26, 1864.
[29] Pryor Lea to Guy M. Bryan, October 21, 1864, *ibid.,* October 26, 1864.
[30] LaGrange *True Issue,* quoted *ibid.,* December 7, 1864.
[31] October 19, 1864.
[32] Quoted in Houston *Daily Telegraph,* September 14, 1864.

Murrah wrote numerous letters to Kirby Smith, explaining the course taken by the legislature and himself and urging the general commanding to issue specific orders that there would be no interference with the transportation of Texas cotton to the Rio Grande. In reply Kirby Smith discussed in detail the problems of securing supplies and the plans by which he had hoped to solve the problem. He made no claim to superior talents as a civil administrator, he explained, but he recognized the seriousness of his problems and attempted to solve them in the most efficient manner. When he arrived west of the Mississippi he found the soldiers poorly provided with those supplies necessary to the waging of successful war. Neither was there money with which to buy. Little support could be expected from east of the river; consequently, he found it necessary to solve his own problems.

Through the highly respected personnel of the Texas cotton office he made his appeal to the people for one half of their cotton and promised to exempt the other half. In his mind there was no doubt of the power to impress cotton, but he had hoped that planters, recognizing the government's urgent need for cotton, could be induced "to acquiesce and furnish it." Although disappointed thus far, he was confident that Congress would validate the certificates given in payment for cotton. He felt it his duty to state that "but for the interruption of our plan the cotton office would have succeeded in obtaining the cotton needed by the army." In short, the interference of the Texas governor and legislature was responsible for many troops now being "without arms, clothing, hospital or ordnance stores for an effective campaign." He wished to state clearly that "I have not received from you the co-operation to which I think the support of the army entitled at your hands."

Although convinced of his power to impress and determined to do his duty, he had a strict regard for law. "If the courts decide that I cannot impress cotton I shall not attempt to impress it nor claim power of exemption based upon such." However, in such a case, he would clearly state to the people of Texas that no longer having power to acquire cotton he was without the means to supply their soldiers.

In all his actions as department commander, he had sought to conform to the wishes of state officials as far as possible. "Collision by me with the State authorities would only be deplored less than to yield the country to the enemy." But the request for noninterference with transportation could not be granted by him, since the cotton contracted for remained the property of the vendor until delivered. Such an exemption would be in violation of the recent law of Congress which forbade exportation of cotton except according to uniform regulations made by the President. State interests would no doubt be affected by this decision, but he wished to point out that all the states and all the people were vitally interested in the proper enforcement of the laws of Congress. A concession, of questionable legality, granted to Texas might put specie in the state treasury but it would do nothing for the destitute soldiers. The general commanding would be pleased to grant the conference suggested by Governor Murrah.[33]

The conference between Murrah and Kirby Smith was held near Hempstead, and the results were all that could be hoped for. Murrah returned to Austin and announced that he had held a "full, free and unreserved" conference with Kirby Smith. He now appealed to the people of Texas to co-operate in supplying the military needs of the Trans-Mississippi Department and promised every assistance

[33] E. Kirby Smith to Pendleton Murrah, July 5, 1864, *Official Records*, Ser. I, Vol. LIII, Suppl., 1010–15.

within his power.[34] For this expression of genuine support, Kirby Smith thanked him profusely.[35]

On August 3, 1864, the War Department sent Kirby Smith a message notifying him that henceforth the acquisition and sale of cotton would be handled by the Treasury Department. There would no longer be any need for a cotton bureau. Broadwell would report to department headquarters for reassignment. Hutchins would be shifted to the Treasury Department and continue his connection with cotton. The military power to impress might still be exercised, if necessary, when requested by the assistant secretary of the treasury for the Trans-Mississippi Department.[36]

A glance at the military situation within the department during late winter 1864 tends to justify Kirby Smith's gloomy outlook. In Arkansas, Holmes was attempting to hold the line of the Ouachita. Mouton was in the vicinity of Monroe, Louisiana, waiting to protect the passage of the arms which had not arrived. Taylor, expecting few if any arms to be crossed over the Mississippi, was urging that Mouton be recalled to the Red River. An estimated 13,000 Federal troops were still in Lower Louisiana and almost certainly being prepared for a Red River campaign. On the coast of Texas, a Federal base had been established at Matagorda Bay with Houston or San Antonio probable objectives. This would cut off Mexican trade and gain control of the Texas railroads. Green's division from Louisiana had arrived in Texas, and W. H. Parsons' brigade from Arkansas had recently been ordered to the same district. With these re-enforcements and the Texas

[34] Houston *Daily Telegraph,* July 20, 1864.

[35] E. Kirby Smith to Pendleton Murrah, August 25, 1864, *Official Records,* Ser. I, Vol. XLI, pt. 2, 1083–84.

[36] J. A. Seddon to E. Kirby Smith, August 3, 1864, *ibid.,* Vol. LIII, Suppl., 1016–18.

state troops, Magruder could muster probably 15,000 men for the defense of Texas. A Federal march on either San Antonio or Houston with such a force on its flank would at least be hazardous.

Kirby Smith was correct in his belief that the "only true line of operation" by which the department could be invaded advantageously was the Red River Valley. With supplies in abundance and with river navigation possible for several months to come, a combined land and naval force could move up the valley, seizing and destroying, shifting its base as it progressed, and driving straight into the heart of the department. The possible prize would be valuable. Planters, ever reluctant to destroy their own property, would allow thousands of bales of cotton to fall into enemy hands. And if Shreveport and Marshall were reached, foundries, powder mills, clothing factories, and warehouses could be destroyed. Jefferson, Tyler, and the wheat fields of Texas would be next. It was not reasonable to expect that Federal officers, fully informed of the advantages of such a route, would delay much longer an invasion along this line.[37]

Taylor's informers reported that in New Orleans it was generally understood that the main movement was to be up the Red River. Already no fewer than seven gunboats were engaged in sounding the bars at the mouth of the river. But since the river was at present falling rather than rising, a delay would be necessary. Taylor hoped that the delay would be sufficient to permit further strengthening of the small forts along the river. "We shall all be put on our mettle during the spring," he commented.[38] Kirby Smith agreed.

[37] E. Kirby Smith to Jefferson Davis, January 20, 1864, *ibid.*, Vol. XXXIV, pt. 2, 895–96.
[38] Richard Taylor to W. R. Boggs, January 16, 1864, *ibid.*, 879.

Magruder, always convinced that the greatest danger was in Texas, continued to send in exaggerated reports. He had recently heard that 20,000 more troops were at the mouth of the Mississippi ready to steam for the coast of Texas. Already, he reported, the Federals had 4,000 or 5,000 men at Brownsville and between 12,000 and 22,000 at Saluria. In view of the state law and the governor's attitude he had no idea how many Texas state troops could be depended upon. He urged that Kirby Smith come to Texas for a survey of the situation.[39] Kirby Smith made the suggested trip to Texas to inspect the military situation and confer with Governor Murrah.

There was a misunderstanding about the Texas state troops. These troops had been raised during the previous summer. In appealing for state troops Magruder had hoped to get the services of more men than were coming in under the poorly enforced conscription law. Furthermore, in view of the shortage of arms, it was hoped these men would bring in private arms with them. Subsequently, the legislature had been urged to vote these men into the Confederate service for the duration of the war. Instead, it had voted to keep them in service for only six months longer, but made no claim to control over men subject to the conscription law. The governor, however, issued a proclamation advising men liable for military service to join the state troops.

While in Texas, Kirby Smith, Magruder, and Murrah held a conference at Houston early in February. Kirby Smith disagreed with the governor's claim of state control of men of conscript age. But realizing the difficulty in drafting men under such circumstances, he agreed that conscripts might form new organizations, join old units, or join the state troops. Those in state troops would be

[39] J. B. Magruder to W. R. Boggs, January 22, 1864, *ibid.*, 905–906.

subject to Confederate service after the expiration of their six months terms. But many state troops had already gone home and others claimed furloughs following their six months of service. The result, Kirby Smith complained, was that about "6,000 able-bodied fighting men within conscript ages remain idle, while their services are of vital importance in the field."

"Many companies have met, I am told, elected themselves teamsters and their captains wagon-masters to the Governor and then dispersed," reported Magruder. If this chasm between state and Confederate authority could not be bridged, he would "leap it." "I cannot wait. Action now or never."

Governor Murrah denied that conditions within the Texas state troops were as bad as pictured, but reluctantly agreed "to look no longer to an organization under the State laws."

Conditions in Texas were not so serious as Magruder had feared; the large scale invasion which he had predicted was not attempted. And on March 8 Kirby Smith instructed him to mobilize and prepare his entire force, garrisons excepted, for rapid movement to Louisiana.[40]

While Kirby Smith was away in Texas, General Holmes requested relief from command in Arkansas. He had learned of a communication from Kirby Smith to President Davis asking that Holmes be replaced by a younger and more energetic officer. Kirby Smith held Holmes's request for a month and then forwarded it to Richmond with a recommendation that Buckner, Cleburne, or Stevenson

---

[40] *Id.* to *id.*, February 16, 1864, *ibid.*, 973–75; *id.* to E. B. Nichols, April 2, 1864, *ibid.*, pt. 3, 726–27; Pendleton Murrah to J. B. Magruder, April 7, 1864, *ibid.*, 747–50; E. Kirby Smith to Magruder, March 31, 1864, *ibid.*, pt. 2, 1103; *id.* to Jefferson Davis, March 28, 1864, *ibid.*, 1095; S. S. Anderson to Magruder, March 8, 1864, *ibid.*, 1029.

be sent to Arkansas. Price was placed in command there temporarily.[41]

To Holmes, Kirby Smith sent copies of letters written to the President. "I have never, general, in the course of my official duties been so much embarrassed in making a decision," Holmes was assured. "I know that the District of Arkansas will never have a purer, more unselfish, patriotic commander; no one more willing to sacrifice himself for our cause. A succession of circumstances, involving a loss of country, loss of confidence, loss of hope approaching almost to despair, necessitates a change in the administration of the district." The greatest service Holmes could now render the Confederacy would be to seek a personal conference with Davis at Richmond and explain to him "the true condition of affairs" in the Trans-Mississippi Department.[42]

Holmes's removal gave general satisfaction. The Arkansas delegation in Congress had unanimously requested such a step. And Governor Reynolds of Missouri had for months been urging it. The poor discipline of Arkansas troops was attributed to Holmes's weakness as a commander. Yet those familiar with conditions could see no hope for a miracle even after Holmes was replaced. "It is idle to expect that Gen. Smith can fully remedy such abuses," Reynolds had previously written W. P. Johnston, "for he cannot be at once district commander and chief of the department. In his own sphere he has effected great reform, and elevated the tone both of the army and the people. He has also prestige and a military air & bearing to aid him." [43] President Davis further increased the pres-

---

[41] T. H. Holmes to S. S. Anderson, February 1, 1864, *ibid.,* 935.

[42] E. Kirby Smith to T. H. Holmes, March 11, 1864, *ibid.,* Vol. XXXIV, pt. 2, 1035.

[43] T. C. Reynolds to E. Kirby Smith, May 23, 24, 1863, Reynolds Papers;

tige of the Trans-Mississippi commander by promoting him to full general in February, 1864.[44]

---

*id.* to W. P. Johnston, December 24, 1863, *ibid.; id.* to J. O. Shelby, March 26, 1864, *ibid.*

[44] This promotion came immediately after Congress had by law authorized the appointment of a general for the Trans-Mississippi Department and an unlimited number of lieutenant generals wherever needed. *The Statutes at Large of the Provisional Government of the Confederate States of America* (Richmond, 1864), 195. Although Kirby Smith's name was not mentioned in the bill, it was generally understood who the new general was to be. His critics offered spirited opposition in both houses of Congress. *Journal of the Congress of the Confederate States* (Washington, 1904), III, 716, 749, 760, 784, 789; VI, 838, 860.

## CHAPTER XIII

# THE RED RIVER VALLEY

Events crowded upon each other. Before calm and confidence could be restored in Arkansas, Taylor was reporting threatening enemy action in Louisiana. On February 16 he notified headquarters that the Mississippi was "rising rapidly." Backwater had brought a three-foot rise in the Red River at Fort De Russy. Every effort was being made to complete fortifications and obstructions. The fort was now complete except for the nine-inch guns that had been promised from Shreveport. Below De Russy timbers had been sunk "blocking the river completely." Above the obstruction had been driven strongly braced piles and Walker's division was busily engaged "in filling in floating timbers above the piles." For several miles both above and below the obstruction "rifle pits and positions for light guns had been constructed."

In accordance with a suggestion from Kirby Smith, Taylor had swept the Atchafalaya country of mules, horses, and vehicles which might be used by the advancing enemy. Owners protested vigorously, but Taylor would not heed. As the enemy approached Red River the previous year he had listened to owners' protests and as a result General Banks had seized transportation "of incalculable value." "Not one owner in ten thousand," Taylor observed, "will admit the necessity of surrendering his prop-

erty until the enemy is at his door, when it is too late."
Consequently, Taylor had resolved to follow the suggestion
of Kirby Smith and remove all property that might fall
into enemy possession.[1]

Almost daily reports of further enemy concentrations
arrived at Kirby Smith's headquarters. More troops were
arriving at Berwick's Bay. A part of Sherman's command
was said to be near Vicksburg. Cavalry was harassing the
country east of the Atchafalaya and across to Opelousas.
Taylor had practically no cavalry to send in pursuit. Fort
De Russy was alerted. Seven Federal gunboats were entering Red River. Pickets along the river awaited their appearance. But instead of proceeding up the Red they turned
up the Black River moving on to Harrisonburg. They did
no damage, for low water soon forced them to retire.

Such stepped up activities, however, could mean nothing less than enemy concentration for a Red River campaign. Kirby Smith wired Magruder to send Green's cavalry to Alexandria immediately. A few days later two
more Texas regiments were also ordered to Louisiana.
Magruder was to use his own judgment whether to accompany the Texas troops to Louisiana or remain on duty
within his district.[2]

From Arkansas came news that the enemy was withdrawing forces from Fort Smith and concentrating at Little
Rock. Brigadier General S. B. Maxey, commanding in
the Indian Territory, was instructed to prepare for co-
operation with Price or movement into Louisiana. Price
wrote urging Kirby Smith to decide in favor of an all-out
campaign in Arkansas. An army of 20,000 led by Kirby
Smith in person, he insisted, would be sufficient to retake

---

[1] Richard Taylor to W. R. Boggs, February 16, 21, 1864, *Official Records*,
Ser. I, Vol. XXXIV, pt. 2, 971, 977–78.
[2] S. S. Anderson to J. B. Magruder, March 5, 1864, *ibid.*, 1027; W. R. Boggs
to *id.*, March 11, 1864, *ibid.*, 1034.

the Arkansas Valley. From there a force led by either Kirby Smith or Price could enter Missouri where "thousands and tens of thousands of recruits" could be added to the Confederate army.[3]

Governor Flanagin also urged immediate action in Arkansas, but with a somewhat different idea in mind. The Federal government had called a state election for March 14. Under Lincoln's plan the state could be reconstructed if one tenth of the voters participated in the election. Federal success in this undertaking could be prevented only by a Confederate advance toward the Arkansas. This would encourage Confederate sympathizers and destroy the confidence of the Federals. "Those who might under other circumstances vote would hesitate; those who would accept office, refuse." [4]

Kirby Smith agreed with Price both as to what an army of 20,000 could do in Arkansas and as to the importance of reconquering the Arkansas Valley. Yet he saw no means of putting the plan into operation. There could be concentration at one point only and that should be the one at which the enemy threatened the most serious damage to the department. Furthermore, the latest reports available gave the infantry under Price at 5,000, that under Taylor 7,000–8,000, and that under Magruder, since the disbandment of the Texas state troops, at 2,000. Clearly there could be no great concentration of forces within the department until the infantry was increased. This could best be done by dismounting unnecessary and poorly mounted cavalry units. If Price would dismount one half his cavalry and instill discipline in the remainder, Kirby Smith insisted, he would do "more to relieve our people and bene-

---

[3] E. Cunningham to S. B. Maxey, March 12, 1864, *ibid.*, 1038–39; Sterling Price to E. Kirby Smith, March 8, 1864, *ibid.*, 1028–29.

[4] H. Flanagin to E. Kirby Smith, February 27, 1864, *ibid.*, Vol. LIII, Suppl., 969–70.

fit our cause than by gaining a victory." [5] Since simultaneous movements from Berwick's Bay, Vicksburg, and Little Rock were to be expected, Price should strengthen his position at Camden, and be ready to strike at the flank of any force which should attempt to move into the department from Vicksburg by way of Monroe, and with his great superiority of cavalry, he should also be ready to deal Frederick Steele a destructive blow, should he move from Little Rock into "our exhausted and impoverished country." [6] Price should also see that an adequate depot of supplies was established at Calhoun in order to facilitate the movement of troops from Arkansas to Louisiana or vice versa. [7]

As Kirby Smith was writing Price, the Federals were on the move in Louisiana. In mid-January, General Banks, still occupied on the coast of Texas in a plan to capture Galveston, received dispatches from Washington urging that he give attention to Red River. General Sherman on the Mississippi and General Steele in Arkansas both agreed, Halleck wrote, "that the Red River is the shortest and best line of defense for Louisiana and Arkansas and as a base of operations against Texas." As long as Banks confined his operations to the coast of Texas, Halleck continued, Steele must remain on the Arkansas and the greater portion of Sherman's strength must be used to keep the Mississippi River open. But Steele was ready to move to the Red River, if he could rely upon Banks's co-operation and "be certain of receiving supplies on that line." The best military opinion then seemed "to favor operations on the Red River, provided the stage of water will enable the

---

[5] E. Kirby Smith to Sterling Price, March 15, 1864, *ibid.*, Vol. XXXIV, pt. 2, 1043–44.

[6] *Id.* to *id.*, March 14, 1864, *ibid.*, 1041.

[7] E. Cunningham to *id.*, March 14, 1864, *ibid.*, 1042.

gunboats to co-operate." Banks would please confer with Sherman and Steele and with Admiral Porter.[8]

Banks readily concurred in the opinion "that the Red River is the shortest and best line of defense for Louisiana, and as a base for operation against Texas"; yet he felt that he and Steele alone could not succeed in such a campaign if operating separately. However, with the co-operation of Sherman much might be accomplished. He would "cordially co-operate" with Steele, Sherman, and Porter. With his own command alone, he stressed, he could do nothing more than operate on the coast of Texas with no hope of moving far into the interior or of controlling any country except that west of San Antonio. "On the other line, with commensurate forces, the whole State, as well as Arkansas and Louisiana, will be ours, and their people will gladly renew their allegiance to the Government. The occupation of Shreveport will be to the country west of the Mississippi what that of Chattanooga is to the east, and as soon as this can be accomplished the country west of Shreveport will be in condition for movement into Texas." Banks immediately opened up correspondence with Steele and Sherman, enclosing maps of the Red River country, and received an enthusiastic reply from the latter.[9]

Banks next began to estimate the probable Confederate strength that could be concentrated on the upper Red River. Magruder, in Texas, he thought, had about 15,000 serviceable men, 10,000 of which could be spared. In Louisiana, Taylor had at least 13,000, and Price had in Arkansas about 5,000 infantry and 7,000 to 10,000 cavalry, of which probably 5,000 could be spared. Thus, according to Banks's calculations, Kirby Smith should have 25,000 to

[8] H. W. Halleck to N. P. Banks, January 4, 11, 1864, *ibid.*, 15–16, 55–56.
[9] N. P. Banks to H. W. Halleck, January 23, 1864, *ibid.*, 133–34.

30,000 men available for the defense of the Red River Valley. The authorities at Washington were justified in thinking Banks's estimate much too high.

For an invading force Banks counted on the assistance of 10,000 from Steele, 10,000 from Sherman, and 15,000 to 17,000 of his own command, making a total of 35,000 to 37,000 men.[10]

Sherman visited Banks in New Orleans early in March. It was agreed between them that Sherman would lend Banks 10,000 men for one month. This, it was thought, should be ample time for crushing the heart of the Trans-Mississippi resistance. These borrowed troops could then be returned to the more important theater of war east of the Mississippi. Under no condition was Banks to send these borrowed troops further than Shreveport or to detain them longer than was necessary.[11] Since Banks wished to command in person, Sherman did not accompany his troops but sent Major General A. J. Smith instead.

Banks ordered the suspension of operations at Galveston and began concentrating his own forces in the Berwick's Bay area under the command of Major General W. B. Franklin, while he himself delayed in New Orleans looking after political matters. Franklin was directed to begin moving northward on March 7 and make junction with A. J. Smith at Alexandria on March 17. Sherman had instructed Smith to proceed from Vicksburg to the mouth of the Red River, where he would be met by Porter's fleet, and thence to Alexandria.

Steele, in Arkansas, had already been notified that Franklin would probably move on March 7. A junction of Arkansas and Louisiana forces at Natchitoches was first

[10] *Id.* to E. M. Stanton, April 6, 1865, *ibid.,* pt. 1, 194 ff.

[11] W. T. Sherman to N. P. Banks, March 4, 1864, *ibid.,* pt. 2, 494; *id.* to A. J. Smith, March 6, 1864, *ibid.,* 514–16.

suggested, since the road from Monroe to that place was probably the best during that season. A few days later, however, Steele was advised to move on Shreveport by way of Camden and Overton. In reply, he expressed enthusiasm but warned that he would be delayed on account of the state election scheduled for March 14. Unless the troops were present to assist in distributing poll books and oaths of allegiance and "to protect the voters at the polls," the election would not be a success. Steele was convinced that the rebel forces in Arkansas were much demoralized and would no doubt desert to the Federals by the thousands once the campaign was under way. The Missouri troops were expected to desert en masse. Rebel officers no longer trusted their men. He himself would have 3,000 copies of the amnesty oath distributed among the demoralized troops.

It was rumored that Price himself had "deserted the sinking ship and gone to Europe." Steele believed it. There were also reports that Kirby Smith would attempt to hold the line of the Red River, but Steele prophesied that the rebels would "run to Texas," without fighting a general battle. It was certain that Banks's and Sherman's combined forces could "drive Kirby Smith's whole command into the Gulf." As for himself, Steele had decided to move to Washington, Arkansas, "and if necessary, to Shreveport." [12]

A. J. Smith arrived at the Red River at noon March 11. There he was handed a dispatch from Banks stating that his forces had been delayed by heavy rains and would not arrive at Alexandria before March 21. And from Porter, Smith learned that Fort De Russy must be reduced before an advance to Alexandria could be made. It was agreed

---

[12] N. P. Banks to Frederick Steele, February 19, March 3, 1864, *ibid.*, 372, 491; Steele to Banks, February 28, March 7, 10, 1864, *ibid.*, 448–49, 518–19, 542.

that Smith would attack the fort by land and Porter would move against the obstructions on the river. On March 12 Smith landed his force at Simmesport on the Atchafalaya. On the following day he began moving overland toward Fort De Russy.[13]

There was no element of surprise in the Federal movements. The Confederate commanders knew of Sherman's trip to New Orleans and suspected the agreement with Banks. Both Taylor and Kirby Smith, however, expected Sherman to accompany his troops west of the Mississippi. To meet the Federal advance Taylor moved all his forces south of the Red River except the small command of Brigadier General St. John R. Liddell, which remained west of the Ouachita to harass the enemy in the advance up the Red. Mouton and Polignac were stationed on the Boeuf some twenty-five miles south of Alexandria. Walker was just beyond Marksville toward Simmesport. W. G. Vincent's Second Louisiana Cavalry waited on the Teche near Opelousas. Green was on his way from Texas but moving very slowly. Taylor later stated that his entire force south of the Red River at the beginning of the campaign numbered 5,300 infantry, 300 cavalry, and 300 artillerymen.[14]

At his Alexandria headquarters Taylor, usually very successful in securing accurate information as to enemy strength and intentions, learned of the withdrawal of Federal troops from the coast of Texas to re-enforce Franklin on the Teche. He knew Franklin was to move up the Teche with cavalry and some infantry, yet considering Franklin "a slow man" he did not expect the expedition to get under way before March 15. The total Federal force available for the Red River campaign would be about

---

[13] A. J. Smith to W. T. Sherman, September 26, 1865, *ibid.*, pt. 1, 304 ff.
[14] Taylor, *Destruction and Reconstruction*, 154–56.

22,000 including more than 7,000 mounted. Frederick Steele was expected to be active in Arkansas, but nothing was to be feared in Texas. In forwarding this information to Kirby Smith's headquarters, Taylor added: "The above information is strictly correct, and can be relied upon with as much confidence as if the plans had been laid here instead of New Orleans." [15] He was not far wrong.

To meet the expected attack Taylor rushed tools and Negroes to finish Fort De Russy, which he hoped would "be ready in time." The first Confederate troops met by the advancing Federals were of Walker's division, but Walker, not yet ready to fight, fell back to Marksville, hoping to form junction with Mouton near Evergreen. [16] Unfinished Fort De Russy, defended by only 300 men and having little strength against a land force, was left to its fate and immediately fell into Federal hands. Porter's fleet broke through the obstructions and soon arrived at De Russy. The combined land and naval forces moved on toward Alexandria. [17]

Franklin's force, brushing aside Vincent's Second Louisiana Cavalry, began arriving at Alexandria on March 25. Banks had arrived in person on March 19. Loquacious Federal officers, said to be of high rank, were soon telling the populace of their plans. The Federals would march directly to Shreveport, form a junction with Steele from Arkansas, and then move on to Marshall and Tyler, Texas, to destroy stores and depots. [18]

Taylor, now in personal command of Walker's and Mouton's troops, had retired from Alexandria the morning before the Federals arrived. Steamers heavily loaded with

[15] Richard Taylor to W. R. Boggs, March 5, 1864, *Official Records,* Ser. I, Vol. XXXIV, pt. 1, 572–73.

[16] E. Cunningham to Sterling Price, March 16, 1864, *ibid.,* pt. 2, 1046.

[17] A. J. Smith to W. T. Sherman, September 26, 1865, *ibid.,* pt. 1, 304 ff.

[18] Richard Taylor to W. R. Boggs, March 20, 1864, *ibid.,* 500.

Confederate property were sent up the river toward Shreveport. Taylor's withdrawal was along the Natchitoches road to Carroll Jones's, where he had previously established a depot. Here he hoped to remain until joined by Green's force from Texas. Vincent's Cavalry came in on March 19, but Green was still many miles away. From his location on the Kisatchie River, Taylor informed Kirby Smith on March 23 that "as soon as Green joins me I shall assume the offensive, and hope to be able to do so without the assistance of Price, as I do not doubt the intention of the enemy to move from Arkansas." [19]

While Taylor was writing the above, Price's infantry divisions under Churchill and Parsons, 4,000 to 5,000 strong, was nearing Shreveport. They arrived on March 24. The advance of Steele's force had marched out of Little Rock on March 23. Six days later Arkadelphia was occupied, in spite of the sting of Marmaduke's and Shelby's cavalry on front, flank, and rear.[20]

"Retard the enemy's advance," Kirby Smith wired Price on March 27. "Operate on their communications with your cavalry if practicable. Time is everything with us. Do not risk a general action unless with advantage to yourself. You fall back toward re-enforcements." [21] On the following day Maxey was ordered to move his entire Indian Territory command to the support of Price.[22]

Since Steele was advancing in the direction of Washington, Arkansas, Kirby Smith was undecided whether to send his infantry re-enforcement to Taylor or to send it back to meet Steele. He detained it for reorganization and to await developments. In the meantime Congressman D. F. Kenner wrote Taylor from Shreveport stating that

[19] *Id.* to *id.*, March 23, 1864, *ibid.*, 505–506.
[20] Report of Sterling Price, May ?, 1864, *ibid.*, 779 ff.
[21] E. Kirby Smith to Sterling Price, March 27, 1864, *ibid.*, pt. 2, 1095.
[22] W. R. Boggs to S. B. Maxey, March 28, 1864, *ibid.*, 1096.

Kirby Smith had quoted the Louisiana commander as not desiring re-enforcements, citing his communication of March 23 as evidence. Taylor was angry. "If to obtain re-enforcements it is necessary to set up a clamor and urge the abandonment of all the department for selfish ends," he snapped, "I cannot do it." He was "deeply grieved," he told Kirby Smith, "that so little anxiety should be manifested to strengthen my forces. When Green joins me, I repeat, I shall fight a battle for Louisiana, be the forces of the enemy what they may." [23]

Kirby Smith advised the greatest caution. Steele was at Arkadelphia with 10,000 to 12,000 men and thirty pieces of artillery. Should he advance by Washington, as seemed likely, he "comes in the most favorable direction for our operations." For columns pushing in along this route gave the greatest opportunity for Confederate concentration. Price could do no more than delay Steele. If Banks was in the strength reported, Kirby Smith advised Taylor to fall back upon Pleasant Hill and Mansfield. "A general engagement should not be risked without hopes of success."

While occupying the attention of Banks's huge force, Kirby Smith thought the Trans-Mississippi armies were giving valuable assistance to Confederate armies in Georgia and Virginia. Rash action resulting in destruction of either of the Trans-Mississippi armies "would be fatal to the whole cause and to the department. Our role must be a defensive policy where the enemy is largely our superior, and where our columns come within a practical distance of each other, concentrating rapidly upon and crushing one or the other of the enemy's columns." [24]

To Taylor's complaint about re-enforcements, Kirby Smith replied: "While I know you do not call for re-

23 Richard Taylor to W. R. Boggs, March 28, 1864, ibid., pt. 1, 512–13.
24 E. Kirby Smith to Richard Taylor, March 31, 1864, ibid., 516–17.

enforcements unless compelled by necessity, that you appreciate the inadequate means at my disposal, and have always given me a hearty and cordial support, I object to the tone of your letter, which is an unjust complaint, founded on a private letter of a civilian." Kenner had been permitted to see Taylor's communication of March 23 in order to "relieve his anxiety" as to Taylor's position. It was certainly not expected "that he would write anything to impair or interrupt the harmony and good understanding that has always hitherto characterized our official relations." [25]

Taylor was not satisfied with what he considered Kirby Smith's interpretation of his letters of March 23 and 28. "I certainly would have been the first commander possessing ordinary sense who voluntarily declined re-enforcements while retreating before a superior force," he replied to Kirby Smith. Furthermore, he could see nothing disrespectful in his recent letter.[26] Both generals could have spent their time more profitably in preparing to meet the advancing enemy rather than arguing whether or not Taylor had originally desired re-enforcements.

When the enemy, moving on toward Natchitoches, crossed Cane River, cutting off all forage from that direction, Taylor fell back to Beasley's and dispatched a courier to tell Green where to find him. The advance of the Texas cavalry arrived on March 30, and Green himself joined Taylor two days later. By this time the Confederates had evacuated Natchitoches. Banks's cavalry had entered the town on March 31 and his infantry was up by April 2, Franklin moving by land and A. J. Smith by the river. "Our troops now occupy Natchitoches," Banks proudly reported to Washington, "and we hope to be in Shreveport

[25] *Id.* to *id.*, March 31, 1864, *ibid.*, 517.
[26] Richard Taylor to E. Kirby Smith, April 3, 1864, *ibid.*, 519.

by the 10th of April. I do not fear concentration of the enemy at that point. My fear is that they may not be willing to meet me there." Should the rebels not choose to fight there, he would pursue them "into the interior of Texas." [27]

At Shreveport Kirby Smith nervously looked one way and then the other, attempting to calculate probable speed, potential strength, and the intentions of the advancing Federal armies. Citizens were becoming jittery. Those who could conveniently do so were moving to places of safety in Texas. Kirby Smith sent his wife and daughter to visit in the house of a Colonel Kirby, a wealthy planter near Hempstead, Texas. Colonel Kirby and his young wife had met the Kirby Smiths in Shreveport during the previous winter and immediately claimed kinship. They would be delighted, they insisted, to have Mrs. Kirby Smith visit them. The general had never before heard of the colonel, but "being a clever man," he laughingly wrote his mother, he was not inclined to dispute the claim to kinship.[28]

It was not until April 3 that the larger Federal gunboats were able to get above the falls at Alexandria. The river continued to fall, and their advance was stopped at Grand Ecore. Meanwhile A. J. Smith's command had moved on toward Pleasant Hill. Taylor, keeping a safe distance in advance, moved on to Mansfield. Although Green's full force was still not available, Taylor reported that he had twice offered battle, but Banks declined, contenting himself with minor skirmishes.[29]

On the Arkansas line Steele was becoming a serious threat. On April 3 he crossed the Little Missouri at Elkins Ferry. Marmaduke made a dashing attack, temporarily

[27] N. P. Banks to H. W. Halleck, April 2, 1864, *ibid.*, 179–80.

[28] E. Kirby Smith to Mother, May 5, 1864; Mrs. Kirby Smith to Mother, May ?, 1864.

[29] Richard Taylor to W. R. Boggs, April 3, 1864, *Official Records*, Ser. I, Vol. XXXIV, pt. 1, 520–21.

halting the advance. Steele's forces soon recovered and moved on.[30] Kirby Smith was busy calculating. Upon reaching Washington, he figured Steele could choose either of two courses—move directly down the east bank of the Red River or cross that river near Fulton and join Banks either at Marshall, Texas, or Shreveport. Such a junction must be prevented; if the Federal forces were to be defeated it must be done by concentrating on one at a time. No further re-enforcements could be expected. Price had with him about 7,000 cavalry and 1,500 infantry. A brigade of Texas cavalry, concentrating at Marshall, Texas, was about 1,000 strong. Price's infantry commanded by Churchill and Parsons was at Shreveport. All other available troops within the department were under Taylor's command. The commanding general would like to have Taylor's "views and opinions." [31]

Taylor, not being familiar with the country beyond Shreveport, was not in position to designate the place to meet Steele; but he expressed a greater fear of him than of Banks. The latter he considered "cold, timid, easily foiled." And since Banks depended heavily upon river transportation, low water and Confederate obstruction would greatly delay him. Steele was "bold, ardent, vigorous," and being independent of river transportation, would probably "sweep Price from his path." As the more dangerous of the two, Steele "should be met and overthrown at once." Yet in either case, action, immediate and vigorous, was necessary. "King James lost three kingdoms for a mass. We may lose three States without a battle." Taylor would hold himself ready to move in such direction as Kirby Smith might order. If no orders came he would

[30] Report of Sterling Price, May ?, 1864, *ibid.*, 779 ff.
[31] E. Kirby Smith to Richard Taylor, April 3, 1864, *ibid.*, 521–22.

move on Natchitoches as soon as Green's full force was available.[32]

Expecting orders to move against Steele, Taylor began repairs on the road by way of Kingston, the shortest route to Shreveport. But Steele's progress had not been so rapid as was expected. The fact that he had crossed the Little Missouri was not yet known at Shreveport headquarters. The two Federal armies were still about 200 miles apart. It was not yet time to concentrate against either column, Kirby Smith reasoned. Since the fate of the department depended upon this concentration, "The battle must be decisive, whether with Steele or Banks," he advised Taylor. By holding the interior line, the smaller Confederate force had an advantage, and as long as "we retain our little army undefeated we have hopes." The whole cause must not be lost by an ill-advised move. "When we fight it must be for victory." [33]

Considering Taylor in the greatest immediate danger, Kirby Smith, on April 4, ordered Churchill's and Parsons' Arkansas and Missouri infantry divisions to move to Keachie, where they would be in supporting distance. On the following day the commanding general went in person to Taylor's headquarters at Mansfield, discussed details of proposed operations, and returned to Shreveport that evening. A Federal attack did not appear imminent.[34]

On April 7 Major's brigade of Green's cavalry engaged the enemy in a "severe skirmish" a short distance from Pleasant Hill, which Banks reported as a fight lasting two hours and resulting in the rebels being driven from the field with heavy losses. Taylor, suspecting that this enemy

[32] Richard Taylor to W. R. Boggs, April 4, 1864, *ibid.*, 522.
[33] E. Kirby Smith to Richard Taylor, April 5, 1864, *ibid.*, 525–26.
[34] *Id.* to Jefferson Davis, June 11, 1864, *ibid.*, 478 ff.

advance might be a forerunner of a general movement, wired Kirby Smith for instructions. Should he "hazard a general engagement at this point"? An immediate reply was requested.[35] Taylor later stated that he notified Kirby Smith he would "fight a general engagement the next day if the enemy advanced in force, unless ordered positively not to do so." [36] His telegram does not reveal such a positive intention. Kirby Smith, apparently not considering Taylor in immediate danger, answered by letter rather than wire.

The enemy did not retire during the night. Early on the morning of April 8 Taylor ordered up Mouton's and Walker's divisions and sent for Churchill and Parsons to move in from Keachie to Mansfield. Mouton and Walker took positions three miles from Mansfield, the former on the left and the latter on the right of the road, facing Pleasant Hill. Their line was partly concealed in the edge of a woods, and in front lay cleared field 1,000 yards in width.[37]

The Federal advance halted shortly before reaching the Confederate position in order to close ranks. It was no small task to move a large army along a narrow road bordered by pine woods, and Franklin, to whom the movement had been intrusted, had already committed the error that was to defeat him. Out in front of the column was Brigadier General Albert L. Lee's cavalry and a small body of infantry, which had been ordered up on the previous evening. Next came Lee's wagon train, with artillery, which blocked the road, and then came Banks's infantry under W. H. Emory and T. E. G. Ransom. Miles to the rear was A. J. Smith. Accompanying this slow-moving

[35] N. P. Banks to U. S. Grant, April 13, 1864, *ibid.*, 181–85; Richard Taylor to W. R. Boggs, April 7, 1864, *ibid.*, 526.

[36] Report of Richard Taylor, April 18, 1864, *ibid.*, 560 ff.     [37] *Ibid.*

army was a wagon train twelve miles long, carrying twice the amount of supplies needed.

About midmorning April 8 Lee, made a bit bolder by the presence of infantry, began skirmishing with Confederate cavalry. Banks rode forward to investigate, and found the rebels offering unexpected resistance. Neither he nor Franklin had expected serious resistance short of Shreveport. Lee sent back a call for heavy re-enforcements. Banks, instead of ordering him to fall back until the infantry could be brought up, directed that he hold his present position.[38]

Intermittent firing continued during the early afternoon. About 4 P.M. the Confederates opened a "tremendous fire" all along the line. Taylor, growing impatient and correctly suspecting that the enemy's arrangements were incomplete, had directed Mouton to attack from the left of the road. "The charge made by Mouton across the open was magnificent." The woods beyond the clearing was reached "under a murderous fire of artillery and musketry," and Mouton's men "sprang with a yell on the foe." Mouton fell; C. J. Polignac took over and continued the charge. Major's and Vincent's cavalry dismounted and moved up on Polignac's left. Then came Randal, who had just been shifted from the right to the left of the road, moving with "vigor, energy and daring." Walker came up on the right while Bee led Debray's and Buchel's cavalry around to get at the enemy's rear.

Lee had made an error; Banks had encouraged him in it. He had joined battle with Taylor's main force without waiting for re-enforcements. Left almost entirely alone, he resisted "until, utterly overpowered by numbers," and then attempted to fall back. But there could be no orderly retreat; the way was blocked by the wagon train. Midst

[38] Report of A. L. Lee, April 13, 1864, *ibid.*, 449 ff.

the squeal of horses, the curses of wagon drivers, and the yell of onrushing rebels, brave Yankee soldiers became a "disorganized mob of screaming, sobbing, hysterical, pale, terror-stricken men." [39] Even the lowly mules, by nature calm and sturdy, joined in the flight, dragging broken wagons through trees torn by the aimless firing of Federal artillery. The few officers who tried to rally their men were ignored as "the fierce pursuit of a victorious and desperate force for the moment seemed to paralyze individuals and masses." [40]

"We have driven the enemy at this hour 3 miles . . . ," Taylor wired Shreveport at 6 P.M. "We are still driving him." An hour and a half later the enemy had fallen back three more miles, abandoning much material and with heavy losses in killed and captured.[41] A complete rout was prevented by the arrival of Emory's infantry, and nightfall stopped the Confederate advance.

Banks had lost "about 2,000 prisoners, 20 pieces of artillery, 200 wagons, and thousands of small-arms," but Taylor had paid rather dearly for the victory.[42] Banks blamed the disaster on "the fatally incautious advance of the large cavalry train and the surplus artillery." Yet he added: "It is always difficult to ascertain the position of a concealed adversary, and temporary defeat is to be expected when the front of an advancing column encounters the base of that of the enemy." [43] Taylor offered another explanation: "The defeat of the Federal army was largely due to the ignorance and arrogance of its com-

[39] Quoted in Fred Harvey Harrington, *Fighting Politician, Major General N. P. Banks* (Philadelphia, 1948), 156.

[40] N. P. Banks to U. S. Grant, April 13, 1864, *Official Records*, Ser. I, Vol. XXXIV, pt. 1, 181–85.

[41] Richard Taylor to W. R. Boggs, April 8, 1864, *ibid.*, 527.

[42] *Ibid.* There were three dispatches under this date.

[43] N. P. Banks to U. S. Grant, April 13, 1864, *ibid.*, 181–85.

mander, General Banks, who attributed my long retreat to his own wonderful strategy." [44]

Kirby Smith had no knowledge of the fighting at Mansfield (or Sabine Crossroads) until after it was over. When he received Taylor's telegram of the previous evening is not known. He replied on the day of the battle, too late to restrain Taylor. There should be no general engagement, he advised, until all re-enforcements were up. Yet "if we fall back without a battle you will be thrown out of the best country for supplies." The enemy should be compelled to reveal his intentions and then forced to fight at a point chosen by the Confederate commanders. "Let me know as soon as you are convinced that a general advance is being made," he urged Taylor, "and I will come to the front." [45] Taylor could not have received this message until after the battle.

During the course of the day's fighting, Taylor had used probably 8,000 men and Banks about 6,000. A. J. Smith's command, far to the rear, saw no action. And the Confederate forces under Churchill and Parsons did not arrive on the scene until the night of April 8. Taylor was elated over the victory. At 10:30 P.M. he wired Kirby Smith: "Churchill's and Parsons' divisions . . . have been ordered to the front before daylight to-morrow morning. I shall continue to push the enemy with utmost vigor." [46]

Banks, expecting the victorious Confederates to renew the offensive on the morning of April 9, had to decide whether to attempt to hold his position while waiting for A. J. Smith to move up or to fall back during the night and join Smith at Pleasant Hill. He chose the latter. The Con-

[44] Taylor, *Destruction and Reconstruction*, 164.

[45] E. Kirby Smith to Richard Taylor, April 8, 1864, *Official Records*, Ser. I, Vol. XXXIV, pt. 1, 528.

[46] Richard Taylor to W. R. Boggs, April 8, 1864, *ibid.*, 527.

federates followed on the next morning, moving in a long column along the Pleasant Hill road, with Green, commanding the entire cavalry force, in the lead and followed by the infantry units of Churchill, Parsons, Walker, and Polignac. For twelve miles they met no opposition. Then near the village of Pleasant Hill, Green found Banks's army in position, with the train well to the rear. Taylor was particularly eager to drive Banks beyond Pleasant Hill so as to deprive him of the use of the road from that point to Blair's Landing on the Red River. About 3 P.M. the Confederates began moving into position. Churchill and Parsons cut off to the right through a woods leading to the Sabine road with instructions to turn the enemy's left. Walker came up on their left, and Bee held Debray's and Buchel's cavalry on the Mansfield road with orders to charge into Pleasant Hill as soon as the enemy's left had been driven in. Left of the road Green was to send Major's cavalry to drive in the enemy's right and seize the Blair's Landing road. Polignac's division, the hardest hit during the previous day's fighting, remained in reserve.

About 4:30 Green opened artillery fire from the left of the Mansfield road in order to divert attention from Churchill on the right. Churchill and then Walker moved forward. Walker fell wounded. Bee, not waiting for the full development of the attack, rushed toward Pleasant Hill, and was repulsed with heavy losses. He and T. B. Debray were wounded; Buchel was killed. Polignac was called into action. Churchill, not moving far enough to his own right, was flanked and thrown into confusion. Green and Polignac were thrown back; again and again they reformed their lines and renewed the attack. Fighting continued until 9 P.M. when Taylor withdrew his troops and fell back six miles to ample water supplies. The cavalry, except Debray's regiment which remained on picket duty, fell back to Mansfield for water, forage, and rest. "We had driven them in at every point," Taylor reported, "and but for the mistake and consequent confusion on the right we would have captured most of his army." [47]

Kirby Smith arrived on the scene shortly after the battle. At 4 A.M. he had received word of the fighting of the previous day; he left for the battlefield immediately. Upon arrival he found Taylor's army "completely paralyzed and disorganized by the repulse," only Polignac's division being intact. Kirby Smith and Taylor went into conference. Soon stragglers from the battlefield reported that Banks's army was retreating, thus, as Kirby Smith later remarked, "converting a victory which he might have claimed into a defeat." "Had Banks followed up his success vigorously he would have met but feeble opposition to his advance on Shreveport." [48]

Although they had repulsed the enemy, the victorious Federals were left without adequate water, and their food supplies were some distance to the rear. Faced with this shortage of food and water and not being in touch with the fleet on the Red River, Banks considered it necessary to fall back. During the night of April 9–10, he began a retreat to Grand Ecore "to the great disappointment of the troops who, flushed with success, were eager for another fight." In an effort to justify his decision, Banks reported that in its present condition his army could not "have sustained another battle." [49] He believed that at Pleasant Hill he had met the entire Trans-Mississippi army, 22,000 to

[47] Report of Richard Taylor, April 18, 1864, *ibid.*, 560 ff.; N. P. Banks to U. S. Grant, April 13, 1864, *ibid.*, 181 ff.; Taylor, *Destruction and Reconstruction*, 166–69.

[48] E. Kirby Smith to Jefferson Davis, June 11, 1864, *Official Records,* Ser. I, Vol. XXXIV, pt. 1, 478–482; E. Kirby Smith, "The Defense of the Red River," in *Battles and Leaders,* IV, 369 ff.

[49] N. P. Banks to U. S. Grant, April 13, 1864, *Official Records,* Ser. I, Vol. XXXIV, pt. 1, 181 ff.

25,000 strong, commanded by Kirby Smith in person and ably assisted by "the most distinguished generals of the rebel army." [50] Actually Taylor had between 12,000 and 15,000 men. The former is Taylor's estimate; the latter is that of Kirby Smith. Confederate killed and wounded were reported as 2,000.[51]

Before reaching Natchitoches on his forward movement Banks had instructed the transport fleet, commanded by Brigadier General Kilby Smith, to advance up the Red River to Springfield Landing with supplies for the land forces. The transports moved up as far as Boggy Bayou, but upon hearing of Banks's retreat, turned and began to descend the river. Taylor sent Bee's and Green's cavalry forces to attempt the destruction of the retreating fleet. Severe damage was inflicted upon the transports, and even the gunboats were forced to close their portholes to escape Confederate fire. The fleet was closely pursued until it reached Grand Ecore and the protection of Banks's army. The chase was scarcely worth the cost; General Green was killed by grape from a gunboat.[52]

Banks now pondered his next move. What Steele was doing to relieve the pressure upon the Red River army he did not know; he had heard nothing from the Arkansas general for a week. Despite a temporary setback and apparent retreat, he resolved to renew his advance immediately but along a line "less dependent upon a river proverbially as treacherous as the enemies we fight." Shreveport remained the main objective. And he vowed to destroy the rebel force facing him and with it all strong resistance within the Trans-Mississippi Department, "if our movement is not interrupted" by too early a withdrawal of A. J. Smith's command. There was still hope that the job

[50] *Ibid.*    [51] E. Kirby Smith to S. Cooper, April 12, 1864, *ibid.,* 476.
[52] Report of Richard Taylor, April 18, 1864, *ibid.,* 560 ff.

could be finished on time, yet he urged Grant to consider
the probable cost of recalling Smith too early. "It will lead
to the sacrifice of the army and the navy, as well as the
abandonment of the expedition." And this would leave a
rebel army of 25,000 men on the Red River ever remaining a constant threat to Federal navigation on the Mississippi River.[53]

Although continuing to harass Banks with small-scale
cavalry operations, Kirby Smith and Taylor had no plans
for an immediate attack. Below Natchitoches the country
was barren of supplies. Taylor had removed or destroyed
all that he could as he retreated up the valley, and Banks
had taken the remainder. Should the Confederates pursue
Banks in force, they must take their supplies with them.
And obstructions placed in the river above Grand Ecore
by the Confederates themselves rendered the river temporarily useless for the transfer of supplies from above.
These difficulties were discussed at length by Kirby Smith
and Taylor. The general commanding doubted the wisdom
of chasing a retreating army through a barren country
while Steele, moving in from Arkansas, threatened the
depots and shops at Shreveport and beyond.

Shortly after Steele had crossed the Little Missouri,
Price evacuated Camden and arrived at Prairie D'Ane on
April 5. There he found Marmaduke and R. M. Gano's
brigade, recently arrived from the Indian Territory, drawn
up for battle. J. O. Shelby's cavalry was to the front
skirmishing with Steele's advance. Brigadier General J. M.
Thayer's command from Ft. Smith had now joined Steele,
adding an estimated 5,000 to the Federal force. Moving
"slowly and cautiously," Steele attacked Shelby "with
great fierceness" on April 10. Shelby fell back, and on the
following day Price ordered a general retreat to a more

[53] N. P. Banks to U. S. Grant, April 13, 1864, *ibid.*, 186–87.

advantageous position eight miles from Washington, hoping to draw the enemy beyond the prairie and then fall upon his wagon train. Steele advanced a few more miles and then turned toward Camden, heading for the fortifications there, which Price had recently abandoned. The Federals needed the supplies that could be brought up the Ouachita.[54]

Kirby Smith, not knowing of Steele's change of course, decided to return Price's infantry divisions and further to re-enforce him by a division from Taylor's command. He later stated that Taylor approved the plan, selected Walker's division for the campaign, designated Polignac as commander of the forces remaining on the Red River, and requested that he himself be permitted to accompany Walker's division to Arkansas.[55] Taylor later reported that, feeling certain Steele would begin a retreat when he learned of Banks's retreat, he opposed an immediate campaign into Arkansas, preferring instead to pursue Banks, destroy his army, and capture his supplies. However, since the "general's views" differed from his, he expressed a willingness to march to Arkansas and serve as a subordinate to Price "until Steele's column was destroyed or driven back." [56]

Kirby Smith returned to Shreveport on April 11 to make ready for the Arkansas campaign. Taylor wrote him at 8 P.M. on the same day. He was making every effort, he said, to get cavalry and artillery below the boats on the river with the hope of cutting off their escape. Only the lack of forage could prevent success. "Let me know the news from Arkansas." Surely Steele would soon be in re-

---

[54] Report of Frederick Steele, April 17, 1864, *ibid.*, 661–62; Report of Sterling Price, May ?, 1864, *ibid.*, 779 ff.

[55] E. Cunningham to Richard Cunningham, June 27, 1864, *ibid.*, 550–60; E Kirby Smith to Jefferson Davis, June 11, 1864, *ibid.*, 478–82.

[56] Report of Richard Taylor, April 18, 1864, *ibid.*, 560 ff.

treat. If so, "let me push my whole force south as rapidly as possible, to follow and prevent the escape of the enemy. I will strike for New Orleans, or, at least, Algiers." Many recruits would no doubt join him. He had already ordered all jayhawkers shot on sight "without benefit of clergy." "Should the remainder of Banks' army escape me I shall deserve to wear a fool's cap for a helmet." [57] The Louisiana commander was certainly not lacking in either enthusiasm or confidence.

Kirby Smith was not convinced. A vigorous pursuit of Banks he considered unnecessary, hazardous, and less likely to result in permanent advantage than the defeat of Steele. A captured dispatch from Sherman revealed that Banks must soon return A. J. Smith's force east of the Mississippi. This fact plus the falling water in the Red River would force Banks to retire to Alexandria, even if not pursued. Granting that Taylor might inflict further losses upon the retreating Federals and eventually reach the Mississippi, the country would be so exhausted of supplies as to preclude his remaining there. And as for the capture of New Orleans, the presence of the enemy fleet made such an attempt impractical. In his crippled condition, Kirby Smith thought Banks would not soon take the offensive and would probably fall back to Alexandria. Certainly, at present, Steele, "bold to rashness" and probably pushing on "without thought or circumspection," was the more dangerous of the two.

"Should you move below," Kirby Smith explained to Taylor, "and Steele's small column push on and accomplish what Banks has failed in, and destroy our shops at Jefferson and Marshall, we will not only be disgraced, but

[57] *Id.* to W. R. Boggs, April 11, 1864, *ibid.,* 530. For a copy of Taylor's jayhawker order see Louis A. Bringier Papers, Louisiana State Archives, under date of May 18, 1864.

irreparably deprived of our means and resources." He thought that the loyal people of Arkansas had been patient and long-suffering and Price had willingly sent his entire infantry to Taylor's support. Such unselfishness "merits a return." "Prepare your command and organize your trains for rapid movement [toward Shreveport]," he ordered Taylor.[58] Regardless of the merits or demerits of the proposed campaign, Taylor demonstrated his usual reluctance in the return of borrowed troops. This attitude on the part of the Louisiana commander had long been known to Holmes, Magruder, and Price.

At daybreak, April 14, Walker's, Churchill's, and Parsons' divisions took up march for Shreveport. Taylor himself arrived at Kirby Smith's headquarters on April 15. News of Steele's change of course toward Camden had also arrived.

For days Steele had heard nothing from Banks. Scouts sent out had not returned. Then came the rumor that Banks had been defeated. Finally a returning scout confirmed the fact. Steele increased his pace toward Camden. Kirby Smith had instructed Price that should Steele move for Camden every effort must be made to obstruct him. If Price thought himself strong enough to hold Camden, he might reoccupy it. But a weak force should not be sacrificed in an effort to hold the fortifications there.[59] Price, now re-enforced by Maxey from the Indian Territory, tried to block Steele. Marmaduke was sent around to Steele's front; another force attacked his rear. Steele, fearing Price might intend reoccupying Camden, redoubled his efforts, driving Marmaduke before him "from position to posi-

[58] E. Kirby Smith to Richard Taylor, April 11, 1864, *ibid.*, 531–32. E. Kirby Smith, "Defense of the Red River," in *Battles and Leaders*, IV, 372.

[59] E. Cunningham to Sterling Price, April 15, 1864, *Official Records*, Ser. I, Vol. XXXIV, pt. 3, 767.

tion," and arriving on April 15.[60] This was the day Taylor arrived at Kirby Smith's headquarters.

Kirby Smith decided to command the Arkansas campaign in person, leaving Taylor in nominal command at Shreveport, with instructions to return to his troops near Natchitoches should he see fit. Before departing for Arkansas on April 16, he wrote President Davis of his plans and added that should any contingency arise "whereby the command of the Trans-Mississippi might devolve on another," he had issued a special order elevating Taylor to lieutenant general. This seemed necessary since Taylor was the junior of Major Generals Price and Magruder, yet he was the only one of the three "suited to take charge of the affairs of the department." The commanding general hoped his action on this matter would "meet with the approbation and sanction" of the President.[61]

Kirby Smith established headquarters at Calhoun on April 17, keeping in telegraphic connection with Shreveport. Steele was now in the fortifications previously constructed by the Confederates at Camden. The strength of his position was well known. When Kirby Smith learned of Steele's arrival in Camden, he ordered Walker's division to halt at a point twenty miles from Minden and await developments. From there it would be in position to move on to Camden, return to Shreveport, or turn toward Campti. A dispatch from Taylor had stated that Banks was throwing a pontoon bridge across the Red River at Grand Ecore. This indicated a possible intention of Steele and Banks to join forces and march on Shreveport. Not intending to attack Steele in the Camden fortifications, Kirby Smith was thinking of sending Walker back to Taylor.

[60] Report of Frederick Steele, April 17, 1864, *ibid.*, pt. 1, 661.
[61] E. Kirby Smith to Jefferson Davis, April 16, 1864, *ibid.*, 476.

Price had been instructed to throw a cavalry force to the north of the Ouachita and cut off Steele's supplies from Little Rock and Pine Bluff. Upon conferring with Price, Kirby Smith found that no cavalry had been thrown across to the north of the river. Steele was still receiving supplies from Pine Bluff. No fewer than 200 wagons had arrived on April 18. Kirby Smith immediately sent Brigadier General J. F. Fagan, with 4,000 select horsemen from Shelby's and W. L. Cabell's divisions, across the Ouachita to destroy depots at Little Rock, Pine Bluff, and Devall's Bluff. He was then to hold his force in position between Camden and Little Rock. Effective execution of these orders would threaten Steele with disaster; "neither man nor beast," Kirby Smith believed, "could be sustained in the exhausted country between the Ouachita and White Rivers." [62]

Steele must then surrender or evacuate Camden and attempt retreat through a barren country, with enemy cavalry on his rear, flank, and front. Walker's division was called up, and Taylor was notified that since Banks was still retreating, the Arkansas campaign took on even greater importance. Unless Steele could be driven from Camden, all the fruits of recent victory in Louisiana would be endangered, Kirby Smith explained. If Taylor was convinced that Banks was headed for New Orleans, he might leave Polignac or Wharton in command on the Red River and hurry to the Arkansas front. "I can place you on duty with your increased rank, and would feel that I had left the conduct of operations in safe hands." [63]

Within the Camden fortifications Steele felt fairly safe from attack, but he realized his weakness. Until gunboats on the Ouachita came to his assistance, he must depend upon the Arkansas for supplies. And the operations of a

[62] *Id.* to *id.*, June 11, 1864, *ibid.*, 478–82.
[63] *Id.* to Richard Taylor, April 22, 1864, *ibid.*, 534–35.

strong Confederate cavalry made this source uncertain. There was no need to attempt to live off of the exhausted country. He might be able to handle Price, he notified Sherman, but would be unable to cope with the re-enforcements being advanced by Kirby Smith. Why had Banks fallen back and allowed troops to be shifted from the Red River? [64]

Fagan's cavalry reached Eldorado Landing on April 24, and there learned from scouts that a long enemy wagon train, well-protected by infantry, had recently left for Pine Bluff to secure supplies. The destruction of this train would be just the type of work Kirby Smith had assigned. Fagan hurried in pursuit, overtaking the train near Marks Mill. Action began at dawn, April 25. Shelby rode to the front, blocked the road, and drove in the advance. Cabell's men dismounted, and moved in from the side. Resistance was fierce but of short duration. The Federal losses—500 killed and wounded, 1,300 prisoners, 6 pieces of artillery, 300 wagons. The Confederate losses did not exceed 150 killed and wounded.[65]

Steele, now unable to sustain himself within the fortifications at Camden, evacuated on April 27. On the previous day, Walker's division having arrived, Kirby Smith had officially assumed command of the Army of Arkansas. Price took over the Arkansas and Missouri troops. His infantry crossed the Ouachita on April 28 and began pursuit of Steele. Heavy rain and deep mud made progress slow. About daybreak, April 30, the tired Confederates came up with the retreating Federals near Jenkins' Ferry, on the Saline. All night desperate efforts had been made to get troops and trains through the muddy bottoms. Marmaduke's dismounted cavalry opened battle. Churchill was

[64] Frederick Steele to W. T. Sherman, April 22, 1864, *ibid.*, 662–63.
[65] Report of James F. Fagan, May 7, 1864, *ibid.*, 788–90.

thrown forward. Parsons moved to his support. Two batteries were brought up but became stuck in the mud; those
pieces not captured were soon withdrawn. Price's entire
command, "tired, exhausted, with mud and water up to
their knees and waists," wavered, then fell back. By this
time Walker's division was in position and the "contest
now raged with great violence." Price reported that the
enemy "yielded the ground." Steele claimed he drove back
the Confederates "with great slaughter" and crossed his
forces over the river.

Marmaduke's was the only Confederate cavalry force
present. Fagan, after the battle at Marks Mill, had set out
to complete the task assigned him. Unable to cross the
Saline at a lower point, he had gone up the river for forage,
hoping to cross over at Benton. He missed the fight at
Jenkins' Ferry. Had Fagan thrown his cavalry across the
path of retreat, Kirby Smith later explained, Steele would
have been compelled to fight before reaching the Saline
bottoms, and would have been "utterly destroyed." Although Kirby Smith referred to the results at Jenkins'
Ferry as a complete victory, his statement is not convincing; Confederate losses were heavy, including Brigadier
Generals W. R. Scurry and Horace Randal, and Steele got
across the river.[66]

Once across the flooded Saline, Steele could continue his
retreat toward Little Rock without much fear of pursuing
Confederates. Kirby Smith left Price in command, and
ordered Churchill, Parsons, and Walker to rejoin Taylor
on the Red River. Maxey had returned to the Indian Territory before the battle. Before leaving Arkansas in person
Kirby Smith issued congratulations to soldiers of the

[66] Report of Sterling Price, May ?, 1864, *ibid.*, 779–84; E. Kirby Smith to
Jefferson Davis, June 11, 1864, *ibid.*, 478–82; Frederick Steele to H. W.
Halleck, May 4, 1864, *ibid.*, 667–71; E. Kirby Smith to J. B. Magruder, May
2, 1864, *ibid.*, pt. 3, 802.

Trans-Mississippi Department on their glorious and brilliant success—"eight thousand killed and wounded, 6,000 prisoners, 34 pieces of artillery, 1,200 wagons, 1 gun-boat, and 3 transports are already the fruits of your victories." And the "path of glory" was still open. Moving "shoulder to shoulder," they would "free the soil of our beloved country from the invader's footstep." The thanks of a grateful people were theirs. "You living will be respected; your dead honored and revered." [67]

Back in Louisiana, Banks had made no advance upon Shreveport, although he must have known of the transfer of troops to Arkansas. The Red River continued to fall, and the Union commander did not possess the courage to break away from the fleet and advance independently. Taylor, returning from Shreveport much disgruntled, continued to harass the enemy with his reduced force. Banks, fearing that he might be cut off, retreated to Alexandria, arriving on April 25–26.

The river was now so low that the gunboats could not get over the falls. Admiral Porter feared his fleet might be deserted by the land forces. Banks, however, decided there was no choice but to remain and protect the fleet. His proud army, which had entered the valley for a quick thrust into the heart of the Trans-Mississippi Department, must now spend many days in building a winged dam to control sufficient water to float gunboats over the falls. The last boat passed over on May 12. Both army and navy continued the retreat toward the Mississippi, continually harassed but never in great danger. As Banks's forces evacuated Alexandria, clouds of smoke from the burning town billowed to the sky.

Churchill, Parsons, and Walker were too late. The first two were stopped en route and ordered to return to Cam-

[67] May 4, 1864, *ibid.*, pt. 1, 550.

den and "rest your command." Had Banks "delayed but one week longer," Kirby Smith explained, "our whole infantry force would have been united against him." [68] Banks's only consolation was his belief that the invasion of the Red River Valley had occupied Confederate troops that otherwise would have been used against New Orleans or in an invasion of Arkansas and Missouri.[69]

[68] E. Kirby Smith, "Defense of the Red River," in *Battles and Leaders,* IV, 373.

[69] N. P. Banks to U. S. Grant, April 30, 1864, *Official Records,* Ser. I, Vol. XXXIV, pt. 1, 189–92.

## CHAPTER XIV

# GENERALS DISAGREE

THE RED RIVER campaign was over, but the resulting disputes over causes for failure reverberated for years to come. When Banks reached Simmesport he found orders to turn over his military powers to Major General E. R. S. Canby. He was permitted to retain the rather empty title of Commander of the Gulf Department, but henceforth his powers would be civil. Canby assumed command of a newly created Trans-Mississippi Department.[1]

Taylor, angered by Kirby Smith's decision in favor of the Camden campaign, spoke out in an inexcusable manner. Long distrustful of the commanding general's military judgment and now physically ill, he made no further attempt to suppress his feelings. While Kirby Smith's troops were crossing the river at Camden on April 28, Taylor was composing a long letter to his superior. He had just learned that Walker had been ordered to move on into Arkansas, and could see no logical excuse for such a move. Steele had been "completely foiled" by Price and had already retreated 100 miles. What justification could there be in "abandoning the certain destruction of an army of 30,000 men, backed by a huge fleet, to chase after a force of 10,000 in full retreat with over 100 miles start"? He charged that Kirby Smith had allured him to Shreveport "by compli-

[1] Harrington, *N. P. Banks,* 159.

ments" and "there unexpectedly deprived" him of the major portion of his army. Daily since that time other smaller units had been withdrawn "without even the usual official courtesy of sending the orders through my hands." Furthermore, on the eve of the recent great battle for the department the commanding general had continued on detail duty some 400 or 500 men belonging to Walker's and Mouton's divisions, but these men were ordered to rejoin their commands when Kirby Smith himself marched "after a retreating foe with re-enforcements equal to his original strength."

What had happened to cause the commanding general to invite him to come to Arkansas with an increase in rank?

What has occurred since you removed the conduct of operations from my hands after Pleasant Hill to change your opinion of my capacity? General, had you then left the conduct of operations in my hands Banks' army would have been destroyed before this; the fleet would have been in our hands or blown up by the enemy. The moral effect at the North and the shock to public credit would have seriously affected the war. By this time the little division of Polignac and Vincent's Louisiana Cavalry would have been near the gates of New Orleans, prepared to confine the enemy to narrow limits; I would have been on the way with the bulk of my army to join Price at Camden, enriched with captured spoils of a great army and fleet; Steele would have been brushed from our path as a cobweb before the broom of a housemaid; we would have reached St. Louis, our objective point, by midsummer and relieved the pressure from our suffering brethren in Virginia and Georgia. All this is as true as the living God and required no more than ordinary energy for its accomplishment. You might have had all the glory; I would have been contented to do the work either under you or General Price. Your confidential staff might have thrown the blame of every failure on me unrebuked, and claimed the credit of every success for you without contradiction. Not a word should have passed my lips when I heard it announced, as lately at Shreveport, that the signal victories at Mansfield and Pleasant Hill were triumphs of your skill and strategy—victories which your communications to me show you to have had as little connection as with the "army in Flanders."

As for the increase in rank offered by Kirby Smith, he did not desire it. If President Davis should see fit to promote him as a reward for service, he would be "exceedingly grateful"; until then he would be content with his present rank. He had learned from his ancestors, he said, that it was the "duty of a soldier so to conduct himself as to dignify titles and not derive importance from them." Kirby Smith had been only just when he recently complimented the major general for his "hearty support." For a year, Taylor explained, he had supported the commanding general, even when the policy was "fatally wrong," for he believed it his duty to give "warm and earnest co-operation." But now he was discouraged and no longer felt able to do his duty under Kirby Smith's command; therefore, he wished to be relieved.[2] Kirby Smith received this astonishing letter on May 2 and returned it to Taylor with a brief indorsement: "This communication is not only improper but unjust. I cannot believe but that it was written in a moment of irritation or sickness."

After returning to his Shreveport headquarters, Kirby Smith received a second letter from Taylor. The Louisiana commander's dissatisfaction had greatly increased. His troops were worn out from marching, he complained. Walker's and Polignac's divisions had "dwindled to nothing." The ranks could be filled within a month, however, if he were "relieved from the incubus of the Conscript Bureau and not interfered with by department headquarters." Many of his troops were without shoes. "The Clothing Bureau is liberal in promise and utterly barren in performance." The artillery was without horses. Those promised a month ago had never arrived. "They will never be supplied under the present system." The system of de-

---

[2] Richard Taylor to E. Kirby Smith, April 28, 1864, *Official Records,* Ser. I, Vol. XXXIV, pt. 1, 541–43.

tails should be abolished. Laborers and guards, "including that at Shreveport," could be supplied from state troops.

Although stating that the condition of his health would preclude his participation in a proposed Missouri campaign, Taylor gave detailed suggestions as to what preparations were necessary and how the campaign should be conducted. But he could not refrain from again venting his spleen in what he characterized as a respectful and frank expression of opinion. "No campaign dependent on the present system of bureaucracy will succeed," he exclaimed. "The rage for what is termed organization has proceeded so far that we are like a disproportioned garment —all ruffles and no shirt. The number of bureaus now existing in this department, and the army of employees attached to them, would do honor to St. Petersburg or Paris. Instead of making the general staff a mere adjunct to promote the efficiency of the little army in the field, the very reverse is the case. . . . The conscript laws are a snare and a delusion." Every day orders came for more details of trained men. The troops were without pay, and suffering from the lack of food and clothing. "Requisitions for the most important articles upon which depend the fate of a campaign are lost in a mingled maze of red tape and circumlocution." These were the opinions of "every intelligent officer of this army." He wished to repeat his recent request to be relieved from duty.[3] This expression of opinion was no doubt frank, but it could scarcely be considered respectful.

Kirby Smith's reply was calm and brief. He considered the tone of Taylor's complaints "objectionable and improper." He pointed out that Taylor had approved the transfer of troops from Louisiana to Arkansas, designat-

[3] *Id.* to *id.*, May 24, 1864, *ibid.*, 543–45.

ing which should go and which should stay. "The fruits of
your victory at Mansfield were secured by the march of
that column. The complete success of the campaign
was determined by the overthrow of Steele at Jenkins'
Ferry." [4]

Taylor's irritation had increased. When he received
Kirby Smith's reply he almost exploded. He had made no
complaints, he fired back. He had stated facts. He had
learned from the story of "Gil Blas and the Archbishop"
that "truth is often considered 'objectionable by superiors,' " but he had "not drawn the moral that it is therefore
'improper in subordinates to state it.' " Kirby Smith was
accused of bad faith. Through compliments, Taylor
averred, the commanding general had persuaded him to
leave his command and travel to Shreveport to participate
in the campaign against Steele, "which you had determined
I was not to make." Furthermore, he was assured that
should Steele retreat his troops would be restored, yet at
that very moment Kirby Smith knew Steele was retreating.
As for the battle of Jenkins' Ferry making secure the
fruits of victory at Mansfield, Banks had already retreated
to Alexandria before the battle in Arkansas. But even in
that exaggerated victory, the attack had been by infantry
alone, leaving 8,000 men idle. Why could not those 8,000
men have taken the place of Walker's division? Instead
of a "complete success," Taylor considered Jenkins' Ferry
a badly bungled affair. The Confederate losses exceeded
those of the Federals, and Steele moved on to Little Rock
where he had started. The battle of Jenkins' Ferry won
not one foot of Arkansas territory. "In truth," Taylor
lashed out, "the campaign as a whole has been a hideous
failure. The fruits of Mansfield have been turned to dust
and ashes. Louisiana, from Natchitoches to the Gulf, is

[4] E. Kirby Smith to Richard Taylor, May 26, 1864, *ibid.*, 545–46.

a howling wilderness and her people are starving. Arkansas is probably as great a sufferer." And Banks's army was now ready to co-operate with Grant and Sherman to crush "our overmatched brethren in Virginia and Georgia." Kirby Smith's strategy had "riveted the fetters" on the entire department. The "tactical skill" in failing to use 7,000 cavalry while Churchill, Parsons, and Walker's infantry division were being beaten back successively was a worthy successor to that strategy that substituted a chase after the "comparatively insignificant force of Steele" for the certain destruction of Banks's army and Porter's fleet.

Having got this much off his chest, Taylor added a self-righteous conclusion: "The same regard for duty which led me to throw myself between you and popular indignation and quietly take the blame for your errors compels me to tell you the truth, however objectionable to you. The grave errors you have committed in the recent campaign may be repeated if the unhappy consequences are not kept before you. After the desire to serve my country, I have none more ardent than to be relieved from longer serving under your command." [5]

While Taylor, near Alexandria, was penning this severe indictment, Kirby Smith, at Shreveport, was composing an item by item reply to Taylor's letter of May 24. Instead of Walker's force having "dwindled to nothing," he insisted that it had been increased by about 500 men. If the Conscript Bureau and the laws it was trying to enforce had failed, it was due to Taylor's failure to give adequate military support. In this matter the Louisiana commander had not carried out orders from department headquarters. The Clothing Bureau, Kirby Smith believed, had exerted every effort to supply the troops and in general had been

[5] Richard Taylor to E. Kirby Smith, June 5, 1864, *ibid.*, 546–48.

remarkably successful, in view of its being "crippled in its resources and cut off from its supplies by the loss of the Rio Grande and the action of the Governor of Texas and its State Legislature."

If the artillery was short of horses, it was due to the severity of the recent campaign. The inspector of field transportation was laboring to correct the deficiency. As to the men assigned to guard duty at the arsenals and shops near Shreveport, most of them were absentees who had reported at headquarters. Their work was most important. Taylor, although frequently ordered to do so, had never sent a garrison to Shreveport. And as for the number of men employed in the various bureaus, they totaled sixteen, most of whom were either above conscript age or unfit for service. According to the report of the chiefs of pay and commissary departments there were adequate funds and supplies for all Louisiana troops.[6]

When Kirby Smith received Taylor's letter of June 5, he removed him from command and ordered him to Natchitoches to await instructions from the President. John G. Walker succeeded to command of the District of Louisiana. Kirby Smith forwarded to Davis copies of the correspondence that had passed between himself and Taylor. He would not attempt to answer Taylor's untrue charges, he told the President; the reports of the campaign would do that. The good of the service demanded that one of the two be removed from command. Should the President think best, "I will willingly, with no feeling of envy or abatement of interest in the service of my country, turn over my arduous duties and responsibilities to a successor."[7]

This controversy between Taylor and Kirby Smith

[6] E. Kirby Smith to Richard Taylor, June 5, 1864, *ibid.*, 538–40.
[7] Special Orders, No. 145, June 10, 1864, *ibid.*, pt. 4, 664; E. Kirby Smith to Jefferson Davis, June 11, 1864, *ibid.*, pt. 1, 540–41.

placed President Davis in a dilemma. He and Kirby
Smith were personal friends. Davis' first wife was Taylor's
sister.

In verbal combat, as in the clash of arms, the heat and
smoke of battle must clear before there can be a fair appraisal; even then, when it becomes a matter of one man's
word against another's, the appraiser can never be certain. That Kirby Smith erred is true, but there is no
foundation for Taylor's absurd statement that "from first
to last, General Kirby Smith seemed determined to throw
a protecting shield around the Federal army and fleet." [8]
Those risks that turn out well are praised as superior
strategy; those which prove disastrous are denounced as
stupid blunders. Taylor took a great risk in making his
stand near Mansfield, but he won a distinct victory and
became a hero among Confederates who were hungry for
a victory. Kirby Smith's advice to Taylor not to risk a
general engagement until there could be a concentration
of forces was sound. At the most, Taylor had available
8,000 to 9,000 men to hurl against an enemy with a potential strength of three times that number. Yet had he waited
even one more day he could have had the assistance of
Churchill's and Parsons' divisions, more than 4,000
strong.

No doubt Kirby Smith did wish to be on the scene when
the great battle was fought. His wife, at Hempstead, Texas,
secretly accused Taylor of planning to fight before her
husband took command in person, and there may be some
truth in her accusation.[9] Boggs, Kirby Smith's chief of
staff, later stated: "Taylor was to harass Banks up to
the last moment and then General Smith was to move down
with additional troops, take command and carry off the

[8] Taylor, *Destruction and Reconstruction*, 189.

[9] Mrs. E. Kirby Smith to Mrs. Frances K. Smith, May ?, 1864.

glory of the pitched battle." [10] But since Boggs's account was written after he had turned sour on Kirby Smith and Dr. S. A. Smith, his statement must be taken with caution.

Although years later Taylor claimed to have been in possession of such knowledge,[11] there is no evidence that he knew Banks and A. J. Smith were separated by many miles and a long supply train. Taylor was simply impatient and irritated at Kirby Smith's delay in sending reenforcements.[12] The bombastic statement that "when Green joins me . . . I shall fight a battle for Louisiana, be the forces of the enemy what they may" reads well after a victory. However, had his numerically inferior force been crushed these words would have labeled him a reckless incompetent. Had his force been severely defeated, it would have doomed the Trans-Mississippi Department.

But he won. And with victory came a self-confidence that gave to Taylor a feeling of invincibility. He used good strategy in pursuing Banks toward Pleasant Hill, for flushed with victory and re-enforced by Churchill and Parsons, his army was in much better condition than on the previous day. Yet he was defeated at Pleasant Hill. This fact was not altered by the Federal withdrawal during the night. Timidity and fear on the part of Banks were responsible for the Federal retreat. Both Kirby Smith and Taylor should have offered thanks for the good fortune that brought Banks, rather than Sherman, to the Red River Valley.

It was but natural for Taylor to wish to pursue Banks, and no doubt severe damage could have been inflicted

[10] Boggs, *Reminiscences*, 76.

[11] Taylor, *Destruction and Reconstruction*, 162.

[12] Boggs later credited Dr. Smith's influence with the decision to delay the Arkansas and Missouri divisions at Shreveport, Dr. Smith, he stated, hated Taylor as much as he loved Kirby Smith.

upon the Union army. There was a great danger, however, that his enthusiasm might destroy his better judgment; even retiring forces sometimes fight back viciously when there is danger of being trapped. There was reason to Kirby Smith's statement: "If we could not whip him [Banks] at Pleasant Hill in a fair fight, it would have been madness to have attacked him at Grand Ecore in his entrenchments, supported by a formidable fleet of gunboats." [13] It must always be a close approach to madness to hurl an unprotected army against a well-entrenched foe twice as strong, particularly when the foe is almost certain eventually to yield the coveted ground without a fight. As for destroying the enemy supply line, that was a game at which both sides could play, for as Banks retreated, his line became shorter and the Confederate line correspondingly longer.

Kirby Smith's fear for the safety of Shreveport was well founded, but both he and Taylor misjudged Steele when they considered him a bold and vigorous warrior; he exhibited neither of these characteristics in his movement toward Shreveport. The lack of close co-operation between him and Banks was inexcusable. The same was true of his very slow movement after leaving Little Rock.

Protection of the shops and stores in the vicinity of Shreveport and Marshall was essential to continued resistance in the Trans-Mississippi Department. No amount of damage that might be inflicted upon Banks could have compensated for their destruction. Taylor understood this as well as did Kirby Smith and undoubtedly was willing to leave Banks in check and go to Arkansas in person. His real opposition to the movement against Steele dates from the time he learned that he himself was not to ac-

---

[13] E. Kirby Smith to Jefferson Davis, August 28, 1864, *Official Records,* Ser. I, Vol. XXXIV, pt. 1, 482–88.

company the expedition. Resentment and bitterness almost nullified his many soldierly qualities after he returned to his reduced command near Natchitoches.

Kirby Smith, on the other hand, was not blameless. It was quite unnecessary to take so many troops to Arkansas after Steele had changed his course. After it was quite clear that Steele would make no effort to join Banks, it was poor strategy to order Walker from Minden to Camden. Walker's division should have been sent back to Red River Valley, probably to join with Liddell's force operating on the north bank of the river. Yet on the whole Kirby Smith's general plan was sound.

When the campaign opened, there was no hope of defeating Banks on the lower Red River. Neither was there hope of turning back Steele as he began his movement from Little Rock. To fall back and lure the enemy deeper and deeper into hostile territory near Shreveport and then concentrate against one column at a time was the only sensible plan that could have been adopted. It was equally as sensible to allow Banks to retreat while Steele was being cut off by a superior cavalry and crushed by a superior infantry and then to rush all available troops to Alexandria to deal with Banks and Porter. Had the plan worked, Kirby Smith's praises would have been sung by untold thousands of loyal Southerners. But Fagan's failure to throw his cavalry across the route of retreat permitted Steele to escape, and the ingenious dam-building at Alexandria enabled Banks and Porter to escape. And disgruntled "Prince Dick" Taylor by making public his grievances, real and imaginary, did much to undermine confidence in the commander of the Trans-Mississippi Department.

After years of reflection, Taylor was not proud of his conduct in this controversy with his superior; no mention is made of it in his memoirs. "Prostrated by two years of constant devotion to work," he explained, "—work so severe, stern, and exacting as to have prevented me from giving the slightest attention to my family, even when heavily afflicted—and persuaded that under existing administration nothing would be accomplished in the 'Trans-Mississippi Department,' a month after the close of the Red River campaign I applied for relief from duty. After several applications this was granted, and with my wife and two surviving children I retired to the old Spanish-French town of Natchitoches." [14]

Although it is difficult to see how Kirby Smith could have avoided a choice between the removal of Taylor or the submission of his own resignation, the fact remained that Taylor's loss was serious. His connections in Louisiana and his recognized ability as a commander caused many to think as did Judge Barth Egan. He did not profess to know the details of the difficulty between the two generals, but he knew that people were "greatly chagrined at the loss of General Taylor's services." Every one knew that they could not "get a general who loves Louisiana more ardently or who could better use for her defense all the resources at his command." [15]

Some other judges, however, were not so willing to remain neutral. The newspaper accounts of the Red River campaign had "very thoroughly exposed" Kirby Smith's faults, announced Judge Thomas C. Manning.[16] And upon learning that Colonel Lang Lewis, a Congressional candidate said to be friendly to Kirby Smith, was being supported by persons in Rapides Parish, Judge E. Warren Moise wrote former Governor Thomas O. Moore: "Are

[14] Taylor, *Destruction and Reconstruction*, 196.
[15] B. Egan to T. O. Moore, July 9, 1864, Thomas O. Moore Papers, Louisiana State Archives.
[16] T. C. Manning to T. O. Moore, March 30, 1865, *ibid*.

you down there going to unite and send to Congress a man to support the character of Kirby Smith? By God! if you do, you deserve all you have suffered, and I have no sympathy for those who are willing victims of his immeasurable stupidity." [17]

The cause for the bitterness of the judges is obscure. Although law and military necessity were sometimes in conflict and civil judges were generally fearful of military usurpation, there is no evidence that Kirby Smith attempted to disregard the courts. On the contrary, from the beginning of his administration he was careful to avoid clash with civil authorities except in cases of deliberate obstruction of military action. "I am sorry to see that there is a probability of your being brought into collision with the civil authorities," he wrote Assistant Adjutant E. Surget at Alexandria on June 8, 1863; "it is to be avoided if possible—a writ of habeas corpus when rightly and properly presented cannot be resisted—if the object in invoking the aid of the civil authorities be to test a principle, it is always better to comply gracefully, taking such steps as will insure the Confederate rights being properly represented and succored." However, those whose policy was to obstruct military action should first be warned and, should they persist, then be unhesitatingly seized as dangerous men and sent beyond the Confederate line. This should also be the policy toward those who proved disloyal during the temporary occupation of the country by the enemy.[18]

No doubt the hostile judges were a part of and in sympathy with the property owners in the Red River Valley who had suffered at the hands of the invaders. These were severe in their denunciation of the general command-

---

[17] E. W. Moise to *id.*, September 24, 1864, *ibid.*
[18] E. Kirby Smith to E. Surget, June 8, 1864, Kirby Smith Papers.

ing and his strategy in luring the enemy deep into Confederate territory before giving battle. This desertion of them and their property they considered poor compensation for their efforts to keep the valley producing for the Confederacy. Only a few months earlier, when some were seriously considering migrating, Kirby Smith had urged them "to remain where they are, sow their crops, and sell their surplus produce to the Government, and trust to it for protection, which I assure them shall be extended to the utmost of my power." He considered the Red River Valley as safe as the Texas locations to which they talked of migrating.[19]

Now many of those planters who had decided to stay saw their plantations in ruin. Their cotton had been burned by the Confederates or carried off by the Yankees. Seeing no future security in the valley, a number of the planters, including former Governor Moore, began migrating to Texas.[20]

Among the discontented in the Alexandria area were also found the home town enemies of Dr. Sol A. Smith, who was correctly suspected of having considerable influence with Kirby Smith. Yet it is not clear why Alexandrians could blame Dr. Smith for their losses when he too suffered heavy losses. Mrs. Smith escaped from the Alexandria fire with a few personal articles only. Small wonder the doctor should express belief in the proverb that "a prophet finds honor save in his own country."[21]

Outside Taylor's circle of friends and the devastated area of the lower Red River Valley, public opinion was more friendly to the department commander. "The ability of Gen. Smith as a department commander and a strategist

[19] *Id.* to L. L. Johnson, November 20, 1863, *Official Records*, Ser. I, Vol. XXVI, pt. 2, 428–29.
[20] R. C. Hyson to T. O. Moore, January 3, 1865, Moore Papers.
[21] S. A. Smith to *id.*, October 5, 1864, *ibid.*

has been signally evident," Governor Reynolds of Missouri wrote to Richmond. He did not know the details of the controversy between Taylor and Kirby Smith, but he observed the general public considered the latter in the right. "It has done him at least this good that it has shown that with all his amiability he will not permit his legitimate authority to be disputed." Everybody recognized his zeal and ability "except some persistent croakers, few in number." [22]

To Kirby Smith himself Governor Reynolds expressed his satisfaction in the strongest terms: "Having closely observed all your movements during the past six months, I should do you injustice did I not assure you that I have been unable to detect a single blunder in them: in substance and detail they seem to me to have been the very best which, amid the almost overwhelming difficulties of your situation, you could have adopted." The "tranquil masses" were convinced, regardless of "whatever might be the cavilling of some few uneasy politicians." [23]

Wishing to reward his principal subordinates for their services during the recent campaign and to give them rank proportionate to the duties they performed, Kirby Smith urged a number of promotions, including the elevation of Churchill, Fagan, Marmaduke, Maxey, Parsons, and Polignac to the rank of major general. Pending approval by the President, these officers were placed on duty with increased rank. Copies of these orders were forwarded to Richmond.

Months passed and no approval came from Davis. Along with department returns dated October 28, 1864, Kirby Smith sent a special request for approval of his tem-

[22] T. C. Reynolds to W. P. Johnston, April 13, July 14, 1864, Reynolds Papers; *id.* to C. B. Mitchell, May 21, 1864, *ibid.; id.* to J. L. Orr, May 21, 1864, *ibid.*

[23] *Id.* to E. Kirby Smith, May 18, 1864, *ibid.*

porary appointments. Davis refused promotion to all except three colonels. With proper reorganization, he advised, the present eight major generals should be sufficient. No other promotion to brigadier general would be approved "until it appears that there are vacancies in properly organized brigades." "In this connection," Adjutant General Cooper added, "the President instructs me to say that it is improper for you to announce the promotion of general officers and assign them to duty before they are appointed by him." [24]

Kirby Smith was embarrassed and discouraged if not peeved. Some of these officers had been acting with increased rank since May, 1864. What he wished was assurance from Richmond that whatever promotions or assignments he made within his department would be approved in Richmond. He solicited the influence of the Congressional delegations from the Trans-Mississippi states in securing for him such necessary powers. To Senator R. W. Johnson of Arkansas he complained: "If I cannot be trusted another commander should relieve me with whom these powers can be safely confided. I do not court the responsibility of this vast command. I shall labor conscientiously to discharge them, but the greatest kindness the President could confer upon me would be to relieve me by some one in whose ability as well as correctness he can implicitly confide." [25]

Criticism by those whom he felt should be more appreciative of his efforts to protect them and their property had a telling effect upon the commanding general. Despondent

[24] E. Kirby Smith to S. Cooper, October 28, 1864, *Official Records*, Ser. I, Vol. XLI, pt. 4, 1016–17; Cooper to Kirby Smith, December 23, 1864, *ibid.*, 1121–22.

[25] E. Kirby Smith to R. W. Johnson, March 16, 1865, *ibid.*, Vol. XLVIII, pt. 1, 1428–30.

and disgusted, he secretly longed for relief from responsibilities. His staff, although intensely loyal, was almost as discouraged as their general. "Old Doctor" Smith, depressed by his own personal loss at Alexandria and the criticism to which he had been subjected, wanted to resign. Kirby Smith would not hear to it. "I tell him," the latter wrote his wife, "[that] as a friend in the goodness of my heart I would let him go, but as his General, conscientiously discharging my duty I can not listen to his request." Instead, he insisted that Dr. Smith bring his wife to headquarters "bag and baggage . . . if the Yankeys have left her either."

Kirby Smith's wife remained at Hempstead during the summer, and the general hurried there himself to be present at the birth of a second daughter on June 9. She was christened Frances Kirby. Carrie, the other daughter, was ill all summer. Dr. David W. Yandell prescribed by telegraph. The general urged his wife to give the child plenty of exercise and ripe tomatoes. If professional attention was necessary, she should contact Dr. Howard Smith at Houston.[26]

When Banks evacuated Alexandria and gave evidence of his intention to retire from the Red River Valley, Kirby Smith immediately notified Price that he proposed "to make the Arkansas Valley and Missouri the theatre of operations." Price was instructed to begin collecting supplies and information. Through friends in Missouri he was to ascertain the amounts of supplies that might be found there, the strength of the enemy force, the prospects for adding recruits to his army, the condition of roads and

[26] *Id.* to Wife, May 25, 27, 29, 1864. Dr. Yandell had replaced Dr. John M. Haden as medical director in March, 1864. Haden became chief of the Medical Bureau. Yandell was relieved from duty in October, 1864, and Dr. Sol A. Smith became medical director of both the hospitals and the department.

bridges, location of telegraph stations, and if possible obtain copies of United States military maps.[27]

Following the retirement of Federal troops from the Red River Valley, Canby stationed the majority of his force at Morganza and A. J. Smith returned up the Mississippi. Canby's intentions were of much concern to Confederate commanders both east and west of the Mississippi. Those east of the river, including General Bragg and President Davis, were convinced that Mobile would be the objective. On July 9 Confederate General S. D. Lee, commanding east of the river, reported Canby moving toward Mobile with 20,000 men. Bragg had instructed Lee to confer with Kirby Smith on the possibility of crossing troops over the Mississippi. A week later Lee relayed to Kirby Smith a message that the President expected him to assist in defeating the enemy's plans by sending troops east of the river.[28] Then came a dispatch from Bragg, also relayed by Lee: "Inform General E. K. Smith that the President orders a prompt movement of Lieutenant-General Taylor and the infantry of his corps to cross the Mississippi. Such other infantry as can be spared by General Smith will follow as soon as possible. General Taylor on reaching this side of the Mississippi will assume command of the department." [29] At the time he sent this dispatch, Bragg was at Columbus, Georgia. It later developed that Davis had not been consulted. Davis, however, had conferred such power upon Bragg.

Taylor was at Natchitoches awaiting orders from Richmond. Bragg had not yet learned of his suspension. Kirby Smith forwarded Bragg's dispatch to Taylor and ordered him to Alexandria to assume command of the two infantry

[27] W. R. Boggs to Sterling Price, May 19, 1864, *Official Records*, Ser. I, Vol. XXXIV, pt. 3, 828; *id.* to *id.*, June 3, 1864, *ibid.*, pt. 4, 642–43.
[28] S. D. Lee to E. Kirby Smith, July 9, 16, 1864, *ibid.*, Vol. XLI, pt. 1, 89.
[29] Braxton Bragg to S. D. Lee, July 22, 1864, *ibid.*, 90.

divisions of West Louisiana and begin preparations to cross them over.[30] General Walker was informed of the action and given his choice of resuming command of and crossing with his old division or remaining in command of the district. Colonel H. T. Douglas, chief engineer of the Trans-Mississippi Department, was ordered to report at Walker's headquarters and furnish such assistance as was necessary in making preparations for the crossing. A company of pontoniers, with twenty-four boats then at Shreveport, was directed to proceed to Alexandria, pick up eighteen other boats at that point, and report to Walker.

Taylor, at Natchitoches, received Kirby Smith's dispatch on July 29. "If troops can be crossed at all," he replied, "it can only be effected by a diversion in the direction of New Orleans from this side." Could he expect the necessary assistance in making preparation? He wished his old personal staff to rejoin him. Since secrecy was a most important element, he suggested that he not assume command formally until preparations were complete. In the meantime, he would himself cross over "to hasten any assistance possible there, and communicate with Richmond."[31]

Kirby Smith recognized the importance of secrecy, yet he favored "dealing openly and frankly with the troops." They should know where they were going and who would lead them. He prepared a special order appealing to their patriotism:

Your President appeals to you. Your comrades east of the Mississippi River call to you for aid. Events are transpiring. A campaign is there progressing which is to decide the destiny of our country. It is to you to give success to that campaign and to restore peace to our beloved land. Your mission is a holy one. Your commander wishes he

[30] W. R. Boggs to Richard Taylor, July 28, 1864, *ibid.*

[31] *Id.* to H. T. Douglas, July 29, 1864, *ibid.*, 91; *id.* to J. G. Walker, July 29, 1864, *ibid.*, 91–92; Richard Taylor to W. R. Boggs, July 29, 1864, *ibid.*, 92.

could accompany you. He parts with you with regret. He is confident that you will illustrate in the armies of Georgia and Tennessee the deeds which have made your names glorious in this department.

This order was sent to Walker on August 1, with instructions to publish it only if he and Taylor agreed with the policy of making the plan known to the troops.

Walker joined with Taylor in counseling secrecy as long as possible. He contemplated no serious difficulty in persuading his old division to obey the President's order, but he had some question about the probable conduct of "less disciplined" troops. Immediate publication of Kirby Smith's appeal he feared would prove fatal to the whole plan. Let it be delayed until secrecy had broken down.[32]

Kirby Smith contacted Richmond. Since receiving the telegram ordering Taylor to cross over with infantry, he explained, the proposed expedition in Arkansas had been called off. He would, however, throw some cavalry into Missouri. Walker's and Polignac's divisions and Brigadier General Allen Thomas' brigade would cross the Mississippi with Taylor. This would leave too few troops in Louisiana to offer any serious resistance should the enemy take the offensive there. Major General Simon B. Buckner had arrived from east of the Mississippi; Kirby Smith wished him promoted to lieutenant general "as it will relieve me from embarrassment in assigning him to duty." [33] Buckner was the junior of other major generals in the Trans-Mississippi Department. There is evidence that the commanding general originally planned to assign him administrative duties as a "quasi Secretary of War." [34]

---

[32] E. Kirby Smith to Richard Taylor, July 31, 1864, *ibid.*, 93–94; J. G. Walker to E. Kirby Smith, August 3, 1864, *ibid.*, pt. 2, 1038; Special Orders, No. ——, August 1, 1864, *ibid.*, 1035.

[33] E. Kirby Smith to Jefferson Davis, July 30, 1864, *ibid.*, pt. 1, 93–94.

[34] T. C. Reynolds to E. Kirby Smith, July 25, 1864, Reynolds Papers.

Kirby Smith was not enthusiastic about the proposed crossing of troops. "I fear the practicability of the movement," he wrote Taylor, "yet no effort must be spared in securing its execution. You must yourself in person superintend the arrangements and accompany the column." The forty-five boats now on the way would be sufficient, he calculated, to carry over 1,000 men each trip. The point of crossing would be selected by Taylor. He thought the proposed diversion in the direction of New Orleans injudicious. "It would throw a body of cavalry into a distant and sickly country when their services are needed for operations in Arkansas and Missouri." Complete secrecy he thought impossible; too many persons handled dispatches. Not only would the enemy become suspicious, but worse still, sooner or later, "our own people and troops" would learn the secret. "I fear that your command may prove refractory when they find they are ordered across the Mississippi." [35]

General Bragg continued to urge immediate and forceful action. The situation east of the river was desperate. General R. E. Lee at Petersburg was hard pressed and barely able to protect his communications. General Early, operating in the valley of Virginia, was confronted by stiff resistance and needed every available man to protect the grain supply. General J. B. Hood had replaced Johnston at Atlanta and was confronted by Sherman with a superior force. Alabama and Mississippi, although at present almost free from enemy troops, were open for invasion by troops from Arkansas. Unless troops from Kirby Smith's command could move into Mississippi and Alabama, these Federal troops from Arkansas might overrun those states and send assistance to Sherman. [36]

[35] E. Kirby Smith to R. Taylor, July 31, 1864, *Official Records,* Ser. I, Vol. XLI, pt. 1, 93–94.
[36] Thomas Butler to E. Kirby Smith, July 29, 1864, *ibid.,* pt. 2, 1029–30.

How to get the troops across the Mississippi remained the big problem. Colonel Douglas worked out a plan for bridging the river. Since it was necessary to move troops en masse, their artillery and train must also be carried over. This could be done by no other plan than bridging the river on pontoons. For this construction Douglas asked for the services of two companies of engineers, one in Arkansas, the other in Galveston, Texas. Further, he would need large quantities of rope and chain which, he thought, might be procured in Houston.[37]

Taylor approved Douglas' plan, but Kirby Smith declared it "impracticable and visionary." "It necessitates the concentration of engineer troops from Arkansas and Texas—virtually the establishment of a navy yard at Shreveport and building of boats. It makes requisition for materials on the city of Houston, Tex., which in all probability will have to be imported." All of this, the commanding general pointed out, would necessitate a two months' delay and require materials which were probably not available within the department. The use of boats he considered the only practical method for crossing the river. A long delay "would neutralize any good results which might come from crossing this column." [38]

General Taylor, knowing there was no longer a real opportunity west of the Mississippi, was eager to cross over and assume his new duties as department commander. He was much irritated when Kirby Smith refused to give permission to cross immediately. His irritation gave way to anger when Kirby Smith refused to permit him to carry with him former chief commissary A. H. Mason and Colonel J. L. Brent, chief of ordnance. Walker had been

---

[37] H. T. Douglas to *id.*, August 4, 1864, *ibid.*, pt. 1, 96–97.
[38] E. Kirby Smith to J. G. Walker, August 7, 1864, *ibid.*, 100; *id.* to Richard Taylor, August 11, 1864, *ibid.*, 103–104.

consulted to see which of Taylor's former staff members could be spared. Walker replied that "the administration of this district absolutely requires that some of the officers named should remain here, at least for the present." He named Mason as one who definitely could not be spared.[39]

Short of efficient staff personnel, with no assurance of supplies on the other side, with no means of controlling how troops were to be passed, with the plan of crossing devised by the commanding general, rather than himself, and being powerless "to remedy these vital deficiencies," Taylor was unwilling to accept the "responsibility either for the failure or success of the undertaking," which Kirby Smith directed.[40] He took the matter up with Bragg directly. Did Bragg wish him to come east of the river if crossing troops proved impracticable? Did the general wish him to precede the troops? Taylor suggested that Wharton's cavalry and an infantry division from Arkansas also be ordered to cross. However, should the infantry division be so instructed, it should be specified that General Price should not accompany it. If not forbidden to do so, Kirby Smith, Taylor explained, would certainly send Price across the river in order to get rid of him.[41]

Taylor was clearly meddling. However, it was true that Kirby Smith was planning an extensive reorganization of his department. Already, on August 4, he had signed an order transferring Major General J. B. Magruder from Texas to Arkansas, moving Major General J. G. Walker to Texas, and assigning Major General S. B. Buckner to command in West Louisiana.[42]

On August 13 Walker wrote Kirby Smith that in spite

39 J. G. Walker to E. Kirby Smith, August 3, 1864, *ibid.*, pt. 2, 1038.

40 Richard Taylor to *id.*, August 8, 1864, *ibid.*, pt. 1, 100–102.

41 W. Stevens to Braxton Bragg, August 11, 1864, *ibid.*, 103; Thomas Butler to *id.*, August 12, 1864, *ibid.*, 104–105.

42 General Orders, No. 60, August 4, 1864, *ibid.*, pt. 2, 1039.

of the fact that it was of the greatest importance that Taylor superintend in person the passage of the troops, he had learned that the general intended to leave immediately to assume command on the other side.[43] On the following day Taylor wrote in person to relay a dispatch from Bragg directing that he assume his duties east of the river "as soon as practicable." Taylor proposed to leave at once.[44]

"This I positively forbid," Kirby Smith replied. If orders had come from authority higher than the department commander, he wished copies of such orders. In any case, Taylor would remain with his troops, for Kirby Smith would "object to a compliance of those instructions" until the troops had been passed over.[45]

Before Taylor could disobey Kirby Smith's positive order not to leave the troops, information arrived convincing him of "the impracticability and impossibility" of crossing troops. The enemy, learning that a crossing would be attempted, had stationed their ironclads between Vicksburg and the mouth of Red River at twelve mile intervals with gunboats patrolling the intervals. Not a four-hour period passed, it was said, but that a gunboat passed every point where a crossing might be attempted. Furthermore, the troops, learning of the plan to cross over, began deserting by the hundreds. These facts Taylor reported to both Kirby Smith and the War Department at Richmond.

To Kirby Smith, Taylor wrote that he could not "recognize the propriety of expression" used by the general in forbidding him to cross over the river immediately. Neither could he recognize that the general had a right to control his obedience to orders from the President. When orders came from the President he intended obeying them. If

---

[43] J. G. Walker to E. Kirby Smith, August 13, 1864, *ibid.*, Vol. XLI, pt. 1, 106.

[44] Richard Taylor to *id.*, August 14, 1864, *ibid.*, 108–109.

[45] E. Kirby Smith to Richard Taylor, August 15, 1864, *ibid.*, 109–10.

Kirby Smith was displeased with the channel through which the commander in chief was instructing him, then he should take the matter up with higher authorities.[46]

On August 22, 1864, Kirby Smith ordered Taylor to suspend the attempt to transfer troops, relieved him of command, and directed that he cross the river himself. This order followed a message from Adjutant General Cooper requesting, if Taylor could be spared, that he be sent to Mississippi immediately.[47] If there was any officer within the Trans-Mississippi Department that General Kirby Smith felt he could "spare" it was certainly Taylor! Three days later, Taylor, now east of the river, wired Bragg: "I would have been over four weeks ago but was positively forbidden by the department commander, General E. Kirby Smith."[48]

The plan to transfer troops east of the Mississippi was unsound from its inception, and both Kirby Smith and Taylor knew it. As long as ironclads and gunboats patrolled the river there was little chance of crossing any large body of troops and necessary supplies. Secrecy was impossible; Federal authorities soon knew of the general plan. As later reported by Buckner, the only feasible plan for crossing at that time was to send the men over in small squads at numerous points. This would have left the force without organization, and in its disaffected condition, would have resulted in a probable dispersion of two thirds of the army. General John A. Wharton, commanding the cavalry, was not far wrong when he observed "that a bird,

[46] Richard Taylor to E. Kirby Smith, August 19, 1864, *ibid.*, 111–12.

[47] W. R. Boggs to Richard Taylor, August 22, 1864, *ibid.*, 117. Taylor crossed over by canoe on a dark night.

[48] Richard Taylor to Braxton Bragg, August 25, 1864, *ibid.*, 120. His participation in the plan to cross troops is another topic not discussed in Taylor's memoirs. He merely mentioned his own crossing and commented: "Though individuals, with precaution, could cross the great river, it was almost impossible to take over organized bodies of troops or supplies, and Confederates on the west were isolated." Taylor, *Destruction and Reconstruction,* 197.

if dressed in Confederate gray, would find it difficult to fly across the river." [49]

To say the plan for crossing was unsound is not to excuse those whose mistakes made its execution impossible. Taylor desired nothing quite so much as to get outside the Trans-Mississippi Department. He was sympathetic to the proposal to cross troops, for those troops would strengthen him in his new command east of the river and leave Kirby Smith weak. But he did not wish to remain in Louisiana and execute Kirby Smith's orders; he no longer had confidence in or respect for the department commander. And Kirby Smith, himself suffering from rheumatism and then dysentery, did not give the project the proper personal attention. His whole heart was not in the undertaking, particularly after he learned that on July 18 Johnston had been superseded by Hood in command of the army of Tennessee. This he considered a mistake forced upon President Davis "in an evil hour." "Hood is a protege of mine—was one of my boys," he wrote his wife. "He is brave generous openhearted and impulsive—he will fight and his fine personal appearance his frank manly address will attach his men strongly to him but has not the judgment the mind, the comprehension the forethought or the military knowledge or experience of Johnson— If we are defeated at Atlanta and lose that army we lose our cause except through the miraculous interference of Providence. I for the first time since the war fear the result. I know Sherman & I know Hood." [50] A few days later the general confided to his mother that, although still believing in the goodness

---

[49] S. B. Buckner to J. F. Belton, January 5, 1865, *Official Records*, Ser. I, Vol. XLV, pt. 2, 765–66.

[50] E. Kirby Smith to Wife, August 10, 1864. Kirby Smith later lamented that it was unfortunate that throughout the war two "great characters" like Davis and Johnston continually "antagonized each other." Kirby Smith to Bradley Johnson, December 17, 1891, Bradley Johnson Papers, Duke University.

of God, he felt "great anxiety" and was "apprehensive of disaster." Davis appeared to have staked all on his order for Hood to fight Sherman at Atlanta. A crushing defeat at Atlanta would leave the defense of the Confederacy in the hands of armed bodies rather than armies. He knew both Johnston and Hood well. The former he had lived with "in the closest intimacy & friendship" at the beginning of the war. The latter had been his pupil at West Point and his lieutenant in Texas. "Hood is a soldier Johnson the General—Hood is bold, gallant, will always be ready to fight but will never know when he should refuse an engagement. Hood is a man of ordinary intellect, Johnson's brain soars above all that surrounds him. Johnson would have destroyed Sherman. Sherman will defeat Hood." [51]

There were other mistakes connected with the proposed crossing of troops. Walker should have been directed to accompany his old command. His great popularity with Louisiana troops would have done much to relieve the discontent, which eventually resulted in wholesale desertion. But Kirby Smith had suddenly decided to send Walker to Texas and to place Buckner in command in Louisiana. The proposal to place the unpopular Major General John H. Forney in command of Walker's old division was most unfortunate. Taylor positively refused to take Forney east of the river, and no doubt a number of men deserted to keep from passing under his command.

Deserters fled in all directions. Buckner, now in command in West Louisiana, sent out cavalry to round them up. Kirby Smith instructed him to make it known that plans to cross the Mississippi had been abandoned. Where soldiers voluntarily returned to their commands "no notice will be taken of their absence." Buckner talked with divi-

[51] *Id.* to Mother, August 17, 1864.

sion officers and then replied that in his opinion the suggested pardon for deserters "would destroy the discipline of the command." In a few cases desertion had taken the form of mutiny, encouraged by a few officers. The leaders had been arrested and were being tried. In awarding punishment, however, it was believed wise to make a distinction between those deserters who were captured and those who voluntarily returned.[52]

Although already east of the Mississippi and completely outside Kirby Smith's department, Taylor could not refrain from taking a parting shot. He had just heard that Kirby Smith had pardoned all the deserters who refused to cross the river, he wrote Bragg from Selma, Alabama, after he himself had had most of them captured. Under such circumstances, he thought it would be "useless to send further orders to cross the troops." Bragg agreed, and forwarded Taylor's views to the Secretary of War who in turn brought the matter to the attention of President Davis. "Require General Smith to explain his conduct," Davis ordered. If as reported, the action of the Trans-Mississippi commander had placed a premium on desertion. There was no truth in the report Kirby Smith replied. There had been no general pardon of deserters. Instead, every effort had been made to capture and punish them. "The ringleaders were tried, convicted and shot." "In acting on any communication personal to myself from General Taylor I beg the President to remember that General Taylor's systematic misrepresentation of my motives and acts exhibit a violence and prejudice restrained neither by respect for himself nor his superiors." [53]

[52] S. B. Buckner to W. R. Boggs, August 20, September 3, 1864, *Official Records,* Ser. I, Vol. XLI, pt. 1, 113, 120; Boggs to Buckner, August 22, 1864, *ibid.,* 118.

[53] See *ibid.,* 121–22. Taylor told Thomas L. Snead (who was disgruntled over what he considered blunders in the defense of Arkansas) that Buckner's

After examining the correspondence relative to the attempt to cross troops to the east side of the Mississippi, Davis mildly criticized Kirby Smith. More support should have been given to the hard-pressed armies of the East either by a more vigorous effort to send re-enforcements or by a more aggressive program within the Trans-Mississippi region. The latter, Davis believed, would have prevented the transfer of so many enemy troops to the East. But with this mild criticism from the President there came assurance of confidence in Kirby Smith's "zeal and ability" and intense loyalty to the Confederate cause.[54]

promotion was a result of Kirby Smith's constant urging. Taylor considered the promotion unfair to Price, Magruder, and Walker. Snead immediately relayed the information to Price. Further discontent resulted. See Snead to Price, October 21, 1864, *ibid.*, Vol. LII, pt. 2, 763–64.

[54] Jefferson Davis to E. Kirby Smith, December 24, 1864, *ibid.*, Vol. XLI, pt. 1, 123–24.

## CHAPTER XV

# CRITICS AND DEFENDERS

THE PLAN TO send a relief expedition east of the river having been abandoned, Kirby Smith again turned to Arkansas. As early as June 3, 1864, he had instructed Price to make use of friends and agents in Missouri to learn the condition of affairs there, the amount of supplies which might be obtained, the location of enemy troops, the condition of roads, and the "prospects of obtaining recruits." [1] Following up these instructions, Price had been able to compile considerable information on conditions within his home state. Most of the Federal regulars had been removed, it was reported, leaving local defense in the hands of state troops of doubtful loyalty. Many towns, impressed with reports of recent Confederate victories, were flying the Confederate flag, and large guerrilla bands of Confederate sympathizers were operating in the southern section of the state. With the hope of relieving the friends of the Confederacy in Missouri and of welding together the numerous guerrilla bands, Price insisted that he be allowed to lead an army into Missouri. [2]

Even before the idea of crossing troops had been abandoned Kirby Smith had instructed Price to prepare to move

[1] W. R. Boggs to Sterling Price, June 3, 1864, *Official Records,* Ser. I, Vol. XXXIV, pt. 4, 642–43.

[2] Sterling Price to E. Kirby Smith, July 23, 1864, *ibid.,* Vol. XLI, pt. 2, 1023–24.

into Missouri with his entire cavalry force. "You will scrupulously avoid all wanton acts of destruction and devastation, restrain your men, and impress upon them that their aim should be to secure success in a just and holy cause and not to gratify personal feeling and revenge." The principal purpose of the expedition was to rally the loyal people of Missouri and to fill up with recruits the skeleton brigades marched into that state. Most recruits, Kirby Smith pointed out, would probably be mounted. Price must deal frankly with them, making it clear that they might be dismounted if the lack of forage made the maintenance of so large a cavalry force impossible.

Price was to head for St. Louis with the intention of capturing supplies and military stores there. When withdrawal became necessary, it should be "through Kansas and the Indian Territory, sweeping that country of its mules, horses, cattle, and military supplies." [3]

Price left Camden on August 28. On the following day he joined Marmaduke's and Fagan's divisions at Princeton and took command of the cavalry of the District of Arkansas.[4] Moving by way of Dardanelle, the command was at Pocahontas by September 13, where it was joined by Shelby's cavalry from northeastern Arkansas. On September 19 the combined command, 12,000 strong, moved into Missouri.

Major General William S. Rosecrans, commanding the Department of Missouri, had learned of Price's general plan even before the expedition got under way. Over-zealous Confederate sympathizers in Missouri were openly predicting the early arrival of Price, and guerrilla bands were bolder than usual. On September 6 Rosecrans tele-

---

[3] W. R. Boggs to Sterling Price, August 4, 1864, *ibid.*, 1040–41.

[4] The most objective study of Price's Missouri campaign is Norman Potter Morrow, "Price's Missouri Expedition, 1864" (unpublished M.A. thesis, University of Texas, 1949).

graphed Halleck, giving a picture of conditions and requesting that A. J. Smith, then at Cairo on his way to join Sherman, be halted until Price revealed his intentions. Halleck ordered Smith to "operate against Price & Co." should the Confederates attempt an invasion of Missouri. Smith moved to a point near St. Louis and awaited developments.

At Fredericktown, Price learned of Smith's presence in Missouri with an estimated 8,000 men on the Iron Mountain Railroad near St. Louis. Shelby was sent by way of Farmington to destroy bridges on the railroad so that Smith would be unable to re-enforce rapidly smaller garrisons, which were to be attacked by Marmaduke and Fagan. Falling back as Fagan approached, a Federal force under Brigadier General Thomas Ewing occupied the strong fortification at Pilot Knob. Price ordered an attack on September 27 and was repulsed. However, during the night Ewing destroyed the fortification and began a retreat toward Meramac Valley. Although severely harassed by Shelby and Marmaduke, he escaped to Rolla.

Rosecrans expected Price to move against one of the important depots of supplies—St. Louis, Jefferson City, or Rolla. He called for re-enforcements from Arkansas and Illinois. For the defense of St. Louis he had not more than 6,000 men to match a Confederate force estimated by him at 15,000 mounted men. The city was panic-stricken. But Price, after hearing that the Federals in St. Louis would outnumber him two to one, decided to move on Jefferson City instead.

Turning westward, Price sent different brigades to tear up the Pacific railroad, burn bridges, and destroy stations at Franklin, Cuba, De Sota, Washington, and other points. A. J. Smith followed, and Rosecrans called General John

B. Sanborn at Springfield and General John McNeil at Rolla to rush to the defense of Jefferson City. Price crossed the Osage near Castle Rock on October 6 and camped within a few miles of the city. On the following day he crossed the Moreau, driving the Federals into their fortifications, but made no serious attack upon Jefferson City. He had been informed that the works were manned by 12,000 troops and more re-enforcements were coming up; therefore, he decided to move on toward Kansas. A. J. Smith and General Alfred Pleasanton followed, and Major General S. R. Curtis, commanding in Kansas and the Indian Territory, was notified of Price's approach. Curtis ordered Major General James G. Blunt toward Lexington to hold Price in check until Smith and Pleasanton could catch up.

By this time Price had learned from a scout, sent to St. Louis soon after the Confederates had entered the state, that he was being followed by probably 24,000 Federals from St. Louis and another 15,000 from Jefferson City. As later reported by him: "I then abandoned my former determination to issue an address to the people calling upon them to rally to me, as they were already pouring in on me so rapidly that I knew I would not be able to protect and feed them, and as it would require that my army should be kept together to protect them on a rapid and dangerous retreat from the State."

Price's advance under Shelby began sharp fighting with the forces of Blunt near Lexington on October 20. Blunt fell back to Big Blue River west of Independence, skirmishing as he went. By this time Pleasanton was closing in on the Confederate rear. Heavy fighting occurred on October 22 and 23. Price continued his march, turning southward along the state line. "The number of the enemy's troops engaged that day [October 23] exceeded 20,000 well armed men," he reported, "while I did not have 8,000 armed men."

Only light skirmishing interfered with the march on October 24. But on the following day Fagan and Marmaduke reported the enemy approaching from the rear. Shelby, out in front, was ordered to their support, and Price himself galloped back to look over the situation, only to be met by "the divisions of Fagan and Marmaduke retreating in utter and indescribable confusion, many of them having thrown away their arms. They were deaf to all entreaties or commands, and in vain were all efforts to rally them." Generals Marmaduke and Cabell had been captured. The Federals claimed 1,000 prisoners, but Price reported the loss of not more than 400.

Having lost heavily in men and supplies, Price must hasten his march or be completely destroyed. Blunt, Sanborn, and McNeil followed. Forage was becoming short, men and horses tired, and desertions from the Confederate force became numerous. Near Newtonia in southwest Missouri, Blunt overtook Price's weary columns on October 28. A brief but furious engagement followed; each side claimed a victory. Price continued his march to Arkansas without further serious hindrance.

Reporting to Kirby Smith's headquarters, Price tried hard to picture his "raid" as a great success. While marching more than 1,400 miles, fighting more than 40 engagements, capturing and paroling more than 3,000 prisoners, collecting great quantities of military supplies, and destroying "miles and miles of railroad" and property valued at $10,000,000, he had lost not more than 1,000 men including the wounded left behind. Furthermore, he had brought with him "at least 5,000 new recruits," and others were arriving daily. "After I passed the German settlements in Missouri my march was an ovation. The people thronged around us and welcomed us with open hearts and hands. Recruits flocked to our flag in such numbers as to threaten to became a burden instead of a benefit, as they were mostly unarmed. In some counties the question was not who should go to the army, but who should stay at home. I am satisfied that could I have remained in Missouri this winter the army would have been increased 50,000 men." [5]

A few days after Price had left on his invasion of Missouri, Major General John B. Magruder, the new district commander, arrived in Arkansas. Immediately he began to flood Kirby Smith's headquarters with exaggerated reports of enemy strength. As when in Texas, he constantly pictured his insufficient force about to be overwhelmed by a vastly superior opponent. Including the re-enforcement recently arrived from Morganza, Steele must have no fewer than 21,000 men, exclusive of the troops at Fort Smith, he reported. Since Texas and Louisiana were no longer menaced, he urged that all infantry in Louisiana and a considerable portion of the cavalry in Texas be rushed to Arkansas. Along with these re-enforcements should also be sent every available mule and wagon for the hauling of corn from the Red River to Arkansas "even if cotton be stopped for the present." [6]

Magruder's long repetitious letters continued to arrive day after day. He had detailed plans for all districts within the department. Kirby Smith did not share his belief that large scale Federal operation in Arkansas was imminent. As long as Price remained in Missouri, Kirby Smith did not expect too much trouble in Arkansas; the main ob-

[5] Report of W. S. Rosecrans, December 7, 1864, *Official Records*, Ser. I, Vol. XLI, pt. 1, 307–17; Report of Sterling Price, *ibid.*, 625–40.

[6] J. B. Magruder to W. R. Boggs, September 10, 11, 1864, *ibid.*, pt. 3, 917–18, 922.

jective would be to destroy Price. But should Price be defeated and compelled to retire, Steele would no doubt take the offensive on the Arkansas. As for Magruder himself taking the offensive, Kirby Smith would not advise it until the demand for more Federal troops in Missouri had greatly weakened Steele. The best disposition Magruder could make of his forces was to hold them in readiness, replenish supply depots, improve organization and discipline, and keep "a careful watch."

Although news had arrived that the Federal movement against Mobile had been discontinued because of yellow fever, Kirby Smith did not expect Canby's troops to open immediately a new campaign up the Red River. It seemed more likely that, with a large Federal fleet available, an attack would be made on Galveston.[7]

By the last of October Magruder was convinced that the Federal concentration at Little Rock was for the purpose of moving to the vicinity of Ft. Smith and destroying Price should he be forced out of Missouri. Accordingly, he urged Kirby Smith to permit him to concentrate on Little Rock immediately and thus prevent Federal forces from moving to Ft. Smith. Kirby Smith thought well of the idea, and the two went into conference at Lewisville.

It was agreed that Magruder should move on Little Rock, if upon careful investigation such action seemed practicable. If not, he was to make Ft. Smith his objective. The capture of this strong point in northwestern Arkansas would protect Price upon his return and also make it possible to collect there in advance those supplies that would be badly needed by Price's tired army.[8]

Before Magruder could attack either Little Rock or Ft.

---

[7] E. Kirby Smith to J. B. Magruder, September 22, October 3, 1864, *ibid.*, 950, 978–79.

[8] J. B. Magruder to W. R. Boggs, October 30, 1864, *ibid.*, pt. 4, 1020; E. Kirby Smith to S. B. Maxey, November 4, 1864, *ibid.*, 1028–29.

Smith, Price's "totally demoralized" troops were entering Arkansas. Supplies of beef, corn, meal, and flour were ordered up from Texas and the Indian Territory. "Price's men have been arriving here for four or five days, singly, in squads, and every way," reported Maxey from the Indian Territory. "Their horses are miserably poor . . . and many are being abandoned on the prairies." [9] But Kirby Smith, not having seen the miserable remnant of Price's army, painted a much more pleasing picture. "He [Price] drew the Sixteenth Army Corps (A. J. Smith's) from Memphis, and Grierson's cavalry from Mississippi, leaving Forrest free to operate on the communications of the Federal army in Northern Georgia, compelled the concentration in Missouri of 40,000 or 50,000, and diverted re-enforcements which would otherwise have been sent to General Sherman or left to operate against Mobile, besides destroying large amounts of property valuable to the enemy. I consider General Price as having effected the objects for which he was ordered into Missouri, and the expedition a success." [10]

The most immediate and pressing problem now confronting the commanders within the Trans-Mississippi Department was the shortage of corn. Numerous complaints began arriving at headquarters. Price's horses were devouring all the forage on the upper Red River. Kirby Smith ordered Magruder personally to supervise the dismounting of a large portion of Price's cavalry. Many men belonging to cavalry units had lost their horses. They should be placed in the infantry before they procured new mounts. Magruder encountered great difficulty. Price's men were still straggling in from Missouri. Others had been granted furloughs. Should the order to dismount be

[9] S. B. Maxey to W. R. Boggs, November 17, 1864, *ibid.*, 1058–59.
[10] E. Kirby Smith to Jefferson Davis, November 21, 1864, *ibid.*, 1068–69.

issued many would not return to their commands; therefore, both animals and men would be lost.[11]

Wharton's cavalry was ordered to the vicinity of the
Trinity River in Texas to winter where forage was available. The Red River Valley being stripped of supplies,
Polignac's and Forney's divisions were directed to the
vicinity of Minden for the winter. From these locations
Wharton could co-operate with either Buckner in Louisiana or Walker in Texas; Polignac and Forney could move
to either the Red River or Arkansas. Magruder, always
feeling that his district was forced to suffer for the benefit
of the others, complained that some of Maxey's troops
from the Indian Territory were camped in western Arkansas. And his dissatisfaction increased when Kirby
Smith refused to allow him to send troops to winter on
the upper Red River without Maxey's permission. "Give
me my district," he wrote to headquarters; "I will promise
to defend it to the full capacity of its resorces [sic], but
situated as I am and have been, the energy of Napoleon,
with the wisdom of Solomon, cannot insure success." [12]

The ravages of marching armies had cut heavily into
the supplies of the Trans-Mississippi Department during
the year 1864. Federal scouts reported Arkansas as
literally "starved out." Louisiana was better off, yet no
army of any size could any longer live off the country.
Even small cavalry units had difficulty in finding sufficient supplies. Texas, however, was "full to repletion,"
but many people there had lost confidence in the Confederacy and refused to sell except for specie.[13]

It was quite evident that both soldiers and civilians had

[11] Id. to J. B. Magruder, December 9, 1864, ibid., 1103–1104; Magruder to
W. R. Boggs, December 12, 13, 1864, ibid., 1107–1108, 1111.
[12] E. Kirby Smith to S. B. Buckner, November 29, 1864, ibid., 1082–83;
J. B. Magruder to W. R. Boggs, December 27, 1864, ibid., 1125–26.
[13] Report of C. S. Bell, n.d., ibid., Vol. XLVIII, pt. 2, 398–403.

grown weary and discouraged. "This side of the Mississippi River is badly whipped," reported a Confederate observer who had recently arrived at Marshall, Texas. "They receive little news here except Yankee accounts, and they believe everything they hear in regard to reverses to our arms. General Smith has a large army, and I believe is very industrious and active. He is much abused by many citizens. I have discovered since I arrived on this side of the river that there is more loyalty, more patriotism, and better armies on the east side of the river." [14]

While the unoccupied armies in "Kirby-Smithdom" moved to winter quarters where supplies were available, their more unfortunate comrades east of the river were facing destruction. After hard fighting around Atlanta during July, Hood had evacuated the city on September 1. Believing that further penetration of the Deep South by Sherman could be prevented only by an attack upon his communications, Hood moved across north Alabama in preparation for an invasion of Tennessee. Early in December, General Beauregard, commanding the Division of the West, informed Kirby Smith that Hood had penetrated Middle Tennessee as far as Columbia; but across his path near Nashville, General Thomas was concentrating all available Federal forces. The commands of A. J. Smith from Missouri and Steele from Arkansas were said to be on their way to join Thomas. To secure Hood's success, Beauregard urged, it was "absolutely necessary" that Kirby Smith either send at least two divisions east of the river or so seriously threaten Missouri as to compel the recall of A. J. Smith and Steele. "The fate of the country may depend upon the result of Hood's campaign in Tennessee." Even if Sherman were successful in his "venture-

14 J. P. Jones to S. Cooper (?), December 27, 1864, ibid., Vol. XLI, pt. 4, 1124–25.

some march across Georgia" to destroy public and private property and eventually assist Grant in compelling Lee to evacuate Richmond, Hood's successes in Tennessee and Kentucky "would counterbalance the moral effect of the loss of Richmond." [15]

A few days later Secretary of War Seddon, apparently still uninformed of the bloody battle of Franklin on November 30, joined Beauregard in urging Kirby Smith either to cross troops over the river or make a serious diversion. He had learned that Steele, with 15,000 men, had reached Memphis en route to re-enforce Thomas. To Richmond authorities, this meant that the campaign west of the Mississippi had been abandoned.[16]

Kirby Smith sent both dispatches to Buckner and requested his opinion. Should a crossing be attempted it would be he who must furnish the troops and the supervision. Buckner joined Kirby Smith in the opinion that such a crossing, especially during the winter season, would be impracticable. The country near the Mississippi was exhausted of supplies, and the high water made of every bayou an obstacle to Confederate progress and an invitation to Federal gunboats. Any force brought east of the Ouachita, Buckner explained, would almost certainly be cut off by Federal gunboats, for he had no guns that could destroy these boats. A successful crossing would require the establishment of heavy-caliber batteries both above and below the place of crossing, and these batteries must be protected by sufficient land forces. But there were no such guns available, and, besides, the experiences at Port Hudson and Vicksburg proved that even heavy batteries could not blockade the Mississippi. "The utmost that can be

[15] G. T. Beauregard to E. Kirby Smith, December 2, 1864, *ibid.*, Vol. XLV, pt. 2, 639–40.

[16] J. A. Seddon to E. Kirby Smith, December 7, 1864, *ibid.*, Vol. XLI, pt. 1, 123.

done," he concluded, "is to pass men in small squads, with the disorganization and demoralization attendant upon such a proceeding." [17]

Buckner's statement of opinion convinced Kirby Smith that he himself was correct in considering the crossing of any large body of troops utterly impracticable. He now notified Beauregard that high water, the shortage of supplies in eastern Louisiana and most of Arkansas, and the lack of heavy artillery made either a crossing or a serious diversion impracticable. "Appreciating our necessities in your department and ardently desiring the transfer of this army to your aid," he explained to Beauregard, "I am powerless to assist you either by crossing troops or by operating in North Arkansas and Missouri." [18] Kirby Smith forwarded to Richmond copies of the letter from Beauregard and Buckner, and added that nothing could possibly be done before early summer.[19]

Beauregard was not convinced. In forwarding Kirby Smith's letter to the War Department, he added: "Notwithstanding the opinions of General Smith and Lieutenant-General Buckner, I am still of the opinion that troops can be crossed to this side of the Mississippi River, even if it be in canoes constructed by the troops near the points selected for them to cross. No reference is made as to why a movement cannot be made against New Orleans, that troops may be drawn off from the armies of the United States now operating on this side of the Mississippi." [20]

[17] S. B. Buckner to J. F. Belton, January 5, 1865, *ibid.*, Vol. XLV, pt. 2, 765–66.

[18] E. Kirby Smith to G. T. Beauregard, January 6, 1865, *ibid.*, 766–67.

[19] *Id.* to S. Cooper, January 6, 1865, *ibid.*, 764.

[20] *Ibid.*, 767. Beauregard later said of Kirby Smith: "He was an honest, intelligent & zealous officer—but with not much energy or force of character. He was a good subordinate commander, like Bragg, Longstreet, Hood & some others, but inferior as a com[man]der-in-chief. He had not the 'feu Sacre' as Napoleon called it." Beauregard to Mrs. S. A. Dorsey, June 23, 1869, Beaure-

On January 31 Davis, apparently not having seen Kirby Smith's reply to the War Department, was still toying with the idea of a crossing. Federal troops from the Trans-Mississippi were still re-enforcing the armies to the east, he wrote Kirby Smith. "Under these circumstances I think it advisable that you should be charged with military operations on both banks of the Mississippi; and that you should endeavor, as promptly as possible, to cross that river with as large a force as may be prudently withdrawn from your present department." [21]

It was February 23 before Kirby Smith received this dispatch; he could only reply that such a crossing was impossible during the winter months. It might be undertaken early in the summer. But even then if he himself crossed the river he wished someone designated as his successor in the Trans-Mississippi region. He could not control operations on both sides of the river when "communications by individuals is uncertain, dangerous, and difficult in the extreme; by bodies it is impossible." [22]

Public opinion west of the river strongly supported Kirby Smith in his stand against a futile attempt to cross troops over the Mississippi. The Louisiana senate passed a resolution protesting against any attempt at crossing, and Governor Allen prepared to send a special representative to Richmond to confer with President Davis. And through Guy M. Bryan, assistant adjutant general on Kirby Smith's staff, he urged Governor Murrah to join him in protest. Bryan added a personal appeal to both governors for continued support of the general's policy. The departure of a large body of troops, even were a

---

gard Papers, Duke University. It is doubtful whether Beauregard's associations with Kirby Smith were sufficient to make him a competent judge.

[21] Jefferson Davis to E. Kirby Smith, January 31, 1865, *ibid.*, Vol. XLI, pt. 1, 124.

[22] *Id.* to *id.*, February 28, 1865, *ibid.*, Vol. XLVIII, pt. 1, 1406.

crossing possible, he reasoned, would leave the Trans-Mississippi region in a dangerous condition. "I am satisfied that every effort is being made by Taylor & his friends to place Genl Smith in a position to compel him to ask to be relieved." Personally Bryan felt that "Genl Smith under the circumstances is the best man we can get & he should not be removed for Taylor or Bragg." [23]

Bryan was correct. The friends of Taylor were very active, and the general opinion east of the Mississippi that Kirby Smith had failed to give full co-operation greatly strengthened their cause. On December 14, 1864, the editor of the Richmond *Whig* began a severe attack. Thomas had been re-enforced by troops from the Trans-Mississippi region, it was asserted. This was made possible by the lack of fear of "the languid and indecisive operations" of the Confederate commander in that department. The Confederate failure to accomplish great results west of the Mississippi was due "to the hesitancy and the lassitude" of General Smith. Had he listened to Taylor, Banks would have been destroyed and New Orleans retaken. But Taylor was weakened, Banks escaped, and Federal forces, even as far away as Washington, were re-enforced. "Thus the loss of Atlanta, General Sherman's march through Georgia, and the failure to capture Washington . . . are directly traceable to the unaccountable blunder committed by Lieut. Gen. Kirby Smith in Louisiana." [24] Such an absurd statement could result only from prejudice or ignorance or both. The only fair remark the editor could make was that in the early days of the war Kirby Smith had shown considerable brilliance. He might do so again if relieved of civil duties.

[23] Guy M. Bryan to Pendleton Murrah, February 6, 7, 27, March 8, 1865, Murrah Papers.
[24] Richmond *Whig*, December 14, 1864.

The *Whig* editor was determined. Taylor must be vindicated and Kirby Smith removed from command. He returned to the attack on January 18, 1865, in a masterpiece of misstated facts and manufactured quotations to support his efforts. Taylor sent Kirby Smith word on the eve of the battle of Mansfield, the editor asserted: " 'I have determined to give the enemy battle on the morrow. Gen. Green and myself have just selected the battle ground.' " This was quite different from the message actually sent by Taylor.

The editor further erroneously stated that Kirby Smith could have been on the scene when the battle of Pleasant Hill was fought, for he spent most of the day at nearby Mansfield within hearing of the guns. And when he did arrive about 10 P.M. it was not to prosecute a vigorous campaign but to weaken Taylor and prevent his securing "the ripening fruits of his splendid victories." [25] These were cutting words. Although prompted by malice and founded upon false statements, they would be widely read and believed.

West of the Mississippi Kirby Smith also had vigorous critics. Now that the Confederate cause was shrouded in gloom, someone must be blamed for failure. The commanding general had been too easy-going and had pursued a do-nothing policy, some asserted. He should have concentrated all available forces and crushed the enemy. But these critics disagreed on the place for concentration. Should it have been in Arkansas, Louisiana, or Texas? The answer depended much upon the critic's place of residence. Others saw the general as a military dictator, disregarding both orders from Richmond and the rights of private property. However, the unbiased who knew the situation accepted him for what he was—an honest soldier

[25] *Ibid.*, January 18, 1865.

of considerable ability who was forced to attempt too much with too little. An Arkansas editor, who had been close to the scene, gave an excellent summary of the problems of the commanding general:

He must quietly direct general operations from the centre, being himself almost unseen and unknown to the soldiers and citizens. Briareus-like he must from his position, reach forth a hundred arms in all directions, and strike with each. Hercules-like, he must fight a many-headed Hydra, one of whose heads being lopped, two grow in its place. . . . It is only by general results that he can be judged. He must see at once the Rio Grande and the Missouri—the Indian Nation, and Balize—the Mississippi and the coasts, and (sometimes weakening himself at one point) act in all, as may best subserve the interest of the whole. . . .[26]

As his friend went to press with this understanding description of the problems of the Trans-Mississippi commander, Kirby Smith was almost ready to let those who criticized demonstrate their talents. "I have been attacked in the columns of the Richmond Whig," he wrote President Davis.

I know that efforts have been made through other journals east of the Mississippi to prejudice the public mind and destroy confidence in the purity of my motives and in my ability to command. . . . I have faithfully and honestly, to the extent of my abilities, discharged the great duties confided to me. I do not know that I have given you entire satisfaction. I do know that you are often embarrassed in doing what you believe to be for the general good. I desire to aid and not embarrass you in your action, and request that this letter may be regarded an application to be relieved from the command of the department whenever you believe that the public interests will be advanced thereby.[27]

Two days later, after reading the mild criticism expressed in Davis' letter of December 24, Kirby Smith was even more desirous of being relieved. Again he wrote the

26 Washington (Arkansas) *Telegraph,* March 8, 1865.
27 E. Kirby Smith to Jefferson Davis, March 9, 1865, *Official Records,* Ser. I, Vol. XLVIII, pt. 1, 1417.

President at length. As a conclusion to a defense of his course during the recent months, he explained:

The Mississippi was an impassable barrier, and by the expedition into Missouri I made the only diversion in my power. The various promotions conferred upon me by yourself and the confidence which you have always reposed in my abilities have more than done me justice. I have always endeavored to merit this confidence, and I earnestly desire to promote the common welfare, and would willingly sacrifice every personal consideration to that end. I will as a soldier strive honestly and faithfully to obey your instructions. If you doubt my ability or believe that another can better execute them, I request that he may be sent to relieve me of the responsible and onerous duties with which I am charged.[28]

Financial demoralization had proved more disastrous to the Trans-Mississippi Department than military reverses. As the value of Confederate currency continued to decline at a ruinous rate even army officers attached to the district headquarters found it difficult to sustain themselves. General Walker, recently assigned to command in Texas, sought to allow his officers to secure supplies through army channels. Kirby Smith revoked the order as being contrary to orders from Richmond but could do nothing to help the situation. Walker protested that his plan was founded upon "justice, equity, and necessity." Either some such plan must be put into operation or officers must resign in order to earn bread for their families. Or if they remained in the service they must "resort to fraudulent practices." How could the family of a captain survive when his whole month's salary would be required to buy "fifty pounds of flour or three bushels of corn meal?" In Houston a single room suitable for officers' quarters rented for $150 to $200. Most loyal and patriotic men were in the army. Why should they be exploited by

28 *Id.* to *id.*, March 11, 1865, *ibid.*, 1418–19.

those who remained in civilian life to get rich? [29] Walker presented a real problem; Kirby Smith had no solution.

Magruder complained on October 17, 1864, that the Arkansas troops had not been paid in fourteen months and were becoming "dangerously restive." Only their patriotism kept them quiet.[30]

The financial condition grew steadily worse. By the close of 1864, Kirby Smith reported, the unpaid certified claims against the Confederate government held by people in the department amounted to $40,000,000. Public credit was "so seriously impaired" that supplies could scarcely be secured except by impressment; to impress without paying was definitely a violation of law. In every district morale, soldier and civilian, was low and in the armed forces discipline was seriously affected.[31]

W. H. Haynes, chief quartermaster, found that practically every farmer had some of the Confederate "promises to pay" but were not at all interested in acquiring more. "We cannot use certified accounts," he explained to headquarters; "cannot use the large size certificates of indebtedness; cannot impress; have no currency; the army is in want; it cannot be supplied." [32]

Kirby Smith forwarded Haynes's letter to Secretary Seddon by special courier. Farmers and others holding claims against the government, he added, who could not even use these claims to pay their taxes now "absolutely refuse to sell" to the government. State legislatures had passed laws against illegal impressment, and Confederate officials without funds could do no other kind. The com-

[29] J. G. Walker to W. R. Boggs, October 10, 1864, *ibid.*, Vol. XLI, pt. 3, 994–96.

[30] J. B. Magruder to *id.*, October 17, 1864, *ibid.*, pt. 4, 1001–1002.

[31] E. Kirby Smith to S. Cooper, December 28, 1864, *ibid.*, 1129–30.

[32] W. H. Haynes to W. R. Boggs, February 8, 1865, *ibid.*, Vol. XLVIII, pt. 1, 1382–83.

manding general hoped the bearer of this could bring back some $30,000,000 or $40,000,000.[33] This was scarcely a hope; it was a dream.

A copy of Haynes's letter was also forwarded to P. W. Gray, Treasury agent for the Trans-Mississippi Department, with a plea that something be done immediately. "Cannot a temporary loan be negotiated, or cannot you, by a timely and patriotic appeal to the different executives, use the State credit until you can obtain funds?" Kirby Smith anxiously inquired. "Cannot the certificates of indebtedness be made available to the citizens in payment of their taxes for the present at least? In short, can there not be some means resorted to by which money can be obtained for the use of the Government?"[34]

Copies of Haynes's letter and also those to Seddon and Gray were forwarded to Texas Senators L. T. Wigfall and W. S. Oldham with an earnest plea that they consult with members of the Congressional delegations from all the Trans-Mississippi states and "enlist them all, if possible, in a common effort to secure funds at once for this department."[35]

Gray replied that he knew Kirby Smith's picture of conditions was not exaggerated, yet he himself was helpless. He possessed no authority to negotiate a temporary loan. And even if he exceeded his authority and attempted such, he would get little if any money. Neither would the acceptance of certificates of indebtedness in payment of taxes bring much relief. The only hope was an appeal to the states. Possibly they would respond favorably. They should, for this was definitely their cause. A "failure to sustain the army would be their overthrow." Gray had

---

[33] E. Kirby Smith to J. A. Seddon, February 11, 1865, *ibid.*, 1381–82.
[34] *Id.* to P. W. Gray, February 11, 1865, *ibid.*, 1383–84.
[35] February 11, 1865, *ibid.*, 1384.

himself made an urgent appeal to Richmond; there was little hope of substantial relief.[36]

Kirby Smith knew that the Trans-Mississippi Department, if not the entire Confederacy, was doomed unless assistance came from the French. Making use of General Polignac, who was given a leave to visit his native France, he informed John Slidell that "our cause has reached a crisis to call for foreign intervention." The French government must be made to see that the security of the Empire in Mexico demanded "immediate interference to restore peace and establish firmly the nationality of the Confederate States." Kirby Smith was convinced that the great majority of Trans-Mississippi planters would "willingly accept any system of gradual emancipation [of their slaves] to insure our independence as a people." [37]

Turning more directly to imperial authorities in Mexico, the Trans-Mississippi commander attempted to make use of Robert Rose and W. G. Hale, two gentlemen traveling to Mexico on private business, to notify authorities there of his "ardent desire to cultivate and extend still further the amicable relations already existing, and which I trust will continue to exist between two coterminous nations having like aims and pursuits, and perhaps the same great and glorious destiny." Further, Rose was requested to say to the Emperor that should the Confederacy collapse, it was Kirby Smith's "fixed purpose to leave my native land and seek an asylum in Mexico." Trained and experienced in arms, with years of service along the Mexican border, and with some knowledge of the French and Spanish languages, he felt that his services and influence might be of use to the Emperor. "I therefore authorize you to tender

---

[36] P. W. Gray to E. Kirby Smith, February 24, 1865, *ibid.*, 1401–1402.
[37] E. Kirby Smith to John Slidell, January 9, 1865, *ibid.*, 1319–20.

them to him in the possibility of the contingency alluded to." [38]

In spite of the serious shortage of money and the threatened want of essential supplies, military leaders in the Trans-Mississippi region never lost their determination to repulse all Federal attempts at invasion. Before Kirby Smith received Davis' suggestion of January 31 relative to crossing troops the department was again being threatened. The recent movement of Federal troops to the east seemed now to have been reversed. An estimated 30,000 men, drawn from Arkansas and Tennessee and including A. J. Smith's corps from Nashville, were reported concentrating at New Orleans. If this were true, Kirby Smith reasoned that either Mobile or the coast of Texas was the objective. In either case, a naval expedition up the Red River might be used as a diversion. The scattered units of the Trans-Mississippi army were alerted. Wharton was to be ready to move his cavalry to the support of either Walker in Texas or Buckner in Louisiana. Forney was ordered from Minden to Shreveport, which was on the route to either Houston or Natchitoches. Churchill was to move from Lewisville, Arkansas, to Forney's evacuated winter quarters at Minden. Maxey was directed to rush Gano's brigade to join Wharton and to hold the remainder of his command ready to re-enforce Magruder should the enemy attempt a movement from Little Rock.[39]

Kirby Smith notified Walker to expect an attack at either Galveston or Sabine Pass. Since Galveston could not be successfully defended with the guns and troops available, Walker was to hold it until the enemy approached and then evacuate, removing guns and garrison.

[38] *Id.* to W. G. Hale, January 25, 1865, *ibid.*, 1343; *id.* to Robert Rose, February 1, 1865, *ibid.*, 1358–59.

[39] *Ibid.*, 1337–40.

Every effort, however, should be made to defend Houston. In this he could depend upon the assistance of Wharton's cavalry and Forney's infantry. Owing to a shortage of forage, nine regiments of Wharton's cavalry were to be dismounted and organized into an infantry division to be commanded by William Steele.[40]

Forney's division, en route to Texas, was stopped at Shreveport. News had arrived that a Federal force was moving on Monroe apparently with the intention of making the Ouachita a base of operation for a spring campaign. Kirby Smith urged Buckner to throw his entire disposable cavalry in front of this Federal advance, but at the same time he expressed doubt that the condition of the country was such that even cavalry could operate. Heavy rains had made the low country almost impassable. Cavalry horses must be protected in order that they might be in condition for the expected spring campaign.[41]

The Federal threat toward Monroe did not prove serious, and excitement was soon cooled by heavy rains and cold winds. On March 7 Kirby Smith sat at his desk composing a letter to President Davis. He wished to do all within his power to help the hard-pressed armies east of the Mississippi, he began, but neither a crossing nor an invasion of Missouri was possible before early summer. Between his armies and the Missouri line lay 400 miles of destitute country. And the Mississippi River "carefully guarded by iron-clads, with at least 200 miles of exhaustion" separated them from the East. While awaiting instructions from Richmond he would push preparations for both possibilities. "My effective strength in department is 19,000 enlisted men of infantry and artillery; 17,000 en-

[40] *Ibid.*, 1338–39, 1351, 1353.

[41] J. F. Belton to S. B. Buckner, February 2, 1865, *ibid.*, 1362; *id.* to J. G. Walker, February 2, 1865, *ibid.*, 1363; *id.* to J. F. Fagan, February 4, 1865, *ibid.*, 1366.

listed men of cavalry, of which seventeen regiments (6,000 enlisted men) are being dismounted; in addition 4,000 enlisted men are absent on furlough, 10,000 absent on details, including all details under conscription law; 6,000 Reserve Corps in Texas, 2,000 in Louisiana, and 2,000 in Arkansas. Reserves only in part armed." If the President did not intend ordering an invasion of Missouri, Kirby Smith concluded, he would like to leave Lieutenant General Buckner in command to push preparation for a crossing while he himself came to Richmond "to justify in person to you my administration of this department." [42]

Before Kirby Smith had completed his letter to the President, the telegraph instrument at headquarters began clicking off a message from Houston. A secret service agent had just arrived from New Orleans, Walker said, bringing important information from Catholic Bishop Jean Marie Odin and others. A Federal force 40,000 strong commanded by Canby in person would set out for the coast of Texas within three days! [43]

There was no time to lose. Kirby Smith relayed the message to Buckner and President Davis, and began preparation to meet the invasion. The Engineering Bureau, headed by Colonel H. T. Douglas, was instructed to draw up plans for defense. Forney's infantry was ordered to Huntsville, Texas, there to await further developments. Churchill's Arkansas division was sent to Marshall, Texas; Parsons' Missouri infantry and Shelby's cavalry were ordered closer to Shreveport from which point they could be rushed to Texas if needed.

The plan to send Forney to Texas presented a problem in command. He was Walker's senior in the rank of major general and would expect to assume command. Kirby

[42] E. Kirby Smith to Jefferson Davis, March 7, 1865, *ibid.*, 1411–12.
[43] J. G. Walker to E. Kirby Smith, March 7, 1865, *ibid.*, 1412.

Smith had little confidence in Forney's ability and was conscious of his unpopularity with the troops. A transfer of Magruder back to Texas seemed to be the only solution. Since Price, having requested that his conduct in the recent invasion of Missouri be investigated by a committee of inquiry, could not be immediately reassigned to command in Arkansas, Magruder was instructed to place Fagan in command and leave for Texas immediately. Walker was given his choice of either taking command of an infantry division or the District of Arkansas.[44]

But there was to be no major attempt to invade Texas; the days of the Confederacy were fast drawing to a close. On April 9 General Robert E. Lee surrendered his army to General U. S. Grant at Appomattox Courthouse. The terms were generous, but the result was decisive. Officers and men were to give their parole not to fight again until exchanged. All arms and other materials of war save officers' side arms and privately owned horses and baggage were to be surrendered.

[44] W. R. Boggs to J. G. Magruder, March 8, 1865, *ibid.,* 1416; E. Kirby Smith to J. G. Walker, March 22, 1865, *ibid.,* 1442.

## CHAPTER XVI

# "A GENERAL WITHOUT TROOPS"

Nᴇᴡs ᴏꜰ ʟᴇᴇ's surrender reached the Trans-Mississippi region within ten days. Kirby Smith registered no surprise and quickly realized that the best he could hope for was more honorable terms than those generally accorded to a defeated army. "The crisis of our revolution is at hand," he announced to the soldiers of the Trans-Mississippi army on April 21.[1]

Great disasters have overtaken us. The army of Northern Virginia and our Commander-in-Chief are prisoners of war. With you rests the hopes of our nation, and upon your action depends the fate of our people. I appeal to you in the name of the cause you have so heroically maintained—in the name of your firesides and families so dear to you—in the name of your bleeding country, whose future is in your hands. Show that you are worthy of your position in history. Prove to the world that your hearts have not failed in the hour of disaster, and that at the last moment you will sustain the holy cause which has been so gloriously battled for by your brethren east of the Mississippi.

You possess the means of long-resisting invasion. You have hopes of succor from abroad—protract the struggle and you will surely receive the aid of nations who already deeply sympathize with you.

Stand by your colors—maintain your discipline. The great resources of this department, its vast extent, the numbers, the discipline, and the efficiency of the army, will secure to our country terms that a proud people can with honor accept, and may, under the

[1] *Official Records,* Ser. I, Vol. XLVIII, pt. 2, 1284; Shreveport *Semi-Weekly News,* April 22, 1865.

Providence of God, be the means of checking the triumph of our enemy and of securing the final success of our cause.

Such words of encouragement were as hollow to the soldiers who received them as to the commander who uttered them. A Federal scout, who had been drafted into Confederate service and stationed near Shreveport, reported that "the effect of this order upon the troops was marked in the extreme. The men instantly became dejected. Mutiny and wholesale desertion was openly talked of. This soon gave way to a general apathy and indifference, but through all could be seen by a close observer that the Army of the Trans-Mississippi was in spirit crushed." [2]

Magruder, however, still expecting an all-out attack upon the Texas coast, publicly pronounced the surrender rumor untrue and urged Kirby Smith to take drastic, even dictatorial, steps to save the department. But the commanding general knew surrender was inevitable unless he could secure foreign aid. He removed Brigadier General Boggs as chief of staff "at his own request," appointed Buckner to this key position "until further orders," [3] and then turned his eyes toward the Rio Grande. Through the medium of Robert Rose he hoped to make favorable contact with the Emperor of Mexico. Rose was to explain to the Emperor that, although as department commander Kirby

---

[2] Report of C. S. Bell, n.d., *Official Records*, Ser. I, Vol. XLVIII, pt. 2, 400.

[3] General Orders, Nos. 41, 43, April 24, May 9, 1865, *ibid.*, 1285, 1295. For Boggs' version of his removal see *Reminiscences*, 81–84. Buckner's appointment was more a result of availability than personal preference on the part of Kirby Smith. As late as March 16, the latter was still urging the promotion of Dr. Smith to brigadier general "that I may make him chief of staff." (E. Kirby Smith to R. W. Johnson, March 16, 1865, *Official Records*, Ser. I, Vol. XLVIII, pt. 1, 1428–30.) Years later Boggs characterized Dr. Smith as "a man of immense frame and immense intellect; but indolent and selfish. He was undoubtedly very fond of General Smith and endeavored to serve him to his, General Smith's, advancement and glory. But the Doctor having gotten back among his own people (he belonged to Alexandria) was influenced by local relations to such an extent that his advice was not always beneficial." *Reminiscences*, 60.

Smith had no expressed power to appoint diplomatic agents or open negotiations with foreign nations, it was his desire to assure the Emperor of a probable disposition on the part of the Confederacy to enter into a "liberal agreement" with the Empire. Kirby Smith readily admitted the seriousness of the crisis now confronting the Confederacy and wished to stress its probable effect upon Mexico also. According to private and public statements of men high in authority in the United States, the crushing of the Confederacy would not end their aggressive designs. The "signs of the times" indicated great jealousy of the Mexican Empire and a determination to destroy it. In view of this imminent danger, the Emperor must be impressed with the fact that many excellent soldiers in the Trans-Mississippi region were ready to join hands with their neighbors across the Rio Grande in defense against a common aggressor. Nine thousand Missourians, driven from their homes by the invader, and at least 10,000 other "daring and gallant spirits from other States," all ably led veterans of many battles, would gladly rally around any flag that could save them from "a state of vassalage to the Federal Government." Should Rose find the Emperor receptive, he was to inform himself "as to the probable terms and conditions upon which an agreement for mutual protection could be determined upon." [4]

As the shock of Lee's surrender gradually spread over the Trans-Mississippi states, soldier and civilian alike realized that the cause was lost. Yet among those whose opinions were recorded there was a widespread demand for continued resistance, even in the face of overwhelming odds. Mass meetings were held at Shreveport and Houston. The one at Shreveport on April 29 seems to have been or-

[4] E. Kirby Smith to Robert Rose, May 2, 1865, *Official Records,* Ser. I, Vol. XLVIII, pt. 2, 1292–93.

ganized by Governor Allen. Kirby Smith, Buckner, Price, and other military leaders were present, but none of these high-ranking generals addressed the crowd. Governor Allen was the principal speaker. Nothing was required, he explained, but "a little patience and perseverance, bringing into requisition all our available strength to secure the great end of the struggle, viz: the independence of our country." Several lesser military men addressed the meeting, urging, in the words of Brigadier General Harry Hays, that the people "continue true to their colors and the cause would be triumphant beyond the possibility of failure." [5] At Houston speakers urged the people never even to think of giving up. Houston, they asserted, was the nerve center not only of Texas but of the entire Trans-Mississippi. Toward Houston then all eyes would be turned.[6]

Governor Murrah issued an appeal to the people of Texas to remain firm and united. All able-bodied men should rush to the service and all others to the production of essential supplies. "Look at the bloody and desolate tracks of the invader through Georgia and South Carolina," he exclaimed, "and see the fate that awaits you. . . . Rally around the battle scarred and well known flag of the Confederacy and uphold your state government in its purity and integrity—*There is no other hope of safety for you and yours.*" [7]

The Austin *Weekly State Gazette* applauded Governor Murrah, and assured its readers that revolution could "never go backward" as long as the people remained "united and true to themselves." With the "bulwark of space that Texas presents" and the unity and determina-

[5] Shreveport *Semi-Weekly News,* May 4, 1865.
[6] Galveston *Tri-Weekly News,* April 23, 1865.
[7] Murrah Papers, April 27, 1865.

tion of its people "to fight this war to an honorable peace, which shall bring the fruits of unconditional independence, Texas, alone, can prolong the conflict at will." [8]

All hope did not vanish with the surrender of Lee and Johnston, declared the Galveston *Tri-Weekly News* from Houston. Many troops from east of the Mississippi would soon join their Confederate comrades west of the river, and the United States was almost certain to have trouble with Maximilian. General Smith and the governors were "determined to fight it out," and the Yankees, finding the war interminable, "will finally let us alone." "To a brave, high minded man there can be no choice. To a determined, loyal people there can be but one course. Let us follow this course fearlessly and unhesitatingly." [9]

In the meantime, Lieutenant Colonel John T. Sprague, chief of staff to Union General John Pope, commander of the military Division of Missouri, had arrived at the mouth of the Red River under a flag of truce, bringing an important message from his commander. Two staff members were sent down from Shreveport headquarters to receive the message, but Sprague insisted upon seeing the commanding general in person. There were oral explanations to be made.

John N. Edwards, a member of Shelby's command, who was not in Shreveport at the time, later related that, when news of Sprague's arrival at the Red River reached Shreveport, Governor Allen invited "General [Alexander T.] Hawthorne, Colonel [George] Flournoy, Major [?] Watkins, Gen. [Sterling] Price, and Colonel [R. H.] Musser" to meet at his home. Flournoy did most of the talking. Kirby Smith, Flournoy said, was preparing to go down the river to meet Sprague; on board his boat he had "several millions" worth of cotton, the proceeds from which were to

<hr>

[8] May 3, 1865.            [9] May 12, 1865.

be "held subject to his order," and Kirby Smith had made arrangements to take his family out of the country, "leaving the Confederacy to its fate." Flournoy claimed to have seen Kirby Smith's signature on important papers but did not explain the "precise nature" of the papers. According to Edwards, the group then discussed at length Kirby Smith's administration of the department. A number of officers and citizens later called upon Kirby Smith and urged that an immediate surrender would be "impolitic and unnecessary" and urged that he remain at Shreveport. "Smith yielded gracefully and Colonel Flournoy went to confer with Pope's envoys." Edwards, in relating this story, although he thought Kirby Smith incompetent, stressed the fact that Kirby Smith had by neither word nor action "exhibited the least intention of surrendering." Furthermore, there was no evidence that he ever "made one dollar by his position or sent abroad for individual use one single cotton bale."

Edwards further related that about this same time Price held a conference at his Shreveport quarters, but he was certain of the names of only three persons who attended— Price, Colonel Musser, and Colonel L. M. Lewis. Price was attempting to test sentiment. It was proposed that Kirby Smith be arrested should he *"prove troublesome"* and insist on conferring with the Federal commissioners. And Shelby, stationed near Shreveport and awaiting just such an eventuality, stood ready "to hurl his splendid and massive division upon Shreveport, seize the reins of government, call upon the good and the true, march at once against the enemy and attack him for courage's sake."

There was no arrest, and Edwards states that Shelby upon arrival in Shreveport had several meetings with Kirby Smith and was assured that if the troops would stand by the commanding general he would "fight unto the end";

he considered it "nothing more than a supreme duty" that he should continue to fight "at least until President Davis reaches this department, or I receive some definite orders from him."

Had an attempt actually been made to arrest Kirby Smith, Edwards believed it would have meant the death of the general, for he later said to Governor Reynolds that he could have been killed but not arrested. "A calm, pure, God fearing man," Edwards concluded, "yet weak and indolent, willing to die for the right, and conscientious in the discharge of every duty as he interpreted it. . . ." [10]

The separation of fact from rumor in this story is impossible. Certainly Price was disgruntled and Shelby and his Missourians were bitterly opposed to surrender. The part alleged to have been played by Governor Allen is not in harmony with his known sentiments at the governors conference a few days later. There was a meeting at Price's quarters, however, and Colonel L. M. Lewis, commander of a brigade of Missouri infantry, went to Kirby Smith and told him that a conspiracy was forming; when Kirby Smith named Price as the leader Lewis admitted as much. The secret service had already reported the plot to the commanding general. [11]

Colonel Sprague arrived in Shreveport on May 8 and presented General Pope's message. General Lee had surrendered to Grant it said, and Joseph E. Johnston and Sherman were negotiating a similar agreement in North Carolina. There was also an unconfirmed report that the Mobile garrison had surrendered to Canby. "In view of these results, accomplished and in progress of speedy accomplishment," Pope was authorized by Grant to offer Kirby Smith the same terms as given to Lee. With a mighty

---

[10] John N. Edwards, *Shelby and His Men* (Cincinnati, 1867), 520 ff.
[11] E. Kirby Smith to Governor ?, n.d., Kirby Smith Papers.

Federal force now available for an invasion of the Trans-Mississippi region, further effective resistance would be impossible, Pope urged. Should Kirby Smith insist upon a continuation of such a hopeless struggle he must "be made responsible for unnecessary bloodshed," devastation, and misery. "The duty of an officer is performed and his honor maintained," Pope explained, "when he has prolonged resistance until all hope of success has been lost." Resistance beyond that point must result in the infliction upon the people "all the horrors of violent subjugation." "Wisdom and humanity alike" required an end to suffering and bloodshed.[12]

Sprague was instructed to add to this formal demand such oral argument as might appear helpful. He was to picture the devastation and misery that would surely result from a Federal invasion into the heart of Texas and to stress that the terms now offered were much more lenient than could be expected after invasion. Under no circumstances was Sprague to commit the United States government to any policy; however, if soldiers or citizens wished to withdraw themselves to Mexico he was to offer no objection. It was probable, Pope thought, that Louisiana and Arkansas troops might wish to disband and go home without surrendering or giving parole. Sprague was to offer no objection but sign no written permission for such action. The same applied if organized bodies wished to march to Mexico, taking their materials of war with them. He might suggest, as his opinion only, that should Kirby Smith disband his army and no longer occupy military posts in Texas and Louisiana, those posts would be occupied by well-disciplined Federal troops instructed not to "molest private property or interfere with citizens except

[12] John Pope to E. Kirby Smith, April 19, 1865, *Official Records*, Ser. I, Vol. XLVIII, pt. 1, 186–87.

so far as directed to do so by the authorities in Washington." Further, Sprague might allude to the shock resulting from the recent assassination of President Lincoln and remind Kirby Smith that continued resistance would intensify the feeling against rebels in general "to whom the mass of the people in the North attribute, however remotely, the atrocious deed." Should Kirby Smith agree to the terms proposed, Colonel Sprague was to "make immediate arrangements to take the paroles of all concerned." [13]

Before conferring with Sprague, Kirby Smith had officially notified the Trans-Mississippi governors of the surrender of Lee and "the perilous situation" in North Carolina and Alabama. "The army under my command," he explained, "yet remains strong, fresh, and well equipped. The disparity of numbers . . . between it and our enemies may be counterbalanced by valor and skill. Under these circumstances it is my purpose to defend your soil and the civil and political rights of our people to the utmost extent of our resources, and to try and maintain untarnished the reputation which our soldiers have so nobly won in many fields." Continued resistance, however, would "require the perfect concord of the civil and military authorities, the application of all our energies, and the united and devoted support of the people." There was some chance, that owing to the evacuation of Richmond, the seat of the Confederate Government might be moved west of the Mississippi. In this time of crisis, although completely cut off from contact with President Davis, Kirby Smith wished to "avoid any appearance of usurping functions not intrusted to my discretion." Accordingly, he wished to confer with the governors of the Trans-Mississippi states on all matters pertaining to powers of the

[13] *Id.* to J. T. Sprague, April 19, 1865, *ibid.,* 187–88.

commanding general and the common defense and general welfare of the people. He requested an immediate conference at Marshall, Texas, with the hope that the chief executives would there indicate the policy which they believed wise and honorable.[14]

Sprague was invited to remain at Shreveport until the results of the Marshall conference could be known. The governors in conference decided that further resistance was impracticable and advised surrender on the following terms: (1) The army to be disbanded and all men to be sent to their homes "to remain as good citizens" free from all disabilities. (2) No officers, soldiers, or citizens to be prosecuted for alleged offenses against the United States during the war. (3) All soldiers and citizens to be unmolested should they wish to migrate to other states or countries, carrying with them their "arms and effects." (4) Existing state governments to be recognized pending the meeting of conventions to settle "all conflicts between the people of the respective States." (5) Military authority to be turned back to the states, and each state to be permitted to keep a guard sufficient for the protection of the lives and property of the people. And in order that the Trans-Mississippi situation might be adequately explained, Governor Henry W. Allen of Louisiana was requested to go to Washington to confer with Federal authorities.[15]

Thomas C. Reynolds, governor of the "Confederate State" of Missouri, long an exile in the other Trans-Mississippi states, was most reluctant to give up the struggle. He realized what would be the status of ex-Confederate Missourians. But Confederate Missourians, he asserted, would stand by whatever decision the other peoples be-

[14] E. Kirby Smith to Henry W. Allen et al., May 9, 1865, ibid., 189–90.
[15] Ibid., 190–91.

lieved wise. However, should surrender be decided upon, they wished sufficient time to collect adequate facilities and supplies for leaving the country with their personal property.[16]

According to the Edwards story, another conference was held in Marshall concurrently with the meeting of the governors. Those present included Generals Churchill, Hawthorne, Shelby, and Preston, and Colonel Flournoy. The object of the meeting was to formulate a plan of action to "replace the reign of indecision" and give to soldiers and citizens something tangible. After much discussion, Shelby proposed that Kirby Smith be informed "that a change of commanders was necessary"; consequently, he must turn over command of troops to Buckner, send Preston to Mexico to consult "Liberals and Imperialists," order a concentration of troops on the Brazos River, and, should everything else fail, he was "to take service with one or the other of the contending parties in Mexico and establish either an Empire or a Republic." The plan was said to have been unanimously adopted.

Shelby was sent to consult Buckner and finally secured from him a definite promise to take command and "fight the issue out." The entire group then called upon Kirby Smith. "This proposal affected General Smith to tears," Edwards related. "He replied at last with a voice full of emotion, in which pride and grief struggled for the mastery." He was grieved that his soldiers no longer had confidence in him after he had done all within his power for the common good. In spite of the doubts cast upon him by others in an effort to hide their own cowardice, he had never seriously considered surrendering. He was eager to fight it out and "only asked for sympathy and support." Being assured that his patriotism and sincerity were not

[16] Memorandum to Marshall Conference, May 10, 1865, *ibid.*, 191.

questioned but also that the conditions within the army were such that a change was necessary, Kirby Smith turned to Buckner and directed a concentration on the Brazos, relinquished "all command by himself," and instructed Preston to proceed to Mexico. The conference then ended with a *"full and free understanding on the part of all, that no surrender should be resorted to, and no steps taken whatever, looking to an abandonment of the contest."* [17]

There is a thread of truth running through Edwards' story, but no account of such details seems to have been left by any of the alleged participants. Smoldering dissension dares raise its head and point an accusing finger when the cause seems irretrievably lost. Name-calling and speculation in "ifs" become a favorite pastime among those who are unable to adjust themselves to the inevitable. Edwards never claimed to be in attendance at any of the meetings described; he apparently built his story around a few facts told him by Shelby. His intense disappointment over Confederate defeat and his adoration of Shelby, who in turn was loyal to Price, robbed him of all sense of objectivity. The war in the West was lost, he maintained, because there was no "genius, intellect, will, nerve, or enthusiasm" in high places. He could scarcely have been farther from the truth; genius alone of these attributes was lacking. Of Kirby Smith himself, Edwards wrote: [18]

Smith by his inaction at one time seemed a poor blind pilot in an unknown sea, and he neither grappled with the winds and waves bearing him to destruction, nor exhibited one manly effort to escape the coils gathering around him. Sultan in the heart of a magnificent country at other times, surrounded by sixty thousand devoted guards, he yet had no bowstrings for the incapable Pachas, and no Bosphorus for the thousands of traitors spreading their disaffection and their lies almost upon the steps of his throne.

[17] Edwards, *Shelby,* 524–25.   [18] *Ibid.,* 515.

His patriotism was all heart and no brains. His ability all uniform and no fame. His mind all theory and no practice. He was not responsible for being decked out in the robes of power, and he labored faithfully to preserve those robes clean from the stains of battle and the dust of conflicts. He succeeded. Before his eyes, one after another of the South's warriors fell trampled to the earth. He heard their shouts for help. Jackson's death knell shook the battlements about his pleasure grounds; Johnson [*sic*] turned his despairing eyes westward, but no friendly banners came, and thus, without one puny blow for the land which gave him birth, without one glorified sacrifice for the homes of his kindred and dead, he abandoned the conflict, abandoned the department, left eternal disgrace upon the Trans-Mississippi Department.

To the author's statement that he would not write of records and figures, he might have added that neither would he write of truth and justice. Such an appraisal could have come only from one whose attraction to the dramatic was stronger than his love for truth—one who had no conception of the problems connected with trying to do much with too little.

Kirby Smith returned to his Shreveport headquarters immediately following the conference of governors at Marshall, and resumed his talk with Colonel Sprague. Before leaving for Marshall he had dictated a short note of rejection to General Pope, dating it May 9, but held it until after his return. He regretted that the proposed terms were not such that his "sense of duty and honor" would permit him to accept, he informed Pope. He further regretted that Pope had used threats in an effort to sway him in his decision as to duty.[19] To Colonel Sprague, however, he admitted that there was no hope that the Trans-Mississippi Confederacy could alone win its independence. But resistance there could be destroyed and the country overrun only after great preparation and considerable expense,

[19] E. Kirby Smith to John Pope, May 9, 1865, *Official Records*, Ser. I, Vol. XLVIII, pt. 1, 189.

probably resulting in serious political complications for the United States.

"As the commander of the military forces," he explained to Sprague, "I cannot accept terms which will purchase a certain degree of immunity from devastation at the expense of the honor of its army." An army such as his, being in no immediate danger of destruction, could scarcely be expected to surrender as prisoners of war; therefore, General Pope's demand was both unreasonable and contrary to "the laws which custom has made binding amongst nations and military men." The implication was that the victorious United States intended to humiliate rather than pacify and restore those people and states "who have contended gallantly in behalf of principles which they believe to be right." The military authorities of the Trans-Mississippi Department were eager to hasten pacification by all honorable means, but they were determined "not to submit to ignominious terms." The following were the terms which the Trans-Mississippi Department could accept:

First. The U. S. authorities to grant immunity from prosecution for past acts to all officers and soldiers and citizens in the Trans-Mississippi Department.

Second. On the granting of this immunity all military resistance to the United States Government to cease.

Third. The Confederate Army to be disbanded and its officers and soldiers to be permitted to return to their homes, transportation to be furnished them as far as practicable.

Fourth. Such officers and soldiers as choose will be permitted, without molestation, to leave the country, with or without their arms, in a reasonable time.

Fifth. The same permission to be granted to citizens.

"Many examples of history," Kirby Smith advised Sprague, "teach that the more generous the terms proposed by a victorious enemy, the greater is the certainty of a speedy and lasting pacification, and that the imposition of harsh terms leads invariably to subsequent disturbances." [20]

On May 15 Kirby Smith handed Sprague the reply to Pope and a personal letter, and the flag of truce began descending the Red River. Sprague reported to Pope that the general attitude among military and civil officials at Shreveport was that more considerate terms were merited. However, he had refused to permit Governor Allen to accompany him to Pope's headquarters. [21]

Kirby Smith was stalling for time and hoping for the best. He knew the game was about over and that all was lost save honor. All he could hope for now was more liberal terms than those offered by Pope. Governor Murrah, of Texas, who owing to illness was absent from the Marshall conference, wired on May 17, urging that the commanding general not surrender without a guarantee of respect for life, property, and constitutional rights. Kirby Smith replied: "I agree with you. If I am supported by the troops and state authorities I do not propose to accept other terms." [22] He did not say, however, how long he expected that support.

Rumors now flew thick and fast. Kirby Smith would no doubt soon surrender, reported a Union scout, for he was a defaulter to the Confederate government to the extent of $5,000,000. [23] If Jeff Davis ever joined Kirby Smith, declared another, they would "fight to the bitter end." "The

[20] Memorandum to Colonel Sprague, n.d., *ibid.*, 192–93. It is not known whether this memorandum was handed to Sprague before or after the Marshall conference.

[21] E. Kirby Smith to J. T. Sprague, May 15, 1865, *ibid.*, 191–92; Sprague to John Pope, May 27, 1865, *ibid.*, 188–89.

[22] Kirby Smith Papers, under date of May 17, 1865.

[23] A. M. Jackson to C. T. Christensen, April 29, 1865, *Official Records*, Ser. I, Vol. XLVIII, pt. 2, 239.

people of the entire Trans-Mississippi infinitely prefer an alliance with a foreign power to a return to old ties. France has the first choice." [24] Kirby Smith would not surrender, explained one Louisiana officer to another; he and Buckner "would bring ruin on Louisiana and Texas merely to enable them to escape with a corporal's guard into Mexico." Louisiana officers must take things in their own hands.[25]

Kirby Smith had delayed surrender in order that a great migration might get under way, reported a Louisiana "scalawag." Buckner was already on the march to Texas with 15,000 men and "the largest transportation train ever known west of the Mississippi." In Texas he would be joined by Magruder and others with possibly 30,000 men. General Preston had already made arrangements in Mexico. Only conciliatory Federal action could prevent this mass migration.[26] Canby endorsed on this report that he had no news that would indicate the truth of it.

The press advised patience and caution until the results of the official meeting were made known. He himself was unable to say what was best, advised the editor of the Shreveport *Semi-Weekly News,* but he had sufficient confidence in Kirby Smith "to await his decision, and abide by it." [27] Soldiers and civilians had "unbounded confidence in the patriotism of General Smith and the Governors," declared the Marshall *Texas Republican.* These men would weigh all facts carefully and then arrive at the correct decision.[28] There were too many "grumblers and croakers," announced the Galveston *Tri-Weekly News,* who advised surrender. "When President Davis bids us

[24] Report of C. S. Bell, n.d., *ibid.,* 398–403.
[25] D. F. Boyd to L. A. Bringier, May 20, 1865, *ibid.,* 1314–15.
[26] F. L. Claiborne to H. N. Frisbie, May 22, 1865, *ibid.,* 538–39.
[27] May 11, 1865.                    [28] May 12, 1865.

lay down our arms and submit, when Gen. Smith says it is no use trying any longer, and when Gen. Magruder tells us that we have done all that men could do, but that the fates are against us, then, and not until then, will it be time for us to be discussing the matter in our minds." [29]

On May 18 Kirby Smith announced a change of headquarters from Shreveport to Houston. Smoldering disaffection among Texas troops had broken into open disregard for organization and discipline. Only through immediate and drastic steps was there hope of continued resistance. Leaving his wife, two children, and "Mammy" Mahala in care of the faithful Aleck with instructions to take them back to Virginia, Kirby Smith set out across Texas on May 20. Every day brought unmistakable evidence that his military organization was crumbling about him. Before he left Shreveport a telegram came from Magruder informing him that a portion of the garrison at Galveston had mutinied.[30]

Maxey, now in command of a division in Texas, reported that he could no longer rely upon his men to resist. Officers of Walker's division expressed a belief that their troops would "fight no longer." Brigade and regimental commanders in Forney's division were unanimously agreed that their men, considering the cause hopeless, would "lay down their arms at the first appearance of the enemy." The Texas cavalry, although remaining quiet, was reported merely awaiting "what they considered the inevitable result, viz. surrender." In the western subdistrict of Texas fully one half of the troops had deserted, and the remaining one half refused to help bring the deserters back. "It

[29] May 17, 1865.

[30] Magruder had arrived in Galveston on May 11 and delivered an appeal to the troops. A reporter observed that the soldiers listened "with silence and respect" but without "manifestation of enthusiasm." Galveston *Tri-Weekly. News,* May 15, 1865.

is useless for the Trans-Mississippi Department to undertake to do what the Cis-Mississippi Department has failed to do," they agreed.

He had done all he could to instill a spirit of resistance, Magruder explained, but had only made himself "antagonistic to the army and an object of their displeasure." There was nothing left to do, he lamented, but to permit the soldiers to divide the government property and return home by regiments "with as little damage to the community as possible." "For God's sake act or let me act," he urged Kirby Smith.[31]

On May 21 at Crockett, Texas, Kirby Smith received another wire from Magruder, stating that Forney's division had disbanded. Four days later he arrived at Hempstead, "having been compelled to remain 36 hours in Huntsville to escape the mob of disorderly soldiery thronging the roads." At Hempstead he found another telegram waiting. The cavalry had disbanded, and all control over troops had been lost, explained Magruder. Still worse news came from Walker. His infantry had mutinied on May 19, seized all transportation and supplies, and carried off to their homes everything they could get their hands on. "In a word," he announced, "there is not an animal, or wagon, or public stores of any description left in their track." [32]

In a half-hearted attempt to exercise his fast-fading authority, Kirby Smith called upon Magruder for a full report on "this most unexpected and humiliating conduct." There was no use. Neither Kirby Smith nor any other commander could have prevented the disgraceful scenes which were about to be enacted. Disintegration had fol-

[31] J. B. Magruder to E. Kirby Smith, May 16, 1865, *Official Records*, Ser. I, Vol. XLVIII, pt. 2, 1308; J. E. Slaughter to Magruder, May 19, 1865, *ibid.*, 1313–14.

[32] E. Kirby Smith to J. B. Magruder, May 26, 1865, Kirby Smith Papers; J. G. Walker to S. S. Anderson, May 24, 1865, *ibid.*; E. Kirby Smith to U.S. Grant, June 15, 1865, *ibid.*; Oldham, "Memoirs," 336–38.

lowed demoralization and would inevitably run its course. Whole companies, even brigades, which, lacking in discipline, had sometimes been the terror of the region in which they were foraging, now became disorganized mobs, thronging the roads, "suspending travel and making life and property insecure." And jayhawkers, bushwhackers, and renegades in general joined in the looting, and threw upon the returning soldiers the credit for their depredations.

By the time of his arrival at his new headquarters on May 27, Kirby Smith was a general without an army. Although he summoned a court of inquiry to investigate the "causes and manner" of disbandment, its decision could do nothing toward bringing back the lost legions. Despondency and hopelessness had crept over the land following the shocking news from east of the Mississippi, the court of inquiry reported; the soldiers merely yielded to the "feeling of non resistance spread among them by the people of the state." And when some deserted and began pillaging, others felt a necessity of returning home to protect their families. The seizure of property was a part of an understanding between soldiers and citizens, and officers were helpless to prevent it. Neither should the officers be held responsible for "the acts of an armed and overwhelming mob who had become deaf alike to the dictates of duty, reason and honor." [33]

Regardless of the commanding general's previous intentions, his course was now no longer in doubt. He appealed to Governor Murrah to make use of state troops to protect public property, and then sent out under date of May 30, 1865, his last message to the soldiers of the Trans-Mississippi Department: [34]

[33] See Kirby Smith Papers, under dates of May 29, 30, 1865; E. Kirby Smith to U. S. Grant, March 15, 1866, *ibid.*

[34] Galveston *Tri-Weekly News*, June 5, 1865; Kirby Smith Papers, under May 30, 1865.

Soldiers—The day after I refused the demands of the Federal government to surrender this Department, I left Shreveport for Houston. I ordered the Missouri, Arkansas and Louisiana troops to follow. My purpose was to concentrate the entire strength of the Department, await negotiations, and, if possible, secure terms alike honorable to soldiers and citizens. Failing in this, I intended to struggle to the last; and with an army united in purpose, firm in resolve, and battling for the right, I believed God would yet give us victory. I reached here to find the Texas troops disbanded and hastening to their homes. They had forsaken their colors and their commanders; had abandoned the cause for which we were struggling, and appropriated the public property to their personal use.

Soldiers! I am left a commander without an army—a General without troops. You have made your choice. It was unwise and unpatriotic, but it is final. I pray you may not live to regret it. The enemy will now possess your country, and dictate his own laws. You have volunteerly destroyed your organizations, and thrown away all means of resistance.

Your present duty is plain. Return to your families. Resume the occupations of peace. Yield obedience to the laws. Labor to restore order. Strive both by counsel and example to give security to life and property. And may God, in his mercy, direct you aright, and heal the wounds of our distracted country.

His last address to the Trans-Mississippi soldiers completed, the "general without an army" reported to Colonel John T. Sprague the change in conditions within the department. "When I gave you, at Shreveport, a memorandum which I hoped might be the basis of negotiations with the United States Government," he sadly explained,

I commanded an army of over 50,000 men and a department rich in resources. I am now without either. The army in Texas disbanded before my arrival here. From one extremity of the department to the other the troops, with unexampled unanimity of action, have dissolved all military organization, seized the public property, and scattered to their homes. Abandoned and mortified, left without either men or material, I feel powerless to do good for my country and humiliated by the acts of a people I was striving to benefit. The department is now open to occupation by your Government. The citizen and soldier alike, weary of war, are ready to accept the authority and yield obedience to the laws of the United States. A conciliatory policy, dictated by wisdom and administered with patient moderation, will insure peace and secure quiet. An opposite course will rekindle the flames of civil war with a fierceness and intensity unknown even in this sad and unfortunate struggle. I myself shall go abroad until the future policy of the United States toward the South is announced, and will return to my family only when I can do so with security to my life and person.[35]

As Kirby Smith wrote the above messages, Union Brigadier General James J. Davis was en route to Galveston bearing an official copy of the terms of surrender agreed to at New Orleans on May 26 between Major General P. J. Osterhaus, chief of staff to General Canby, and Lieutenant General Buckner. What understanding there was between Kirby Smith and his chief of staff when the former left for his new headquarters was never revealed. A telegram sent upon arrival in Houston seems to indicate that Kirby Smith expected Buckner to join him there: [36]

Just arrived. Texas troops all disbanded. Public property all seized. Galveston probably occupied by enemy this morning. No supplies for maintaining troops. Discharge them and send them to their homes. When shall I expect you. Will any troops accompany you? If Headquarters have not left start all who wish to come immediately under escort if practicable otherwise they must protect themselves. Inform General Cooper commanding Indian Territory of conditions of things and tell him to have the Indians take care of themselves.

A north Texas planter, traveling to New Orleans to purchase supplies, reported that Buckner and his brother were busily engaged in selling Confederate property for specie and pocketing the proceeds, and that it was supposed that Kirby Smith would do the same at Houston. He further related that about May 21 Buckner and Price addressed the troops near Shreveport, urging them to march off to Mexico. But the troops refused and threatened to

[35] E. Kirby Smith to J. T. Sprague, May 30, 1865, *Official Records,* Ser. I, Vol. XLVIII, pt. 1, 183–94.

[36] A. M. Stickles, *Simon Bolivar Buckner* (Chapel Hill, 1940), 270, quoting from Buckner Papers.

seize Buckner and surrender him to United States authorities. "About this time Generals Price and Buckner were seen moving down the river for New Orleans." [37]

There is little if any truth in this story. In the first place, Buckner had no brother. There is no evidence that he appropriated any Confederate property. Neither were he and Price in the vicinity of Shreveport on May 21. However, the same feeling of hopelessness which had scattered the Texas troops was also prevalent to a lesser extent among other troops. Although no terms of surrender had been agreed upon, reported Governor Flanagin of Arkansas on May 27, "so far as I know, there is not a man of ours in arms in this State." All had taken furloughs and gone home. "I feel no hesitation in acting as I would act if no such thing as a Confederate force existed." [38]

On May 20 Buckner and Price were at the mouth of the Red River. No doubt Buckner had abandoned whatever idea he had had of moving his command to Texas or going in person to Mexico, although, two days earlier, Colonel Sprague had reported that should Kirby Smith change his mind and decide to surrender, Buckner intended "to cut a way through Texas into Mexico with the more exasperated portion of the army." [39]

On May 24 Buckner, Price, and Brigadier General Joseph L. Brent were at Baton Rouge en route to New Orleans, and Canby was on his way from Mobile to his New Orleans headquarters. The three Confederates conferred with the Federal commander on May 25, received his terms, and promised a reply that evening. The surrender was signed on the following day. [40]

[37] Frank N. Wicker to C. T. Christensen, May 30, 1865, *Official Records,* Ser. I, Vol. XLVIII, pt. 2, 673–75.

[38] H. Flanagin to A. H. Garland, May 27, 28, 1865, *ibid.,* 1320, 1321.

[39] P. J. Osterhaus to E. R. S. Canby, May 20, 1865, *ibid.,* 515.

[40] E. R. S. Canby to F. J. Herron, May 24, 1865, *ibid.,* 581; *id.* to U. S. Grant, May 25, 1865, *ibid.,* 591.

In taking this action the Confederate generals were acting on their own.[41] Buckner made it clear that the agreement on terms was subject to the approval of the commanding general of the department. Those conferring at New Orleans had no knowledge of the disbandment of the Texas troops. The terms of surrender [42] were essentially the same as those between Grant and Lee.

On June 2 Kirby Smith, accompanied by General Magruder, went aboard the Federal steamer *Fort Jackson* off Galveston harbor and affixed his signature to the agreement, endorsing thereon that he understood that "officers observing their parole are permitted to make their homes either in or out of the United States." Considering his signature as his parole, he designated persons to be responsible for paroling those troops which had remained to surrender and to turn over to Federal authorities all Confederate property, and prepared to return to private life.[43]

The last official order issued by Kirby Smith as commander of the Trans-Mississippi Department directed Captain Ernest Cucullu, chief of the secret service, to go to New Orleans and surrender to General Canby the $3,300 remaining in his possession. When Kirby Smith had learned that President Davis would probably escape to Cuba and then cross over to Texas, where he hoped to make a final stand, the commanding general had directed Cucullu to procede to Cuba with $5,000 in gold and see the President across. Before Cucullu could get passage

[41] E. Kirby Smith to U. S. Grant, June 15, 1866, Kirby Smith Papers; Statement of S. B. Buckner in New York *Times,* January 10, 1867, quoting from New Orleans *Crescent*. Magruder also appointed representatives—Ashbel Smith and W. P. Ballinger—to confer with Canby in New Orleans, but they did not carry out their mission. Pendleton Murrah to Ashbel Smith and W. P. Ballinger, May 24, 1865, Murrah Papers.

[42] *Official Records,* Ser. I, Vol. XLVIII, pt. 2, 600–601.

[43] Of the approximately 60,000 troops within the Trans-Mississippi Department only 17,515 remained to be paroled. *Ibid.,* Ser. II, Vol. VIII, 717.

from Galveston, the Texas troops had disbanded and the news of Buckner's surrender had arrived. There was then no need to make the trip. With Kirby Smith's permission, $1,700 were turned over to Generals Walker, Magruder, Hawes, Drayton, and Forney as part of the pay due them. It was the remaining $3,300 that Kirby Smith directed Cucullu to take to Canby.

Cucullu, accompanied by Dr. David Yandell, journeyed to New Orleans and surrendered $3,299. He had spent one dollar for cab fare. Cucullu later quoted Canby as saying "It is just like Kirby, the soul of honor." Learning that Yandell and another unnamed officer had no funds on which to travel to their homes, Canby gave them $270.[44]

It was with deepest humiliation, announced the editor of the Galveston *Tri-Weekly News,* that he accepted the inevitable. But "when a people have, apparently with one accord, determined to submit," it was his duty to "acquiesce in that determination." [45] The editor of the Marshall *Texas Republican,* not so willing to acquiesce, placed to the credit of General Kirby Smith the major portion of the responsibility for failure. The general was totally incapable as an administrator, he contended. The troops "lost confidence in him, and associated him with cotton speculation." While those orderly Arkansas and Missouri troops stationed in the vicinity of Marshall remained loyal to the Confederacy, others, "influenced by Gen. Smith, were demoralized, and broke up in squads and went home." The editor felt that Kirby Smith's greatest weakness was the deficiency "in his judgment of men," which resulted in his being imposed upon "by the insincere and designing." Yet as a man, the editor greatly admired the general as

[44] Ernest Cucullu to E. Kirby Smith, January 29, 1891, Kirby Smith Papers; "Secret Service Funds," in *Confederate Veteran,* Souvenir Number, April, 1894, p. 31.

[45] June 2, 1865.

one "devoted to the cause he espoused, and essentially a warm-hearted, true man." "However much we may condemn the policy he pursued latterly, as a commander, we have no hesitation in saying, that we consider him one of the purest and best men, in a moral sense, connected with the Confederate service, and that the reports circulated prejudicial to his integrity are without foundation." [46]

[46] Marshall *Texas Republican,* May 26, June 2, 1865.

# CHAPTER XVII

# "A LIGHT PURSE BUT
# A HEAVY HEART"

From galveston Kirby Smith went to Hempstead and remained a few days with friends. He was considering settling in Texas. On June 14 he started again for Galveston to give his formal parole. En route he met Dick Howard and Colonel Douglas who had a copy of President Johnson's amnesty proclamation. From them he also learned of the arrest of General Lee. He quickly decided "to place the Rio Grande between myself & harm" until hostile feeling should subside.

Through friends he secured enough money to give him economical support for about four months.[1] Before daybreak, June 15, he set out for San Antonio. There he was joined by Generals Cadmus M. Wilcox and James M. Hawes, a Judge Divine, Colonel Henry Douglas, and others. Traveling by day and night through "bands of robbers and plundering deserters with which the roads were infested," the group reached the Rio Grande and crossed over at Eagle Pass on June 26. Between San An-

[1] He also wrote his rancher friend J. M. Hunter at Fredericksburg, Texas, to sent him $1,000 via Liverpool, but Hunter, unable to find a San Antonio merchant or speculator willing to draw on funds in Europe, was unable to comply with the request. See Hunter to Mrs. Kirby Smith, August 29, 1865; *id.* to Kirby Smith, February 28, 1866.

tonio and the river they had overtaken another party which included Generals Magruder, Price, and Shelby, and Governors Allen, Murrah, and Moore. Mounted on a mule and dressed in shirt sleeves with a silk handkerchief tied around his neck "a la Texas" and armed with revolver and shotgun, the former commanding general of the Trans-Mississippi Department rode into Mexico. "I had left everything behind except a clear conscience and a sense of having done my duty," he wrote his wife, "and with a light purse but a heavy heart I trudged along over the desert plains & under the burning sun of the Rio Grande. . . . Even the darkness and uncertainty of the future could not entirely check the feeling of lightness and joy experienced by me when I felt myself to be plain Kirby Smith relieved from all cares and responsible only for my own acts."

The heat on the cactus plains and fear of attack by both Indians and the "Liberal Robbers" made the trip to Monterey one of torture. In this Mexican town Kirby Smith found a hundred or more "Confederate censorians, fault finding & dissatisfied." Disgusted with their "criminations & selfishness," he, Governor Reynolds, and General Wilcox took a diligence for Mexico City on July 5. Eleven days later they were in the capital city, having traveled 1,200 miles within the past month. While in Mexico City, the party put up at the Hotel San Carlos, which was kept by a former servant of General Buckner who had left his master at West Point and grown wealthy in Mexico.

Kirby Smith found nothing in Mexico to cause him to desire to reside there. The government there, he complained, was too afraid of offending the United States to make any concessions to ex-Confederates. He and Governor Reynolds soon headed for Cuba, arriving in Havana on July 28. They put up at the Hotel America, but Major Minter, former purchasing agent for the Trans-Mississippi Department, soon came for the general and took him to the Hotel Cubano where Minter and his wife were staying.

At the Cubano Kirby Smith found Judah P. Benjamin, who was about to leave for England. General Breckinridge had just left. Kirby Smith thought of joining them, but decided to spare himself the expense of such a trip until he could hear what the situation was in the United States. A few days later other friends took him to Matanzas, where he was entertained royally.[2]

Shortly after arrival in Cuba Kirby Smith wrote privately to General Grant, requesting a candid statement as to what he could expect should he decide to return to the United States. He wished to return only if it could be "without dishonor or humiliation." He was willing to give his parole and take an oath of allegiance.[3] The ex-commander of the Trans-Mississippi Department then settled down to weeks of waiting and meditating.

Former Confederates were fairly numerous in Cuba, and there was much leisure time for discussing the late war and the probable future of the South. Stories, usually exaggerated and highly colored, drifted in. Letters soon began to arrive, and Kirby Smith became the recipient of all kinds of advice from relatives and friends. His wife and family, thanks to the skill and energy of the faithful Aleck, were again safe in Lynchburg, Virginia. By some means Aleck had secured passage for them on a steamer going up the Mississippi. It was hoped that they could travel incognito, but the precocious little Carrie, who had absorbed too much of the army life, including language,

[2] See manuscript diary kept by Kirby Smith during travels to Cuba, Kirby Smith Papers; E. Kirby Smith to Wife, July 4, 10, 28, 1865; also long undated letter written in either July or August, 1865; *id.* to Mother, August 4, 1865.

[3] *Id.* to *id.*, August 4, 1865.

ruined the plan by addressing an officer as a "damn Yankee" and threatening to kill him. No doubt she also told her name. At any rate, the captain, fearing punishment for assisting the family of a Confederate general, put the whole party off at an undisclosed landing. Aleck disappeared and soon returned with a mule and wagon and carted the family off to the next town, where they got railway passage to Virginia.[4]

Sister Frances Webster who had spent the war years in Geneva, New York, much cramped in words and action and cut off from Southern relatives, again felt free to speak. She would not have Edmund return to the United States until the bitterness subsided. As in earlier years, she again dreamed of being near him. Why, she wrote Kirby Smith in Cuba, could not the family open a school? Any place—Yucatan, Andalusia, California—would do. The only requirement was pupils. Her daughters, Fannie and Josie, were accomplished in music and foreign languages, and "with you for the *ologies* & myself for general usefulness I think we might succeed—relieve ourselves of all present embarrassment, provide for the future, and life happily together."[5]

Aged Mother Smith also emerged from her place of involuntary seclusion at Madison, Florida, and decided to visit her sisters Mrs. Belton and Mrs. Russell in Brooklyn and then join Frances. The Putnams were so poverty-stricken that they could scarcely support her any longer. They were now living in "an abandoned shanty without a single pane of glass," and the source of their next meal was never a certainty.

Never-to-be-reconstructed rebel that she was, Mother Smith felt no need to restrain either words or actions.

---

[4] Smith, *All's Fair in Love and War*, 35–37.
[5] Frances Webster to E. Kirby Smith, August 14, 1865.

Stopping for a few days at the Pulaski House in Savannah, she talked frequently with Mrs. Jefferson Davis. She was then accompanied northward by Mrs. Yulee, who was on her way to Washington to insist that her husband be released from Fort Pulaski. At the Belton home, truly a rebel island in a Yankee sea, Mother Smith again met "Cousin Win" Belton of Kirby Smith's staff, who had just returned after a four-year absence from his wife and children. All agreed that the general must not return to the *"so-called"* United States and become "a subjugated man, under Yankee feet, bearing the stamp of dishonor." [6]

Frances planned to take her mother to Geneva to live, at least until her brother's future plans were known, but she soon decided that the social and political atmosphere of Maryland would be more conducive to safety and happiness. She had rented a house in Baltimore, she wrote Cassie. Her mother was much under the influence of "Mrs. Belton & that most miserable Winfield," and they excited and encouraged her in a "violent mode of expression" which, under the existing conditions, was at least impolitic. "I think if I had brought her on here, we should all have been in Fort La Fayette in about a week." [7] But when the old mother learned that her son might be permitted to return with honor, she became quiet again.[8]

Belton remained very belligerent. He could not forgive "these infernal Yankees," he exclaimed. His only regret was that his power to hate was so limited. He despised the so-called Union and wished no league with Yankees and fanatics. Never again would he be a citizen of the United States. If he had possessed the means, he explained, he would have joined "Cousin Edmund" in his flight to Mex-

[6] *Id.* to Mrs. Kirby Smith, July 24, 1865; Mrs. Frances K. Smith to *id.*, August 17, 1865.

[7] Frances Webster to *id.*, October 22, 1865.

[8] Mrs. Frances K. Smith to *id.*, November 5, 1865.

ico. But he was caught in Shreveport without a dollar in his pocket, until he sold his horse for $100, and General Buckner failed to make funds available for the escape of staff members. Only Colonel Douglas got away; as head of a bureau, he had funds. But Belton was still resolved to leave the country and await the proper time to take up arms again. A number of other Trans-Mississippi officers were in New York. Marmaduke called at the Belton home. Dick Taylor was in town too but Belton "avoided him." [9]

Faithful "Old Doctor" Smith from his home at Alexandria, Louisiana, gave thanks for his general's safety. Louisiana was quiet, he wrote. Confederates everywhere seemed to display great "heroism and fortitude" in accepting the results. But "Woe to the Govt if it mistakes their quietness and silence for servility and broken spirit." If the conqueror would but act with magnanimity the South would respond with gratitude, and old enmities would soon be erased. As yet, however, there had been no relaxation of military control. "The South lies mangled rent and palpitating in supreme agony of a ruined and trodden down people." He had considered experimenting with free Negro labor in agriculture, but had about decided to try his profession in New Orleans. His plantation, which before the war was valued at more than $200,000, would not sell at present for $10,000, and there was a $14,000 lien on it.

The former staff, he informed Kirby Smith, was badly scattered. Cunningham had applied for a professorship "in our seminary." Douglas was hoping to become state engineer. Boggs was said to be seeking some commercial connection. Dr. Yandell had gone to Louisville and Haden planned to settle at Galveston. All must abandon their old

[9] J. F. Belton to Mrs. E. Kirby Smith, August 18, 1865.

ideas and adopt the new regardless of the direction taken.[10]

Back in Lynchburg with her mother, Mrs. Kirby Smith was as bitter as the others, but in the interest of the effect it might have upon her exiled husband, she restrained herself. The town was full of Yankees, she wrote her husband, but those in authority conducted themselves well. She was not acquainted with any of them and did not care to be, but their old friend McDaniel was very attentive. Self-interest seemed to govern him. Everybody in Lynchburg was talking poverty.

She advised her husband against returning to the States until he had something in writing. She had resolved to go in person to see President Andrew Johnson. To ask a favor at Washington would be the greatest of humiliations, yet she would do anything honorable to assist his return. If she was unsuccessful, then they could meet in Canada. There was too much cholera in Europe. However, if he were allowed to return, Texas was her choice. All she would ask for was a cabin on the wildest Texas prairie. With the few thousands of dollars they could get together they could buy a piece of land and raise cattle, and remain there until they had accumulated enough to live comfortably elsewhere. She and the children could stay with Cousin Helen until he found a suitable place. "Imagine your city wife a dairy maid." Aleck and Mahala, though free, were still loyal, she assured the general, and would go with the family anywhere except to Europe.[11]

Kirby Smith, impatiently waiting in Cuba, reflected upon the past, pondered future possibilities, and weighed the advice of relatives and friends. His loneliness was intense; he longed to be with his family in Virginia. His

---

[10] S. A. Smith to E. Kirby Smith, September 30, November 13, 1865.
[11] Mrs. Kirby Smith to *id.*, August 15, 16, 19, 28, 1865.

wife's comments on the children kept them constantly in his mind. She must not whip Carrie when it could be avoided, he urged his wife. "I do not believe in whipping children—it is rarely necessary and should not be resorted to until their disposition has been thoroughly studied and when all other means fail." Parents should always be calm and dispassionate, never making promises unless they could be religiously fulfilled; "unbounded reliance in the parents truth and rectitude is the key to a child's affection & the formation of the control which they exercise over them." Carrie was not bad, only mischievous and a sufferer from Mahala's "undisciplined affection & unbounded indulgence." Little Fanny was a much more amiable child, but from what her mother reported, he suspected that she had the Kirby temper.[12]

Kirby Smith, although lonely, accepted the period of separation from his family as a part of God's plan. He refused to believe that God had forsaken him and the cause for which he had fought. In his heart he still trusted and believed "that we will gain and be bettered by the trials & chastisements which in his wisdom he has seen fit to inflict upon us." "The war is over," he reassured his wife, "& our cause irretrievably lost. I may have decided unwisely but I have acted conscientiously in the part I have taken in the struggle—I will never acknowledge I was wrong when I feel I have in every thing acted from a sense of duty." "I did not fight for the negro or for the perpetuation of slavery. I took up arms through a sense of duty and in defense of principles whose complete triumph I shall live to see if not by force of arms, by the awakened sense of the people of the U.S. to their true interests and to wisdom." Loyal Southerners should not seek asylums abroad; their own destinies as well as

[12] E. Kirby Smith to Wife, n.d.

the truth of the principles for which they fought were now in their hands. Every possible effort should be made to re-establish state governments which in the natural course of events would soon replace military rule. If the South would then form a coalition with the Democratic party of the North and Northwest, it would hold the balance of power and assure "the establishment of our rights & the triumph of our principles." He could not agree with his mother that he should expatriate himself and seek a career in some foreign land. "Mother is uncompromising and never forgets. I cannot retain enmity—would assist and relieve my enemy in his misfortune—Mother is ambitious, and would be happy amidst excitements and display. I have no ambition but for the love & happiness of my wife & children and the quiet discharge of my duty —am naturally diffident & retiring and prefer quiet of home to the responsibilities of power and the publicity of fame and greatness." It was his life-long desire that he might be "sufficiently good & fitted for the ministry." And it was his constant prayer that "under God's mercy" he might yet be privileged "to die an humble & faithful teacher of his word." [13]

Since arriving in Cuba Kirby Smith had met a number of persons from Merida, capital of Yucatan, and received from them glowing accounts of life in that quiet secluded place, "probably the cheapest place in the world to live." The luxuriant vegetation and abundance of fruits more than compensated for the rather warm climate. There, Kirby Smith was told, a family could live on forty to fifty dollars per month. Beautiful homes with fountains, gardens, and fruits could be rented for twenty to thirty dollars; servants worked for one to three dollars. "The place is secluded," Kirby Smith explained to his wife,

[13] *Ibid.*; *id.* to *id.*, August 21, 1865.

"has had but little intercourse with the world—the people are primitive & hospitable—have not been contaminated by English or Americans—are honest & kind hearted." [14] What could be more attractive to an exile without funds should it be necessary to remain abroad? "Like your description of Merida," his wife replied, "but don't they have earthquakes there?" [15]

Kirby Smith also thought seriously of going to Europe or to Canada, but his greatest desire was to rejoin his family in the States. He did not possess the unforgiving spirit of his mother, he repeatedly explained to his wife. "I see she [Mother] retains the same unsubdued, uncompromising irreconcilable spirit which has sustained her in all her trials and which with her indomitable will has made everything yield before her, and borne her triumphantly through all the vicissitudes of life and shielded her from all attacks of the grave. . . ." And even now her "Spartan spirit" commanded her to abandon all hope of ever seeing her only son again rather than see him submit to dishonor or humiliation. But as for himself, he viewed life differently. "I look to the future, and removed from the influence which at home excites the imagination & warps the judgment, calmly watch events and dispassionately draw conclusions." Only those who had lived abroad could appreciate the difficulties of life among strangers with whom one has little in common. Supposing that one could be materially successful in a foreign land, what could he expect in the way of the better things of life? [16] The Confederate general longed for the soil of his native South.

Prolonged waiting increased agony, and by late Sep-

[14] *Id.* to *id.*, n.d. Probably written early in August, 1865.
[15] Mrs. Kirby Smith to E. Kirby Smith, August 28, 1865.
[16] E. Kirby Smith to Wife, September 15, 1865.

tember Kirby Smith was almost persuaded to return and take whatever punishment might be inflicted upon him. He was encouraged by news from the South that Federal control was gradually being relaxed. Surely the re-establishment of state governments and the end of military rule could not be delayed much longer, he reasoned. A reuniting of the Democratic party, North and South, he believed to be the aim of President Johnson. Success in this effort might mean the "ultimate triumph of those principles which we failed to establish with the sword & bayonet." [17]

October came and still there was no reply from General Grant. Homesickness had conquered the general in exile. He resolved to wait until November 7 for a reply from Grant and a report of his wife's visit to President Johnson. If neither arrived, he would sail on that date. To pave the way for his arrival, he sent his wife letters to be forwarded to Johnson and Grant. The worst that could happen to him, he reassured his wife, "would be a short imprisonment," and he did not believe that probable.[18]

Much of the sternness of the military leader was gone, and Kirby Smith now became more like a child counting the days until Christmas. Only "Three short weeks!" he exclaimed on October 21. Mrs. Smith should meet him in New York if possible. She must bring a pair of boots from his chest and have "2 flannel undershirts made— long & full." He had shed his flannel underwear in Mexico, "the first time in many years," and had suffered a return of his rheumatism as a result. "You must expect to find me much changed," he warned his wife. Responsibility and suspense had taken their toll. Older in body but still young in heart, he had not ceased to trust the God who had never deserted him, "and with his help,

[17] *Id.* to *id.,* September 22, 1865.    [18] *Id.* to *id.,* October 4, 1865.

energy capacity and the determination to succeed, I will secure success at something." [19]

To add to the joys of the returning exile, a letter from General Grant arrived on the eve of his sailing: [20]

E. Kirby Smith
Late Genl Southern Army

Your letter dated Havanna July 31st 1865 reached me but a day or two since, as I have been absent from this city since the middle of July.

After consultation with the President of the United States, I am of the opinion that you had better return to the United States, take the amnesty oath and put yourself on the same footing with other paroled prisoners. I am authorized to say that you will be treated with exactly as if you had surrendered in Texas and been there paroled.

> Yours &c.
> U. S. Grant

On November 14, 1865, in Lynchburg, Virginia, Kirby Smith took the amnesty oath. Regarding his signature on the articles of surrender as sufficient, the provost marshal thought the requirement of a parole was not necessary.[21]

At home again, tired but happy, Kirby Smith's immediate problem was the same that other former Confederates had been wrestling with during his exile: how to begin life anew and establish a home and security for his wife and children. He immediately contacted his old friend Joseph E. Johnston, who had taken a position as president of the National Express Company. Would Johnston put his name before the board of directors? His connections and long period of residence in the area west of the Mississippi, he believed, especially qualified him for employment in that section. His preference was a superintendency in Texas with supervision over a line

---

[19] *Id.* to *id.*, August 21, October 21, 1865.     [20] Kirby Smith Papers.
[21] See copy, *ibid.*

of steamers between Galveston and New Orleans.[22] No job resulted from the proposition.

Kirby Smith also had some unsuccessful negotiations with the Alexandria Railroad. And for a time he considered going to New Orleans to seek employment. His sister Frances continued to urge that he go into educational work. She had learned of the plan to establish a new college at Annapolis and began immediately to plan a place for her brother on the faculty. She could then be near him.[23] The general spent some time visiting his sister in Baltimore but made no permanent educational contacts. And Frances, forced to give up her rented house in Baltimore, moved her family to York, Pennsylvania, and took up temporary residence in a hotel, thinking it would be an inexpensive place to live. Her old mother was not at all satisfied in that "German Yankefied Pennsylvania place." The rooms, she complained, were not large enough to "swing a cat." She had heard that the town had money, but had seen no indication of it. There was neither beauty nor culture, but there was an abundance of "fat Dutch fraus." [24]

Frances was not so displeased as her mother. She had found many of the people of York to be "copperheads"; consequently, she had made some pleasant contacts. She was concerned over her mother's discontent but attributed it to advanced years and her mother's nature. "I do not believe she will be satisfied anywhere," she wrote her brother Edmund, "unless she is in the midst of gay society & amusements, and where she will receive constant attention & have unlimited control of money." [25]

[22] E. Kirby Smith to Joseph E. Johnston, December 4, 1865.

[23] Frances Webster to E. Kirby Smith, February 6, 1866.

[24] Mrs. Frances K. Smith to Mrs. Kirby Smith, April 12, 1866; *id* to E. Kirby Smith, April 13, 1866.

[25] Frances Webster to E. Kirby Smith, April 16, 1866.

Months of unemployment and waiting gave ample time for reflecting and writing, and the general seems to have written to many old friends. He also read extensively, particularly material relating to the late war. He was much concerned with a portion of Grant's report relative to the surrender of the Trans-Mississippi Department. "Genl Kirby Smith surrendered his entire command to Maj. Genl Canby," Grant had reported. "The surrender did not take place, however, until after the capture of the rebel President and Vice President; and the bad faith was exhibited of first disbanding his army and permitting an indiscriminate plunder of property."

Kirby Smith, vigorously objecting to this accusation of "bad faith," arranged in chronological order the documents bearing upon the disbandment and surrender, and accompanying them by paragraphs of explanation, forwarded them to Grant. "I appeal to you," he concluded, "as a soldier jealous of your own high reputation to remove the imputation of bad faith undeservedly made against a brother whose only legacy the war and misfortunes of his country have left him is the consciousness of having honestly and faithfully discharged his duties and obligations." [26]

Three months later, while on a trip to Washington, Kirby Smith met General Canby, who admitted that his own telegram to Grant following the surrender at New Orleans had been largely responsible for Grant's accusation of bad faith. Since Kirby Smith had "left the country, he jumped at conclusions and hurriedly reported without facts to justify him & without taking the trouble to investigate the circumstances." He later learned that Kirby Smith could not properly be held responsible for the disbandment; therefore, an injustice had been done. [27]

---

[26] E. Kirby Smith to U. S. Grant, March 15, 1866.
[27] *Id.* to Wife, June ?, 1866.

June, 1866, arrived, and Kirby Smith was still in Lynchburg, without steady employment. He had about decided to go to either Kentucky or Tennessee. This decision again brought up the question of parole; so he journeyed to Washington to confer with Grant. Although he had always considered his signature to the surrender as his parole, he was willing to sign another in order that in Kentucky and Tennessee he might not "be placed in a false position." [28]

Following a short visit with relatives in Baltimore, Kirby Smith left for Louisville late in June, 1866. His old friend Dr. D. W. Yandell was waiting at the boat when he arrived. During the next few days he was lavishly entertained by friends and admirers. "If compliments and flatteries from the ladies, and attentions from the men could dazzle & deceive I might believe I had done something to be proud of," he confided to his wife. He was taken to the Board of Trade and introduced to numerous businessmen. Some advised him to go into the commission business either in Louisville or Cincinnati. Others urged Memphis or New Orleans as a more suitable place since his name was so well known in those areas.[29] The inclination for New Orleans was no doubt strengthened by the fact that General Buckner and Dr. Smith had located there. Yet he hesitated to expose his young family to what he considered the unfavorable New Orleans climate. He finally decided to accept the presidency of the Accident Insurance Company in Louisville.[30]

While waiting for necessary supplies for opening his

---

[28] *Id.* to U. S. Grant, June 15, 1866. While waiting for a reply from Grant, Kirby Smith visited friends in Washington and wandered about public buildings. Upon visiting the Smithsonian he found a package of books addressed to Captain E. K. Smith, which the director had been keeping for him for six years. It was rather singular, he wrote his wife, that his books in St. Augustine and Texas were lost while those in the Federal capital were carefully preserved. E. Kirby Smith to Wife, June ?, 1866.

[29] *Id.* to *id.*, June 27, 1866.    [30] *Id.* to *id.*, June 29, July 14, 1866.

new office in Louisville, Kirby Smith visited his friend William Preston in Lexington. The Lexington press gave him very complimentary recognition: "Gen. Smith's last visit to Lexington was in the midst of the war, and while he was in command of a hostile force. His scrupulous regard for private right during that period, when he held the lives and property of the people subject to his own will, won for him the respect of all classes, as has been abundantly testified by the *private* attention shown him during his visit—for with characteristic modesty Gen. Smith has declined anything like public demonstration." [31]

His wife and the two little girls joined the general in Louisville in August, 1866. Shortly after their arrival the family was further increased by the birth of a son. "Name that wonderful boy Joseph Lee for our dear father," wrote sister Frances, "& so give him a good legacy." There would probably be another within about a year and he could be given the general's name. [32] The son was named Edmund Kirby.

The Accident Insurance Company was not a success. Kirby Smith then tried the presidency of the Atlantic and Pacific Telegraph Company, but it too was a failure. Everything appeared uncertain except the increase in family responsibilities. Lydia was born in 1868. Even while otherwise employed, the general had continued to investigate the possibilities of making connection with some educational institution. There was little chance to get the presidency of the Louisiana Seminary, wrote "Old Doctor" Smith; Dick Taylor had killed him "so dead that early resurrection was impossible." [33] Robert E. Lee

---

[31] Clipping from unnamed and undated Lexington newspaper in Kirby Smith Papers; E. Kirby Smith to Wife, July 14, 1866.

[32] Frances Webster to E. Kirby Smith, October 6, 1866.

[33] S. A. Smith to *id.*, April 4, 1866.

was a bit more encouraging. Kirby Smith's name would be put before the Board of Trustees of Washington College. If the people of Kentucky wished to endow a chair of history, no doubt the Trustees would approve their nomination of an occupant.[34] Through his good friend G. R. Fairbanks, Kirby Smith also investigated the opportunities at the new University of the South at Sewanee, Tennessee.[35]

In 1868 Kirby Smith quit the insurance and telegraph business and opened a school at New Castle, Kentucky. The life of the school was cut short by a disastrous fire the following year. In May, 1870, Bushrod R. Johnson and Kirby Smith proposed to reopen the literary department of the University of Nashville and to operate the Montgomery Bell Academy as a preparatory school. The trustees were inclined to reject the proposition until the veteran educator John Berrien Lindsley came to the rescue. In a published communication he severely criticized the trustees for their shortsightedness and gave a good description of the conditions of the University: [36]

In 1870 the board finds itself very much in the same situation as in 1855, with large and valuable college buildings most beautifully situated within the limits of a wealthy, refined, and growing city, and with an income from its college fund not sufficient to pay one-half the salary of the principal or head of the institution, as such officers are now paid. While to the popular eye the institution is wealthy, its buildings and grounds attracting universal attention, it is in reality poor, very poor. Its endowment is utterly inadequate even to the keeping in repair of its large and costly buildings, and to the proper caring for its libraries, apparatus, et cetera. It has always depended, and must for years continue to depend, upon tuition fees for the payment of its corps of teachers. . . .

By accepting these propositions, the University committed to your

[34] Robert E. Lee to *id.,* October 8, 1866.

[35] G. R. Fairbanks to *id.,* February 29, 1868.

[36] John Berrien Lindsley, "The Present Conditions and Prospects of the University," quoted in J. E. Windrow, *John Berrien Lindsley* (Chapel Hill, 1938), 54.

charge can in no event be damaged. All the risk is to be borne by the two distinguished gentlemen who propose to conduct a great school under your charter and with your co-operation, in buildings which are now but partially used, and in the present unsettled condition of Tennessee may soon be not used at all. The only guarantee demanded by these gentlemen is that they shall continue in their professorships for the short period of fifteen years, instead of being at the pleasure of the board, and that they shall have the right to nominate their co-adjutors and associate teachers in the school. When it is considered that these gentlemen must at once obtain from the public several thousand dollars to place the buildings in good repair, that by their individual influence and efforts they are to draw students from distant states to fill these buildings, and that the salaries of the teaching corps will depend entirely upon their success in so doing, surely nothing less could be asked. As the board does not guarantee any pay, it is but fair that a reasonable time should be secured to these gentlemen so that after having faithfully and patiently sown the seed through a number of years, they may hope to reap the harvest through a second more remunerative period. As to nominating their associates, this is a courtesy usually conceded to heads of colleges by boards of trustees. . . .

Of Kirby Smith, Dr. Lindsley remarked: "From the great civil strife he emerged with the happy and rare reputation, universally conceded, of a brilliant military genius combined with untarnished humanity and unblemished integrity." [37]

The trustees accepted the Johnson-Kirby Smith proposal in modified form. The trustees would select and pay the salaries of the faculty and reserved the right to approve the course of study and methods of discipline. At the same time they would furnish rent free both buildings and necessary apparatus. The Kirby Smith family, including the latest arrival—Rowena Selden—moved to Nashville late in 1870.

Johnson and Kirby Smith set to work immediately. A collegiate department was organized, with six professors offering courses in Latin, Greek, French, German, Eng-

[37] *Ibid.*

lish, mental philosophy, political economy, pure mathematics, chemistry, natural philosophy, natural history and geology, agriculture, engineering, and architecture. Kirby Smith taught mental philosophy, political economy, natural history and geology, and agriculture.[38]

The life of a professor in Nashville was not exciting, but Professor Kirby Smith was not seeking excitement. His wife and children made long visits to relatives in Virginia both for pleasure and to escape the cholera, which was prevalent in Nashville; he studied, kept up with the students, got out catalogues, took an active part in church work, delivered a few public speeches, and occasionally strolled along the sand bars of the Cumberland River collecting shells. In 1872 the family was increased by the birth of Elizabeth Chaplin; Reynold Marvin arrived two years later.

The University of Nashville did not prosper under the new mánagement. At times there were definite signs of progress, but they were eventually nullified by cholera epidemics and the financial panic of 1873. Timely assistance from the Peabody Fund made possible a change over to a normal school. The result was the establishment of the State Normal College in 1875.[39] Eben S. Stearns of Massachusetts became president.

Kirby Smith was again forced to seek new employment. With a family of seven children now dependent upon him the economic pressure was greater than ever. He moved to Sewanee in 1875 and became professor of mathematics in the University of the South. His intense loyalty to his church made Sewanee attractive. And his long and intimate friendship with G. R. Fairbanks, of St. Augustine, played

[38] See circular in Kirby Smith Papers.
[39] Later known as Peabody Normal College and then George Peabody College for Teachers.

an important part in his decision to go to the mountain-top. Fairbanks was prominently connected with the University as Commissioner of Lands and Buildings. General Josiah Gorgas was vice-chancellor at that time. He had known Kirby Smith in an official way during the late war, but there had never been any close friendship. Bishop Quintard might also have had some influence; he knew Kirby Smith well. But most important of all, a loyal Episcopalian and competent teacher needed employment.

## CHAPTER XVIII

# ON THE MOUNTAIN

THE LITTLE VILLAGE of Sewanee, situated atop the Cumberland plateau, was a place of peace and quiet. Except for an occasional coal train, working between the Tracy mines and the valley below, there was little to remind one of the hustle and struggle of the world beyond. A number of families had already discovered this peaceful village and there they had built homes for summer comfort and retirement. The University of the South had opened its doors in 1868, and in spite of the hardships of the Reconstruction era, was already giving promise of the important educational institution it was destined to become.

What could have been more attractive to a lover of nature than this mountain scenery, the shade of the massive trees, and the mountain springs beside which wild flowers bloomed profusely? And when to this picture is added the refining atmosphere of a growing university, what could be more attractive to a retired military man who loved books and wished to forget the hardships of war and live a quiet life among those he loved?

At Sewanee the Kirby Smith family took up residence in a University-owned building which became known as Powhatan Hall, a name probably suggested by the general himself. The family continued to grow. William Selden was born in 1876; Josephine, Joseph Lee, and

Ephraim subsequently arrived at two years intervals, bringing the number of children to eleven. But the noise and confusion of so large a family merely added to its attractiveness. The doors of Powhatan Hall were always open to visitors, and the Kirby Smith hospitality is still a topic of conversation among older persons who recall their visits or residence on the mountain.[1]

Life at Sewanee was simple and inexpensive. Under no other conditions could a family of thirteen have lived so well an on annual income ranging from fourteen to eighteen hundred dollars. When a colleague suggested the establishment of a co-operative store, Kirby Smith quickly endorsed the proposal. The general was suffering "under similar difficulties with myself" Dr. John McCrady confided to his diary.[2] Wartime experiences had dulled the general's earlier enthusiasm for hunting, but the boys eagerly took up the sport and kept the family table supplied with small game. When Mrs. Kirby Smith remarked that she was about to write for Carrie and Fannie to come home from their visit with relatives, little Josephine exclaimed "Oh mother don't. It will take two more wabbits."[3]

When General Kirby Smith came to the University of the South the faculty was capable but not distinguished, and the future course of the university had not been definitely charted. Should it seek to excel as a liberal arts institution? Must it maintain close relationship with the Episcopal Church? Would it be wise to establish a strong military department? The only hope for steady development, argued Bishop Charles Todd Quintard, was in remaining a church university. Other colleges had more distinguished faculties and in a strict academic competition

[1] Queenie Woods Washington in *Sewanee* (Sewanee, 1932), 84.
[2] Manuscript diary in Sewanee Archives.
[3] Washington in *Sewanee*, 86–87.

would get the students. In fact, although he respected the ability of the Sewanee faculty, he questioned whether any member but Kirby Smith would attract students to the mountain.[4]

Kirby Smith joined Bishop Quintard in discouraging the establishment of a strong military department. There were already enough military schools. Sewanee should be different—a strong liberal arts institution in close connection with the church. Kirby Smith himself was a great mathematics teacher but not a great mathematician. He knew enough to teach undergraduates; he had neither time nor inclination to become a great scholar. Good students respected him; poor ones feared him, especially some of his embarrassing remarks. During cold winter days he often permitted his two dogs to enter the classroom and occupy choice places around the old "barrel stove" while students worked at the blackboard. When some student made an error the professor would whistle for "Ned" or "Dick," and hand him the eraser. Then with a twinkle in his eyes he would turn to the troubled student. "Rub it out," he would exclaim. "Even Ned knows it's wrong and wants you to erase it." [5]

Through years of strain in rearing so large a family the general's jovial disposition remained unaltered, although he occasionally lost his temper. "He was always gay and cheerful, no matter how darkly loomed the cloud of disaster. He was most courteous to every one." [6] His surviving children, however, recalling the spankings their father sometimes administered, are certain that he soon forgot the earlier lecture he had given their mother against applying the rod. In after years former students and colleagues often

[4] C. T. Quintard to "My Dear Bishop," November 20, 1878, in Sewanee Archives.

[5] William S. Slack in *Sewanee,* 67.

[6] Thomas Claiborne in *Confederate Veteran,* I, 101.

recalled the merry twinkle in his eyes and his sly wit. One morning a student gave him a "lift" as far as the chapel gate. The absent-minded professor alighted without saying good-by. "General won't you shake hands?" the student smilingly suggested. " 'Yes God bless you. I'll kiss you,' " the general quickly replied. "And before I could defend myself, he had done the deed," the student later related.[7] One day after class a student stopped by and suggested that he would like to hear some of the general's "personal recollections of the War of Rebellion." "Rebellion! Sir, Rebellion!" growled the general. "There was no Rebellion. Where are you from?" The student was from Massachusetts. Kirby Smith smiled. "Oh that's all right," he added in a lowered tone. "They don't know any better up there." [8]

General Kirby Smith was not fond of discussing his experiences in the late war, and he had still less desire to write about them. At times, however, he would warm up a bit while talking with friends. "Gen. Kirby Smith turns out to be a man full of adventures and perilous escapes," wrote Dr. John McCrady in his diary. "We brought him out, and were greatly entertained by his wealth of stories of his life at the war. He fully confirms the accounts of the entire incompetency of Gen. Bragg as a field officer." [9]

Although he wished to forget the horrors of war and stressed a restoration of friendly relations between the Blue and Gray, Kirby Smith was bombarded with letters from would-be historians, biographers, and writers of memoirs. As early as 1866 J. Stoddard Johnston, a former member of General Bragg's staff, had begun publishing some accounts of the Kentucky campaign, and urged Kirby Smith to send information. This he did in a long letter designed

---

[7] William O. Thompson to Queenie Woods Washington, September 16, 1889. Copy in possession of Arthur B. Chitty, Sewanee.

[8] William S. Slack in *Sewanee*, 66–67.     [9] Manuscript diary, July 8, 1877.

to correct Johnston's "errors." The following year Joseph E. Johnston wrote urgent letters from Selma, Alabama, where he had taken over the superintendency of the Alabama and Tennessee River Railroad. He was being vigorously assailed, he reported, for his conduct relative to Harper's Ferry and the Valley during the summer of 1861. Would Kirby Smith give his version of the points in controversy? Johnston was thinking of writing a narrative of military operations.[10] Kirby Smith vindicated his former superior on every count relative to Harper's Ferry and Manassas.[11]

Edward A. Pollard was preparing a volume of Southern biographies. He wished Kirby Smith to furnish important notes and recollections touching his own military career.[12] E. L. Drake of Fayetteville was collecting material for the next number of his *Annals* and urged that Kirby Smith throw some light upon Bragg's failure in Kentucky and what could have been done to avoid it. This subject "should receive attention before it is too late," Drake insisted.[13]

As years passed and regimental histories began making their appearance, Kirby Smith continued to receive a flood of requests for assistance. The inspector general of Randal's Brigade wrote from Texas. He was writing up some accounts of battles west of the Mississippi and was ready for Jenkin's Ferry. Would Kirby Smith state just what orders had been given General Fagan prior to that engagement?[14] A. L. Long of Charlottesville, Virginia, called attention to a recent dispute over whether or not the arrival of Kirby Smith's brigade at Manassas was responsible for turning the tide of battle. He had always understood that this was true. Would Kirby Smith write

[10] March 23, May 17, 1867, in Kirby Smith Papers. [11] May 28, 1867.
[12] April 17, 1867. [13] August 10, 1878. [14] February 5, 1891.

him the details or tell him where they could be found? [15]
Kirby Smith furnished both details and opinions. "My
belief is that we were virtually whipped when I came upon
the field, and that the appearance of my command upon
the enemies right flank, together with that of other troops
which . . . came up to the support of our left, caused
the panic which so suddenly changed a victory for the
Union army into a disgraceful flight." [16]

Many friends and former associates urged Kirby Smith
to write his own memoirs or at least a detailed account of
his administration of the Trans-Mississippi Department.
*"Every consideration conspires* to require of you *your*
contribution," insisted R. W. Johnson, a former Confederate Senator from Arkansas. In his own defense, if for
no other reason, the commanding general's account should
be preserved along with the writings of scores of others. [17]
When Richard Taylor published his book entitled *Destruction and Reconstruction,* Kirby Smith's friends were even
more insistent than ever. "You and I are very old men,"
wrote Dabney H. Maury, "and it is but natural and proper
for us to transmit our record fairly to our children." This
he thought could be done by a simple narrative in which
dignity could be preserved and controversy avoided. Such
a narrative would bring peace of mind and set the record
straight. "He [Taylor] was a good friend to me," Maury
concluded, "but with a bitter tongue and pen on occasion."
If Kirby Smith had not read Taylor's attack, he should
avoid doing so before writing his own account. [18]

Out in Texas, General H. P. Bee was not so willing to
see Taylor's account go unchallenged. In addition to being
severely critical of the generalship of Kirby Smith, Taylor
had also been critical of Bee for his conduct at Monette

---

[15] February 21, 1887.    [16] February 27, 1887.    [17] February 7, 1871.
[18] August 25, 1891.

Ferry. Taylor had not told the truth about the battles of Mansfield and Pleasant Hill, Bee assured Kirby Smith. And since Bee felt that he knew more of the details than any other surviving officer, he would gladly put his knowledge at Kirby Smith's disposal should the general decide to reply to Taylor.[19] But Kirby Smith was not interested in reopening old controversies nor in contributing to new ones. He went no further than to write a brief narrative of the Red River campaign, and in that account he leaned heavily upon his own report as dictated to Doctor Smith in 1864.[20]

Attacks upon his military judgment did not greatly worry the retired general, but an attack upon his honor was another matter. When he was informed of the rumor that he and General Banks had planned the Red River campaign so that Federal troops might assist in getting out cotton in which he was personally interested, Kirby Smith pronounced it so clearly false as not to require serious notice. Yet he wrote a lengthy letter to R. U. Johnson of *Century Magazine* pointing out its utter absurdity. Although he had many opportunities for dishonest acquisition of wealth while commanding the Trans-Mississippi Department, he denied acquiring anything beyond his salary. His "poverty" since the war, he thought, should be ample proof. Besides, God had blessed him in a way that dishonesty could never have been rewarded. He had eleven fine healthy children and a wife who grew younger in spite of years and cares. "My home on the Cumberland Plateau is in the midst of beautiful scenery & in a delightful climate where neither politics nor epidemics find extremes and where surrounded by friends life flows along under the refining influences of university life & with the

---

[19] May 18, 1879.
[20] "Defense of the Red River," in *Battles and Leaders*, IV, 369 ff.

comforting & guiding privileges of the Church daily present." [21]

The congenial life on the mountain was made even more enjoyable by correspondence with old army friends, particularly those of West Point years. His West Point buddies always addressed him as "Seminole." Many were the letters from "Baldy" Smith, Fitz John Porter, George W. Morgan, Joseph E. Johnston, Jefferson Davis, and others, expressing great admiration for Kirby Smith both as a man and a military leader. Many too were the notes of respect and admiration from little-known men who had served with him during the late war or on the Southwestern frontier. A Texas friend wrote: "I have a cow named Winnie Davis, and her calf is named Kirby Smith, and one half Durham named Jeff Davis—and a dog named Robert Lee." [22] When Powhatan Hall burned on January 1, 1892, destroying most of the Kirby Smith family possessions, friends from far and near sent checks for hundreds of dollars.

Kirby Smith received many invitations to visit friends and attend reunions at distant points, but he seldom left the quiet of the mountain. In 1888 he did journey to Mexico to visit a son who was engaged in surveying there. And in February, 1892, he travelled east to visit "Baldy" Smith and Fitz Porter who had arranged a grand reunion of West Point buddies. "Baldy" sent round trip tickets, including passes secured from the Pennsylvania Railroad. Nothing was to be said about the passes, he warned, for the new Interstate Commerce Commission might not like it.[23] Kirby Smith liked the idea of joint reunions of Blue and Gray. When a historical society in Sioux City, Iowa, informed him of his unanimous selection as an honorary

[21] March 6, 1887.        [22] W. W. Arnett to Kirby Smith, May 25, 1889.
[23] See numerous letters from Smith and Porter under dates January, February, 1892.

member, he replied that he considered this action "one of the very many evidences that sectional differences are fast disappearing and that, under the blessing of God, we will soon be, if we are not so already, one people in truth and deed." [24]

During 1892 General Kirby Smith was frequently ill with a stomach disorder, which he attributed to unwise eating. Not even the pleasure of having his family settled again in a new Powhatan Hall greatly improved his condition. But in spite of poor health he journeyed to New Orleans in February, 1893, to attend a Confederate reunion. During the previous year General J. B. Gordon, commander of the Confederate Veterans, had made him chairman of a committee to plan the writing of a reliable history of the late war and to recommend suitable United States histories for use in the public schools of the South.

In New Orleans Kirby Smith stopped with a cousin, Mrs. Frederick Tilton. He was ill all the time, yet he wrote his wife about attending numerous parties and dinners. He also held an organization meeting of his history committee. During his stay in New Orleans General Beauregard died. As the only surviving full general, Kirby Smith occupied an honored position in the funeral procession.

His departure for home was delayed by illness; he finally left on March 15. The spring term at the university was just beginning. The declining general was able to meet only one class. He died on March 28, 1893. Three days later, on Good Friday, Bishop Quintard presided as the last of the generals was laid to rest in the Sewanee cemetery.[25]

[24] See dates March 17, 27, 1886.

[25] Among the many messages of condolence received by the family was one from Aleck. The letterhead bore the name A. H. Darnes, M.D. In some unknown manner he had acquired enough medical training to become a practicing physician in Jacksonville, Florida.

# CRITICAL ESSAY ON AUTHORITIES*

In 1907 Arthur H. Noll published a volume entitled *General Kirby-Smith.* In this work Noll was more an editor than an author, for most of the volume was made up of long quotations from letters, connected by a few comments. The letters were not correctly reproduced. The wording was often changed, and sentences and paragraphs omitted without proper indication. The result was a volume of some interest but of little value as a serious study of the subject.

Several graduate students have interested themselves in studies of General Kirby Smith and the problems of Trans-Mississippi administration. At the University of Florida (1935), Joseph B. James attempted to cover the entire subject. The task was too great, but he produced a superior master's thesis. At Louisiana State University (1947), Albert Nutter Garland narrowed his subject to "E. Kirby Smith and the Trans-Mississippi Confederacy," and did an excellent study. At the University of Texas the late Charles W. Ramsdell inspired a number of students to make studies of different phases of Trans-Mississippi administration. The more useful of these theses are Jonnie Mildred Megee, "The Confederate Impressment Acts in the Trans-Mississippi States" (1915); Agnes Louise Lambie, "Confederate Control of Cotton in the Trans-Mississippi Department" (1915); Margaret Nance Goodlet, "The Enforcement of the Confederate Conscription Acts in the Trans-Mississippi Department" (1914); and Florence Elizabeth Holladay, "The Powers of the Commander of the Confederate Trans-Mississippi Department, 1863–1865," in the *Southwestern Historical Quarterly,* XXI (1918), 279–98; 333–59.

## Manuscript Collections

The Kirby Smith papers, now deposited in the Southern Collection at the University of North Carolina, are rich in intimate family material dating as far back as the American Revolution. Among the

* Only those items found helpful in the preparation of this biography are included in this essay. A few works from which single bits of information were secured are given in full in the footnotes, but are not included in this bibliography.

thousands of items are diaries, ledgers, drawings, historical notes, newspaper clippings, and articles, printed and manuscript. But most important of all are the intimate family letters, especially those that passed between Edmund Kirby Smith and his mother and wife. From these letters came the major portion of the nonmilitary material used in writing this biography. A few letters of value, Kirby Smith's United States army commissions and a manuscript genealogy prepared by the general himself are in the possession of Dr. R. M. Kirby-Smith, Sewanee, Tennessee.

Other manuscript letters and diaries in limited quantities are found in several depositories. In the Archives of the University of the South are a few letters from Kirby Smith and several pertaining to him. Here also are the manuscript diaries of Bishop Charles Todd Quintard and Dr. John McCrady. These diaries make numerous mentions of Professor Kirby Smith. Three collections in the Duke University Library contain letters of value. A few such letters are in the Bradley Johnson and P.G.T. Beauregard papers. The Clement C. Clay papers contain several valuable letters covering the period of intimate association of Hugh L. Clay with Kirby Smith.

The papers of Governor Thomas O. Moore are in the Louisiana State University Archives. They include numerous letters relative to conditions within the Trans-Mississippi Department. The Louis A. Bringier papers in the same depository contain considerable correspondence from the field which relate to army organization and morale. In a collection labelled "Confederate States Army Collection" are a few W. A. Broadwell letters.

The papers of Governors Francis R. Lubbock and Pendleton Murrah (Texas State Archives) are rich in local complaints and material relative to the cotton controversy and state troops. Here too are valuable letters from Guy M. Bryan of Kirby Smith's staff.

The most consistent supporter of Kirby Smith among the Trans-Mississippi governors was Thomas C. Reynolds, "Confederate" governor of Missouri. Among his papers (Manuscript Division, Library of Congress) are several letters touching upon the problems and support of the Trans-Mississippi commander. In the same depository the John T. Pickett papers include a number of pertinent items on relations with Mexico.

## Printed Correspondence and Documents, Official and Private

The correspondence between President Thomas Jefferson and Ephraim Kirby concerning the latter's appointment and activities in the Mississippi Territory is found in Clarence Carter (ed.), *The Territorial Papers of the United States* (Washington, 1934———), V.

Since Edmund Kirby Smith was only a second lieutenant in the Mexican War his actions cannot be traced in official records. The only sources of great importance are his own letters to his mother and the letters of his brother published in Emma Jerome Blackwood (ed.), *To Mexico with Scott: Letters of Captain E. Kirby Smith to His Wife* (Cambridge, 1917).

The great storehouse of information on the military phases of the Civil War is *The War of Rebellion: A Compilation of the Official Records of the Union and Confederate Armies,* 128 vols. (Washington, 1880–1901). Some supplementary materials bearing upon the Trans-Mississippi Department are also found in *Official Records of the Union and Confederate Navies in the War of Rebellion,* 30 vols. (Washington, 1894–1927). Dunbar Rowland (ed.), *Jefferson Davis, Constitutionalist, His Letters, Papers and Speeches,* 10 vols. (Jackson, 1923) also contains much material relating to Kirby Smith and the Trans-Mississippi, but most of it duplicates the *Official Records.*

Such records of the Confederate Congress as were kept are found in *Journals of the Congress of the Confederate States of America,* 1861–65, 7 vols. (Washington, 1904–1905) and in five individual volumes edited by James M. Matthews: *Public Laws of the Confederate States of America . . .* (Richmond, 1862–64). The collapse of the Confederacy prevented official publication of the acts of the last session of Congress. The task was completed in Charles W. Ramsdell (ed.), *Laws and Joint Resolutions of the Last Session of the Confederate Congress (November 7, 1864–March 18, 1865) Together with the Secret Acts of Previous Congresses* (Durham, 1941).

## Diaries, Autobiographies, Memoirs, and Reminiscences

The most intimate, if somewhat colored, volume of reminiscences touching the life of General Kirby Smith was that written by his wife about 1901. In 1945 the manuscript was privately printed by her daughter, Mrs. Nina Kirby-Smith Buck, under the title *All's Fair in Love and War or The Story of How a Virginia Belle Won a Confederate Colonel.*

Very few of the numerous memoirs of military men contain material important to a study of Kirby Smith. Some interesting recollections of Manassas are found in McHenry Howard, *Recollections of a Maryland Confederate Soldier and Staff Officer under Johnston,*

*Jackson, and Lee* (Baltimore, 1914). The friendship between Joseph E. Johnston and Kirby Smith gives interest to his *Narrative of Military Operations* (New York, 1874) but it is of little importance. A few observations on the Kentucky campaign are recorded in Basil Duke, *Reminiscences of Basil Duke* (New York, 1911). William R. Boggs, *Military Reminiscences of General William R. Boggs, C.S.A.* (Durham, 1913) is brief and disappointing. Had he written many years earlier and with less bias he could have made a valuable contribution. The best and most controversial of the military memoirs is Richard Taylor, *Destruction and Reconstruction: Personal Experiences of the Late War* (New York, 1879). Taylor was a capable man with a biting tongue. After his disagreement with Kirby Smith he let his bitterness destroy his better judgment. This is quite evident in his book.

Among the memoirs written by civilians only two need citing. The unpublished "Memoirs of William Simpson Oldham, Confederate Senator [from Texas], 1861–1865" (n.p., n.d. Typed copy in University of Texas Library) is interesting and informative. Francis Richard Lubbock, *Six Decades in Texas or Memoirs of Francis Richard Lubbock* (Austin, 1900) give some light on activities during his term as war governor of Texas. J. B. Jones, *A Rebel War Clerk's Diary,* 2 vols. (New York, 1935 reprint) makes several brief references to Kirby Smith and his department.

## Military Biographies and Campaign Sketches

Holman Hamilton, *Zachary Taylor, Soldier of the Republic* (Indianapolis, 1941), Brainerd Dyer, *Zachary Taylor* (Baton Rouge, 1946), and Charles Winslow Elliott, *Winfield Scott, The Soldier and the Man* (New York, 1937) are excellent studies of the campaigns of the Mexican War, but they give nothing on Lieutenant Edmund Kirby Smith.

Of limited value in the study of Kirby Smith's Civil War campaigns are Irving A. Buck, *Cleburne and His Command* (New York, 1908); Basil Duke, *Morgan's Cavalry* (New York, 1909); Cecil F. Holland, *Morgan and His Raiders* (New York, 1942); G. F. R. Henderson, *Stonewall Jackson and the American Civil War* (New York, 1949, reprint); John P. Dyer, *"Fightin' Joe" Wheeler* (Baton Rouge, 1941); and Robert S. Henry, *"First With the Most" Forrest* (Indianapolis, 1944). Of much greater value are Fred H. Harrington, *The Fighting Politician: Major General N. P. Banks* (Philadelphia, 1948); Don Carlos Seitz, *Braxton Bragg* (Columbia, 1924); and Arndt M. Stickles, *Simon Bolivar Buckner, Borderland Knight* (Chapel Hill, 1940). The best account of a Trans-Mississippi campaign is Norman Potter Morrow, "Price's Missouri Expedition, 1864" (unpublished M.A. thesis, University of Texas, 1949); the most biased is John N. Edwards, *Shelby and His Men or The War in the West* (Cincinnati, 1867). Sarah A. Dorsey, *Recollections of Henry Watkins Allen* (New York, 1866) is a eulogistic study of a wartime governor of Louisiana. It is generally unfriendly to Kirby Smith.

## Articles

Although most of the material on the Kirby-Smith families and on the early life of the subject himself is found in the Kirby Smith papers, there are a few articles that should be noted. Thomas M. Owen, "Ephraim Kirby, First Supreme Court Judge in What is Now Alabama," in Montgomery *Advertiser,* December 14, 1902, is a brief sketch of limited importance. But Samuel H. Fisher, "Why Two Connecticut Yankees Went South," in the *Florida Historical Quarterly,* XVIII (1939) brings together essential material drawn from files of rare newspapers. Articles on Edmund Kirby Smith's early life are Joseph B. James, "Edmund Kirby Smith's Boyhood in Florida," in the *Florida Historical Quarterly,* XIV (1936), and Mrs. Nina Kirby-Smith Buck, "The Boyhood Days of General Edmund Kirby Smith Spent in St. Augustine" (typed copy in possession of the author). Both of these articles are based upon the family papers. Shortly after the general's death an article entitled "General Kirby Smith" appeared in *The University of the South Magazine,* IV (1893). It is too eulogistic to be of much value.

The most extensive and important articles on the campaigns of the Civil War are in Robert U. Johnson and Clarence C. Buell (eds.), *Battles and Leaders of the Civil War, Being for the Most Part Contributed by Union and Confederate Officers,* 4 vols. (New York, 1884–88). Kirby Smith's only published article on his campaigns, "The Defense of the Red River," is found in Volume IV. Other useful articles are in the *Southern Historical Society Papers.* Paul Hammond, "The Campaign of General E. Kirby Smith in Kentucky in 1862" appears in Volumes IX and X. It is of considerable value. The files of the *Confederate Veteran* are filled with Civil War information of many kinds, but they yielded little of value on General Kirby Smith.

## Contemporary Newspapers

Where a single item was taken from a newspaper proper citation is made in the footnotes; such newspapers are not included in the list below. Newspaper files found useful in the preparation of this biography are the Shreveport *News* (weekly and semiweekly), 1863–65; Washington (Arkansas) *Telegraph*, 1865; Houston *Daily Telegraph*, 1863–65; Austin *Weekly State Gazette*, 1863–65; Marshall *Texas Republican*, 1864–65; Galveston *Tri-Weekly News*, 1863–65 (published at Houston); and Richmond *Dispatch*, 1861–65.

## Histories and Monographs

Of value in the study of family background are Richard J. Purcell, *Connecticut in Transition* (Washington, 1918), and Melatiah E. Dwight, *The Kirbys of New England* (New York, 1898). Items of interest on early life in Florida are found in Rowland H. Rerick, *Memoirs of Florida,* 2 vols. (Atlanta, 1902); Frederick W. Dau, *Florida, Old and New* (New York, 1934); and Caroline Mays Brevard, *A History of Florida* (Deland, 1924).

The Mexican War is well covered in Justin H. Smith, *The War with Mexico,* 2 vols. (New York, 1919), and Robert S. Henry, *The Story of the Mexican War* (Indianapolis, 1950). They contain nothing on Kirby Smith.

Useful information on Confederate military leaders is given in George W. Cullum, *Biographical Register of the Officers and Graduates of the United States Military Academy,* 2 vols. (New York, 1868); Marcus J. Wright, *General Officers of the Confederate Army* (New York, 1911); and Ellsworth Eliot, *West Point in the Confederacy* (New York, 1941). The most extensive account of Confederate military operations is in Clement A. Evans (ed.), *Confederate Military History,* 12 vols. (Atlanta, 1899). Those volumes covering campaigns in Arkansas, Louisiana, and Texas were found useful. The battle of Manassas receives extensive treatment in R. M. Johnston, *Bull Run: Its Strategy and Tactics* (Boston, 1913) and in Volume I of Douglas S. Freeman, *Lee's Lieutenants,* 3 vols. (New York, 1944–46). Interesting sidelights on activities around Cumberland Gap in East Tennessee are in R. L. Kincaid, *The Wilderness Road* (Indianapolis, 1947). Stanley Horn, *The Army of Tennessee* (Indianapolis, 1941) covers Bragg's invasion of Kentucky. J. Winston Coleman, *Lexington During the Civil War* (Lexington, 1938) is an interesting local study of the Bragg-Kirby Smith campaign in the blue grass country.

The standard work on Confederate foreign relations is Frank L. Owsley, *King Cotton Diplomacy: Foreign Relations of the Confederate States of America* (Chicago, 1931).

# INDEX

cusses Lent, 74-75; illness of, 76; rejoins regiment, 76-77; explains merits of being bachelor, 77; arrives in Texas, 78; describes Texas, 78-79, 83, 84 ff.; fears war with Mexico, 79, 80; ill with fever, 80; accompanies Frances east, 81; returns to Texas, 81; complains of heat, 82; meets West Point friends, 82-83; moves to San Antonio, 83; with boundary commission, 83 ff.; appointed to Second Cavalry, 88; estimate of, of other officers, 87-88; moves to Texas, 88; campaigns against Indians, 89-90, 96-98; describes life of dragoon, 90-91; visits St. Augustine, 92; makes trip to Europe, 92-96; returns to Texas, 96; leads Wichita Expedition, 98-99; at Camp Cooper, 99-102; receives St. Augustine news, 100-102; expresses attitude toward servants, 101; moves to Camp Colorado, 102; describes site of camp, 102-103; visits San Antonio, 104, 105-106; attitude of, on religious toleration, 105; expresses desire to enter ministry, 106; goes into cattle business, 108; sends money to mother, 108; as a hunter, 108-109, 114; and crisis of 1860–61, 109-10; receives advice from Hardee, 113-14; and secession, 115, 116-17; surrenders Camp Colorado, 117; becomes E. Kirby Smith, 117-18; promoted to major, 119; resigns commission, 119; reports to Montgomery, 119; assigned to Lynchburg, 120-21; at Lynchburg, 122-29; estimate of, of Lee, 123; advises nephew, 124-25; romance of, 125-26; at Harper's Ferry, 126; compares military strength, 126-27; estimates recruits, 128-29; serves as Johnston's adjutant, 130; promoted to brigadier, 130; at Manassas, 132-35; explains Manassas victory, 136-37; recuperates, 137, 138, 139; marries Cassie Selden, 139-40; honeymoons in Florida, 140-42; promoted to major general and assigned to northern Virginia, 142-43; begins love letters to wife, 143; in northern Virginia,

143-55; receives report on cattle business, 153-54; appointed to command in East Tennessee, 155; realizes importance of new task, 156; reluctant to leave Virginia, 156; establishes headquarters at Knoxville, 156; reports on conditions, 156-57, 158-59, 160-61, 162, 166, 167; recommends martial law, 159, 166-67; orders re-enforcements to Chattanooga, 162; lacks knowledge of enemy strength, 164, gives Leadbetter *carte blanche,* 164; reports shortage of arms, 165; attempts to compel loyalty, 166, 172-73; sends aid to Beauregard, 168, 169; calls for re-enforcements, 170; cites work of Morgan, 170; orders destruction of bridges, 170, 176; orders threat to Nashville, 170; adopts policy of caution, 171; orders arrest of refugees, 172, 173; replies to Carter, 174; reports on available forces, 175; expresses faith in God, 176; asks Marshall to co-operate, 176; visits Cumberland Gap, 176; learns of Morgan's plan, 178; fears loss of East Tennessee, 179-80; orders supplies moved, 180; resolves to hold Chattanooga, 180-81, 183; goes to defense of Cumberland Gap, 183, 185, 186; again decides to defend Chattanooga, 186-88; orders concentration along railroad, 187-88; calls for re-enforcements, 189; prepares to turn on Morgan, 190; suffers from fever, 191; receives dispatches from Morgan, 191; comments on war in Virginia, 192-93; comments on disloyalty, 194; reorganizes command, 195; recuperates at Montvale Springs, 196; comments on Forrest's raids, 197; urges Bragg to join him, 198, 199; confers with Bragg, 199; reports on effective strength, 199; plans Kentucky campaign, 200-201, 202; staff of, 202-203; invades Kentucky, 203 ff.; describes hardships, 206-207; issues appeal for loyalty, 205; enters bluegrass region, 207 ff.; reports on conditions in Kentucky, 207; sends